W9-AXD-201

RICHARD © FRANCES HOOK

TAYLOR'S BIBLE STORY BOOK

TAYLOR'S

BIBLE STORY BOOK

KENNETH N. TAYLOR

Illustrated by Richard and Frances Hook

Tyndale House Publishers
Wheaton, Illinois

Coverdale House Publishers Ltd.
London, England

Distributed in Canada by
Home Evangel Books Ltd.
Toronto, Ontario

Third printing, March 1973
125,000 copies in print

Library of Congress Catalog Card Number 76-123034
ISBN 8423-6700-4

Printed in United States of America

CONTENTS

I

God Makes a Beautiful World

Long, long ago, long before anyone can remember, God made the world. But it didn't look the way it does now, for there were no people, animals, birds, trees, bushes, or flowers; everything was lonely and dark.

Then God made the light. He said, "Let there be light," and light came. God was pleased with it. He gave the light a name, calling it Day. And when the day was gone and the darkness came again, He called that darkness Night. God did these things on the first day* of creation.

Then God made the sky above the earth; and He gave the sky a name, too, calling it Heaven. God did this on the second day of creation.

Now God said that the waters covering the earth should become oceans and lakes, and the dry land should appear. Then He made the grass grow, and the bushes and trees. All this was on the third day of creation.

On the fourth day God let the sun shine in the daytime, and the moon and stars at night.

On the fifth day He made great sea monsters and all the fish. And He made the birds—some, like the ducks and geese, to fly over the water and swim on it and live near it; and others, like eagles, robins, pigeons, and wrens, to live in the woods and fields.

On the sixth day of creation God made the animals, those that are wild and live out in the forests, such as elephants, lions, tigers, and bears; and those that are tame and useful, such as rabbits, horses, cows, and sheep. And He made the little insects, such as the ants that crawl around on the ground and the little bees that fly from flower to flower.

Then God made a man and named him Adam.

This is how God made him. He took some dust from the ground and formed it into a man's body, and breathed into it, and the man began to breathe and became alive and walked around. And the Lord God planted a beautiful park as a home for the man He had made, calling it

*Older children and parents should understand that the original word in Hebrew, here translated "day," can also mean "period of time." Some authorities believe each "day" was millions of years long. But no one really knows.

the Garden of Eden; in it God planted lovely trees full of delicious fruit for the man to eat. A river flowed through the park and watered it.

God told Adam he could eat any fruit in the garden except the fruit from one tree called the Tree of the Knowledge of Good and Evil. If he took even one bite from that tree's fruit, God said, Adam would begin to die.

Adam was the only person in all the world and he was lonely. God decided it wasn't good for him to be alone, so He made another person to be with Adam and to help him. This is how He did it: He put Adam to sleep; and while he was sleeping, He took one of Adam's ribs and made a woman from it. Then God brought the woman to Adam, and she became his wife. Her name was Eve.

God sent all the animals and birds to Adam so he could give a name to each kind.

Then God looked at all He had made in those six days, and He was very pleased. So the earth and skies and all the plants and animals were finished in six days of creation.

On the seventh day, God rested; so it was a quiet and different day from all the others, a holy day of rest.

QUESTIONS

What was everything like before God created the world?

How did God make Adam?

How did God make Eve?

What happened on the seventh day?

What did God tell Adam and Eve that they must never do?

2
The World's Saddest Day

But there was someone else in the Garden of Eden besides Adam and Eve and God. Satan was there, in the shape of a serpent. Satan is the wicked spirit who tempts us to sin. So now the serpent came to Eve and told her to do something that was wrong. He asked her, "Did God tell you not to eat the fruit of any of the trees in the garden?"

"We can eat any of it except from one tree," she replied. "We can't eat the fruit of the Tree of the Knowledge of Good and Evil, for if we eat it, we will begin to die."

"That's not true!" Satan told her. "It won't hurt you at all! God is just being mean to tell you that! Really it's good and will make you wise!"

Eve should have gone away and not

listened to Satan, but she didn't. Instead, she went over and looked at the tree. It was beautiful! And the fruit looked so good! When she remembered that Satan had said it would make her wise, she took some of the fruit and ate it and gave some to her husband, Adam; and he ate it too.

After they had eaten it they heard a voice calling to them. It was God's voice. But they didn't come; instead, they hid among the trees, for now they were afraid of God. God called to them again.

"Where are you, Adam? Where are you?"

"I'm hiding," Adam finally replied, "for I'm afraid of You."

"Have you eaten the fruit I told you not to?" God asked.

Then Adam began to make excuses and blamed Eve. He said, "The woman You gave me, she gave me some of the fruit and I ate it."

God asked Eve, "What is this you have done?"

"Satan fooled me," she said, "and so I ate some of it."

God was very angry with Adam and Eve and with the serpent. He said that the serpent would be punished by having to crawl on the ground in the dust all its life. He told the woman that when her children were being born she would have sickness and pain. And God sent Adam and Eve out of the beautiful garden and wouldn't let them live there any longer; for if they stayed they might eat fruit from the Tree of Life and live forever. So He sent an angel with a sword made of fire to stop them from ever going back into the garden again.

God told Adam that because he had listened to his wife and eaten the fruit, when the Lord had said not to, the ground would no longer grow lush crops for him as it had in the Garden of Eden; instead, it would grow thorns and thistles. As long as Adam lived, he would have to work hard to get enough food to eat; and when he died, his body would become dust again, like the dust he was made from.

But even though they had sinned, God made a way for Adam and Eve to be saved from punishment after they died. He promised to send a Saviour who would be punished for their sins so that they wouldn't have to be punished. God said that if people would ask God to forgive them and would trust the Saviour to save them, and would try to obey God and be good, God would take them to heaven when they died.

When the Saviour came, he died for Adam and Eve's sins, and for their children's sins too, and also for ours. For we, too, have done bad things and need to be forgiven. That includes you and me and everyone else. We are all sinners. But God forgives us if we ask Him to, because Jesus died to take away our sins.

QUESTIONS

Who else was in the Garden of Eden with Adam and Eve?

What did Satan tell Eve to do? Did she do it?

Why did Adam and Eve hide from God?

How did God punish Adam and Eve?

How did he punish Satan?

Did God have a way to save Adam and Eve from punishment after they died? Do you know what it was?

3
How Abel Pleased God

After Adam and Eve were sent out of the Garden of Eden, God gave them two sons. The older one was named Cain, the younger one, Abel. When they grew to be young men, Cain became a farmer while Abel was a shepherd with a flock of sheep. They both had wicked hearts like their parents, and they often sinned. But Abel was sorry about his sins and believed the promise God had made to send a Saviour.

One day Abel brought a lamb from his flock and offered it as a gift to God by killing it and burning it on the altar. The altar was a pile of stones which was flat on top. He built a fire on the altar and put the dead lamb in the fire to burn up until only ashes and bones were left. Doing this was called a sacrifice. By giving God his lamb, Abel showed God that he loved Him.

God was pleased that Abel worshipped Him in this way, for the lamb was in many ways like the Saviour God would some day send to die for people's sins. The Saviour would be gentle and patient and innocent like the lamb, and would be killed as a sacrifice just as the lamb was.

But Abel's brother Cain did not turn from his sins or believe God's promise to send a Saviour; and when he brought his offering it was not a lamb, which was what God wanted, but some things from his garden. So God was not pleased with Cain or his offering.

When Cain realized that God wanted a lamb as a sacrifice, and had accepted Abel's sacrifice but not his, he was angry with God. Yet God spoke kindly to him and asked why he was angry. If Cain would bring a lamb, God told him, then God would accept his gift and be pleased with him.

Cain was angry with God but took his anger out on Abel. One day when they were in the field together, Cain killed Abel; and the ground was wet

The first man was Adam, and his first two sons were Cain and Abel. Cain was angry because Abel obeyed God. One day when they were out in a field, Cain killed Abel. God had to punish him severely for doing this.

R. HOOK

with his blood.

Then God called to Cain, "Where is your brother Abel?"

"How should I know?" Cain answered. "Am I supposed to baby sit my brother?"

But God had seen what Cain did, and now declared that all the rest of his life Cain must wander from place to place as his punishment for killing Abel—always afraid, and with no home to stay in. And when Cain planted a garden, it wouldn't grow well, and briars and weeds would spring up and choke it; or it would have leaves but no fruit; so Cain would hardly have enough to eat.

Cain told God that this punishment was too much, and that everyone who met him would hate him and want to kill him. But God said that anyone who killed Cain would be punished with a very dreadful punishment; for God Himself chose to punish Cain, and no one else was to do it. So God put a mark on Cain. We are not told what sort of mark it was, but it was something other people could see; and when they saw it, they knew he was Cain, and remembered God's command that no one was to kill him.

Adam lived for many years after this. Finally, when he was 930 years old, he died, and his body became dust again as God had said it would, because he ate the forbidden fruit in the Garden of Eden. Nine hundred and thirty years is a very long time for a man to live, but in those days God allowed people to live much longer than now.

During those years Adam and Eve had many children, and the children grew up and had children, and then those children grew up and had children until there were many, many people in the world. One of them was Enoch. The Bible tells us that Enoch walked with God. This means that he loved God and thought about God all the time. It was as though he and God were walking along like friends, with Enoch listening to what God was saying and trying to please Him and obey everything He said.

When Enoch was 365 years old, God did a wonderful thing for him: He took him up to heaven while he was still alive! So Enoch didn't die like other men, for God just took him away to live with Him.

Enoch had a son named Methuselah who lived to be 969 years old. The Bible doesn't mention anyone else who lived to be older than that; so Methuselah is called the oldest man who ever lived.

QUESTIONS

What were the names of Adam and Eve's first two sons?

What did Abel offer to God? What did Cain offer to God?

Why didn't God want Cain's offering?

How did Enoch get to heaven?

Who was Methuselah?

Here is a picture of the oldest man who ever lived.
His name is Methuselah. He was 969 years old when he died.

4
Saved from Drowning

As the years went by the world became more and more wicked. People did all kinds of bad things. They didn't want to please God and didn't even try to obey Him. So God was angry with them and said He would punish them by sending a flood to cover the earth with deep water, drowning them all.

But there was one good man whose name was Noah. God loved Noah and told him about the flood He was going to send, so Noah could get ready for it.

God told Noah to build a huge boat as high as a three-story house, filled with many large rooms, and having a long window and a big door in the side. He said that when the boat was finished, Noah and his sons and their wives would live in it and float away safely when the flood came.

God also told him to bring into the boat a father and mother animal of every kind there was, and birds and even insects, so that when the flood came, some of each kind would still be alive; for everything not inside would be drowned.

So Noah began to build the boat. It took him a long, long time, more than a hundred years; but as you know, at that time men lived much longer than they do now.

Noah did something else, too, besides building the boat—he was a preacher, so he talked to the people about God and warned them about the flood that was going to come because of their sins. But the people didn't believe him and they weren't sorry for their sins. All during those long years while he was building the boat, he heard them say bad things about God, and saw the wicked things they did. He patiently kept on working until at last the boat was finished.

Then God told Noah to bring all his family and the birds and animals

God told Noah to build a huge boat on dry land! It took 100 years for him to finish building it. Then, at God's command, animals and birds of every kind came to live in it. Noah and his family and the animals and birds were saved from the terrible flood.

into the boat, for in seven days the rain would begin and the flood would come, and everyone outside the boat would be drowned.

So Noah brought his wife and his three sons and their wives into the boat. And he brought in at least two of each kind of animal and bird. These were in pairs, a father and a mother of each kind. We don't know how Noah found all the different animals and birds or how he got them to come into the boat, but they came, for God was helping him. Two of some kinds came and seven of other kinds.

When all were safely inside, God closed the door and locked it.

Seven days later it began to rain; in fact, it poured. It rained without stopping for forty days and forty nights. The rain came down as if it was being poured from great windows in the sky. The creeks, the rivers, and the great oceans all began to rise; and water covered the land. After a while there was so much water all around the boat that it was lifted off the ground. Higher and higher the water rose, with the boat floating on it.

But what about those people who had refused to obey God and wouldn't listen to Noah's warning? They had laughed at Noah for saying there would be a flood; they said Noah was only trying to scare them. But now, too late, they saw that all he had told them was true. Oh, if they could only get into the boat, but now it was too late.

They climbed the highest hills and mountains, but soon the hills and mountains were covered with water, too; and there was nowhere else for them to go. So all the people in the world were drowned except those in the boat. And every animal and bird and insect, except those in the boat, died in the flood, for all the earth was covered with the water. There was no land to be seen anywhere; only the boat could be seen, floating alone upon the water.

God did not forget Noah. All through that dreadful storm He took care of him and of all those who were with him. God kept the boat safe. Finally the rain stopped and the water began to go down again.

After Noah had been in the boat for 150 days, almost half a year, the water had gone down so much that the boat rested on the top of a mountain called Ararat, but Noah and his family stayed inside, for God wasn't ready to let them out yet. Two months later the flood had gone down even more, so that the tops of other mountains could be seen peeping above the water.

Now Noah opened a window in the boat and let a raven out. The raven flew over the water and didn't come back to Noah again.

Then Noah sent out another bird —a dove. Noah wanted to find out whether the ground was dry yet, but it wasn't. When the dove found no trees or flowers, she came back to the window of the boat, and Noah put out his hand and brought her back in.

Noah waited seven days longer and sent the dove out again. That evening she returned to the boat with an olive leaf in her mouth. Then Noah knew the water must be almost gone or the dove could not have found the leaf.

He waited another seven days and once more sent out the dove; and this time she didn't come back, for the woods had become pleasant to fly around in.

Then God told Noah and his wife and his sons and their wives to come out of the boat and to let out all the animals and birds. At last they could walk around outside.

Then Noah built an altar, as Abel had done, and sacrificed animals and birds upon it to the Lord. This was his way of thanking God for saving him and his family from the flood, though all the other people in the world had drowned.

God spoke kind words to Noah and his sons and said they were in charge of everything living on the earth and that they could kill the animals for food. Adam had been permitted to eat only the fruit growing on the trees and bushes. But now, after the flood, God said the people could eat meat.

God promised that He would never send another flood to drown all the people. As proof, He gave Noah a sign—a beautiful rainbow in the sky where Noah could often see it when it rained; and whenever he saw it, he would remember God's promise not to send a flood like that again.

Noah lived many years after the flood, and died when he was 950 years old.

QUESTIONS
Why did God send the flood?
What animals did Noah take into the boat? How many of each kind? Are you sure?
When the boat was finished, who lived in it?
Why did Noah build an altar?
What was God's promise to Noah? What should you think about when you see a rainbow?

5
A Huge Tower

Soon after the flood ended, Noah became a grandfather, for God gave children to Noah's sons and their wives. These grandchildren grew up and had children, too, until after a while the world was full of people again.

Don't you suppose these people would be very careful not to make God angry? They knew about the terrible flood and what had happened to all the people before. But no, they didn't care, and kept on doing all sorts of bad things. Perhaps they weren't afraid of God, because of the rainbow and God's promise not to send another flood. But there were many other ways for God to punish them. He could send sickness or war or not enough food, or He might send down fire from heaven to burn them up. But they seemed to forget this; their hearts were bad so they acted just like the people before the flood, and constantly sinned against God.

There was only one language in the world at that time. Today there are hundreds of languages, like English, Spanish, French, and German. (Can you name five more?) But in those days the people all talked alike, so everyone in all the world could understand everyone else!

One day the people said to each other, "Let's build a high tower, as high as heaven!"

So they began to build it. We are not told why they wanted this tower, but probably it was because they were proud and wanted everyone to see how great they were to build such a high tower. But it is sinful to be proud, and God knew what they were thinking.

One day the Lord came down from heaven to see the tower, and He was not happy about it. He decided to stop the people from building it. So He made them begin to speak in different languages! Now they couldn't understand each other! One man would ask another for a hammer, but the other man couldn't understand him! This made them angry with each other, and soon they stopped working and went home.

They didn't even want to live near each other anymore, so all those speaking the same language lived together, and moved away from those who didn't speak their language. That is why different languages are spoken in different parts of the world today.

So the tower, which was called the Tower of Babel, was never finished. The word "Babel" means "mixed up." When people began to talk in different languages and couldn't understand each other anymore, they got all mixed up. That is why the tower was called the Tower of Babel.

QUESTIONS

Did the people try to obey God?
What did they decide to build? Why?
What did God do about it?
Why was the tower called the "Tower of Babel"?

God wasn't happy about this tower, because the people building it were trying to prove that they could get along without God. See how high it is? And they did it all without asking God for His blessing. So God made people talk new languages, and suddenly they couldn't understand each other. They were so upset by this that they quit building and went away.

6

The Story of God's Friend

Far away in the land of Ur (or Iraq, as we call it today), there lived a man named Abram. The people of his country worshipped idols made of wood and stone. This was very wrong of them, for God had said that they must worship only Him. God told Abram to go away from people like that and to move to another country.

So Abram left his home and relatives and friends and travelled far away to a distant land with his wife Sarai, his nephew Lot, and his servants. He had never been in that land before, but he believed God would take care of him. Abram was seventy-five years old at that time.

It was a long, hard journey. They had to cross wide rivers and a desert where the country was lonely and wild. Yet God took care of them and brought them safely to the promised land. It was called the land of Canaan. Today we call it Israel.

"I will give all this land to you—this whole country," God told him. "It will belong to you and to your children forever."

Then Abram built an altar and worshipped God by killing an animal and burning it on the altar.

Other people were living there in the land who might have harmed him, but God kept them from doing it. It was a time of famine when Abram arrived. Famine means that the grass and the grain didn't grow well, so the people had little to eat.

Now Abram went away for awhile to still another country called Egypt, and waited until there was more food for them in Israel. Then he and Lot and their families returned to Israel again, and Abram sacrificed to the Lord again by killing a lamb and burning it on the altar.

Soon Abram became very rich and owned many, many cows, goats, and sheep. Lot had many of them too.

But the men who took care of Lot's

One day God told Abraham to move far away to another country. He took his family, his servants, his sheep, and his goats and started out. There were no cars or trains or airplanes in those days, so they all walked for many weeks, and God took care of them.

animals quarreled with the men who took care of Abram's animals. When Abram heard about this, he talked to Lot about it. Do you think Abram said, "This is my land, Lot, and you get out—God has given it to me, and you must move away somewhere else?" No, Abram was very nice to Lot and said, "Let's not have any fighting and quarreling between us."

Then Abram and Lot divided the land. Abram gave Lot first choice, even though he didn't need to—it was his land, for God had given it to him.

Lot chose the very best part of the country, the valley of the Jordan River. One of the cities there was named Sodom. The men of Sodom were very bad, but Lot went to live among them anyway. He was not a bad man himself, for he worshipped God; but he went to live among these wicked men because he thought he would have better pasture for his cattle in their country and that he soon would become rich. He shouldn't have done this, and we will soon see how much trouble it caused.

After Lot had moved away to his new home, the Lord said to Abram, "I will give you all of the good land Lot chose. Lot is living there now, but some day it will all be yours!"

God also said He would give Abram so many children and grandchildren and great-grandchildren that they would become a great nation. That promise has come true and today we call Abram's people the Israelis, or Jews.

QUESTIONS

Why did God want Abram to move? Did Abram obey?

What were Abram's men and Lot's men quarreling about?

Did Lot make a good choice? Why or why not?

Abram could have kept all the land for himself, for God had given it to him. Instead, he offered to divide it with his nephew, Lot, and he let Lot take first choice.

7
What Happened to Lot?

Then Abram moved to a place called Hebron and built another altar to the Lord. That was the third altar he had built since he arrived, for he loved to have an altar near him wherever he moved, so that he could sacrifice to the Lord and worship Him.

But before long there was a war. Four kings came with their armies and attacked the city of Sodom where Lot lived, and conquered it. They went into the houses and took food, money, clothing, and everything else they wanted. They took some of the people, too, and Lot was taken away to be a slave. When Abram heard about it, he called together his 318 servants and some of his friends and chased after the army to try to rescue Lot.

Soon Abram and his men caught up with the four kings and their armies and attacked them, and God gave him the victory. So all the captives were rescued.

On the way back to Sodom, Melchizedek, the godly king of a city called Salem, came out to meet Abram, bringing him bread and wine. Then Melchizedek blessed Abram. He asked God to be good to him, and he thanked God for giving Abram the victory. Abram gave Melchizedek a tenth of everything he had taken away from the enemy army.

How happy the king of Sodom was when he saw Abram returning with the captives! "Give me back my people," the king said to Abram, "but you can keep everything else for yourself—all the food, clothes, and jewelry—keep it all for yourself."

But Abram said no, he wouldn't keep anything for himself, for he had promised God that he wouldn't. The men who had helped him could take some of the things, he said, but he would take nothing, so that no one could ever say, "I made Abram rich." He wanted only God to be able to say that!

One day God told Abram, "I am your friend." So Abram reminded his great friend that he wanted a son, for he had no children. God promised to give him one.

Then He took Abram out under the night skies and told him to look up at the stars, and asked him whether he could count them. Abram couldn't do it because there were so many. Then God told him, "You will not only have a son, but many, many grandchildren and great-grandchildren. Their families will be like those stars up there—too many to count!"

But God also told Abram that these people of his would be taken away to another country as slaves and be treated cruelly for many years. "But afterwards," God said, "I will punish those who hurt them, and I will bring them back again to the land of Israel, and they will be very rich."

God also said that Abram would live to be an old, old man, and would die happy.

Abram's wife, Sarai, owned a slave girl named Hagar. She was Abram's other wife. But Sarai was angry with her and punished her. Then Hagar ran away into the lonely wilderness where no one lived.

The angel of the Lord found her beside a spring and asked her where she had come from and where she was going. She answered that she had run away from Sarai. Then the angel told her to go back to Sarai again and to obey her.

The angel also said that Hagar would have a son whose name would be Ishmael and that he would be a fighter—he wouldn't like other people, and they wouldn't like him! So Hagar went back to Sarai, and afterwards God gave her the son He had promised, and she named him Ishmael.

When Abram was ninety-nine years old, God talked with him again. (Abram lay face downward on the ground while God talked to him.)

God said again that He would give Abram, many, many grandchildren and great-grandchildren—a whole country full of them—and some of them would be kings. God now made a promise to Abram and his children: "I will be your God," He said, "and you will be my people."

Then God promised again to give the land of Israel to the Jews.

Now God gave Abram a new name! "Your name isn't Abram anymore!" God said. "From now on it is Abraham!" (Abraham means "the father of a whole country.")

And He gave Sarai a new name too. Her name was Sarah (which means "princess"). So the Lord changed both their names, and promised again to give them a son, whose name would be Isaac.

QUESTIONS

Whom did the armies of the four kings capture?

Why wouldn't Abram keep any of the loot for himself?

What did God promise Abram?

What did God tell Hagar?

What was Abram's new name? What does it mean?

What was Sarai's new name? What does it mean?

8
God's Visit with Abraham

One hot day as Abraham was sitting at the entrance of his tent, he looked up to see three men coming toward him.

He ran to meet them and threw himself down in front of them with his face to the ground, for that is the way strangers were welcomed in that land. Abraham invited the men to rest in the shade of a tree while he brought some water to soothe their tired feet. In those days people either went barefoot or wore sandals, so their feet became very dusty. One of the things a friendly man did for his guests was to give them water to wash their feet after a long, hot walk.

Abraham ran to the tent and told Sarah, "Quick, bake some bread." Next he ran out to where the cows were and selected a fat calf to be killed and cooked.

When the meat was ready he set it before the men, with some butter and bread and milk, and they had a picnic beneath the tree while Abraham stood nearby to serve them.

After they had finished eating they started off toward the city of Sodom, and Abraham walked along beside them.

Now I must tell you that these three men were really not men at all. Two of them were angels, we believe, and the other one was God.

Could God look and talk like a man? Yes, several times in the Bible He appeared in the form of a man and talked with someone.

God told Abraham that He had decided to burn up the cities of Sodom and Gomorrah. Why was He going to do this? It was because the people who lived there were so bad. Abraham was very sad when he heard about this, for Sodom was the city where his nephew Lot lived. He was afraid Lot would be burned up too. Abraham talked to God about it.

"Perhaps there are some good people living in the city," he said. "Must they die too?"

God replied that if there were only fifty good people in the entire city, He wouldn't destroy it.

"But perhaps there are only forty-five!" Abraham said.

And God replied, "If there are even ten good people there, I won't destroy it."

Then God went on to Sodom, and Abraham returned to his tent.

That evening Lot was out by the city gate; for in that country the cities had walls around them to keep out enemies, and there were gates in the walls to go in and out.

As Lot was sitting there, suddenly the two angels stood before him. But Lot didn't know they were angels because they looked just like men. They were the same angels who had come with God to Abraham's tent. Lot stood up to meet them and invited them to come to his house to spend the night.

"No," they replied, "we'll just camp out here."

But Lot was afraid of what the bad people of the city might do to them, so he begged them to go home with him. Finally they agreed.

After supper the angels asked him whether he had any other sons or daughters in the city beside those who were with him at home.

"Go and warn them to leave Sodom at once," they told him, "for the Lord is going to destroy this city."

Lot ran quickly to the homes of his married daughters and said to his sons-in-law, "Quick, get your families out of the city, for the Lord is going to destroy it."

But they didn't believe him, and Lot had to come back home without them.

Early the next morning, while it was still dark, the angels said to him, "Leave the city at once, or you will be burned up along with all the other people living here. Take your wife and your two girls and get out right now. *Hurry!*"

But Lot stayed a little longer, perhaps to save something out of his house. Then the angels caught hold of his arms and pushed him out of the house. They told him to go as fast as he could or it would be too late.

"Don't look behind you," they said. "Hurry to the mountains where the fire won't kill you."

There was another small city near Sodom, named Zoar. Lot begged the angels not to destroy it and to let his family go there instead of up on the lonely mountain where wild animals might kill them. God agreed and gave them permission to go to Zoar.

But as they were going, Lot's wife looked back toward Sodom, even though the angels had told her not to. She died right there and became a statue of salt.

The sun was just rising when Lot and his two daughters arrived at Zoar.

Then the Lord rained down fire from heaven on Sodom and Gomorrah, completely destroying both cities. All the people in them died, and all the grass and plants and trees were destroyed.

God saved Lot and his two daughters, but Lot lost everything, including all the nice things he took to Sodom when he and Abraham left each other.

Early that morning when Abraham came out of his tent, he saw a great cloud of smoke rising from Sodom and

Gomorrah. He knew God hadn't found even ten good people in the entire city of Sodom, for God had promised not to destroy it if He found even that many good people there.

QUESTIONS
Did God save Lot and his family? All of them?
Tell what happened to each one in the family.
Why did Lot's wife turn to a statue of salt?
Did God find ten good people in Sodom?

9
God Keeps His Promise

Abraham moved again, this time to a place named Gerar, in what is now the land of Israel. The king of Gerar gave Abraham a present of sheep, oxen, and slaves, and told him he could live anywhere he wanted to in his country.

At this time God gave Abraham and Sarah a little baby son, just as He had promised them. Abraham named him Isaac, for that is the name God had said to give him.

Abraham was 100 years old when Isaac was born. What a happy day it was!

The baby grew and was soon old enough to play with other children. So his father gave him a nice party. But during the party another boy, whose name was Ishmael, made fun of Isaac. Ishmael was the son of Abraham's other wife, Hagar, who was a slave girl. When Isaac's mother saw the slave girl's son mocking her son, she was very angry.

Sarah told Abraham to get rid of Ishmael and his mother, because she couldn't stand the sight of them. Abraham didn't want to send them away, but God told him to do as Sarah demanded. So Abraham got up early in the morning, gave some bread and a bottle of water to Ishmael and his mother, and sent them away.

They walked a long way into the wild country. Soon all the water in the bottle was gone. Ishmael became so weak with thirst that his mother thought he was going to die. She laid him under a bush in the shade and

This is a picture of Abraham, the founder of the Hebrew race. He was the very first Jew, and he loved God very much. In the picture you can see him with his wife Sarah and his son Isaac.

L+R.HOOK

went a little farther on and sat down and cried, for she didn't want to see him die.

But God heard her, and the angel of God called to her out of heaven, "What's the trouble, Hagar?"

The angel told her not to be afraid and showed her where there was a well! So Ishmael had a drink and felt all right again.

God was kind to Ishmael and took care of him. Growing up in the country, far away from any city or town, he learned to shoot birds and animals with a bow and arrow. When he grew up, his mother brought him a wife from the land of Egypt where she had lived when she was a girl.

Meanwhile Abraham was still living at Gerar. When the king of Gerar realized that God was Abraham's friend, he asked Abraham to be his friend too.

Abraham promised to be friends, but he told the king about a problem. Abraham's servants had dug a well. But then some of the king's servants said it was theirs, and they wouldn't let Abraham use it! It was hard work to dig a well in the rocky ground of that country, so Abraham didn't want to have to dig another one.

The king said he didn't know his servants had done this and he was sorry about it. Then Abraham took seven lambs from his flock and gave them to the king. The king asked him why he was giving these lambs to him. Abraham replied that they were a present to remind the king that Abraham had dug that well and that it belonged to Abraham.

So the king and Abraham made an agreement always to be friends. Abraham called the name of the place Beer-sheba, which means "the well of promise," because it was there that he and the king had promised to be friends.

Abraham planted trees beside the well, and lived there a long time.

QUESTIONS

Why was Sarah angry? What did she tell Abraham to do?

What happened to Hagar and Ishmael when their water ran out?

What problem did Abraham tell the king about?

What did the king and Abraham promise each other?

One of Abraham's wives was Hagar, and one of his boys was Ishmael.
But they were punished by being sent away from home into the hot, dry desert.
Ishmael is dying from thirst. But God sent them water and he got well again.

10

Abraham Gives Isaac to God

Do you remember that Abel sacrificed a lamb to God? Do you remember how pleased God was with him for doing this?

Well, one day God said to Abraham, "Abraham, take your son Isaac whom you love so much, and go to the land of Moriah and burn him as a sacrifice upon one of the mountains I will point out to you!"

Yes, Abraham was commanded to sacrifice Isaac upon an altar just as Abel had sacrificed that lamb so long before. How could Abraham ever do this? How could he kill his own dear son?

But God told him to do it; Abraham heard Him speak. He knew that he must do whatever God said, and he knew that even if Isaac were burned on the altar so that nothing was left but his ashes, God could take those ashes and make him live again.

So Abraham got up early in the morning and saddled his donkey. He took two young men with him, some wood to lay on the altar, and Isaac, his son.

They started toward the mountain God had told him about. They travelled all that day and the next day and the next, before Abraham finally saw the mountain far ahead of them. Then he told the young men to stop and wait. He and Isaac would go to the mountain and worship, he told them, and then would come back to them.

Why do you think Abraham said that both of them would come back? I think it was because Abraham believed God would bring Isaac back to life.

Isaac carried the wood, and Abraham took some fire to light the wood (since they had no matches in those days). The two went on together.

Isaac did not know what God had told his father to do, nor why his father was taking him to the mountain. He knew they were going to offer a burnt offering, but he didn't know he was going to be burned up on the altar as a sacrifice. So, as they walked along together, he said to his father, "Father, we have the fire and the wood, but where is the lamb for a burnt offering?"

Abraham answered, "My son, God will find Himself a lamb for the burnt offering."

When they came to the place God had sent them to, Abraham built an altar and laid the wood on it. Then he tied Isaac and laid him on the wood, and Abraham lifted the knife to kill his son.

But at that instant the angel of God shouted to him from heaven, "Abraham! Abraham! Stop!"

Then the angel told him not to hurt Isaac. Abraham had proved that he feared God. He had been willing to obey God's command even if he had to sacrifice his only son.

Then Abraham noticed a ram caught in the bushes by its horns. God had sent it there to be used as a burnt offering instead of Isaac. Abraham killed it and burned it on the altar.

God was greatly pleased with Abraham for being willing to obey. Then the angel of God spoke to him from heaven again and told him that God would bless him by giving him many, many grandchildren and great-grandchildren. His family would some day be so large, the angel said, that no one could even count them! And they would help all the other people in the world.

(The angel said this about helping other people everywhere, because the Saviour of the world was going to be born into Abraham's family.)

Then Abraham and Isaac came back to the young men who were waiting for them, and they all returned home.

Sarah, Isaac's mother, died when she was 127 years old. Abraham and Isaac cried a lot because she was dead. Then Abraham asked the people who owned that country to sell him a piece of land where he could bury her.

In that country people were buried in caves made in the sides of hills. Then a great stone was rolled against the opening of the cave to close it. When anyone died the stone was rolled away and the dead person was laid inside the cave. Then the stone was rolled back again and the cave was shut up until someone else was to be buried there.

There was a man in that land whose name was Ephron, who owned a field with a cave at one end of it. Abraham wanted to buy this cave to bury Sarah in. So he asked Ephron's friends to tell him that Abraham wanted to buy it.

Ephron said Abraham could have the cave without paying, but Abraham preferred to buy it. Ephron agreed to sell it, and Abraham gave him four hundred pieces of silver for the cave and the nearby field and trees. So he buried Sarah there.

Abraham was getting very old, and the Lord had blessed him in every way.

Isaac was a full-grown man and wanted to get married. But his father Abraham didn't want him to marry any of the girls in that country, because they all worshipped idols instead of worshipping God. He wanted Isaac to marry a girl from the country where his relatives lived, where the people obeyed God and didn't worship idols.

But that country was far away. So Abraham called his oldest servant, the one who was in charge of all his business, and asked him to go to that distant land where his relatives lived and to bring back a girl for Isaac to marry.

"But what if I can't find a girl who is willing to come so far?" the servant asked.

Abraham told him, "God will send an angel ahead of you to help you find the right girl to come and be Isaac's wife."

So the servant loaded ten of Abraham's camels with beautiful presents and started off.

After many, many days of hard travel he finally arrived at the town where Abraham's relatives lived. He made the camels kneel down by a well that was just outside the city.

QUESTIONS
What did God tell Abraham to do?
What happened just as Abraham was about to sacrifice Isaac?
What did Abraham use as a burnt offering?
Why didn't Abraham want Isaac to marry a girl from his own country?
What did Abraham tell his servant to do?

II
God Answers a Prayer

It was evening when Abraham's servant arrived at the town, and the girls were all coming out to draw water from the well. As the servant watched them coming, he asked God to help him find the right one to be Isaac's wife.

How could he ever know? This is what he decided to do. He would ask one of the girls to give him some water from her pitcher. If she answered him with a smile and said, "Yes, and I will water your camels too," then she would be the one God had chosen to be Isaac's wife. But if she was grouchy and wouldn't give him the water, then she wouldn't be the right one.

While he was still praying, a beautiful girl named Rebekah came, carrying her pitcher on her shoulder; she went down to the well and filled it with water.

The servant ran over to her and said, "Please give me a drink from your pitcher."

"Certainly, sir," she replied, "and I'll water your camels too!"

She let down her pitcher from her shoulder and gave the servant a drink,

Abraham sent his old servant across the desert to find a wife for Isaac. The servant asked God to help him find the right one, and here she is, talking to him. Her name is Rebekah. Do you think they called her Becky?

F.&R. Hook

then ran back to the well and began drawing water for his camels!

After the camels had finished drinking, the man gave Rebekah a gold earring and two gold bracelets. He asked her whose daughter she was and whether there was room at her father's house for him and his men to spend the night. Rebekah told him she was the daughter of Bethuel and that there was plenty of room.

When the servant heard her say she was Bethuel's daughter, he realized that she was a cousin of Isaac's, for Abraham was Bethuel's uncle. He was glad, so he bowed his head and worshipped the Lord, thanking God for helping him find the right girl so quickly.

Rebekah ran home to tell her mother that the men were coming. When her brother Laban heard about it and saw the earring and the bracelets, he ran to the well to find the man and to bring him home. After Laban had helped him unload the camels and feed them, it was time for supper, so Laban took Abraham's servant in to meet the family.

But the servant said he couldn't eat until he had told them why he had come to their country. He said that he was Abraham's servant and that the Lord had blessed Abraham and made him very rich. He had silver and gold, flocks and herds, camels and donkeys; God had also given him a son, Isaac, who needed a wife.

He told how he had come to the well that day and had prayed that God would help him find the right girl to be Isaac's wife. He had prayed that if she was the right one she would answer pleasantly when he asked for water. He told them that while he was still praying, Rebekah had arrived. When he had asked her for a drink, she had said, "Of course, and I'll water your camels too!"

Then the servant asked them whether or not they would let Rebekah go with him to marry Isaac. They said yes; since it was the Lord who had brought him to them, Rebekah could go.

When the servant heard this he was very happy and worshipped the Lord. He brought out other beautiful presents—jewels of silver and gold, and beautiful clothing—and gave them to Rebekah. And he gave her mother and her brother presents too.

At last he and his men were ready to eat, and afterwards they stayed at Laban's house all night.

QUESTIONS

How did Abraham's servant find the right girl?

What was her name?

How did she show that she was the right girl?

12
Rebekah Says Yes

In the morning, Abraham's servant wanted to take Rebekah and leave at once to return to Abraham.

But her mother and brother said, "Let her stay with us a few days at least, and then she may go."

The man begged them not to delay him, for he felt that he should hurry back to his master again.

They said, "We'll call Rebekah and ask her if she is willing to go so soon."

She replied, "Yes, I'll go now."

So they sent her to Isaac and never saw her again, for Isaac's home was hundreds of miles away.

After many long, hot, weary days of camel travel, they came at last to Canaan just as the sun was going down. Isaac had gone out into the field for a walk, to be alone with his thoughts. Perhaps he wondered whether the servant would soon be back and whether God had helped him find a girl to be his wife. What would she be like?

Just then he looked up, and the camels were coming!

When Rebekah saw Isaac walking in the field, she asked the servant who it was, coming to meet them. The servant told her it was Isaac. Then she took a veil and covered her face with it. Isaac brought her into the tent that had been his mother's before she died. And Rebekah became his wife, and he loved her.

Abraham gave all that he had to Isaac and died at the age of 175. He was buried in the cave he had bought from Ephron, where he had buried Sarah.

QUESTIONS

Was Rebekah willing to go right away?

What was Isaac doing when he saw the camels coming?

What did Rebekah do when she saw Isaac?

How old was Abraham when he died?

13
Esau's Terrible Mistake

After Isaac and Rebekah were married, God gave them twin sons! The babies' names were Esau and Jacob. Esau was born first, and Jacob was born a few minutes later. So Esau was the older.

In those days the oldest son in every family had what was called the birthright. This meant he got more of the money and property when his father died. In fact, he got twice as much as the other children.

In Isaac's family, Esau was born first and had the birthright.

When Esau and Jacob grew up to be men, Esau was a hunter; he went out into the fields and woods and killed deer and brought the meat home to his father, Isaac. How his father loved that meat!

Jacob stayed home and helped care for his father's flocks and goats.

One day Jacob was at home cooking some especially good food when Esau came in from his hunting. Esau was very tired and hungry and asked Jacob to give him the food. Jacob said he would if Esau would give him his birthright! Esau didn't care about it, so he told Jacob he could have it; then Jacob gave him some food.

It was wrong for Esau to sell his birthright. God had given it to him, and he should not have sold it. It was wrong, too, for Jacob to take it.

QUESTIONS

What did Isaac and Rebekah name their twins?

Which one was older?

What is a birthright?

When did Esau give away his birthright to Jacob? Was this right?

14
Isaac Digs Some Wells

One time there was a famine in the land. A famine means that there isn't enough food. Isaac moved back to Gerar, hoping to find more food there. Gerar was the city where his father Abraham had lived many years before, after Sodom was destroyed.

God talked to Isaac at Gerar and told him to stay for a while. He promised to bless him. So Isaac planted crops. When the grain grew and became ripe, he reaped a hundred times as much as he had planted, because the Lord made it grow so well.

The Lord made Isaac very rich and great and gave him flocks and sheep, herds of cattle, and many servants.

But the Philistines, the people who lived in Gerar, were not pleased to see him so much richer than they were. They envied him and wished they had his flocks and herds. Then the king of the country came and told Isaac to go away.

So Isaac went away and found another place to live, a valley where there were some wells his father Abraham had dug when he was in Gerar. But the Philistines had filled them with dirt, so he couldn't get any water from them.

Isaac took out the dirt, and his servants dug a new well too. But the Philistines came along and said the wells belonged to them and took them away from Isaac's men.

Isaac told his men to dig another well, but the Philistines came and took it too. He tried once more, and this time the Philistines let him have the well.

Later Isaac moved to Beer-sheba, another place where his father Abraham had once lived. That night the Lord spoke to Isaac and told him not to be afraid of the people living there. They would not harm him, for God would be with him and take care of him and bless him. Then Isaac built an altar and worshipped the Lord.

Soon afterwards the king of the Philistines, who had told Isaac to go away, came from Gerar with two friends to visit Isaac. Isaac asked them why they had come, since they hated him and had sent him out of their country.

They said they wanted Isaac to promise never to harm them, for they saw that God was his friend. They knew this because of all the good things God had done for him. Isaac was nice to them and promised never to hurt them, and they promised not to harm him, either.

Isaac's servants dug a new well at Beer-sheba and found water. They were glad, because sometimes the water was very deep in the ground, and they had to dig a long time before they found it, and sometimes they couldn't find water at all.

During this time Isaac's son Esau had married two wives. Both of them were girls from Canaan. His father and mother were very sorry, because the girls of Canaan worshipped idols.

QUESTIONS
What is a famine?
What did the Philistines do when Isaac built the wells?
What did God tell Isaac in a dream?
What did Isaac and the king of the Philistines promise each other?
Whom did Esau marry?

15
Jacob Lies to His Father

Isaac was getting very old and couldn't see; he called his oldest son, Esau, and told him to take his bow and go out into the field and get a deer. "Then cook the meat just the way I like it best; then I will bless you."

He meant that he would ask God to be kind to Esau and give him many good things. So Esau went out into the field to hunt the deer for his father.

Rebekah heard what Isaac said, and she wasn't happy about it. She didn't want Esau to get the special blessing from Isaac, even though he was her oldest son; she wanted the best for Jacob.

When Esau had gone to hunt the deer, Rebekah told Jacob to kill two lambs from their flock of sheep and bring them to her. She cooked them so the meat tasted just like the deer meat Jacob's father loved so much. Then she got some of Esau's clothes for Jacob to put on and she put goat skins on the back of his hands and neck. She told him to take the food to his blind father and to say that he was Esau.

So Jacob took the food to his father. His father was surprised that Esau was back so soon. Because he was blind, he asked if it really was Esau. Jacob said yes, and that he had brought the deer meat his father had asked for.

His father put his hands on Jacob's hairy neck—remember, Jacob's mother had put a goat skin around his neck! —and smelled his clothes and was convinced that it was really Esau, even though his voice sounded more like Jacob's. And of course, it *was* Jacob, and not Esau at all. Jacob had fooled his father. So his father ate the food and blessed Jacob.

This was a very wicked thing that Jacob and his mother had done; for though Esau had sold him his birthright, Jacob should not have lied to his father.

As soon as Isaac had finished blessing Jacob, and Jacob had left the room, Esau came in from his hunting, with the deer meat he had cooked.

Isaac asked him, "Who are you?"

Esau answered, "I am Esau, and I have the meat you told me to get for you."

Isaac began to tremble, "Who was it, then," he asked, "who was just here? I have given him your blessing!"

Isaac knew now that it was Jacob who had come in first, and he told Esau that his brother had been there before him and had stolen his blessing.

Esau cried and begged his father to bless him too. So Isaac did, but he had already promised the best things to Jacob, and now he couldn't take them away from him.

Esau hated Jacob for what he had done, and said to himself, "My father will soon die and then I will kill Jacob."

Esau was not a good man; he did not love God. When a good man has done something wrong, he is sorry afterwards and asks God to forgive him and tries not to do it again. But when a bad man has been wicked, he does not repent and ask to be forgiven; he goes on and does the same thing again. Jacob did a wicked thing in lying to his father, but afterwards he became a good man who loved and served God as long as he lived, and God forgave him for his sin. But Esau was not willing to forgive Jacob; instead, he said he would kill him after his father died.

When Rebekah heard what Esau was saying, she sent for Jacob and told him to leave home and to go away to the country where she used to live, to the home of her brother Laban, so that Esau could not hurt him. But how could she get Isaac to agree? This is the way she did it:

She reminded Isaac that the girls of Canaan didn't love God, but prayed to idols. She reminded him that Esau had married two of these girls; she said she would rather die than see Jacob marry a girl who didn't love God.

Isaac agreed that Jacob must not marry a Canaanite girl. He called Jacob to him, blessed him again, and told him not to marry a girl of Canaan, but to marry one of his mother's relatives who lived far away in another country.

Then Isaac sent Jacob away to that far-off land where his uncle Laban lived, to see if he could find a girl there who would marry him. It was the same land from which Isaac's mother had come with Abraham's servant.

QUESTIONS
What did Isaac tell Esau to do for him?
How did Rebekah and Jacob fool Isaac?
Who did Jacob pretend he was?

Who got the first blessing from Isaac?
What did Esau say he would do to Jacob when he found out what Jacob had done?

Where did Jacob go to escape from Esau?
What excuse did Rebekah use for sending Jacob away?

16

Jacob Leaves Home

As Jacob travelled, he had a dream one night. He thought he saw some stairs in front of him reaching to heaven, and angels were going up and down them. God stood at the top of the stairs and told Jacob about the country He was going to give him and his children. And God said He would be with Jacob and take care of him wherever he went and would bring him safely home again.

Jacob woke up, and was afraid because God had been there and had spoken to him. So, very early the next morning, he got up and worshipped the Lord. He called the place Bethel, which means "the house of God."

Jacob promised that if God would take care of him—if He would give him enough food and clothes and would keep him from harm until he got back to his father's home again—then he would obey God and give Him a tenth of everything he had. Jacob meant that he would help the poor and the sick with his money and would build altars and would sacrifice burnt offerings. That is the way he would give a tenth of all that he had to God.

Jacob kept travelling a long, long time until he came to Haran where Laban lived. He saw a well there in a field, three flocks of sheep lying around it, and the shepherds with their flocks. A large rock was rolled over the mouth of the well to cover it; when all the flocks arrived each evening, the shepherds would roll away the stone and get water for the sheep. Afterwards the stone would be rolled back over the mouth of the well again.

Jacob asked the shepherds where they lived, and they told him at Haran.

"Do you know Laban?" he asked them.

"Yes," they said, "we surely do."

Jacob worked for Laban for many years
so that he could marry Laban's beautiful daughter Rachel.

Jacob asked if he was well.

"Yes, he is," they replied, "and look, here comes his daughter Rachel with his sheep."

Jacob went over to the well and kissed Rachel, then rolled away the stone and watered her sheep for her. He explained to her that he was her cousin, her Aunt Rebekah's son, and she ran and told her father.

When Laban heard that his nephew had arrived, he ran out to meet him. He gave him a warm welcome and brought him home. After Jacob had been there about a month, Laban asked him to stay and work for him.

By this time Jacob was very much in love with Rachel, and he told Laban he would work for him seven years if he could marry Rachel afterwards.

Laban was delighted. So Jacob worked for him the next seven years. Even though it was a long time, the years went by so fast they seemed like only a few days to Jacob because he loved Rachel so much.

But when the time was up Laban would not let him marry Rachel. He said her older sister Leah should be married first, so Jacob had to marry her in order to marry Rachel afterwards. He had to work seven more years for Rachel. This was very unfair of Jacob's uncle, but Jacob agreed to it because of his love for Rachel. So he stayed and worked seven years more, and both Leah and Rachel were his wives. Afterwards, he married two more girls, so he had four wives in all.

Jacob wanted to take his wives and children back home to the land of Canaan to see if his father and mother were still alive. He also thought that perhaps after all this time Esau would forgive him for stealing his blessing.

But Laban wouldn't let Jacob go. Laban said he realized that the Lord was blessing him because of Jacob's being there, and he asked what wages Jacob wanted in order to stay longer.

Jacob said that if Laban would give him some of his sheep and goats he would stay. So Laban did. Jacob's flock soon grew very large. After a while he was rich and had many slaves and camels and donkeys, as well as large flocks of sheep.

One day Jacob heard Laban's sons talking angrily about him. They said he had stolen their father's sheep and that was why he was so rich. Jacob noticed that Laban was not as friendly to him as he used to be.

Then God told Jacob to return home to his father in the land of Canaan. God said He would be with Jacob and take care of him and keep him from harm.

Jacob sent word for Rachel and Leah to meet him out in the field where he was caring for his flock. He wanted to talk with them where Laban couldn't hear what he said. He told them that their father wasn't friendly to him anymore and that the Lord had told him to go back to Canaan.

Rachel and Leah both agreed he must do whatever the Lord wanted him to.

QUESTIONS

What was Jacob's dream?

What was the name of the girl Jacob met at the well?

What did Laban say Jacob had to do before he could marry Rachel?

Who was Leah?

Why did Jacob decide to return home to his father?

17
Jacob Returns

Jacob got ready to return home to Canaan, to see his father and mother again after being away so many years. He put his wives and children on camels, took everything that belonged to him, and started back toward the land of Canaan, driving his sheep and goats ahead of him.

Laban was away when Jacob left, for Jacob had kept it all a secret. But three days after Jacob was gone, someone told Laban about it. Laban quickly took off after him. He was angry, for he didn't want Jacob to go. But that night, in a dream, God spoke to Laban and told him not to harm Jacob or even speak roughly to him.

It took seven days for Laban to catch up with Jacob, for Jacob had gone a long way—across a river and through a wide, lonely country—to a mountain called Gilead.

There Laban finally found him.

He asked Jacob why he had gone away secretly, taking his daughters Rachel and Leah and their children, without letting him know; for he wanted to kiss them all good-bye before they left.

Jacob said he had kept it a secret because he was afraid Laban wouldn't let Rachel and Leah go. Then Jacob got angry. He reminded Laban of the twenty years he had worked for him taking care of his sheep and goats, day and night, winter and summer, in the heat and the cold. And now, he said, Laban would have sent him away without paying him a penny for all the work he had done.

Laban replied, "Your wives are my daughters, and your children are my grandchildren. I would never harm them. Let's be friends and promise that we will never hurt each other."

Jacob agreed, and they made a huge pile of stones as a monument to remind them of their promise. If they were ever angry and came to harm each other, they would see that heap of stones and, remembering their promise, would go back home again.

Jacob then built an altar and offered up a sacrifice. Afterwards he and Laban and the men who were with him ate together and camped together that night.

Early the next morning Laban kissed Rachel and Leah and their children good-bye and blessed them.

He went back home and never saw them again.

As Jacob and his family travelled on toward Canaan, some angels met them. Perhaps God sent them to help Jacob, for soon he would be coming to where his brother Esau lived. Esau might try to kill Jacob for stealing his birthright so long before.

Jacob sent messengers to tell Esau about all that had happened during the twenty years he had been away. He was afraid. Though it had been twenty years since he had lied to his father and stolen Esau's blessing, Jacob still remembered his sin and was afraid of what Esau might do to him in revenge.

Jacob's messengers returned with the fearful news that Esau was coming to meet him with four hundred men. Jacob's heart sank. He divided all his flocks, herds, camels, and men into two groups. If Esau attacked one group, the other group might be able to escape.

Jacob prayed and asked God to save him from Esau, for he was afraid Esau would kill him and his wives and his children. He thanked the Lord for being so very kind to him before. He admitted he did not deserve the good things God had given him. When he had left Canaan twenty years before, he had owned only the staff he carried in his hand. But now, coming back, he had all these men with him, plus flocks and herds and camels. He had been very poor before, but God had made him very rich. He thanked God for this.

The next morning he sent some of his cattle as a present to Esau—220 goats, 220 sheep, 30 camels with their colts, 40 cows, 10 bulls, 20 donkeys, and 10 donkey colts.

He didn't send them all together, but put them into different flocks and sent the flocks one at a time.

His idea was that when Esau met the first flock, he would ask the man who was driving it, "Whose cattle are these, and where are you going?"

The man would say, "They are Jacob's; he has sent them to you as a present." The man driving the next flock would tell him the same thing, and this would continue until all the flocks had been given to Esau.

Jacob hoped these gifts, given one at a time, would make Esau so happy that he wouldn't hurt Jacob or his family or steal his flocks and herds.

QUESTIONS

Why did Jacob keep it a secret when he left Laban?
What did God tell Laban in a dream?
How long did it take Laban to catch up?
Why was Jacob afraid of Esau?
What did Jacob send to Esau as a present?

18
Is Esau Still Angry?

That night Jacob got up, awakened his family, and sent them across the river while he stayed behind alone.

Then a Man came and wrestled with him until dawn. Jacob was strong and kept on wrestling until the Man touched Jacob's thigh. Just by that touch, Jacob's thigh was put out of joint, and he became lame.

The Man said, "Let me go, for dawn has come."

But Jacob replied, "I won't let You go until You bless me."

"What is your name?" the Man asked.

So Jacob told him. (In their language Jacob's name means "tricky" or "unfair.")

The Man said, "I am giving you another name. You are no longer Jacob, but Israel." (Israel means "a prince of God.")

Who was this Man? He was the same person who had talked with Abraham about destroying Sodom and Gomorrah: this Man was the Lord. The Lord was glad that Jacob wanted God's blessing so much that he kept on asking for it all night; for Jacob refused to quit wrestling with God until God had given him a blessing.

Then Jacob said to the Man, "Now tell me *Your* name."

But the Lord answered, "Do not ask!" And the Lord blessed Jacob there.

Jacob was afraid something dreadful would happen to him because he had seen God and talked to Him. But God blessed him instead. Then Jacob (or Israel, as we can call him now) named that place Peniel, which means "the face of God." For he said, "I have seen God face to face."

The sun was rising as he limped back across the stream. He limped for the rest of his life because the Lord had touched him. Probably the Lord did this to make him always remember that God had blessed him.

When Jacob saw his brother Esau coming with four hundred men, he divided his wives and their children into groups. If Esau attacked, perhaps some of them could run away and escape, and not all be killed. Then Jacob went on ahead by himself to meet his brother.

He bowed low before him seven

times. Esau was pleased at Jacob's humility and ran to meet him. He put his arms around him and kissed him on the cheek, as men still do in that country when they meet friends. Then they both started crying.

God had promised Jacob to be with him and keep him from harm, and now we have seen how God kept His promise. First, He hadn't let Laban hurt Jacob or even speak roughly to him; then, He made that angry brother Esau, who had wanted to kill him, feel so good towards him that he cried!

Then Esau asked, "Who are these women and children?"

"They are all mine," Jacob replied. Then the slave-wives and Leah and Rachel came with their children, and the children met their Uncle Esau for the first time.

Esau asked Jacob "Why did you give me all of these sheep and goats?"

"They are a present for you," Jacob replied.

"No, you shouldn't do that," Esau said, "I have enough, my brother; keep them." For Esau had plenty of flocks and herds of his own.

But Jacob said, "Please accept my present," and he begged him until Esau finally did.

Esau suggested to Jacob that they travel together as they returned home, but Jacob was afraid to. He told Esau to go on ahead while he followed more slowly.

"Some of the children are too little to go very far at a time," he explained, "and the flocks and herds cannot be driven too fast or they will get sick and die."

Esau agreed and offered to leave some of his men with Jacob to help him and to protect him from robbers; but Jacob said he didn't need them. Finally Esau went back home.

QUESTIONS

What did Jacob and the Man do until dawn? Who was the Man?

What happened when the Man touched Jacob's hip?

What was Jacob's new name? What does it mean?

What did Jacob and Esau do when they met each other?

These two brothers haven't seen each other for many, many years! The one with the bow and arrows is Esau, and the other one is Jacob. Once they were angry with each other, but now in this picture they are friends again. The children of Esau are the Arabs and the children of Jacob are the Jews.

F.+R. Hook

19
Jacob Comes Home

After Esau had gone, Jacob went on to a place called Succoth. Here he stopped and rested his cattle before he went on to the land of Canaan.

Now God spoke to Jacob again. He told him to go to the city of Bethel and to build an altar there. Bethel was the place where Jacob had dreamed many years before about the stairs reaching to heaven with angels going up and down on it. In that dream God had promised to be with him wherever he went and to bring him back safely, and now God had done this.

Although it was more than twenty years since he had gone away, the Lord had taken care of him all that time, and at last he was safely home in his own country again. That is why God told him to go back now to Bethel where the promise had been given him and to build an altar there and worship the Lord.

So Jacob said to Rachel and Leah and to his sons, "Let's go to Bethel and build an altar there to God."

He told them how kind the Lord had been to him many years before when he was in trouble, when he was running away from his brother Esau, and how the Lord had been with him ever since and had taken care of him.

On the way to Bethel they passed through cities where the people might have robbed or killed them. But God made the people afraid, and they didn't try to harm Jacob and his family in any way.

They arrived safely at Bethel and built an altar there and sacrificed to God to show Him their thanks.

Then God spoke to Jacob, blessed him, and told him again, "Your name isn't Jacob anymore, but Israel." (Remember, Israel means "a prince with God"; this new name showed how much God loved him.)

God told him again that He would give all the land of Canaan to him and his children and his children's children, that they would become a great nation, and that some of them would be kings.

Then Jacob set up a great pile of stones at Bethel, so that everyone would always remember that this was the place where God had spoken to him.

Afterwards Jacob and those with

him started off to Bethlehem. Before they arrived, Rachel had another baby, and they named him Benjamin. But Rachel died soon afterwards, and they buried her beside the road. Jacob was very sad, for he loved Rachel very much. He piled stones over her grave to show where she was buried, and the stones stayed there for hundreds of years.

Finally Jacob came to Hebron where his father lived. Yes, Isaac, his father, was still alive. Though it had been so long since he had become old and blind, God had kept him alive until Jacob came home again.

But Isaac died soon afterwards and his sons, Jacob and Esau, buried him in the cave where Abraham and Sarah were buried. He was 180 years old at the time of his death.

Then Esau took his wives, his sons, his daughters, his cattle, and moved everything he owned to the land of Edom. For he and Jacob had so many cattle that there was not enough food for all of them to live together in the same part of the country.

QUESTIONS
Why did God tell Jacob to go to Bethel?
What was the name of Rachel's baby?
Did God keep Isaac alive until Jacob came home?

20
Joseph's Dreams

One of Jacob's twelve sons was named Joseph. He was the youngest in the family, except for Benjamin.

When Joseph was seventeen years old, he went out into the fields one day to help his ten older brothers who were taking care of the sheep and the goats. But while he was there he saw his brothers do something they should not have done. That night when he got home, he told his father. This was a good thing to do, for then his father could talk to his brothers about it, so that they would not do it again. But of course his brothers were angry with him for telling on them.

Joseph was his father's favorite son, so his father gave him a present of a beautiful coat. But this made his brothers jealous. From then on they couldn't seem to find one good thing to say about him!

One night Joseph had a strange dream, and the next morning he told his family about it.

"In my dream," he said, "all of us were out in the field tying bundles of grain stalks. Then your bundles stood around mine and bowed to it!"

This dream made his brothers even angrier. They thought Joseph was saying that they should bow to him as though he were their king.

"Do you think you are better than we are?" they demanded.

Then Joseph had another dream. This time he dreamed that the sun, the moon, and the eleven stars all bowed to him. His eleven brothers knew he was talking about them when he talked about the eleven stars bowing to him; and the sun and moon must mean their father and mother. This made them angrier than ever.

When he told his father about the dream, his father scolded him.

"Do you think your mother and brothers and I are going to bow to you?" he asked. "Don't be foolish!"

Soon after this his brothers took their father's flocks to Shechem to find pastures for them there. Shechem was a long way off. It took several days to walk there with the sheep.

Not long afterwards Jacob said to Joseph, "Go and find your brothers and see how they are getting along and how the sheep are." So Joseph went to find them.

But his brothers weren't at Shechem. He was wandering around in the fields looking for them when he met a man who told him, "Your brothers are at Dothan. I heard them say that they were going there." So Joseph went on to Dothan.

When his brothers saw him coming, they began talking to each other about killing him.

"Here comes that dreamer," they said. "Come on, let's kill him and throw him into a well, and we'll say some wild animal has eaten him. Then we'll see what happens to his dreams!"

When Joseph's brother Reuben heard them talking like that, he didn't like it at all. He wanted to save Joseph, so he persuaded his brothers to put Joseph into the well without hurting him. Reuben planned to come back after the others were gone and take Joseph out and get him home to his father again.

Joseph came, and they grabbed him and took away his beautiful coat and put him into a well that did not have any water in it.

Then they sat down to eat their lunches. Just then they saw some men coming along on camels: these men were taking things to the country of Egypt to sell. When Joseph's brother Judah saw them, he said, "Let's sell Joseph to them! We'll get rid of him and get some money, too."

The other brothers thought this was a good idea, so they pulled Joseph out of the well and sold him for twenty pieces of silver. The merchants put him on a camel and took him far away to the land of Egypt.

Reuben had not been there when Joseph was sold. When he came back to the well to get Joseph out and send him home, he was very sad.

"Joseph is gone," he exclaimed. "Oh, what shall I do?"

The brothers killed a young goat and dipped Joseph's coat in the blood.

Joseph was his father's favorite child. He gave Joseph a very pretty coat, but this made his brothers jealous and angry. Here you can see Joseph's father, Jacob, giving the coat to him.

R. HOOK

They brought the coat to their father and told him they had found it on the ground.

"Is it Joseph's coat?" they asked.

Jacob knew it was and began to cry. "Yes," he said, "it is Joseph's coat; a wild animal must have eaten him. Joseph is dead."

Then Jacob tore his clothing and dressed himself in sackcloth. Sackcloth is a dark, scratchy kind of cloth that people used to wear to show their sadness. Jacob said that he would mourn for his boy all the rest of his life.

QUESTIONS
What did Jacob give Joseph to wear?
What did Joseph dream about?
What did Joseph's brothers do to him? Why?
What did they tell their father had happened?

21
Joseph in Jail

The men who had bought Joseph took him to Egypt and sold him to a man named Potiphar, who was an Egyptian army officer. Joseph became his slave and lived in his house.

The Lord helped Joseph to work hard. His master was pleased with him and put him in charge of all his other servants. God blessed Potiphar because Joseph was in his home.

But after awhile Potiphar's wife wanted Joseph to do something very wrong. Joseph said no, and that made her angry. She decided to get even with him, so she told her husband a lie. She said that Joseph had tried to hurt her. Her husband believed her and put Joseph in jail.

But the Lord was kind to Joseph and made the man in charge of the prison feel friendly to him. He put him in charge of all the other prisoners. Joseph took the full responsibility of taking care of them. And the Lord helped Joseph do everything just the way it should be done.

One day Pharaoh, the king of Egypt, became angry with two of his officers; one of them was his baker, and the other was the man who brought him wine whenever he wanted a drink. Pharaoh put them

Joseph dreamed one night that someday he would be very great and famous, and everyone would bow to him.

both in the jail where Joseph was.

One night both of these men had dreams. When Joseph came in to see them the next morning, they looked very sad.

"What's the matter?" he asked. "Why so sad this morning?"

"We had strange dreams last night," they told him, "and there is no one to tell us what the dreams mean."

"Tell me your dreams," Joseph said, "and I'll ask God what they mean."

First the man in charge of the king's wine told Joseph his dream. He had dreamed about a grapevine with three branches. As he was looking at it, buds appeared on the branches and became bunches of ripe grapes. He was holding King Pharaoh's wine cup in his hand, so he took the grapes and squeezed out the juice from them into the cup. Then he gave the cup of juice to Pharaoh to drink.

God told Joseph what the dream meant. Joseph told the man that the three branches he had seen in his dream meant three days; in three days Pharaoh would let him out of jail and give him back his job.

"When you get out, don't forget about me!" Joseph said. "Ask the king to let me out, too."

Then Joseph told him how he had been sold by his brothers and brought to Egypt. He said he had done nothing wrong and shouldn't be in jail.

When the chief baker heard what a nice meaning the first man's dream had, he told Joseph his dream, too. He said he was carrying three baskets on his head, one above the other. In the highest basket were all kinds of food for Pharaoh, and the birds flew down and ate it.

Then Joseph told him what his dream meant. The three baskets meant three days. Within three days, King Pharaoh would kill him and hang him on a tree, and the birds would eat him!

Both dreams came true just as Joseph said. Three days later was the king's birthday, so he had a big party for all of his officers. He sent a messenger to the jail to bring back to the palace the man who was in charge of his wine, to work as he had before. But he hanged the chief baker, as Joseph had said.

I'm sorry to say that the officer in charge of the wine promptly forgot all about Joseph and didn't bother to tell Pharaoh about him or try to get him out of jail.

Two years later King Pharaoh had a dream. He was standing beside the Nile River in Egypt and saw seven cows coming up out of the water. They were fat and healthy, and they went into a meadow to eat grass. Then seven more cows came up out of the river. These cows were thin and scrawny, and they ate the fat and healthy cows! Just then King Pharaoh woke up.

Soon he went back to sleep and had another dream. This time he thought he saw seven ears of corn growing on one stalk. They were plump ears, well filled with grain. But afterwards seven other ears of corn grew on the stalk. These were thin and withered, and they ate up the seven good ears! Then Pharaoh woke up and realized it was all a dream.

The dreams bothered him so much that he sent for all the wise men of Egypt and told them his dreams, but they couldn't tell the king what his dreams meant.

Then the man in charge of the king's wine remembered the young man in jail who had told him and the chief baker what their dreams meant. He remembered that the dreams came true just as Joseph had said.

So the king sent for Joseph. He quickly shaved and put on other clothes and was brought to Pharaoh.

Pharaoh said to Joseph, "I had a dream last night, and no one can tell me what it means; but I'm told that you can."

Joseph said he could not do it, but that God would. Then Pharaoh told Joseph his dreams: the one about the seven thin cows who ate the seven fat ones and still looked so thin and starved afterwards; and the dream about the shriveled-up ears of corn eating the fat ears of corn.

Joseph told him that both dreams meant the same thing: God was telling Pharaoh what was going to happen in the future. The seven fat cows and the seven good ears of corn meant seven years of wonderful crops, when everyone's gardens would grow; and the seven thin cows and the seven withered ears of corn meant seven years when nothing would grow. First there would be seven good years in Egypt. The corn would grow tall, and there would be plenty to eat. But afterwards there would be seven years of poor crops when people would be hungry, for nothing would grow in their gardens.

Joseph told Pharaoh to put someone in charge of making the people of Egypt save up corn during the seven good years. Then during the hungry years, the people would have enough food. The king thought this was a good idea and he put Joseph in charge!

QUESTIONS

Was Joseph a good worker?
Why did Potiphar put him in jail?
What did the king's cupbearer dream?
What did the king's baker dream?
What did Joseph say the dreams meant? Was he right?
What were King Pharaoh's two dreams?
What did Joseph say the dreams meant? How did he know?
What job did Pharaoh give to Joseph?

22
Joseph Meets His Brothers

So Pharaoh didn't send Joseph back to jail any more, but made a great man of him instead. The king took off his own ring and put it on Joseph's finger and dressed him in beautiful clothing and put a gold chain around his neck.

He gave him a chariot to ride in, with soldiers running along ahead of him shouting, "Bow down." And all the people bowed low before him wherever he went. He was in charge of all the land of Egypt and was almost as great as the king. Everyone had to do whatever Joseph told him to do.

During the first seven years, when all the farms had such good crops, he went to all the farmers and made them give some of their corn to Pharaoh. Joseph took this grain and stored it in the nearby cities, keeping it safe until the seven years of famine came. Soon he had so much grain stored away that he stopped counting it.

Then the seven years of good crops ended, and the seven years of poor crops began. Soon everyone began to be hungry because there was so little to eat. When all their food was gone, the people came to Pharaoh to ask for something to eat.

"Joseph is in charge," Pharaoh said, "Go to him and he will tell you what to do."

Then Joseph opened up the buildings where the grain was kept and sold it to the people.

Joseph's brothers were still living in the land of Canaan when the famine came. Soon their grain was gone, and they needed food for their father and for their families. They looked at each other blankly, not knowing what to do.

Then their father said to them, "Don't just stand around looking at each other! I hear there is grain in Egypt; go and buy some for us, so we won't starve to death."

So Joseph's ten brothers got on their donkeys and rode for many days until they came to Egypt. Joseph's youngest brother, Benjamin, stayed with his father in Canaan, for his father was afraid to let him go. He was afraid something might happen to him just as it had to Joseph.

Since Joseph was the governor of Egypt, he was in charge of selling the grain to the people. But his brothers didn't recognize him in his Egyptian robes. They came and bowed low before him, never imagining he was their brother! But Joseph knew them right away.

Do you remember Joseph's dream that had made his brothers so angry? He had dreamed that his brothers' sheaves of grain bowed to his sheaf, and that the sun and moon and eleven stars had bowed to him. And now it had come true—here were his brothers bowing to him now!

Imagine Joseph's surprise and joy to see his brothers again, even though they had been so cruel to him. But he pretended he didn't know them at all. He spoke roughly to them and asked them, "Where are you from?"

"From the land of Canaan," they said. "We have come to buy food."

Then Joseph said, "No, you are spies and have come here to see what trouble we are in, so that you can bring an army and attack us."

"Oh, no, sir," his brothers answered, "we have come to buy food. We are all one man's sons. We are men who speak the truth. We are not spies."

Joseph pretended he didn't believe them and said again that they were spies. They told Joseph more about themselves and why they had come. They said one of their brothers was with their father in the land of Canaan far away, and one was dead.

Joseph still pretended not to believe them and said he would find out whether they were telling the truth or not. This was what he would do. He would send one of them back to Canaan to get their youngest brother they had told him about and bring him to Egypt. All the others must stay until he returned.

Then he put them in jail for three days.

On the third day he talked with them again. This time he said that only one of them must stay, and all the others could go home to take food to their families. One must stay so that Joseph would be sure the others would come back again and bring their youngest brother with them.

When his brothers heard this, they were very sad. They said God was punishing them for their sin of selling their brother as a slave long ago. Reuben (the one who had intended to take Joseph out of the well and bring him back to his father) said to his brothers, "Didn't I tell you not to sin against the child? But you wouldn't listen to me."

Joseph listened to them talking to each other. They didn't know he could speak their language and understand them, for he had talked to them only in Egyptian, and a servant had told them in their own language what he was saying to them. But of course Joseph understood every word they said.

When he realized how sorry they were for what they had done to him, he had to go away and cry. Afterwards he came back again and talked to them some more, but he still pretended that he thought they were spies.

Then he took Simeon and tied him up while all the others watched, for Simeon was the one he chose to stay in Egypt while the others went home after Benjamin.

Then Joseph told his servants to fill his brothers' sacks with grain and to put into the tops of their sacks the money they had paid for the grain;

but he didn't tell his brothers that the money was there.

Finally their donkeys were loaded, and all except Simeon started back home to Canaan. That night when they stopped to eat, they opened a sack to get some food. There was the money right at the top of the sack! They were frightened, for they didn't know how it got there.

QUESTIONS
How great did Joseph become?
What did he do during the seven good years?
Why did Joseph's brothers come to Egypt?
Did they recognize Joseph?
Was Joseph happy to see his brothers?
What did he pretend he thought they were doing in Egypt?
Why did Joseph keep Simeon in jail?
What did Joseph tell his servants to do with the brothers' money?

23
Joseph's Favorite Brother

After many hard days of travel Joseph's brothers finally returned home and told their father what had happened.

"The governor of Egypt spoke roughly to us," they said, "and thought we were spies. 'Oh, no,' we told him, 'we aren't spies. We are honest men. We are twelve brothers, though one is dead, and the youngest is with our father in the land of Canaan.'

" 'Well, I can find out easily enough whether you are telling me the truth,' the governor said. 'Leave one of your brothers here and take food for your families, and go get your youngest brother and bring him to me. Then I will know that you aren't spies.' "

When they went out to unload their donkeys and empty the grain out of their sacks, can you imagine their surprise when each of them found his money at the top of his sack? There it was, lying right on top of the grain! When Jacob saw the money, he was afraid.

"You have already robbed me of two children," he said, "for Joseph is gone and Simeon is gone. And now you want Benjamin, too."

Then Reuben said to his father, "Kill my two sons if I don't bring Benjamin safely back to you! I will take care of him."

But Jacob said Benjamin couldn't go. Joseph was already dead; and if anything happened to Benjamin, it would be too much to bear.

The famine became worse and worse. Soon the grain brought from Egypt was almost gone and Jacob said to his sons, "Go back to Egypt again, and buy us a little more food."

But Judah told his father they couldn't go unless Benjamin was with them; for the governor had told them, "You must not return without your brother."

"But why did you tell him you had another brother?" Jacob cried out.

"The man asked us," they replied. "He said, 'Is your father still living? Have you another brother?' How could we know he would say, 'You must bring your brother here?' "

Then Judah told his father he would take care of Benjamin.

"I'll see that nothing happens to him," Judah said, "and if I don't bring him safely back again, then I will bear the blame forever. If we had not stayed home so long, we could have gone to Egypt and been back by now."

Finally their father agreed. He told his sons to take a present to the governor.

"Take some honey, spices and myrrh, and nuts and almonds. Take extra money with you, along with the money that came back in your sacks before; perhaps it was a mistake. And take your brother, and go."

Then Jacob prayed for his sons and begged God to make the governor kind to them; for if his children were taken away from him, he would die with sorrow.

The brothers took the presents, the money, and their brother Benjamin and went back to Egypt. Soon Joseph saw them standing before him again.

When Joseph saw Benjamin with them, he said to his servants, "Take these men home to my house and get dinner ready for them, for they are going to eat with me."

Joseph's brothers were frightened when they saw where the servant was taking them. They thought Joseph was going to keep them as his slaves and never let them go home again. They thought it was because of the money they found in their sacks.

They went to Joseph's servant and told him all that had happened: that when they were going home to Canaan, they had opened their sacks and found their money there. But they hadn't stolen it, and now they had brought it back again.

Joseph's servant told them not to worry, there was nothing to fear. He brought their brother Simeon to them, the one who had been left as a prisoner while they went home for Benjamin.

The servant gave them water to wash their feet and hay for their donkeys. Then they got out the present their father had sent to the governor, to give it to him when he came home at noon, for now they knew they were to eat there.

When Joseph arrived, they brought his present to him and bowed low before him.

He spoke kindly to them and said, "Is your father well, the old man you told me about? Is he still living?"

They answered, "Yes, he is in good health, he is still alive." And they bowed to him again.

Then Joseph saw his brother Benjamin and said, "Is this your youngest brother you told me about? May God be good to you, my son."

Then Joseph hurried away to find a place where he could be alone. He went into his bedroom and started crying because he was so happy at seeing his little brother again. But then he washed his face, and when he came out again he kept back the tears so that his brothers didn't know what he had been doing!

Then they all sat down to eat. Joseph ate by himself at one table, and his brothers were at another table; for Egyptians never ate with Hebrews, and everyone thought Joseph was an Egyptian!

Joseph seated the oldest brother at the head of the table, with the next oldest next to him, and so on down the line according to their ages. Who could have told him their ages, they wondered! But you and I know that no one had to tell him, for he knew it all the time!

Joseph served all the food from his table, and waiters took it over to the table where the brothers were. He gave Benjamin five times as much as any of the others! You see, he loved Benjamin more than the others because he and Benjamin had the same mother, Rachel, who died when Benjamin was born. (All the brothers had the same father, Jacob, but there were four different mothers.)

QUESTIONS

What did Joseph's brothers tell their father?
Why did they have to take Benjamin to Egypt?
Would their father let Benjamin go?
Why did Jacob send presents to the governor? Did he know it was Joseph?
For whom did Joseph tell his servants to prepare dinner?
Why were Joseph's brothers frightened?
Which brother did Joseph love best? How do you know?
Do you know why he loved him best?

24
A Big Surprise

Joseph told one of his servants to fill the men's sacks with grain and to put back their money in the top of the sacks, just as he had before.

"And," Joseph said, "put my silver cup in the sack of the youngest boy, Benjamin." So that is what the servant did.

In the morning, as soon as it was light, the men got on their donkeys and started happily back to Canaan.

But they were hardly out of the

city when Joseph told his servant to chase after them and stop them and ask them why they had stolen his silver cup? So the servant hurried and caught up with them.

They were very much surprised and wondered what the servant was talking about when he asked them about the cup.

"God forbid that we should do such a thing as to steal the governor's cup," they said.

They reminded the servant that they had proved their honesty by bringing back the money they found in their sacks before, and they certainly wouldn't steal a silver cup.

"If any of us stole it, we ourselves will kill him," they said, "and all the rest of us will go back and be slaves."

The servant said that only the one who had stolen the cup would be a slave; the rest of them could go on home.

Then they all took down their sacks from the backs of their donkeys and opened them so the servant could look. He began with the sack of the oldest, but the cup wasn't there. He went on down the line, but none of them had the cup. Then he came to Benjamin. And there was the cup, right at the top of Benjamin's sack.

Now the poor brothers didn't know what to do. They tore their clothes in sorrow and finally loaded up their donkeys and went back to the city with Benjamin and the servant.

When they saw Joseph they all fell to the ground before him. Joseph pretended that he thought Benjamin had really stolen his cup and said they should have known that he would find out about it. Judah stood up and spoke to Joseph for all of them.

"Oh, what shall we say to my lord?" he asked. "God has found out our wickedness; we are all your slaves."

But Joseph said that only the one who had stolen the cup would be his slave; the rest of them could go on home to their father.

Judah pleaded with Joseph. He reminded him about the first time they had come to Egypt for food, and how Joseph had asked them whether they had a father and a brother at home. And they had told him yes, their father was an old man now, and their brother was still very young. They had told him that their father dearly loved his youngest son, for he was all he had left from his wife Rachel, who was dead.

But Joseph had said that they must bring their younger brother to Egypt with them the next time they came. They said then that the boy could not leave his father, for if he did, his father would die. But Joseph had told them that if they didn't bring their brother, they could never come back.

Judah explained to Joseph that when they went home, they had told their father what he had said. And when their father wanted them to go back to Egypt to buy more food, they had told him, "We can't, unless Benjamin goes with us, for the man told us not to come back without him." Then their father told them that if they took Benjamin, and anything happened to him, he would die of sorrow. So now, Judah said, if they went home without Benjamin, their father would die of shock and sorrow. Then Judah begged Joseph to let him stay and be a slave instead of Benjamin, and to let Benjamin go home to his father.

Joseph couldn't stand it any longer. He ordered all of his servants to leave the room, and Joseph was left alone with his brothers. Then he began to cry. His brothers watched in surprise.

Finally, when he could speak, he told them, "I am Joseph! Oh, tell me more about my father!"

His brothers were too surprised and frightened to say anything. Then Joseph called them over to him.

"I am your brother Joseph!" he said again.

Then at last they realized what he was saying—and what excitement there was as they all hugged and kissed each other!

Joseph told them to stop being sad for what they had done to him, because God had turned it all into good. Joseph loved his brothers and didn't want them to be unhappy and afraid, and that is why he told them this.

He explained to them that the famine would last another five years, for God had said that there would be no crops for all that time.

"Hurry back to my father," he told them, "and tell him that his son Joseph says, 'God has made me ruler over all of Egypt. Come down to me, and you will live in the best part of the land. Bring your children, your flocks and your herds, and all that you have, and I will take care of you.' Tell my father how great I am in Egypt, and describe all you have seen. Hurry home and bring my father here."

Then Joseph hugged his brother Benjamin and cried again, for he was so glad to see him. And Benjamin cried too, and so did all the brothers.

QUESTIONS

Why did Joseph tell his servant to hide a silver cup in Benjamin's sack?

What did Judah offer to do, if Joseph would let Benjamin go home?

Did Joseph forgive his brothers for doing wrong to him years ago? Why?

25
Israel Moves to Egypt

When Pharaoh heard that Joseph's brothers had come, he was very glad.

He told Joseph to tell them to return for their father and their wives and children and bring them all to Egypt where there was plenty to eat.

"Take some of my wagons for your wives and little ones to ride in," he said, "Don't bother to bring any of your furniture and other things, for I will give you everything you need."

Then Joseph gave new clothes to

each of them—giving Benjamin more than any of the others! And he sent his father twenty donkey-loads of food and other good things. Then at last he let his brothers start home again to get his father and their families.

When they finally arrived home, what joy there was!

"Joseph is alive," they shouted. "He is governor over all the land of Egypt!"

It seemed too wonderful to be true, and Jacob did not believe them at first; but when he saw Pharaoh's wagons that he had sent, he finally realized that his sons were telling the truth.

"It is proof enough," he said at last. "Joseph is alive! I will go and see him now before I die."

So Jacob and his children and their families all left their homes in Canaan and started off to the land of Egypt. They stopped briefly at Beer-sheba, where grandfather Isaac had built an altar many years before and had sacrificed to God.

That night God spoke to Jacob and said, "Don't be afraid to go down into Egypt, for while you are there I will make your family grow into millions of people."

God told Jacob that He would take care of him in Egypt, and that when the time came for him to die, Joseph would be by his side.

So Jacob and his sons and their families left Beer-sheba and went on to Egypt. They took their cattle with them and all of their belongings.

Jacob sent Judah ahead to tell Joseph that his father was on the way. When Joseph heard this, he jumped into his chariot and raced out to meet him. He and his father wept for joy when they finally saw each other again after all those long years apart.

Israel—that was Jacob's other name, remember?—said to Joseph, "Now I can die in peace, for I have seen you again. To think, that you are still alive!" He could scarcely believe it.

Then Joseph invited some of his brothers to come with him to meet Pharaoh and to tell him that they had arrived with their flocks and herds. When Pharaoh asked them what kind of work they did, they told him they were cattlemen just as their grandfathers had been. Joseph told them to say this because it was the truth, and also because Joseph wanted Pharaoh to send them to live in Goshen, which was the best part of the land of Egypt for raising cattle. So Pharaoh gave them permission to go there.

Then Joseph took his father to meet Pharaoh and to bless him.

QUESTIONS

How did Pharaoh show his friendship for Joseph and his family?

Describe the reunion of Joseph and Jacob.

What kind of work did Joseph's brothers do?

What was the name of the part of Egypt where Jacob and his sons lived?

26
Joseph Saves the Egyptians

The famine was dreadful everywhere. No one had enough to eat. The people of Egypt had used up all of their grain, and now their gardens and fields didn't give them any more food, for nothing would grow.

They came to Joseph to buy the corn he had stored away during those seven wonderful years when everything grew so well. But soon all their money was gone. Although there was plenty of food for sale, they did not have any money to buy it.

Then Joseph told them to bring their cattle, for Pharaoh would give them food if they would give him their animals.

But after awhile all their cattle were gone, too—all sold to Pharaoh in exchange for food. Now the people had nothing left but their land and themselves. They said they would give their land to Pharaoh and be his servants if he would give them more food. So Joseph traded them food for land, until all the land of Egypt belonged to Pharaoh.

At last the seven years of famine ended, and Joseph gave the people seed to plant. For he knew that now the corn would grow again.

He told them that since they had sold all their land to Pharaoh, it wasn't theirs any longer, but Pharaoh would let them use it if they would give him a fifth of all the food they raised on it. The people were glad to do whatever Joseph said, for they were thankful to him for saving them from starving. So from then on they gave twenty percent of all their crops to the government as taxes.

QUESTIONS

Why didn't the people have enough to eat?

Where did Joseph get so much corn to sell?

How did the people buy corn when they ran out of money?

After the famine, why did the Egyptians still give part of their crops to Pharaoh?

27
Jacob Blesses His Children

Jacob lived in the land of Goshen with his children and their families for seventeen years, but at last the time came for him to die. He became very sick, and a messenger came to tell Joseph that his father was getting worse and wouldn't live very much longer.

So Joseph took his two sons, Manasseh and Ephraim, and went to visit his father. Jacob sat up in bed and talked with him, and told him how kind God had been to him all during his long life. And he told Joseph about the time when God had spoken to him in a dream as a young man—the dream about a stairway going up to heaven, with angels walking up and down on it.

Joseph told his father that he had brought his two sons with him so that Jacob could bless them. Jacob said to bring them close to him. Then he put his arms around them and kissed them and asked God to help them. What a happy day that was for Jacob and Joseph and the two boys!

Then Israel called in all his other sons and blessed each one of them. He told them he was going to die, but that God would be with them and bring them back to the land of Canaan. He commanded his sons to take his body back and bury it in the same cave where his grandfather Abraham was buried, and his grandmother Sarah, his father and mother—Isaac and Rebekah—and his wife Leah.

When Jacob had finished all he had to say to his sons, he lay back on the bed and died. Joseph put his face down to his father's face and wept over him and kissed him. Then he commanded his servants to embalm his father. This meant to put spices and other things into his body to prepare it for burial. All the Egyptians mourned for him for seventy days.

Joseph told Pharaoh that his father had made him promise not to bury him in Egypt, but to bury him back in Canaan. So Pharaoh granted him permission to leave the country for awhile.

Joseph and his brothers went up to Canaan to bury their father, and many of Pharaoh's government officials and other wealthy men from the land of Egypt went with them.

After the funeral, Joseph's brothers were afraid. They thought that now, with their father dead and unable to defend them, Joseph would surely punish them for all the bad things they had done to him.

They sent a message to him saying that before their father had died, he had expressed the hope that Joseph would forgive them. When Joseph heard this he cried, for he knew they were afraid of him. His brothers now came and fell down before him and said, "Don't kill us; we will be your slaves." But he told them not to be afraid, for though they had wanted to hurt him by selling him as a slave, yet God had turned the harm into good by putting him in Egypt where he could save many people from starving to death from the famine. And he spoke kindly to them and comforted them.

Joseph was in Egypt all the rest of his life, and lived to see the birth of his great-grandchildren. But after many years he sent for his brothers and told them that the time had come for him to die.

He asked that his bones be taken back to Canaan when God took the nation of Israel back there again. This didn't happen for four hundred years, but when Moses led the people of Israel back into the Promised Land of Canaan, he took along Joseph's bones just as Joseph had requested.

So Joseph died when he was 110 years old. His body was embalmed and put into a coffin in Egypt.

QUESTIONS

Whom did Joseph and his two sons go to visit?

Where did Jacob want to be buried?

What did Joseph's brothers think would happen to them after the funeral? Why?

Where did Joseph want his bones to be buried?

28

The Princess Finds a Baby

After hundreds of years Jacob's children and grandchildren and their children became a great nation in Egypt. There were so many of them that it took many days to count them all.

Then a new king began to rule over Egypt who didn't care anything about Joseph and all he had done to save Egypt. When the new king saw how many of Jacob's descendants there were, he was afraid of them. He thought that some day when his enemies came to fight against him, Jacob's huge family would turn against him and help his enemies, then run away and go back to their own country. He didn't want that to happen; he wanted them always to stay in Egypt as slaves to do his work.

So this wicked king persuaded the Egyptians to treat Jacob's family (now known as the Israelis, or people of Israel) very cruelly. They made slaves of them, making them build houses for the Egyptians and work in their fields. But the more cruelly the Israelis were treated, the more of them there were. God had promised Abraham and Isaac and Jacob that their children would become a great nation, and now God was doing as He had promised.

Pharaoh told the women who took care of the babies to kill all the Israeli boys as soon as they were born. The girls could live, he said, because they would never be able to fight against him.

But these women feared God and did not obey the king. They let the little boys live, too, and God blessed these women for doing this. Then Pharaoh told all his people that whenever they saw a baby boy among the Israelis, they must throw him into the river so he would drown or be eaten by the crocodiles. What a cruel king he was! But God protected his people from this evil king.

Now I'm going to tell you about what happened to one of the little Israeli babies, whose name was Moses. Moses became one of the greatest men in all the world when he grew up.

His mother and father loved him very much, and they were afraid that the Egyptian king's men would come and take their baby away and kill him. So the baby's mother hid him at home for three months after he was born. Then she made a little basket from the stems of long weeds that grew by the river and smeared the outside of it with tar to keep the water out. It was a little boat that would float safely on the water.

She put her baby in the little boat and floated it out among the bushes at the edge of the river. She told her daughter, whose name was Miriam, to hide there and watch to see what would happen to the baby and to try to help him in any way she could.

Soon a princess came along. She was one of the daughters of Pharaoh and had come to bathe in the river. She and her maids were walking along the river's edge when she saw the little boat in the bushes. She sent one of her maids to get it and bring it to her so that she could open it and see what was inside. And when she opened it, there was a little baby! She felt sorry for him and decided to adopt him as her own son.

"This must be one of the Hebrew children," she exclaimed. Miriam, the baby's sister, had been watching; and now she went over to the king's daughter and asked, "May I go and get one of the Hebrew women to take care of the baby for you?" The princess said yes, so Miriam ran home to get her mother! When her mother came, the princess said to her, "Take care of this baby for me, and I will pay you well!"

So the baby's mother took him home again!

QUESTIONS

What did the new king do to the Israelis?

Why did Moses' mother put her baby in a boat in the water?

Who found the baby?

What did the baby's sister do?

29
Moses Runs Away

When the little baby was older, the princess sent for him to come and live in her palace and be her son. She called him Moses, an Egyptian word that means "taken out," because she had taken him out of the water. He lived with her for many years and was a prince.

One day when Moses was grown up, he went home to visit his real father and mother and the other people of Israel to see how they were getting along. While he was with them, he saw an Egyptian hitting an Israeli. Of course this made Moses very angry, for the Israeli was one of his relatives. Moses looked to see if anyone was watching, then killed the Egyptian and hid his body in the sand.

The next day as he was walking around he saw two Israelis quarrelling. He scolded the man who was in the wrong and asked him why he had hit the other man. This made the man who had done wrong very angry.

"You can't tell *me* what to do," he shouted. "Are you going to kill me as you killed that Egyptian yesterday?" Then Moses realized that someone had seen him kill the Egyptian and that everyone knew about it.

When Pharaoh heard what Moses had done, he wanted to arrest Moses and have him executed for murder; but Moses ran far away to the land of Midian, where Pharaoh couldn't find him. He sat down beside a well trying to think what to do next. Soon some girls came to get some water. There were seven of them, all sisters. They wanted to water their father's flock, but some shepherds who were standing beside the well told them to go away.

Moses told the shepherds to be quiet, and he helped the girls water their flocks. When the girls got home, their father asked why they had come back so quickly. They told him that an Egyptian had saved them from the shepherds and helped them get the water.

"Where is the man?" their father

A princess found baby Moses in the little boat his mother made for him. She adopted him and he became her son—a grandson of the king of Egypt!

Y. Hook

asked. "Why didn't you bring him home with you?" He told them to go back and find him and invite him home for dinner. So Moses went home with them. They all wanted him to stay and help them. He liked it so well that he married one of the girls and lived there many years, caring for their father's sheep.

QUESTIONS
Why did Moses get to live in a palace?
Why did Moses run away?
How did Moses help the girls at the well?

30
God Asks Moses to Help Him

All the time Moses was living in the land of Midian, the Egyptians were being very cruel to the people of Israel. Finally the people of Israel cried to the Lord because of their sufferings, and the Lord heard them and looked down from heaven and pitied them. He decided to send Moses to help them.

One day while Moses was taking care of his sheep out in the country near Mount Horeb, suddenly he saw fire flaming up out of a bush. Moses ran over to see what was happening and saw a strange thing: the bush was on fire but didn't burn up! Just then God called to him from the bush, "Moses! Moses!"

We can hardly imagine how surprised and frightened Moses was, but he said, "Yes, Lord, I am listening." God told him not to come any closer and to take off his sandals because the place where he stood was holy ground, for God was there.

God said, "I am the God of your fathers—the God of Abraham, Isaac, and Jacob." Moses hid his face, for he was afraid to look upon God.

Then God told him that He had seen the sorrows of the people of Israel, and had heard their cries, and had come down from heaven to set them free from the Egyptians.

There was a new king in Egypt by this time, not the one who had chased

Moses was surprised to see a bush on fire—and it kept burning and burning without burning up! It was because God was there. He had come to talk to Moses about rescuing the Israelis.

Moses out of the country. This new king was called Pharaoh just like all the other kings of Egypt. The Lord told Moses to go to Pharaoh and to tell him to stop hurting the people of Israel and to let them leave Egypt and go back to Canaan. The Lord told Moses he was to lead them out of Egypt and to bring them to that very mountain where He was talking with Moses.

But Moses was afraid to go; he was afraid that Pharaoh would hurt him or kill him if he said to stop hurting the people of Israel.

But God told him, "I will be with you and help you."

God told Moses to tell the people of Israel that God wanted them to leave Egypt and to follow Moses to a good land where there would be plenty to eat and where everyone would be happy and free.

Moses said he was sure that no one would listen to him or believe that the Lord had really sent him. He had a shepherd's rod in his hand, which the Lord told him to throw on the ground. Moses did, and God made it change into a snake! Moses was afraid of it and ran away.

Then the Lord said, "Grab it by the tail." Moses did, and it was changed back into a shepherd's rod again!

Then the Lord said to Moses, "Put your hand into your coat." When he took it out, his hand had turned white! It was covered with a dreadful disease called leprosy that made it white.

"Put your hand back into your coat again," God said. When Moses took it out this time, it was well again!

God gave Moses power to do these two wonderful miracles so that when the people of Israel saw him do them they would believe that God had sent him. But if they still would not believe him, even after he had done these two miracles, then Moses must take some water out of the Nile River and pour it on the ground, and the water would change to blood!

Moses still didn't want to go, and he began to make one excuse after another. He could not speak well in front of people, he said.

But the Lord told him again to go to Pharaoh, and Moses begged the Lord to send someone else. Then the Lord became angry with Moses for refusing.

Moses had a brother whose name was Aaron. God finally said that Aaron could go with Moses and make the speeches to Pharaoh and the people of Israel. God would tell Moses what to say, Moses would tell Aaron what to say, and Aaron would tell the people and the king what God wanted them to know.

When the Lord had finished talking with him from the burning bush, Moses went back home and received permission from his father-in-law, whose name was Jethro, to return to Egypt to visit his people.

QUESTIONS

What was strange about the bush Moses saw?

What did God tell Moses to do? Why?

What did Moses' rod turn into? How did he get his rod back?

What happened to Moses' hand when he put it into his coat?

Why did God give Moses power to do these two miracles?

31
Pharaoh Won't Listen

The Lord told Moses' brother, Aaron, to go and meet Moses at Mount Horeb. When he got there, Moses told him all about everything that had happened and what God had said for him to do.

Moses and Aaron went together to Egypt and talked with the Israeli leaders, and showed them the two miracles. He threw down his shepherd's rod and it became a snake; then he put his hand into his coat, and it became white with leprosy. When the leaders saw these two miracles, they believed that God had sent Moses and Aaron, and that Moses was to lead them out of Egypt.

Then Moses and Aaron went to Pharaoh and told him, "The Lord God of Israel says, 'Let my people leave Egypt and worship Me in the desert.' "

"Huh!" Pharaoh scoffed. "Who is the Lord, and why should I obey him? I've never heard of that god, and I certainly won't let these Israeli people out of my sight."

Moses and Aaron begged Pharaoh to let the people go. They said that God would punish Pharaoh if he didn't obey. But Pharaoh was angry. He asked Moses and Aaron what right they had to get the people all excited about going on a trip and keeping them from their work. "Stop this foolishness right now," he shouted. "Get out of here, and get to work!"

One of the jobs of the Israeli slaves was to dig clay and make bricks by drying the clay in the sun. The clay was mixed with pieces of straw to make the bricks tougher and stronger. This straw was given to them by Pharaoh.

But now Pharaoh was so angry that he said from now on they must get their own straw, but still make just as many bricks as before. Pharaoh said they were lazy, and that was why they wanted time to go and worship their God.

So the people of Israel went out into the fields and gathered straw. But though they worked very hard, they could not make as many bricks as when the straw was brought to them. Some of the people were brutally beaten because of this.

The leaders of the people of Israel told Pharaoh that he wasn't being fair. How could he expect them to make as many bricks now that he was not giving them the straw?

He replied, "You're lazy! You're lazy! That's why you say, 'Let us go and sacrifice to the Lord.' " And he told them to get to work, for no straw would be given to them anymore.

Then the Israelis saw that they were in real trouble, and some of them went to Moses and Aaron and accused them of making things worse for them instead of better.

Moses complained to the Lord about it and asked why He had sent him. He had only made things worse for the people, and now the Egyptians were more cruel than before.

"Just wait," the Lord told Moses, "and you'll see what I am going to do. Tell My people that I will rescue them from their slavery, and they will be My special people. I will lead them into the land I promised long ago to Abraham, Isaac, and Jacob."

Moses told the Israelis what God said, but they wouldn't listen to him anymore.

Then the Lord sent Moses and Aaron to talk to Pharaoh again. "When Pharaoh tells you to do a miracle, throw your shepherd's rod on the ground," the Lord said, "and it will change into a snake, just as it did before."

So Moses and Aaron went to Pharaoh. Aaron threw down his rod, and sure enough, it changed into a snake. Then Pharaoh called for his magicians. They brought some shepherd's rods and threw them down, and their rods changed into snakes too. The Lord let the magicians do just as Aaron had done!

But Aaron's snake swallowed up all the other snakes! Yet even so Pharaoh wouldn't let the people go.

QUESTIONS

Who was Aaron?

What two miracles did Moses perform in front of the Israeli leaders?

What did Pharaoh do to make the work harder for Moses' people?

What happened when the magicians threw down their sticks?

32
The Terrible Troubles Begin

The Lord told Moses to go to Pharaoh the next morning when he would be taking a walk beside the river. When Pharaoh came along, Moses must go up to him and say, "The God of the Hebrews has sent me to tell you, 'Let My people go. They must sacrifice to Me in the desert.' "

So the next morning Moses went to the river. Sure enough, Pharaoh was out for a walk, and Moses told Pharaoh what the Lord had said. But Pharaoh refused to let the people go.

The Lord told Aaron to strike the river with his shepherd's staff, while Pharaoh and his men were watching. When Aaron did this, the water in the river changed to blood! Suddenly all the water in Egypt, in all the streams and ponds, changed to blood too! So the fish died, and the Egyptians had no water to drink.

Then Pharaoh's magicians came; and they, too, turned water into blood, because the Lord let them do it. So Pharaoh went back home to his palace and wouldn't let the people go.

The Egyptians dug holes in the ground near the river to get water fit to drink, for the blood stayed in the river seven days.

The Lord now told Moses to announce to Pharaoh that unless he let the people go, God would send millions of frogs that would cover the entire nation and be in the Egyptians' houses and even jump into their beds.

But Pharaoh said he didn't care, he wouldn't let the people go.

So God told Aaron to point his shepherd's staff over the rivers of Egypt. Suddenly, millions of frogs came up out of the water.

Pharaoh's magicians held out their rods over the rivers, and more frogs came out; for again God allowed them to do the same thing Aaron did.

But now Pharaoh and the people of Egypt were in real trouble. Frogs were everywhere. He called for Moses and Aaron and asked them to pray to God to take the frogs away. "If you do," Pharaoh said, "I'll let the people go to sacrifice in the desert."

"When do you want the frogs to die?" Moses asked.

Pharaoh replied, "Tomorrow."

So the next day Moses prayed to the Lord, and the Lord did as Moses asked. The frogs in the houses and villages and fields all died, and the people gathered them in great heaps. The smell of dead frogs was all over the land. It was terrible!

But when Pharaoh saw that the frogs were dead, he wouldn't let the people go.

Then the Lord commanded Aaron to strike the dust on the ground with his shepherd's staff, and the dust changed into very small insects called lice that covered the people and the cattle.

Pharaoh's magicians tried to make lice, too. But this time they couldn't, because God wouldn't let them. So they told Pharaoh that it was God who had changed the dust to lice. But Pharaoh's heart was wicked. He wouldn't listen, and he wouldn't let the people go.

QUESTIONS
What happened to all the water in Egypt?
Tell about the frogs.
What did Pharaoh promise he would do if God took away the frogs? Did he keep his promise?
What did the dust turn into?

33
Flies, Boils, and Hail!

The Lord again told Moses to get up early the next morning to meet Pharaoh as he went to bathe in the river. Moses must tell him again to let the people go. If he still refused to let them go, the Lord would send swarms of flies all over Egypt.

Moses did as the Lord commanded, but again Pharaoh said no, he wouldn't let the people go. So the Lord sent the flies and they covered the whole country. The houses of the Egyptians were swarming with them, and the ground was covered with them.

But in the land of Goshen where the Israelis lived, there were no flies at all, because the Lord did not send them there.

Pharaoh was very much upset about the flies, as he had been about the frogs. He called Moses and Aaron and told them, "All right, the people of Israel can sacrifice to their God, but

Flies, flies everywhere. They filled the houses and swarmed outside. No one could escape them.

they must stay in Egypt to do it. They mustn't go out into the desert."

Moses told Pharaoh they must leave Egypt and go three days' journey into the desert to sacrifice to the Lord, for that is what God had told them to do. Then Pharaoh said all right, they could go, but not that far.

"Please," he begged Moses, "pray to your God to get rid of the flies." Moses said he would, but he warned Pharaoh not to lie to him again by not letting the people go. Moses went away and prayed to the Lord, and the Lord took away the swarms of flies from Pharaoh and his people. Suddenly there wasn't one left in all the land! But when Pharaoh saw that the flies were gone, he changed his mind again and wouldn't let the people go.

Next the Lord commanded Moses to tell Pharaoh that a great sickness would destroy the cows and sheep of Egypt, but the cows and sheep of the Israelis would not be hurt at all.

But Pharaoh still said no, the people could not go.

So the Lord sent the sickness. The Egyptian cows and horses and donkeys and camels and sheep began to die. Pharaoh sent to see if any of the Israelis' cattle were dead, but not one of them was even sick! When Pharaoh found that the animals belonging to the people of Israel were all right, his heart grew even harder and more wicked than before, and he would not let the people go!

Then the Lord told Moses and Aaron to stand where Pharaoh could see them and to toss handfuls of ashes into the air. Those ashes, the Lord said, would cause terrible sores to break out all over the bodies of the Egyptians and their animals. So Moses stood before Pharaoh and tossed the ashes into the air; and the sores broke out on the Egyptians and on their animals throughout all Egypt, except where the Israelis lived. This time the magicians didn't even try to do the same thing, for the terrible boils were on them, too.

But Pharaoh's heart was still wicked, and he wouldn't let the people go!

Then the Lord told Moses to get up early the next morning and tell Pharaoh that God would send a great hailstorm—a storm such as there had never been before. Moses told Pharaoh to quickly get all his cattle in from the fields, for everything out in the storm would die. Some of the Egyptians feared the Lord, and when they heard what was going to happen, they brought in their slaves and cattle from the fields and put them in barns where the hail couldn't hurt them. But most of the Egyptians didn't believe what Moses said and left their animals out in the fields anyway.

Then the Lord told Moses to point his hand toward heaven, and suddenly a terrible hailstorm began, and lightning ran along the ground. Never before had there been such a storm in Egypt. The hail crashed down onto the fields, killing men and animals alike. It broke the bushes and trees, and all the grain was broken and spoiled, except for what hadn't yet grown up above the ground.

But in the land of Goshen, where the people of Israel lived, no hail fell at all!

Then Pharaoh sent for Moses and Aaron and said, "I have sinned; the Lord is good, and I and my people are wicked. Beg the Lord to stop the terrible thunder and hail, and I will let you go right away."

Moses said that as soon as he was out of the city he would ask the Lord to stop the thunder and hail. But he knew that Pharaoh still wouldn't obey the Lord. Moses went out into the terrible storm, but God kept the hail and fire from harming him. When he was out of the city he prayed, and the thunder and hail stopped.

And when Pharaoh saw that it had stopped, he changed his mind and wouldn't let the people go!

QUESTIONS

What three plagues are told about in this chapter?

What happened to the Israelis' cows?

Why didn't Pharaoh let the Israelis go?

34 Locusts and Darkness

Moses and Aaron went to Pharaoh again to tell him that if he wouldn't obey the Lord, tomorrow the Lord would send locusts to destroy everything that was left. Locusts are like grasshoppers, but they eat gardens and crops.

Pharaoh's men were very frightened. They remembered about the river turning into blood, and about the frogs and the lice and the flies. They remembered about the sickness of the cattle and about the boils and the hail. They begged Pharaoh to let the Israelis go so that no more punishments would come.

Moses and Aaron were told to come to Pharaoh's palace, and he said to them, "All right, go and sacrifice to the Lord your God; but which of the people do you want to go?" Moses answered that all the people of Israel must go—young and old, sons and daughters, flocks and herds—for they must have a religious holiday.

Pharaoh said that only the men could go—the women and children must stay in Egypt. Moses and Aaron were then dragged away by Pharaoh's guards and told to get out and stay out.

Then the Lord told Moses to lift his hand toward heaven, and the locusts would come. Then the Lord caused the east wind to begin blowing, and it continued blowing all that day and all night too. In the morning the wind brought great clouds of locusts that filled the sky and covered the ground! They were all over Pharaoh's palace and in all the houses of the Egyptians. The locusts ate everything that the hail had left, until there was not a leaf to be seen on the bushes or trees in all the land.

Pharaoh hurriedly called for Moses and Aaron and said, "I have sinned." He asked Moses to forgive him only this one more time and to pray that God would take the locusts away.

So Moses went out and prayed. The Lord sent a very strong west wind that blew the locusts into the Red Sea where they were drowned. There wasn't one locust left in all of Egypt!

But when Pharaoh saw that the locusts were gone, he wouldn't let the people go!

Then the Lord commanded Moses to hold up his hand toward heaven, and it became dark all over the land. The Egyptians couldn't see one another for three days, and couldn't leave their homes.

But in the houses of the Israelis it was as light as usual.

Then Pharaoh called for Moses, and said, "All right, go and worship the Lord! Take your children with you, but not your flocks and herds." But Moses told him no, they wouldn't go without their animals. That made Pharaoh angry. He told Moses again to get out of his sight and never come back again. If he did, Pharaoh said, he would kill him.

QUESTIONS

What did the locusts do to the land of Egypt?

How long did the darkness last?

What did Pharaoh say that the people could take with them? What did he say they couldn't take?

35
The Worst Plague of All

Moses became angry and told Pharaoh that God was going to send one last terrible punishment. The Lord Himself was coming to Egypt and in the middle of some night soon, He would cause the oldest son in every Egyptian home to die. Even Pharaoh's oldest son would die. There would be a great cry of grief all through the land, such crying as there had never been before and would never be again. But not one of the Israeli children would be hurt in any way; then Pharaoh would know that he and his people were the ones the Lord was punishing, and not the Israelis. Moses told Pharaoh that after this punishment the Egyptians would come and beg Moses to take his people and leave the country.

Moses stalked out in great anger, leaving Pharaoh sitting there.

Then the Lord instructed the Israelis to be ready to leave Egypt in four days. He said to ask the Egyptians for jewels and silver earrings and gold necklaces to take with them. And the Lord caused the Egyptians to want to give their jewels to the people of Israel.

The Lord said for each family in Israel to get a lamb and to kill it on the fourth evening. Then they must take the blood of the lamb outside and sprinkle it on each side of the door and up above the door, making three marks of blood on the outside of every Israeli home. They must stay in their houses and not come out again until morning, for that night the angel of the Lord would come and kill the oldest child in every home where the blood was not on the door.

On that fourth evening they must roast the lamb, God said, and everyone in the house must eat some of it. They must be dressed to travel as they ate it, all ready to go, with their shoes on and their walking sticks in their hands. And they were to hurry as they ate, for when the Lord went through the land on that night and caused the oldest sons to die, at last Pharaoh would really let them go.

God promised that He would pass over the houses where the blood was on the door and not harm anyone inside. The supper of lamb they ate that night was called the Lord's "Passover," because the Lord passed over the houses where He saw the blood on the door.

At last the terrible night came. In the middle of the night the Lord passed through the land. Wherever He saw the marks of blood, He passed over that house and no one there was harmed. But there were no marks of blood on the houses of the Egyptians, and the Lord sent his destroying angel into every one of those homes and caused the oldest son to die. Even Pharaoh's oldest son died that night.

The king got up in the night with all his people, and there was a great cry of sorrow and despair through all the land, for in every home the oldest son was dead.

Pharaoh called for Moses and Aaron and told them to leave Egypt at once and to take all the people of Israel with them. "Take all your flocks and herds," he begged, "and leave tonight." All the Egyptians begged them to go quickly, for they were afraid the Lord would kill them all, not just their oldest sons.

So the people of Israel left Egypt that night, carrying their clothes on their shoulders. And the Egyptians gave them jewels of silver and gold, and clothes too; so they went away with great riches. And many of the Egyptians went with them.

The lamb that was killed in every Israeli home that night was in some ways like our Saviour. The lamb died for the people, and its blood saved them. That is what happened again many years later, when Christ the Saviour came as the Lamb of God to die for each of us.

And just as God passed over those who had the marks of the lamb's blood on their houses, and did not punish them, so it will be when Christ comes back again. He will not punish those who have the marks of the Saviour's blood in their hearts—those whose hearts have been cleansed from sin by His blood.

That night as they left Egypt, the Israelis took the body of Joseph with them, for Joseph had made his brothers promise four hundred years before that they would take his body home again to Canaan! At last his dying wish was being fulfilled.

QUESTIONS
What did God command the Israelis to do so that the Lord would pass over their houses?
Why was their supper that night called the Lord's "Passover"?
In what ways were the lambs that were killed that night like Jesus?
What did the Israelis take with them as they left Egypt?

36
The Egyptian Army Dies

Finally the people of Israel had escaped from Egypt. At last they were free. What a wonderful feeling it must have been—they were no longer Pharaoh's slaves.

The Lord led them toward the Red Sea to a place called Etham, on the edge of the desert. There they set up their tents and made camp.

As they travelled along, the Lord was very kind to them; He went before them in a cloud to show them the way. The cloud was shaped like a pillar reaching up toward heaven. They could see it all the time. As they walked along, it moved on ahead of them so that they could follow it and know where God wanted them to go. In the daylight it looked like a cloud, but at night it became a pillar of fire. It gave them light at night, so they could travel whenever the Lord wanted them to, day or night.

Almost as soon as the Israelis left Egypt, Pharaoh and his officers were sorry they had let them go. "Why did we ever let them get away from us?" they asked.

Then Pharaoh and his soldiers got into their chariots and chased after the people of Israel. They caught up to them as they were camping by the Red Sea. The Israelites saw the Egyptians coming and were frightened and cried out to God. Then they turned against Moses and blamed him for getting them into this trouble. It would have been better to stay and be slaves to the Egyptians, they said, than to be killed in the desert. But Moses told them not to be afraid. "Wait and see what the Lord will do for you," he said. "For the Egyptians you have seen today will never be seen again. The Lord will fight for you, and you won't need to do a thing."

When Pharaoh and his army had almost caught up with them, the cloud in front of them moved behind them, and came between them and Pharaoh's army. The cloud was dark on the side where Pharaoh was, and his soldiers couldn't see. But the side of the cloud that was turned toward Israel was as bright as fire and gave the people light in their camp!

The Lord said to Moses, "Tell the people of Israel to start marching to the sea. When they get there, point your shepherd's staff toward the sea, and a path will open up in front of you through the water, and My people will go across on dry ground!"

So Moses pointed his staff toward the sea, as the Lord had told him to, and the water opened up ahead of them, making a path across the bottom of the sea. The water was piled high on each side of them like walls, but they walked across on dry ground and were soon safe on the other side!

The path through the water was still there the next morning, so when Pharaoh saw what had happened, he and his chariots started across between the walls of water. But the Lord made the wheels come off the Egyptian chariots, so they ground to a stop.

Then the Egyptian soldiers panicked. "Turn around! Let's get out of here!" they shouted. "The Lord is fighting against us; He is for the Israelis."

But before they could get out, the Lord told Moses to point his staff toward the sea again. When he did, the water came together and covered the Egyptians, drowning the entire army. Not one soldier was left alive. The Israelis saw them lying dead upon the seashore where the waters washed them up.

But Moses and the Israelis were safe on the other side of the Red Sea. There they sang a song of praise to the Lord for saving them from Pharaoh.

QUESTIONS

How did God guide the Israelis by night and by day?

How did God use the cloud to keep the Israelis safe?

How did the Israelis get across the Red Sea?

What happened when the Egyptians tried to follow?

R. Hook

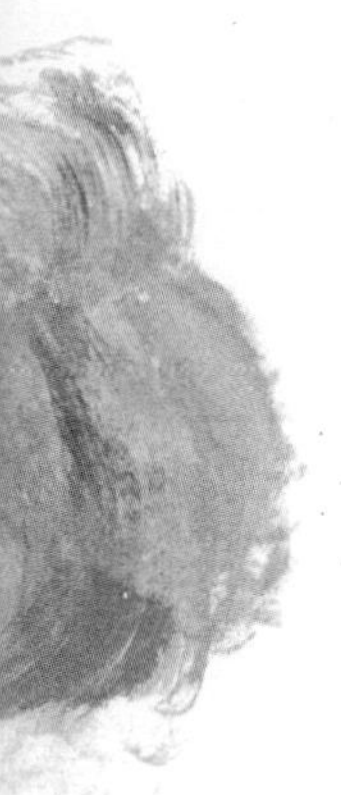

37
God's Patience

The Israelis now found themselves in a great desert between Egypt and the Promised Land, Canaan, where God was leading them. Soon their water was gone and they were thirsty. They finally arrived at a place called Marah and found water there, but it was too bitter to drink. But instead of asking the Lord to help them, they blamed Moses.

Moses prayed to the Lord about it, and the Lord showed him a certain tree and told him to throw it into the water. He did, and suddenly the water was no longer bitter, and the people could drink it!

They travelled on and came to Elim; there were twelve wells there and seventy palm trees. Going on farther they came to the desert of Sihn. But now a rebellion broke out; the people began to riot against Moses and Aaron because they were hungry. They said they had had plenty of food in Egypt and they wished God had killed them there instead of bringing them out into the desert to die of starvation.

The Lord heard their complaints and told Moses He would send meat for them that evening, and as much bread as they wanted in the morning. Then they would know that the Lord was taking care of them.

The Lord did as He promised; for that evening about the time the sun was going down, huge flocks of birds called quail came flying just above the ground. The people killed them with clubs and ate them for supper.

The next morning after the dew was gone, small, white, round things were all over the ground. No one knew what it was, so they called it "manna," which in their language means, "What is it?"

"This is the bread the Lord promised you," Moses told them.

God led Moses and the people by a cloud in the sky. At night the cloud looked like fire burning. When the cloud moved ahead, the people followed, but when it stood still, they knew God wanted them to stop for awhile.

The Lord told the people to go out each day except Saturday and gather as much as they wanted. He told them not to take more than they needed for one day, since there would be a fresh supply each morning. The Lord wanted them to trust Him one day at a time for their daily bread. Some of the people didn't obey, and gathered enough for two days instead of one. The next morning the extra manna was spoiled, with worms crawling around in it. They had to throw it away and get fresh manna off the ground.

Each morning when the sun warmed the ground the manna melted away and disappeared. But early the next morning there was always more waiting for them.

The only exception was on the seventh day of each week. That was the Sabbath day when God told them not to work. On that day there was no manna on the ground. The day before the Sabbath they gathered twice as much as other days, and what they saved to eat the next day didn't spoil. Some of the people went out on the Sabbath anyway to try to get some, but there wasn't any. And the Lord was angry, so they didn't do it anymore. After that they rested on the Sabbath day as the Lord had told them to.

The manna was small and round, and white like coriander seed. It tasted like bread made with honey. Moses told Aaron to get a bottle and fill it with manna. He wanted to keep it forever, so that the children who weren't even born yet would be able to see a sample of the food the Lord fed His people with in the desert. Moses did this, and God kept the manna from spoiling for hundreds of years until they finally lost it.

The Israelis ate manna every day for forty years until they finally came to the land of Canaan.

As they travelled they came to a place called Rephidim, but found no water there. So they complained again. "Get us water," they demanded of Moses.

"Why blame me?" Moses asked.

"Because you brought us here," they retorted.

Then Moses cried out to the Lord and said, "What shall I do? For they are almost ready to stone me."

By this time they were close to Mount Horeb where Moses had seen the fire burning in the bush. The Lord told him to lead the people to a certain rock on Mount Horeb and to strike the rock with his walking stick. Moses did as the Lord said, and water poured out giving everyone enough to drink!

QUESTIONS

How did Moses make the bitter water safe to drink?

How did God provide food for the Israelis?

Why didn't God want the people to collect manna on the Sabbath?

How could several million people get food while travelling through a desert for forty years? God rained down food from heaven! This food was called "manna."

38
God Helps the Israelis

Then some soldiers from the country of Amalek attacked them. There was a brave man among the people of Israel whose name was Joshua. Moses said to him, "Choose the men you want, and go out tomorrow to fight with the army of Amalek. I will stand on top of the hill with the rod of God in my hand."

Joshua did as Moses told him to. As Joshua's men fought with the Amalekites, Moses, Aaron, and a man named Hur went up to the top of a hill where they could watch. Moses pointed his staff toward the men fighting in the valley below. As long as he held it up, the people of Israel were winning; but whenever he let it down, the enemy began to win. Soon Moses' arm became very tired, so Aaron and Hur rolled a rock over to where he was standing, and he sat on it. They stood on each side of him and held up his hands all day until the battle finally ended at sunset. So God gave the victory to the Israelis.

God was displeased with the Amalekites for fighting against His people and said that the time would come when all the Amalekites would be destroyed.

The Israelis arrived at Mount Sinai three months after leaving Egypt. They camped at the bottom of the mountain while Moses went up and talked with God. God told Moses to remind the people of how He had helped them by protecting them from the Egyptians, and He said that He would love them more than any other people if they would obey His commandments.

God told Moses to go down and call the people together. In three days God would return to the top of the mountain to talk with Moses there, and all the people would hear Him. He told Moses to tell the people to wash their clothes and to be very careful not to sin, in order to get ready for God's visit. None of them were allowed to go up onto the mountain, for anyone who did must die. A loud trumpet blast far up on the mountain would be the signal for everyone to gather quickly at its foot and wait there for God to speak.

Moses went down and told the people, and they put on fresh, clean clothing for the awesome occasion.

On the morning of the third day there was a terrible thundering and lightning, and the Lord came to the top of the mountain in a thick cloud. And there was a trumpet blast so long and loud that the people trembled with fear.

Then Moses led them out of the camp to the foot of the mountain. The whole mountain was covered with smoke because the Lord was there. The smoke climbed skyward as from a furnace, and the mountain shook. The trumpet blast grew louder and louder. Moses called, and God answered him, summoning him to the top of the mountain.

QUESTIONS

What did Moses do while Joshua was fighting the Amalekites?

Where did the Israelis go to listen to God speaking to them?

How did the mountain look when God was on it?

39
God's Commandments

Then God gave the people of Israel these Ten Commandments.

1
You Must Not Have Any Other God But Me

This means that we must love God more than anyone or anything else; for anything we love more than God becomes our god instead of Him.

2
You Must Not Make Any Idol, nor Bow Down to One, nor Worship It

Many people in the world make statues, or idols, and believe that they are gods which can help them. But in this commandment God forbids making such statues or bowing down to them or worshipping them. God is the only One who can save men, and we are to worship Him alone. This commandment also means that we are not to worship money or clothes or anything else but God.

3
You Must Not Take the Name of the Lord Your God in Vain

This means that whenever we speak God's name, we must do it reverently, remembering how great and holy a name it is. If we speak it carelessly or thoughtlessly, we offend

R. Hook

Him. This commandment teaches us not to swear.

4

Remember the Sabbath Day, to Keep It Holy

In this commandment God instructed His people not to work on the Sabbath. This was because God rested on the seventh day after His six days of work when He created the heavens and the earth.

5

Honor Your Father and Your Mother

Next to obeying God, we should obey our parents. We must not delay doing what they tell us to, and shouldn't even wait to be told. This is God's commandment.

6

You Must Not Kill

We break this commandment by murdering, but we also break it when we are angry with someone and wish he were dead. For then we have the wish for his death in our hearts, and God sees murder in our hearts.

7

You Must Not Commit Adultery

When a man lives with a woman as his wife when he is already married to somebody else, it is adultery. God says we must never do this, and it is a sin when a man and a woman sleep together when they are not married. He commands us to be pure in all our thoughts, words, and actions.

8

You Must Not Steal

You must not take anything for your own that belongs to someone else. If you have ever done this, whether by mistake or on purpose, God commands you to give it back or pay for it.

9

You Must Not Tell Lies

This means that you must never say anything about another person that isn't true. And when you are saying what is true, you must be very careful how you say it. Don't leave out a little or add a little to make it different from the real truth.

10

You Must Not Covet Anything That Is Your Neighbor's

To covet a thing is to wish it were yours. We must not do this. God, who knows best, gives to each of us just what He wants us to have.

When all the people heard the terrible thunder and the blast of the trumpet and saw the lightning and the smoke and heard God's voice, they were terrified. They said to Moses, "You tell us what God wants, and we will do it; but don't let God speak with us, or we will die." Moses told them God hadn't come down to kill them, but to make them afraid to sin against Him.

The people stood a long way off

God called Moses to the top of Mount Sinai, where He gave him the Ten Commandments, written on two tables of stone.

from the mountain while Moses climbed up to the dark cloud where God was. There God talked with him and gave him many more laws for the Israelis to obey.

When the people heard these laws, they promised to obey all of them.

QUESTIONS
See how many of the Ten Commandments you can remember.
Tell what any two of the Ten Commandments mean.
What did the people promise God?
What does this mean: "You must not covet anything that is your neighbor's"?

40
God Talks to Moses

The Lord told Moses to come up to the top of Mount Sinai again, so that He could give him two tablets of stone with the Ten Commandments written on them. So Moses went up, along with Joshua, his assistant.

Then a cloud came down and covered the mountain for six days. On the seventh day the Lord called to Moses from the cloud. Moses stayed there on the mountain for forty days and forty nights. The people at the bottom of the mountain saw the glory of the Lord like a bright, burning fire at the top.

The Lord told Moses that the people should build a Tabernacle, or church, where they could worship Him. He showed Moses just how to do it; He even gave Moses a pattern of the building, so he would know just what it should look like.

It was to be very beautiful, with many beautiful things in it made of gold, silver, and brass. There were to be curtains of finespun linen, with rich needlework embroidery. God told Moses to ask the people to bring gifts of gold and silver and everything else that was needed, and to give these gifts to the Lord.

God also commanded Moses to make an Ark to be placed inside the Tabernacle. This Ark was a beautiful gold box—it was made of wood and then covered inside and outside with pure gold.

God said that when the Ark was finished, Moses was to put into it the two stone tablets God would give him —the tablets with the Ten Commandments written on them.

The Ark was to have a cover of solid gold, with two gold angels standing on it, one at each end, facing each other with their wings spread out. This

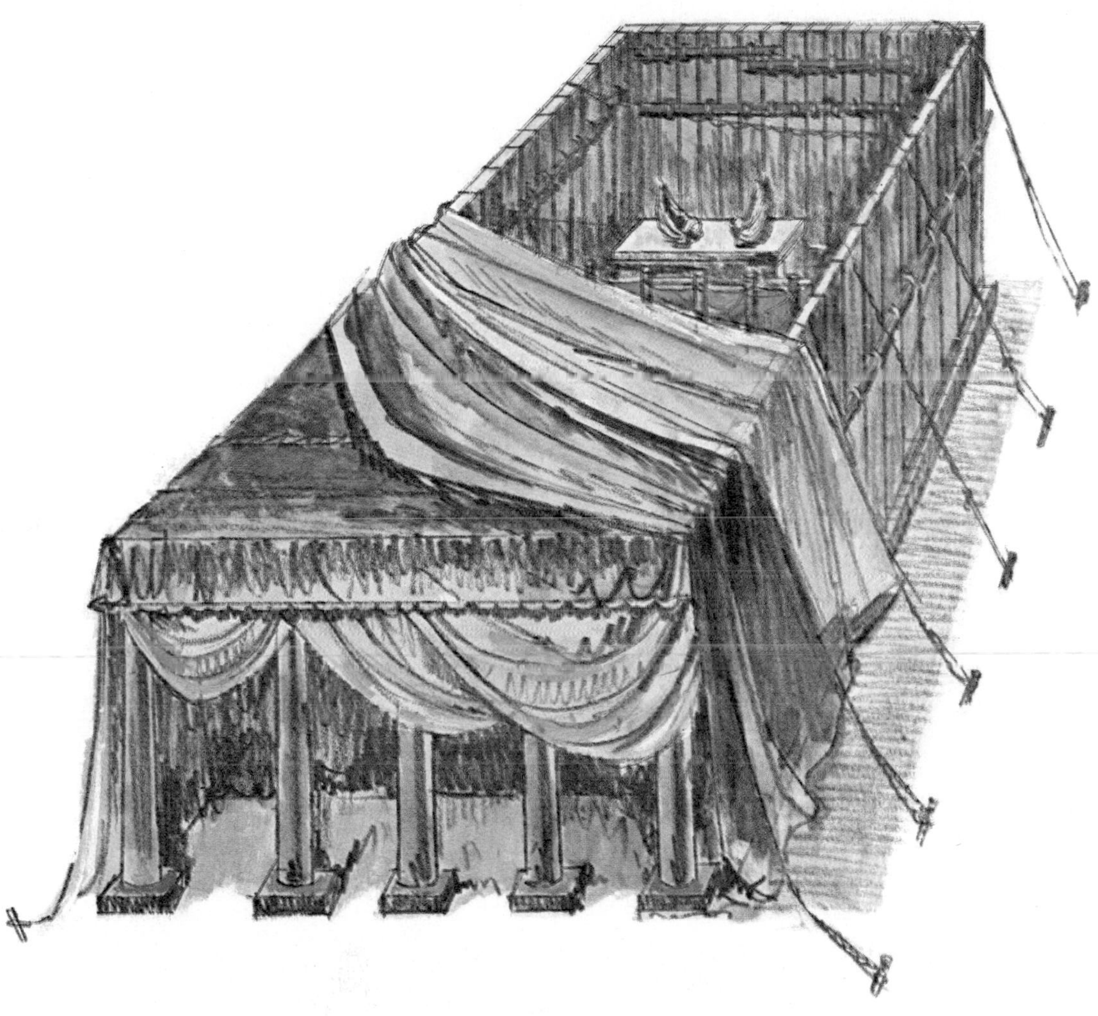

Moses followed God's detailed instructions very carefully so that everything about the Tabernacle would please God.

cover with the angels on it would be called the mercy seat.

There was to be a gold table, too—made of wood and covered with gold—to stand in the Tabernacle, and a gold lampstand to give the Tabernacle light.

God told Moses just how to construct the Tabernacle. It would be portable, easy to take apart and put together again, for the people were to carry it with them on their journey to the land of Canaan.

The sides of the Tabernacle were to be made of boards covered with gold. These boards were to stand on end and be fastened together with a curtain that was spread over them as a roof. The door of the Tabernacle would be a curtain; and another beautiful curtain, called the veil, would hang across the inside of the

Tabernacle, dividing it into rooms. In the inner room Moses was to place the Ark with the mercy seat. The gold table and the gold lampstand would go in the outer room.

There was to be a little yard all around the Tabernacle and a wall to protect the yard. An altar would stand in the yard in front of the door of the Tabernacle. It would be made of wood covered with bronze, large enough to sacrifice oxen, sheep, and goats on it. For until the Saviour came into the world to be sacrificed on the cross, the Israelis were told to sacrifice these animals as illustrations of what would happen to the Saviour when He came.

The Lord said that Aaron and his sons would be God's priests. They would sacrifice to God the animals brought to the Tabernacle by the people of Israel. Aaron would be the High Priest; he would be in charge, and his four sons would be his assistants.

Beautiful clothes were made for Aaron. There was a linen turban for his head, with a plate of gold fastened to the front of it, and these words written on it: "Holiness to the Lord." This reminded Aaron that God commanded him to be holy, and it reminded the people to honor Aaron as God's High Priest.

Next to his skin Aaron wore a robe made of embroidered linen. Over the linen robe he wore a long, sleeveless blue coat. Hanging from the lower edge of this outer robe were decorations made to look like pomegranates —blue, and purple, and scarlet. A pomegranate is a fruit something like an orange. Gold bells were hung between the pomegranates.

Over the blue robe, Aaron wore a many-colored vest, called the ephod.

Over the front of this vest was a square piece of richly embroidered cloth with twelve different kinds of jewels on it, called the breastplate. These jewels were of the most beautiful kinds, including a ruby, a sapphire, and a diamond, each in a beautiful gold setting. So Aaron's clothes were very splendid.

His four sons had special clothes, too; but theirs were not as beautiful as Aaron's, because he alone was the High Priest.

QUESTIONS

What is a Tabernacle? What were some of the things in it?

Why was it portable? (What does "portable" mean?)

What were the doors and walls made of?

Tell about Aaron's clothes.

The Ark was the most important part of the Tabernacle.
Its cover, with the cherubs on it, was called the mercy seat.

41
Aaron Makes an Idol

The Lord told Moses to bring Aaron and his sons to the door of the Tabernacle and bathe them there. Then he put on them the special robes made for them and poured olive oil on Aaron's head, anointing him as God's High Priest. Afterwards Moses gave sacrifices to God on their behalf. That is the way Aaron and his sons became priests.

They sacrificed two lambs every day for the sins of the people. These lambs were killed and then burned before God on the great bronze altar, one in the morning and the other in the evening.

God told Moses to make another altar, too, of wood covered with gold. It was smaller than the bronze altar, and stood inside the Tabernacle in the room with the gold table and the gold lampstand.

This altar was not to sacrifice animals on, but for burning incense. When incense burns, it sends up a smoke that is sweet to smell.

The animals sacrificed on the bronze altar represented the Saviour being offered up for our sins. The incense sending up its sweet smoke from the gold altar represented the prayers of God's people. Aaron was commanded to burn incense on the gold altar every morning and every evening when he came into the Tabernacle to trim and light the lamps on the gold lampstand. It is a good idea for us to have a special time of prayer each morning and evening just as Aaron did.

God also told Moses to make a huge bronze water tank to stand in the court outside the Tabernacle, near the great bronze altar.

The Lord told a man named Bezaleel to make all these things, for God had given him special ability to make beautiful things out of silver and gold, bronze and jewels. Other men would help him, but God told Bezaleel to be in charge.

When the Lord had finished talking with Moses, He gave him the two tablets of stone on which God had written the Ten Commandments. Moses had been with God on Mount Sinai for forty days and forty nights learning about all the things God wanted made.

Meanwhile the people of Israel

were in their camp at the foot of the mountain. They became impatient when Moses stayed so long. They went to Aaron and said, "We don't know what has become of Moses. We want to worship idols, like all the other nations do."

"All right," Aaron said, "bring me your wives' and children's gold earrings." Aaron melted the earrings in a fire and poured out the gold into a big lump, which he then made into the shape of a beautiful gold calf.

The people bowed to the calf and said it was their god who had brought them out of the land of Egypt. Aaron built an altar in front of it and told the people to come back the next day for a big celebration. Early the next morning, they sacrificed burnt offerings to the calf instead of to the Lord. They had a great party, feasting and getting drunk and dancing around the calf.

All this time Moses was still on the mountain. He couldn't see what the people were doing, but God could. "Quick! Go on down," God told him, "for the people have done a very wicked thing. They have made a calf and worshipped it and sacrificed to it and called it their god."

Moses hurried down the mountain with the two tablets of stone in his hand. Joshua, his helper, was with him; and as they came near the camp, they heard the noise of the people shouting.

Joshua said to Moses, "It sounds as if they are getting ready for war."

"No," Moses said, "it isn't the noise of war; they are singing."

When they came nearer Moses looked down and saw the gold calf and the people dancing before it. He could hardly believe it; in great anger he hurled the two tables of stone down the mountain and they broke in pieces as they smashed against the ground.

QUESTIONS

What are sacrifices? Why did God want them? Does He want us to sacrifice to Him?

How was the gold calf made? Why was it wrong to worship it?

What happened to the two stone tablets?

42
The Idol Is Smashed

When Moses saw the people worshipping the gold calf, he ran all the rest of the way down the mountain and smashed the calf and ground it into powder. Then he threw the powder into the water and made the people drink it.

Moses turned to Aaron and demanded, "Why have you helped the people do this great sin?" Aaron tried to excuse himself. He said the people told him to make the calf or they would hurt him. They brought him their gold, he said, and when he put it into the fire, it just happened to come out in the shape of a calf. What a wicked thing for Aaron to say!

A terrible punishment from the Lord came upon His people because of their sin. Moses stood at the gate of the camp and said for everyone who was on the Lord's side to come and stand there with him. All the men of the tribe of Levi came. He told them to take their swords and to go from one end of the camp to the other killing every man they met. In this way God punished the people for their wickedness. That day the Levites killed about three thousand men.

The next day Moses told the people that although they had sinned so greatly he would pray for them, and perhaps their sin would be forgiven. So he talked with the Lord about it. He confessed that the people had sinned terribly because they had made the idol and worshipped it, but he begged God to forgive them. But God said no, He would punish those who had sinned. He would not go with them to the Promised Land and He would not give them the cloud to lead them any more.

Moses begged God to stay with them, and the Lord finally listened to his prayer and promised that He would.

Then God told Moses to make two stone tablets like the ones he had broken, and He would write the Ten Commandments on them again.

He told Moses to come up alone to the top of the mountain in the morning. No one could be anywhere near the mountain, and no flocks or herds were to graze there.

So Moses chipped out two tablets of rock, just like those he had broken, and went up to the top of Mount

Sinai early in the morning, carrying the tablets. And the Lord came down in the cloud and passed before him. When Moses heard His voice, he bowed quickly to the earth and worshipped. He prayed again that the Lord would forgive the people of Israel and would let them be His people again.

The Lord accepted Moses' prayer and took the people back again as His own. He promised that He would do wonderful things for them and drive out the wicked nations of Canaan to make room for His people to live there instead.

QUESTIONS

What lie did Aaron tell Moses about the gold calf?

How did God punish the people?

When Moses asked God to forgive the Israelis, what did God say?

43
God's Workmen

Now Moses invited the people to bring their gifts of gold, silver, bronze, wood, and whatever else was needed, to begin building the Tabernacle. The people gladly brought their gold and silver bracelets and earrings and other ornaments. Some brought jewels for the breastplate for the High Priest, and olive oil for the lamp. They kept on bringing more and more. Finally there was enough, but still they kept on bringing it. Moses had to tell them to stop! He handed their gifts to Bezaleel and Aholiab and the other men chosen and trained by the Lord to do the work.

These men made curtains to spread over the top of the Tabernacle as its roof. The curtains were made of soft linen cloth, colored blue, purple, and scarlet; other curtains were made of goats' hair and rams' skins, dyed red. They also made a beautiful curtain to hang inside the Tabernacle, to divide it into two rooms, and a curtain for the front door. The sides of the Tabernacle were made of boards covered with gold.

Outside the Tabernacle was a fence made of bronze posts with curtains hanging between them. This fence enclosed a small yard around the Tabernacle.

It was at this time that Bezaleel and Aholiab made Aaron's beautiful clothes—his linen coat, and the blue, purple, and scarlet vest.

Some of the threads used in making

his coat were solid gold! The gold was beaten into a very thin sheet, then cut into little strips. These strips, or threads, were then worked in among the purple, blue, and scarlet.

Then they made the breastplate with twelve jewels attached to it. Each jewel was set in gold. Aaron wore this breastplate over his chest, suspended by two gold chains coming down from his shoulders.

The robe beneath the vest was all blue, and around its lower edge hung what looked like blue, purple, and scarlet pomegranates. Between the pomegranates were gold bells that tinkled as Aaron went in and out of the Tabernacle.

Then Bezaleel made the Ark. It was a wooden box covered inside and outside with solid gold. The cover of the Ark, called the mercy seat, was pure gold without any wood. The Ark was the most important part of the Tabernacle because God was there.

Then Bezaleel made two gold angels to stand, one on each end of the cover. Their faces were turned toward each other, with outspread wings.

The table in the Tabernacle was made of wood, then covered with solid gold. There were gold dishes for the table, gold bowls and spoons, and a gold lampstand. This lampstand had three branches coming out from each side, with lamps and gold flowers on each branch.

The incense altar too was made of wood covered with gold. Bezaleel made special incense to burn on this gold altar, and he prepared special olive oil to pour on Aaron's head to anoint him as the High Priest.

The altar for the burnt offerings was built of wood covered with bronze. The huge wash tank for Aaron and his sons to wash their hands and feet in was also made of bronze. God had told Aaron and his sons always to wash their hands and feet before going into the Tabernacle to sacrifice at the altar.

Coats and trousers of soft linen were made for Aaron's sons, too, and a turban for Aaron's head, with a gold plate on it that read: "Holiness to the Lord."

At last the different parts of the Tabernacle were finished and ready to be put together. The workmen brought them to Moses, and he inspected them to be sure everything was just as God had said to make them.

God told Moses to go ahead now and put the parts together to make the Tabernacle. First he set up the gold-covered boards for the sides. Then he spread the curtains over them for a roof; the curtains covered the Tabernacle and hung down on each side.

He placed the two stone tablets with the Ten Commandments written on them in the Ark, then placed the gold top of the Ark, called the mercy seat, in its place. Then he took the Ark into the Tabernacle and divided the Tabernacle into two rooms by hanging a huge curtain down the middle. The Ark was placed in the inner room.

In the other room he placed the gold table, the gold lampstand, and

These children are bringing their gifts to the Tabernacle. God is pleased because they want to help.

the gold altar, then hung up a curtain as a door at the front of the Tabernacle. Outside the door, but not very far away, he placed the huge, bronze burnt offering altar, and offered a sacrifice on it. He set the wash tank near the altar and put water in it, and Moses and Aaron and his sons washed their hands and feet there.

He set up the curtain-fence around the Tabernacle to enclose the courtyard. Finally, he hung up the beautiful curtain to cover the front entrance.

So the Tabernacle was finished, with the yard around it, and everything in place inside. Then the pillar of cloud that went ahead of the people of Israel as they travelled, came and stood over the Tabernacle and covered it.

And the glory of the Lord filled the inside of the Tabernacle so that Moses couldn't go in.

QUESTIONS

How did Moses get the gold, silver, and jewels he needed for the Tabernacle?

Can you describe Aaron's clothes?

In what part of the Tabernacle were the Ten Commandments kept?

When God's glory filled the Tabernacle, why do you think Moses could not go in?

44

Lambs Died for People's Sins

The cloud (with God in it) entered the Tabernacle. It went into the inner room and stood above the mercy seat where the gold angels stretched out their wings. When Moses was able to go in, God spoke to him from above the mercy seat and gave him many laws for the people of Israel.

God told Moses to bring Aaron and his sons to the door of the Tabernacle to consecrate them there. This meant Moses would make them priests. So Moses called them to come, and all the people came to watch.

First he washed Aaron and his sons and put Aaron's beautiful clothes on him. Then he poured special olive oil on Aaron's head, anointing him. He put the special clothing on Aaron's sons and afterward offered sacrifices to God. So Aaron and his sons became priests; now God would let them burn incense and offer sacrifices to God for all of the people of Israel.

Before this, each man could offer his own sacrifices, as Abel, Noah, and Abraham had done. But now God had chosen Aaron and his sons to be priests, so no one else was allowed to offer a sacrifice. Everyone must bring his offering to the Tabernacle and let the priests burn it for him on the altar.

Then Aaron killed a lamb and laid it on the altar to be burned as an offering for the sins of all the people. He didn't light a fire under it, though, for the Lord sent fire down from heaven that burned up the lamb! When the people saw the fire they shouted for joy, for now they knew that the Lord was pleased with their priest and with his sacrifice.

The priests always kept that fire from heaven burning on the altar. They never let it go out because the Lord had sent it.

The priests were commanded to sacrifice two lambs every day for the sins of the people of Israel. One was sacrificed in the morning and the other in the evening.

If anyone was sorry for his sins and wanted to be forgiven, he would bring an ox, a sheep, or a goat and lay his hand upon the head of the animal there at the door of the Tabernacle. This showed that the man wanted his sins taken away from himself and put on the animal. Then the man killed the animal; and Aaron's sons, the priests, burned it for him on the altar. God was pleased and forgave his sins, not because the innocent animal had died, but because this animal was an example of what the Saviour would do when He came. For the Saviour would come to die for His people, just as the animal was killed and was burned on the altar instead of the person who sinned.

These lambs that were sacrificed each day by Aaron and his sons, were like Abel's lamb and like the Passover lambs that were killed that night in Egypt when the oldest sons of the people of Israel were kept safe because the blood of the lamb was on the door. Killing these lambs was like what would happen to the Saviour who would come many, many years later and die for the sins of the world. God was pleased when these lambs were sacrificed, for He had said to do this to show that the Saviour was coming to die for us.

There were several different kinds of offerings. When someone had turned from his sins and wanted to be forgiven, he brought his offering to the priests and they burned all of it on the altar. It was called a burnt offering.

But when he brought an offering because he was thankful for some blessing God had given him or because he was asking God to answer some special prayer, then the priest took the animal and burned only part of it on the altar. The priests kept some of it for themselves to eat, and some of it they gave back to the man for him to eat. This offering that was partly burned and partly eaten was called a "peace-with-God" offering or a "thank-you" offering.

When the priest gave back part of the animal to the man who brought it, that man often invited his family and friends and perhaps his poor neighbors to feast on it with him. The man was not allowed to save the meat; it had to be eaten that same day or the day afterward.

QUESTIONS

What kind of oil did Moses pour on Aaron's head?

Why didn't Aaron have to light the fire under the lamb when he sacrificed it?

Can you think of two ways in which the sacrificed animals can remind us of Jesus?

45
Two Sons of Aaron Die

Aaron's four sons were in charge of worshipping God at the Tabernacle; they saw to it that everything was done properly, in just the way God wanted it done.

God commanded incense to be burned on the gold altar. This incense was placed in a kind of cup, called a censer, probably made of bronze. The priest carried coals of fire in the cup into the Tabernacle and set it on the gold altar; he sprinkled the incense on the coals so that it would burn and send up its sweet smoke. The fire in the censer was taken from the burnt offering altar, from the fire God had sent down from heaven.

But two of Aaron's sons, Nadab and Abihu, put other fire in their incense cups because they didn't want to obey God. God was angry at their sin and sent down fire from heaven that burned them to death. Their dead bodies were carried away from the Tabernacle, out of the camp. God told Aaron and his other two sons not to show any sign of grief for them, for they had been put to death because of their sin against God.

The Lord told Moses what animals and birds and fish the Israelis could eat, for they were not to eat every kind. They could eat oxen, deer, sheep, and goats, but not camels, rabbits, or pigs. They could eat fish that had fins and scales, but not those with smooth skins. They could eat doves and pigeons and quail, but they were forbidden to eat eagles, ravens, owls, and swans.

Do you remember about the leprosy that came suddenly upon Moses' hand, making it white as snow until he put it back into his coat again? God sent it upon Moses so that he could show this miracle to the people of Israel in Egypt. Leprosy was a very dreadful disease that sometimes spread over people's entire bodies, for no one knew how to cure it. After a while the leprosy would eat away the person's fingers and toes.

God told Moses and Aaron that when a man had a spot or sore on his skin that seemed like the beginning of leprosy, he must go to the priest. The priest could look at it and say whether or not it really was leprosy. If it was, the man had to go away from his family and from all the rest of the people and live in some place alone.

If God made him well, the priest would look at him again and decide whether he was well. If he was, he could come back again and live in the camp.

But he must bring three lambs, or, if he was poor and could not bring so many, he could bring one lamb and two doves or young pigeons to the Tabernacle as offerings to the Lord who had healed him.

QUESTIONS

Why was God angry with Nadab and Abihu? How did He punish them?

Name the two kinds of animal which the Israelis were allowed to eat. Name two which they were forbidden to eat.

Who could decide whether a man had leprosy? Where must he live until he recovered from the disease?

46
The High Priest

Do you remember that there was an inner room in the Tabernacle where Moses put the Ark and where God came in a cloud above the mercy seat? That room was the most holy part of the Tabernacle; it was called the Holy of Holies. The Lord told Moses that no one but Aaron, the High Priest, could ever go in there. Even Aaron could go there only once every year, very carefully.

Before going he bathed thoroughly. He took off his splendid High Priest's robe and put on plainer clothing of pure white linen, for he must go in humbly before the Lord. Before going in, he offered up sacrifices for his own sins and for the sins of all the people. He took the blood of those sacrifices with him into this most holy place and sprinkled it with his finger on the mercy seat and in front of it; there Aaron prayed that the Lord would forgive him and all the people.

What did it mean when the High Priest did these things? He was showing what the Saviour would do for all who trust in Him. For the High Priest went into the most holy place on earth to pray for the people; the Saviour, after He was crucified, went up to heaven to pray for us. The High Priest asked God to forgive the people because animals had been sacrificed for them. The Saviour asks God to forgive us because He died for us. Aaron is dead and cannot ask God to forgive us, but the Saviour is alive in heaven and is there every day asking God to forgive us.

On the day when Aaron went into the most holy place the people were not allowed to work, but spent the time thinking about their sins and being very, very sorry for them. Anyone who did not do this was punished; for that day was the most solemn day of all the year. It was called the Day of Atonement.

God said that when the people of Israel arrived in the Promised Land and went out into their fields to cut their grain and bring it into their barns, they must never bring in quite all of it, but must leave a little. And when the grapes became ripe, they must not pick every grape, but must leave some for the poor who had no fields or vineyards of their own. The poor could come and gather what was left.

The Lord told the people of Israel never to steal or lie to each other. And when a man had been working for them, they should not tell him to wait awhile to be paid; they should pay him right away.

If a person was deaf, people must not talk against him just because he couldn't hear them; if he was blind, they must not put things in his way to make him stumble and fall. If anyone knew something bad about someone else, he must not go and tell everyone about it; he must not be a gossip.

And the Israelis were not to hate each other, but to love each other. If one of them saw another doing wrong, he must tell him kindly not to do it anymore. Then he might repent of his sin.

When people from other countries came to live among them, the Israelis were not to treat them unjustly nor steal their things. They must be as kind to them and love them as much as though they had always lived with them and were their own people.

The nations living in the Promised Land of Canaan where the Israelis were going worshipped a huge idol named Molech.

This idol, with the face of a calf, was made of bronze and was hollow, so that a fire could be lighted inside of it like a furnace. After it was heated very hot, those wicked people would put their little children into the idol's arms, and there the babies burned to death; the people beat drums while the babies were burning, to keep from hearing their screams. They burned their children in this way because they thought it pleased the idol; they called it giving their children to Molech.

God told Moses to kill any of the Israelis who gave their children to Molech. If the people refused to kill a man who did that, pretending not to know what he had done, God said that He Himself would punish the people for not punishing that man.

QUESTIONS

How often could Aaron go to the most holy place? What was this day called?

Tell some ways in which Aaron was like the Saviour.

Tell some ways the Israelis were told to be kind to each other.

Who was Molech?

47
Three Holidays

The Lord commanded the people of Israel to have three religious holidays each year.

The first was called the Passover. This celebration was to remind everyone about the night they came out of Egypt, for it was a great victory over the Egyptians. On the night each year when this event was celebrated, the people ate a lamb during the night, just as they had done that first time. Then for seven days afterward they ate bread made without yeast. God wanted the people to have this celebration each year so that they would always remember how God had punished Pharaoh until he finally set the people of Israel free, even though he was determined not to let them go.

Seven weeks after the Passover, there was the Harvest Festival. This lasted only one day and came after the grain had been gathered into the barns. It was like our Thanksgiving Day. The people thanked God for sending the rain and the sunshine that made their crops grow out in the fields and for giving them food enough for another year. The Lord told them to be glad and to rejoice on this special day.

At the end of the year, there was the Tabernacle Festival. This celebration lasted seven days. During those seven days all the people of Israel moved out of their homes and lived in huts made from branches of trees because the Israelis lived like that for forty years while they were travelling through the deserts. The Lord wanted them to remember this when they arrived in Canaan and were living in houses again.

At each of these three celebrations every man of Israel was to come to the Tabernacle and bring an offering to the Lord.

One kind of gift God told Moses to tell the people to bring was olive oil for the lamps in the Tabernacle. Olives are a fruit that grow in Canaan. When the olives are pressed, a very pure vegetable oil runs out of them. It was this oil that the people were to bring to burn in the seven lamps that were in the gold lampstand. The Lord told Aaron and his sons to clean the lamps every day so that the lights could burn all night in the Tabernacle. Only the priests were allowed to trim them.

God told Moses to take finely ground flour and to bake twelve loaves of bread with it. These were to be placed on the gold table which stood in the Tabernacle near the gold candlestick. He was to put them there on the Sabbath Day and leave them a whole week until the next Sabbath. Then a priest took them away and put fresh loaves in their place. Aaron and his sons could eat the bread after it was taken away, but they must eat it at the Tabernacle because it was holy bread; they could not take it home, for it had been set on the gold table before the Lord.

There was a man in the camp whose father was an Egyptian, but his mother was an Israeli. He quarrelled with another Israeli, and in anger blasphemed God's name; that is, he spoke evil of God.

The people brought him to Moses and put him in a jail until the Lord told Moses what his punishment should be. The Lord told Moses to command the people to take him out of the camp and stone him. The Lord said that whoever blasphemed God's name, whether it was an Israeli or a foreigner living there with them, must be killed; all the people must stone him until he was dead. So they took the man out of the camp and killed him, as the Lord had commanded.

QUESTIONS

What were the names of the three national holidays of the Israelis?

What very wrong thing did the man in this story do? What happened to him?

These children and their parents are celebrating one of the three great national holidays.

R. Hook

48
The Year of Jubilee

God said that when the Israelis came into the land of Canaan, they could plant their crops for six years; but every seventh year they must not plant any seed at all, but just let the land alone. If any grain grew without being planted, they must not cut it, and the grapes on the vines must not be picked; for this seventh year was to be a Sabbath year, a year of rest for the land! Yet there would be enough to eat that seventh year because the Lord would give them enough extra crops the previous year to last for two years.

Every fifty years was the Year of Jubilee. This was a glad and happy year. The day it began, trumpets were blown all through the land. No one planted crops or harvested them that year, for God promised to give large crops the year before, enough to last through the entire Year of Jubilee. If anyone had been so poor that he had had to sell the field his father had given him, he got it back free when the Year of Jubilee came! For the Lord said that the person who bought it had to give it back at that time.

Or if anyone had sold himself as a slave, he became free when the Year of Jubilee began. What a wonderful year!

God told the people that if they would obey His commandments, He would send them rain so that all their crops would grow well, there would be luscious fruit on their trees, they would have plenty of bread to eat, and no one would hurt them. The Lord would destroy or drive away the dangerous wild animals. He Himself would take care of His people and make all of their enemies afraid of them.

But if they didn't obey His commandments, God said they would have sickness and trouble. When they sowed their grain, it wouldn't come up, or if it did, their enemies would come at harvest time and steal it from them. Wild animals would carry off their children and kill their cattle. Only a few people would be left in all the land. The Lord would send disease and famine upon them. Their enemies would make war on them, and the people of Israel would be taken away to other countries where the people would hate them; and many of them would die there.

But if those who were left would confess that they had been wicked and that it was God who had punished them, then He wouldn't punish them anymore. He would be kind to them and bring them back again to the land He had promised to give to the children of Abraham, Isaac, and Jacob.

QUESTIONS

What was a Sabbath year?

Why was the Year of Jubilee such a wonderful year? How often did it come?

What did God tell the people would happen if they obeyed Him?

What if they disobeyed Him?

49
Workers at the Tabernacle

More than a year had passed since the people of Israel left Egypt, but they had gone no farther than Mount Sinai.

They had stayed there forty days and forty nights while Moses was on the mountain getting the two tablets of stone from God, with the Ten Commandments written on them. But Moses had angrily thrown down the two tablets and broken them because the people were worshipping the gold calf.

Then they had waited forty more days and nights while Moses went back up the mountain with two new tablets and the Lord again wrote His Ten Commandments on them.

Afterward they waited while the Tabernacle was built and while God spoke to Moses inside the Tabernacle, giving him many new laws for the people of Israel to obey.

But at last the time had come to leave Mount Sinai and to continue the journey to the Promised Land of Canaan.

The Israelis were divided into twelve large groups, called tribes. Each group was descended from one of the sons of Jacob. One of the groups was the tribe of Joseph, for instance, and another was the tribe of Benjamin.

The Lord told Moses and Aaron to count all the men of Israel who were able to be soldiers. There were 603,550 of them.

The men of the tribe of Levi were not counted along with the others, because the Lord didn't want them to go to war. He chose them to stay near the Tabernacle to take care of it. Whenever God told the Israelis to move to a new location, the men of this tribe took down the Tabernacle and carried the different parts, and whenever the people of Israel stopped and made camp, these men set the Tabernacle up again.

The Tabernacle and all the things in it were holy, and no one except the priests and Levites could enter it. If anyone else did, he was killed.

There was much work for these men of the tribe of Levi to do. Besides sacrificing the two lambs every day, the people brought many other offerings. Wood was cut to burn these. Water was brought for washing. The ashes were taken away from the altar, and the yard where the offerings were killed was cleaned.

Aaron and his sons could not do all these things by themselves, so God chose the Levite tribe to help them. Moses and Aaron counted 8,580 men of the Levite tribe. These men began to help the priests by working at the Tabernacle.

The twelve leaders of the tribes now brought presents for the Tabernacle in six wagons pulled by twelve oxen. Moses gave the wagons and the oxen to the Levites to carry the different parts of the Tabernacle when the people of Israel were travelling. Two wagons were used to carry the heavy curtains; four other wagons carried the boards covered with gold for the sides of the Tabernacle, and the brass pillars that stood around the court. But there was no wagon to carry the ark, the gold lampstand, the gold altar, or the bronze altar; for God said never to carry these in wagons. They had to be carried on the shoulders of the men of the tribe of Levi.

All this time the pillar of cloud stood over the Tabernacle. During the day it was the color of a cloud, but every night it became a pillar of fire. It came there on the very first day when Moses put up the Tabernacle, and there it remained above the roof of the inner room, called the most holy place. It stayed there except when the Lord wanted the people of Israel to move. Then it lifted and waited for the people to get ready to follow, and as the cloud moved forward, the people walked behind it.

As long as it was moving, everyone followed, but whenever it stopped, everyone stopped and set up the camp. If the cloud stayed over the Tabernacle only one day, they stayed only one day. If it stayed two days, they stayed two days; or if it stayed a whole year, they stayed a year. But whenever the cloud lifted, whether by day or by night, they travelled. It was the Lord who made it stay or go, and He was guiding the people through the wilderness.

The Lord commanded Moses to make two silver trumpets for the priests to blow when Moses wanted to call the people together, or when they were about to start travelling.

While travelling, the people of Israel carried banners and flags and marched like an army. Each tribe kept in its own place, and each one had a captain in charge of it.

The Levites carrying the different parts of the Tabernacle were surrounded by the other tribes. Wherever the cloud stopped, the people stopped, and the Levites set up the Tabernacle again.

The Levites put up their family tents next to the Tabernacle, and the other tribes put their tents all around them, farther away from the Tabernacle than the Levites.

QUESTIONS

Why did the Israelis stay so long at Mount Sinai?

What work did the Lord have for the tribe of Levi?

How was the Tabernacle carried when the people moved to a new place?

Tell about the cloud.

50
Always Complaining

Now it was time for the Israelis to leave Mount Sinai for the Lord told them they had been there long enough. They should move on toward Canaan, He said. So the cloud rose from the Tabernacle and moved on before them, and they followed it for three days until they came to the wilderness of Paran. There it stopped and there they camped.

We would suppose that when the people saw the cloud going along in front of them they would be very thankful to God. We would expect them to be satisfied with whatever He chose to give them until they reached that good land to which He was leading them. But no, they complained that there was no meat for them to eat. "We remember the fish we had in Egypt," they said, "and the cucumbers, the melons, and the onions, but now we have nothing at all beside this manna." So they complained and cried, standing at the doors of their tents.

The Lord was very angry with them, and Moses was discouraged. Then he complained to the Lord, too. He asked the Lord why he had been given the care of all these wicked people. It was too much for him, he said, and if the Lord was going to send him such a burden as this to carry, he wanted to die and end it all.

Moses sinned when he talked to God like that, for God had always helped him when he was in trouble, and He was willing to help him again now. Moses should not have complained—he should have trusted God.

God told Moses to tell the people that He would give them meat, for He had heard their complaining. They would have meat not only for one day or five days, but for a whole month until they couldn't stand the taste or sight of it.

Moses could hardly believe it. He said, "Here are 600,000 families, and yet You say You will give them meat to eat for a whole month? Must we kill all the flocks and herds that we brought out of Egypt? Or shall all the fish of the sea be caught to give them enough?"

The Lord answered, "Have I grown weak? Is that why you think I can't do it? Wait, and you will see whether My words will come true or not."

So Moses told the people what the Lord had said.

Then the Lord sent a wind that brought quail from the sea, and they flew down all around the camp. There were so many that the ground was covered with them. The people went out and gathered them all that day, all that night, and all the next day. But as soon as they put the meat in their mouths to eat it, the Lord sent a great plague among them, and many of them died for their sin and were buried there in the wilderness.

Then the cloud lifted again, and the people followed it until it stopped at a place called Hazeroth; there they stopped and made their camp.

Moses was their leader because the Lord had chosen him. Yet the Bible tells us he was more meek and humble than any man alive. But Miriam, his sister, and Aaron, his brother, found fault with him for marrying a woman who was not an Israeli. They said God had chosen them also, and that they, too, should be rulers over the people.

The Lord heard what Aaron and Miriam said, and He was angry. He told them to go with Moses to the Tabernacle. While they were there, the pillar of cloud came down and stood by the door. Then the Lord called to Aaron and Miriam from the cloud and they came and stood before Him. The Lord told them He had chosen Moses, and He asked them why they were not afraid to speak against Moses as they had been doing. When the pillar of cloud rose again, Miriam was covered with leprosy; her skin was as white as snow. God had sent the disease upon her as punishment for their wickedness.

When Aaron saw it, he was terribly frightened and said to Moses, "We have sinned." He begged that Miriam might be healed.

Then Moses prayed earnestly to the Lord for her, saying, "Heal her now, O God, I ask." And the Lord listened to his prayer and healed her from her leprosy.

Then the people travelled from Hazeroth back again to the wilderness of Paran.

QUESTIONS

What did the people complain about?

How did God provide meat for all the people?

How did God show Aaron and Miriam that He had chosen Moses to be in charge?

51
The Spies

The people of Israel had almost reached the Promised Land of Canaan now. Moses told them to go in and conquer it, for the Lord had told them to. But the people begged Moses to send spies first, to go through the land and come back and tell them what it was like.

So Moses sent twelve men, one from each tribe. He told them to look at the land to see whether it was good or bad, what sort of people lived there, how many there were, and whether they lived in tents or in cities with walls around them.

Moses told the spies not to be afraid, and to bring back samples of the fruit that grew in the Promised Land. So the spies walked through the land from one end to the other, and the Lord kept the people who lived there from hurting them. At a place called Eschol, they cut a branch of grapes with a single cluster so large that it took two men to carry it! They hung the cluster on a pole with a man at each end, carrying it between them! They also brought back to Moses some samples of the wonderful pomegranates and figs that grew in the Promised Land.

They were away for forty days before returning with their report and with the samples of fruit they had found. They said the grain and grapevines grew tall and strong and that there was plenty to eat and drink. But there was one problem: there were walls around the cities, and the people were fierce and strong. The spies were afraid and didn't think the Israelis would be able to conquer people like that.

But two of the spies, Caleb and Joshua, remembered God's promise that He would give the land to the Israelis. They knew He would keep His promise, for they had faith in Him. Caleb begged the people to enter the land at once; they were well able to capture it, he told them.

But the other spies persuaded the people not to go; there were giants there, the spies said, so large that ordinary people seemed about the size of grasshoppers in comparison!

So the Israelis refused to enter the Promised Land.

Then they began to cry and murmur against Moses and Aaron. "Why did God bring us here to kill us in this wilderness?" they complained fearfully. "We should never have left the land of Egypt. Now what is going to happen to our wives and to our children? They will all be killed."

Suddenly they decided, "Let's go back to Egypt. Down with Moses! We'll elect someone else to lead us."

Moses and Aaron felt terrible about this; so did Joshua and Caleb, the two good spies. Once more they told the people what a wonderful country the Promised Land was. They begged the Israelis not to be afraid of the people living there, for the Lord would help His people. But the people were angry at Caleb and Joshua for saying this, and wanted to kill them.

Then God was very angry with the people of Israel. He told Moses that He would send a terrible plague to destroy them; they could no longer be His people, He said. Instead He would give many children to Moses, and they would become a greater nation than the people of Israel were.

But Moses begged the Lord not to kill them. Moses said that if God destroyed His people and didn't bring them safely into the Promised Land, all the heathen nations would say it was because God wasn't able to do it!

The Lord listened to Moses' prayer and promised not to kill the people after all. But because the people had disobeyed God so often and wouldn't believe His promises even though they had seen Him do such wonderful things for them, God said they couldn't enter the Promised Land for forty years. They must wander around in the wilderness all that time until all of them were dead. At the end of the forty years, God said, He would bring their children into the land. And He promised that the two good spies, Caleb and Joshua, would live and enter Canaan with them.

Then the people of Israel were sorry for what they had done. They got up early the next morning and told Moses that now they were willing to go into the Promised Land after all. But Moses told them no, it was too late—now the Lord wouldn't help them, and if they went they would be killed by their enemies. But they went anyway, and the people living in the land came and fought against them and chased them as bees chase those who come too close to their hives.

The Israelis returned to their camp and stayed there several days. Then the Lord led them back into the wilderness.

QUESTIONS

Tell about the spies' trip to Canaan.
In what way were Caleb and Joshua good?
Why were the people afraid to enter the Promised Land?
How did God punish the people for not trusting Him?

52
The Rebel

The Sabbath was the seventh day of each week; the Israelites were commanded not to work on Sabbaths.

One Sabbath day a man was noticed at work gathering sticks. Since this was against God's law, he was put in jail until the people could find out how God wanted them to punish him for his sin.

The Lord told Moses to sentence the man to death. "Tell the people to take him out of the camp and throw heavy stones upon him until he is dead," the Lord said.

So they did.

After this, three men named Korah, Dathan, and Abiram, and 250 other Israelis, started a protest movement against Moses and Aaron. They said Aaron had no right to be the High Priest and that they didn't want Moses as their leader.

Korah was one of the Levites. He helped the priests at the Tabernacle, but he was not satisfied with doing this. He wanted to be a priest. That was why he had urged these 250 men to come with him to speak against Aaron.

Moses heard what they had to say and told them to return the next day, each with an incense cup and some incense. Then the Lord would show them whether or not He had chosen Aaron alone as His High Priest.

So they all returned the next day with their incense cups, put fire in them, and sprinkled incense on the fire just as the priests did at the Tabernacle. All the rest of the people of Israel came out to watch and to encourage and support the rebels against Moses and Aaron. But the Lord was very displeased with them for coming. He commanded them to get back away from Korah, Dathan, and Abiram. So the people drew back.

Then Moses announced what God's proof would be that He had chosen Moses and Aaron: the ground would open up under Korah, Dathan, and Abiram and swallow them alive.

Moses had hardly finished speaking before the ground opened up and swallowed them—Korah, Dathan and Abiram, with their tents and families —screaming as they went down alive into the ground, and the earth closed over them again.

All the people standing near them ran for their lives, fearing that the earth would swallow them too. And the Lord sent fire from the sky that killed the 250 other rebels.

But the next day all the people murmured against Moses and Aaron again. "You murdered Korah, Dathan, and Abiram and those 250 other good men," they said.

Then the Lord was very angry. He said to Moses and Aaron, "Get away from these people, for I am going to destroy them." But Moses and Aaron lay flat on their faces before the Lord and prayed for all the Israelis. The Lord refused to listen, for even while they were praying He sent a terrible plague among the people and many of them died.

When Moses realized what was happening, he said to Aaron, "Quick! Take an incense cup and put fire in it from the altar of burnt offering. Sprinkle incense on the fire, and run out among the people, and offer up the incense to the Lord."

Aaron did as Moses said. He ran out among the people and stood with the burning incense between those who had died and those still living, and the Lord stopped the plague. But 14,700 people had already died.

The Lord said for the people of Israel to give a dead stick to Moses, and for Aaron to give one to him too. Then Moses took the two dead sticks into the Tabernacle and left them in front of the Ark all night.

The next day Aaron's dead stick had blossoms and almond nuts growing on it!

Moses brought out the sticks and showed them to the people. God used this miracle to show everyone that He had chosen Aaron as the High Priest and hadn't chosen anyone else.

God told Moses to take Aaron's stick back into the Tabernacle again and to keep it there as a reminder that God had chosen Aaron alone as His High Priest. And when Aaron and his sons were dead, then their sons would be the priests. All the men in Aaron's family in all the years to come would be priests, but no one else could be.

Then God reminded the people again that the men of the tribe of Levi would be helpers to Aaron and his sons and would do the work at the Tabernacle.

The Lord said that all the other tribes of Israel must give the priests and Levites part of their grain and fruit and cattle. The priests and Levites wouldn't have farms in the Promised Land as the other tribes would, for their work was to care for the Tabernacle and to help the people worship. That is why the other tribes were commanded to give a tenth of their grain, fruit, and cattle, and of everything they earned to the priests and Levites.

QUESTIONS

What happened to the man who worked on the Sabbath? Why?

What happened to Korah, Dathan, and Abiram?

What happened to Aaron's stick? What did this prove?

53
Moses' Disobedience

Now all the Israelis moved their camp again, this time to the Zin Desert. Moses' sister Miriam died and was buried there.

Once again they ran out of water, and the people rebelled against Moses. "Why didn't you murder us along with Korah and the others?" they shouted insolently. "You might as well have done that as to kill us now with thirst."

Then Moses and Aaron went to the Tabernacle and threw themselves flat on the ground before the Lord, and the glory of the Lord appeared to them.

Then the Lord told them to take Aaron's stick from the Tabernacle and as all the people watched, to stand before a certain rock God pointed out to them, "Speak to the rock," God told Moses, "and water will gush out before their eyes."

So Moses took the stick from its place in the Tabernacle and summoned the people. But instead of just speaking to the rock as the Lord had told him to, he yelled angrily at the people, "Listen, you rebels, must we get water for you from the rock?" Then he struck the rock twice, though God had not even mentioned striking it. He had only said to speak to it.

Suddenly water began flowing from the rock and all the people and their cattle drank and drank until they had enough.

But God said to Moses, "You didn't believe Me, did you? You didn't think it was enough just to speak to the rock as I told you to. So you struck it twice. The people would have respected Me more if the water had started flowing from the rock when you only spoke a word. Your punishment is that you may not lead My people into the Promised Land."

How sad that Moses did wrong and had to be punished! How he had looked forward to going into the Promised Land! But now he would never get there.

Moses and the people of Israel next arrived at Edom—the country where Jacob's brother Esau had lived four hundred years before. Esau's people were still living there; it was their land. And now the people of Israel, who were the descendants of Esau's brother Jacob, wanted to pass through the land of Esau, now known as Moab, on their journey to Canaan. So Moses asked permission of the king of the land. He sent him this message:

"You know our history—about our ancestor Jacob and his sons and their families. They went to Egypt 400 years ago, and we have lived there ever since. But the Egyptians treated us very cruelly. Then we cried to the Lord, and He listened to us and He has brought us out of our slavery in Egypt. Now please let us pass through your country on the way back to our homeland. We will not go through your fields, or tread down your grain, or drink water from your wells. We will stay on the regular roads."

But the king of Edom said no, the people of Israel must not pass through; and he came with his army to keep them out. So the Israelis turned back and went around by a different, longer route.

When they arrived at Mount Hor, almost forty years had gone by since they left Egypt. Still they were wandering around and camping in the desert. For God had said that all of the people who had refused to enter the Promised Land because the spies said it was too dangerous—all these people must die before Israel could go in. Only their children, who had now grown to be men and women, could go and live in the Promised Land. At Mount Hor the Lord spoke to Moses and Aaron and told them that the time had come for Aaron to die. "You and Aaron and Aaron's son Eleazar are to go up to the top of Mount Hor," the Lord told them. "When you arrive, take the High Priest's garments off Aaron and put them on his son Eleazar. Aaron will die while you are up there, and Eleazar will be the new High Priest."

Moses did as the Lord commanded. While all the people watched, he and Aaron and Eleazar went up the mountain. When they got to the top, Moses took the High Priest's clothes from Aaron and put them on Aaron's son Eleazar. Then Aaron died on the top of the mountain. So Eleazar became the High Priest in place of his father.

When Moses and Eleazar came down from the mountain and told the people that Aaron was dead, they had a time of mourning for him that lasted thirty days. This was to show their respect and sorrow for him because he was dead.

The Israelis were very tired of travelling, and again they sinned by rebelling against God and against Moses. "We have no bread and no water, and how we hate this manna," they complained.

The Lord was angry and sent serpents into the camp to bite the people, causing many of them to die.

They ran to Moses, screaming, "We have sinned, for we have complained against the Lord and against you; please pray that the serpents will go away."

So Moses prayed for them. The Lord told Moses to make a bronze snake that would look like the poisonous snakes that were biting the people.

"Put the bronze snake on a pole," God said. "Whenever anyone is bitten, if he just looks at the snake on the pole, he will get well again."

So Moses made the bronze snake and put it on the top of a pole. Many people looked at it and lived instead of dying from their snake bites.

But it wasn't the bronze snake that made them well. It was the Lord who did it. The bronze snake on the pole reminds us of the Saviour. He was lifted up on a wooden cross to die for our sins. If we look up to the Saviour on the cross, and realize that He died to take away our sins, God will give us eternal life just as He gave life to the people in Moses' time who did as God said, and looked up at the bronze snake.

QUESTIONS

What did God tell Moses to do to get water for the people?

What did Moses do instead? What was his punishment?

Pretend that you are Moses talking to the king of Edom. Ask him to let your people go through his land.

Where did Aaron die? Who became the new High Priest?

How could the people be saved from the serpents? In what way was the bronze snake like the Saviour?

54

Balaam's Donkey Speaks!

As the Israelis went on, they came to the plains of Moab, where Balak was the king.

When Balak saw them coming, he was frightened. He thought they wanted to fight with him, and he knew there were too many of them for his soldiers to win against. So he sent a man named Balaam to curse the people of Israel. To curse someone means to ask God to send some great evil upon him. King Balak thought God would hurt the people of Israel if Balaam asked Him to, because Balaam was said to have great power with God.

The king told Balaam he would make him rich and great if he would curse the people of Israel.

Balaam loved money, so although the people of Israel had done him no harm, he was willing to curse them to get the money the king promised to give him. He got up early in the morning, saddled his donkey, and started off with the men whom the king had sent to bring him.

But God was angry with Balaam for agreeing to curse His people. So God sent an angel with a sword to stand in front of Balaam in the road. Balaam couldn't see the angel, but his donkey did and ran into the field by the side of the road to get away. Balaam beat the donkey and told her to behave!

The angel went on further and stood in the road at a place where there was a wall on each side. When the donkey came to the place, she pressed up very close to the wall to get by the angel; but in doing this she crushed Balaam's foot against the wall, and he hit her again.

Then the angel went on still further and stood in a narrow place where there was no room at all to get by. The donkey saw the angel standing there with the sword and was so afraid that she fell down under Balaam. This made Balaam very angry, and he beat her as hard as he could.

Then the Lord made the donkey speak like a person! She said, "What have I done to deserve your hitting me these three times?"

Balaam said it was because she had disobeyed him and had turned off the road when he wanted her to go straight ahead. "If I had a sword with me, I'd kill you," Balaam said.

Then the donkey spoke to him again and said, "Haven't you ridden on me ever since I was yours until today? And have I ever done anything like this before?"

"No," Balaam said, "you haven't."

Then the Lord opened Balaam's eyes, and he saw the angel standing there in front of him with a sword, ready to kill him. Balaam was very frightened and threw himself flat on the ground before the angel. Then the angel said to him, "Why have you struck your donkey these three times? I came here to stop you from doing wrong. The donkey saw me and got out of the way. If she hadn't, I would have killed you and saved her alive." Then the angel commanded Balaam to go on to the king, but to say to King Balak only what God would tell him to say.

So Balaam went with the king's men, and the king came out to meet him and welcome him. He was very glad that Balaam had come to curse the people of Israel!

The next day the king took Balaam up on a hill where he could look down and see the entire camp of Israel. Balaam told the king to build seven altars and to prepare seven young bulls and seven rams to sacrifice as burnt offerings to God. So the king built the seven altars, and Balaam and the king sacrificed a young bull and a ram on each. Balaam told the king to stay there while he went away by himself. He needed to find out what the Lord wanted him to say and whether the Lord would let him curse the people of Israel.

So Balaam went off by himself, and the Lord met him. Balaam told the Lord about the altars he had built and the animals he had sacrificed. But the Lord wouldn't let him curse the Israelis; He sent him back to the king and made him bless them instead! He said only good things about them and promised that God would care for them and help them.

King Balak was very disappointed and angry when Balaam blessed the Israelis instead of cursing them. He decided to try again. The king took him to a different place from which

Animals don't normally speak in words as men do. But God gave this donkey a special message for Balaam, and Balaam paid attention when he heard his donkey talk to him!

he could look down upon the people of Israel. He built seven more altars there, and again they sacrificed a young bull and a ram on each altar. Balaam thought that by building so many altars and offering so many sacrifices, he could persuade the Lord to let him curse the people. But he should have known that the Lord wouldn't let anyone harm His people no matter how often He was asked, and no matter how many sacrifices or gifts were given to Him.

Balaam told the king to stay there while he went again to ask the Lord for permission to curse the people. The Lord met Balaam but, of course, wouldn't let him curse them. The king was very, very disappointed. But he said to Balaam, "Come with me to a different place; perhaps the Lord will let you curse them from there." He took him to Mount Peor and built seven altars, and they sacrificed a young bull and a ram on each altar, just as before.

Still the Lord wouldn't let Balaam curse the people, but made him bless them instead!

By now King Balak was very angry with Balaam. "I sent for you to curse my enemies, and instead you have blessed them three times," he growled. Then he told Balaam to go home. So Balaam didn't get any of the silver and gold he wanted so much.

When King Balak realized that he couldn't bring evil on the people of Israel by getting Balaam to curse them, he tried another way. He knew he could get the people of Israel to make God angry at them by sinning against Him. For Balaam had told King Balak to invite the Israeli young people to parties honoring idols. This idea worked. The people of Israel came to the parties and bowed to the idols.

The Lord was very angry with the people of Israel for doing this and sent a disease which killed them by the thousands.

QUESTIONS

Why did King Balak send for Balaam?

Tell about Balaam's donkey and why it kept stopping.

What did Balaam do when he got there?

Why did King Balak invite the Israeli young people to parties? What happened?

55
Almost There

The people of Israel wandered around in the wilderness for forty long years. God wouldn't let them go into the Promised Land of Canaan during all that time. Do you remember why? It was because they had refused to go in when God had told them to; they had listened instead to the ten spies who were afraid. So God said they must all die in the wilderness, and only their children could enter Canaan, the land God had promised them.

Those forty years finally ended, and God brought them back again to the edge of the Promised Land. He told Moses and Eleazar to count the men old enough to be soldiers. They discovered that every one of the men who had refused to enter Canaan the first time had died in the wilderness, as the Lord had said they would. Only Caleb and Joshua, the good spies, were still alive, for God had promised that they could go into the Promised Land. Everyone else who had been twenty years old or older at that time had died during those forty years.

But first, before entering the Promised Land, the Lord told Moses and the Israelis to fight the people of Midian because they had encouraged the people of Israel to worship idols. So Moses sent a thousand men from each tribe to attack and kill the people of Midian and their kings, and Balaam too was killed, for he was living with them. The army of Israel took everything that belonged to them, including 72,000 oxen, 61,000 donkeys, and 675,000 sheep. Then they burned their cities and castles.

After the battle was over, the officers of the army of Israel came to Moses and told him, "We haven't lost even one man of all our soldiers; not one has been killed. We want to give a 'thank you' offering to God for taking care of us. Here, give Him these jewels we took from the Midianites." So Moses and Eleazar the High Priest gave the jewels to God by putting them in the Tabernacle.

Now the Lord led the Israelis to the Jordan River where they waited for Him to tell them when to cross. On the other side was the Promised Land of Canaan. But two of the tribes of Israel came to Moses and requested permission to live on this side where they were, instead of on the other side. They asked this because there was good pastureland for their cattle on this side.

At first Moses was angry with them; he thought they wanted to stay behind because they were afraid of the wicked nations in Canaan on the other side of the river.

"You want to stay here while your brothers go over to fight?" he demanded.

"No, no," they replied, "we don't mean that. We'll cross over with the others to fight, but we want to leave our families and cattle here. Then afterwards, when the war is over, we will come back here and live on this side of the river."

So Moses agreed. He spoke to the rest of the people and told them to let the two tribes have the land they asked for. So it was agreed that they should do this.

These two tribes were the tribes of Reuben and Gad. Half of the tribe of Manasseh also asked and received the same permission.

The Lord told Moses that the Israelis must drive out all the heathen nations living across the river. They must destroy all their idols and break down all the heathen altars they would find there.

Every Israeli family was to be given enough land for a home and farm.

The reason why the Israelis must drive out and destroy the heathen nations was so that the Israelis wouldn't be tempted to worship their idols. For if they worshipped them, the Lord would need to destroy His people because of this sin.

QUESTIONS

How long did the Israelis wander in the wilderness? Why so long?

Why did God tell the Israelis to fight the Midianites?

What did two of the tribes want to do?

What must the Israelis do after crossing the Jordan River? Why?

56
Moses' Last Words

While the people of Israel were camped beside the Jordan River, waiting to go across, Moses spoke to them for the last time. He knew he couldn't go into Canaan with them because he had angrily struck the rock with his rod instead of just speaking to it as God had told him to.

He was afraid the people would forget God's laws when he was gone.

In this last talk to them, Moses told them again how kind the Lord had been. He reminded them of the time forty years before when they were so close to Canaan, but they had refused to go in because the spies told them the people in Canaan were too strong to fight against. He reminded them of how angry the Lord had been with them and how God had sent them back into the wilderness for forty years.

Moses told the people that he had begged the Lord to let him cross the river with them, to enter the good land there in Canaan. But the Lord had said no, he must speak of it no more.

But the Lord told him he could see the Promised Land even though he couldn't go into it. So he climbed a high mountain and saw it far away in the distance.

Moses asked the Lord to give the people of Israel another leader to take his place. Otherwise, he said, the people would have no one to guide them and care for them. They would be scattered and lost, like sheep without a shepherd. The Lord announced that He had chosen Joshua as the new leader, so all the people must obey him just as they had Moses.

Moses told the people to teach God's commandments to their children. They must talk about these laws in their homes, and when they were out for walks, and before going to sleep at night, and when waking again in the morning. Everyone must talk about God's laws many times each day and remind each other about how great and good God is.

They must be careful not to forget about the Lord after He had brought them safely into Canaan. He would give them great and beautiful cities that others had built, and would give them houses full of good things, and wells already dug, and vineyards and olive trees which they had not planted. When they had all these things, they must be careful not to forget that it was the Lord who gave everything to them.

They must never forget how God had led them through the wilderness for forty years and fed them with manna. In all that time their clothes had not worn out, and their feet had never become sore from travelling. God had led them through that lonely wilderness to a better land where streams ran through the fields and where springs of water poured down from the hills. In that good land across the river the grain grew plentifully and there were huge crops of juicy grapes; there were fig trees and pomegranates and olive trees—food enough and to spare. And there was iron and copper in the hills, which they could dig out and use to make many wonderful things. They must never become proud and say that they had gotten these things by themselves, for it was the Lord alone who gave everything to them. The Lord said that if they forgot about Him and worshipped other gods, they would be killed.

When the Lord gave them the victory over the people living in Canaan, the people of Israel must never say God had done this for them because they were so good! No, they weren't good at all. Rather it was because the people living in Canaan were so wicked. And it was because God had promised Abraham, Isaac, and Jacob that He would give the land of Canaan to the Israelites.

No, the people of Israel certainly weren't good; they had often disobeyed the Lord from the time when they left Egypt until the time when they arrived there beside the river.

Moses told them that the Promised Land was not like the land of Egypt from which they had come. In Egypt it scarcely ever rained. A river called the Nile ran through the land. Once every year this river rose higher and higher until it flooded the fields and gardens near it. But everywhere except near the river the people had to carry water out to their fields or nothing would grow. This was hard, hard work.

But in Canaan, rain watered all the land. If the people of Israel would love God and obey Him, He would send them as much rain as they needed to make the corn, the grapevines, and the olive trees grow, and to make the grass green in the fields for the cattle to eat.

The people of Canaan worshipped idols on the mountains and hills and under the trees. They built altars to sacrifice to these idols; they even killed their baby sons and daughters by burning them on altars as sacrifices to their false gods. Moses again told the people of Israel that they must destroy every place where idols were worshipped, and knock down all the altars.

If anyone ever tried to get them to sacrifice to other gods, they must take him out and throw great stones at him until he died.

The Lord told His people that everyone must be kind to the poor and lend them whatever they needed, even if the poor person might never be able to pay them back again. Everyone should lend willingly, not feeling sorry about doing it or wishing that they didn't have to. Because of their kindness to the poor, the Lord would bless His people in everything they did.

QUESTIONS

Who was Israel's new leader? Why did God choose him?

Tell some of the things Moses said to his people.

What did the people then living in the Promised Land sometimes do to their boys and girls?

Did God help the Israelis because they were so good?

How were the Israelis supposed to treat poor people? Are there still poor people today? Try to think of something you can do to help one of them.

57
The Cities of Safety

God also told His people that some of their cities must be set aside as safety zones, where a man could run and be safe from punishment if he had accidentally killed someone. For instance, if he was cutting down a tree and the head of the ax flew off the handle, killing someone standing there, the man with the ax must run to a city of safety. Otherwise the dead man's brother or son or some other relative might try to kill him in revenge. But if he escaped and ran to the city of safety, no one could hurt him there. If anyone did, that person would himself be killed.

When a person who had accidentally killed someone arrived at the city of safety, he would tell the judges what he had done. They would take him into the city and give him a place to live. Then if the brother or the son of the man he had killed came and asked for him, they would protect him because he hadn't meant to hurt or kill anyone.

But if some wicked murderer came to the city and asked for safety, the judges wouldn't let him in, and he would be put to death for his sin.

The Lord said that when the people arrived in Canaan, they must bring the first of their grain and fruit to Him at harvest time each year. They would put it in a basket and bring it to the Tabernacle as a gift to the Lord, to thank Him for a good crop. The priest would place the basket in front of the altar, and the person bringing the gift would say, "I have brought the first of my harvest to You, O Lord, to thank You for giving me a good harvest."

Then he would leave the basket of fruit or grain for the priests to eat. God had given this law because the priests had no farms or orchards of their own.

Moses told the people that on the very day they crossed the river and entered the Promised Land, they should build a monument of stones with the laws of God written on them for everyone to read.

Moses said that if the people of Israel obeyed the Lord, the Lord would make them the greatest nation on earth. He would bless them and their children, their land, and their cattle. Their enemies would be afraid of them and would stay far away.

But if the people of Israel didn't obey God, then they would have constant trouble. The seed they planted in their fields wouldn't grow, locusts would come and destroy their growing grain, and worms would eat their grapevines. The people would be weak and sickly, and the Lord would send fierce warriors against them who would not pity the old or the young, but would take them all away as slaves to other countries.

Moses told the people that they must choose between the good and evil ways. He begged them to choose the good way so that they and their children would live long and well.

Then he presented Joshua to them as their new leader.

The Lord now summoned Moses and Joshua to the Tabernacle. He appeared to them there in the pillar of cloud, and consecrated Joshua as the new leader of Israel.

Moses wrote down God's laws and ordered that every seven years the priests, elders, and all the people, including the children, must be called together to listen as these laws were read aloud to them. For they needed to hear them again and again and to remember to obey them. Moses gave the book of laws to the Levites, and told them to keep it inside the Ark.

After this the Lord told Moses to climb to the top of Mount Nebo to look across the Jordan River into the Promised Land. Then he would die on the mountain, just as Aaron had died on Mount Hor.

Moses was an old man now, but still as strong as many young men. He said a last good-bye to his people and climbed to the top of the mountain. There he looked across the Jordan at the Promised Land of Canaan—the land God had promised long before to Abraham, Isaac, Jacob, and to their descendants.

Then Moses died there on the top of the mountain, and the Lord buried him in a valley in the land of of Moab, but no one knows where. He was 120 years old when he died, but he was well and strong until the day of his death.

After that, Joshua ruled the Israelis and they obeyed him as they had Moses. The Lord gave Joshua wisdom and made him able to teach and guide them. But never again until Christ came was there a man like Moses with whom the Lord talked face to face and for whom He did such miracles. But Christ did many more when He came.

QUESTIONS

If a person accidentally killed someone, what should he do to be safe?

Would murderers be safe in the cities of refuge too?

What did the farmers do at harvest time? What can you do?

What happened to Moses? Did God allow him to see the Promised Land? Could he enter it? Do you remember why?

58

A New Leader

Then the Lord said to Joshua, "Moses My assistant is dead, and you must lead the Israelis across the Jordan River into the land I promised them. Be strong and brave, and be careful to obey all of My laws. Then everything you do will be successful. Don't be afraid, for I will be with you and help you wherever you go."

Then Joshua spoke to the Israeli officers. "Go through the camp," he said, "and announce to all the people that three days from now we will cross the Jordan River into Canaan, the Promised Land!"

Meanwhile, Joshua had already sent two spies across. They came to the city of Jericho and went into the house of a woman named Rahab. Someone told the king of Jericho that two spies had come to the city and were at Rahab's house, so the king sent police officers to Rahab's home and told her to bring out the men who were hiding there.

Instead, Rahab took the two men up to the flat roof of her house and hid them under some stalks of flax spread there to dry. The king's messengers looked all over, but since they couldn't find them, they finally went away.

After they were gone, Rahab talked with the men and said she knew that the Lord had given her country to the Israelis. The people of Canaan had already heard how the God of Israel had dried up a path for them through the Red Sea and how He had helped them in fighting against their enemies. Rahab said that when her people heard these things they were very much afraid of the people of Israel. Then she asked the two men to promise that they would remember her kindness in protecting them, and not let any of her family be killed when Israel captured the city of Jericho.

The men said that if she would keep it a secret about their being there, they would protect her. They told her to hang a red rope from the window of her house to help them recognize it again. When the Israeli army came to destroy the city, no one inside her house would be harmed.

The city of Jericho had a high wall around it, and Rahab's house was built on the wall. The king had ordered the gates of the city closed to keep the two spies from getting away, so Rahab let the two men down by a rope on the outside of the wall. She warned them to hide in a nearby mountain for three days until the soldiers quit looking for them.

They did this, then crossed the river to tell Joshua all that had happened.

Joshua and all the people got up early the next morning and travelled to the banks of the Jordan River, where they stayed for three days. Then Joshua told them, "Get ready! Tomorrow we will cross the river, and the Lord will do wonders among you. The priests will go first, carrying the Ark. As soon as their feet touch the water, the river will stop flowing, and the priests will walk through on dry ground!"

Everything happened just as Joshua had said. The next morning the priests carried the Ark toward the river, and all the people followed them. When the priests stepped into the water at the river's edge, the water opened up in front of them, and they walked on dry ground into the middle of the river! The priests waited there with the Ark while all the people walked past them to the other side, into the Promised Land of Canaan!

After all the people were across, the priests carrying the Ark followed. As soon as they stepped out of the river onto the shore, the river began flowing again!

The Israelis made their camp at a place called Gilgal. There they found some corn in the fields, which they roasted and ate. It was the first time they had eaten anything but manna for forty years! The next day, the manna stopped coming. For the forty years while they were in the wilderness where no grain grew, the Lord had sent manna to them every morning without fail. But in Canaan there was plenty of food, so the Lord stopped sending the manna.

QUESTIONS
How did Rahab help the Israeli spies?
How did the Israelis get across the Jordan River?
Did the people find manna to eat in Canaan? Why not?

59
The High Walls Fall Down

Joshua left the camp and went on foot to inspect the city of Jericho with its high walls. Glancing up, he saw a man with a sword in his hand. Joshua strode up to him. "Are you friend or foe?" he demanded.

"I am the general-in-chief of the Lord's army," the man replied. He was telling Joshua that he had come to be their leader and to show them how to win the battles against their enemies. Joshua realized that this Man was the Lord, so he fell to the ground and worshipped Him. It was the same Man who had come to Abraham's tent long before to say that God was going to destroy Sodom. And he was the Man who had wrestled with Jacob when he was returning to Canaan from Laban's house.

The people of Jericho had shut the city gates to stop the Israelis from coming in. But the Lord said He would give Joshua the victory anyway. He even told him how to plan his attack.

All the Israeli soldiers, He said, must march around the city once every day for six days; and the priests must go with them carrying the Ark. Seven priests were to walk ahead of the Ark, blowing trumpets made of ram's horns.

On the seventh day the Israelis were to march around Jericho, not once, but seven times while the priests blew the trumpets. As they finished the seventh time around, the priests must blow a loud, long blast, and all the army must give a mighty shout. Then the walls of the city would fall down flat, and the Israelis could walk right in!

Joshua told his army that only Rahab and those with her in her house would be saved alive. The Lord had commanded that all the rest of the people of Jericho must die for their sins. All the silver, gold, brass, and iron in the city belonged to the Lord and must be put into the treasury where gifts to the Lord were kept. Joshua told the people not to take any of it for themselves, for the Lord would send a great punishment upon them if they did.

The people did as the Lord commanded. The first day they all marched around the city once, the priests following behind blowing the trumpets. Then came other priests who carried the Ark.

On the second day they marched around the city again, and so it went for six days.

But on the seventh day they got up early, before it was light, and marched around the city seven times. The last time around, the priests blew a great blast on the trumpets, and Joshua called out to his army, "Shout, for the Lord has given you the city!"

They gave a mighty shout, and at that moment the walls of the city tumbled down before them, and they rushed into Jericho and captured it. Joshua told the spies who had been at Rahab's house to protect Rahab and everyone with her, just as they had promised her. So they saved Rahab, her father and mother, her brothers, and all who were with her in the house. Afterwards the army of Israel burned the city; but the silver, gold, iron, and bronze were put into the treasury of the Lord.

QUESTIONS

Who was the Man who came to Joshua to lead the Israeli army?

How many times were the Israelis supposed to march around Jericho on each of the first six days?

How many times on the seventh day? Then what happened?

Why was Rahab saved?

60
A Thief Is Killed

Then Joshua sent scouts to Ai, another city of Canaan. When they came back they told him that it was a small city and not many people lived there, so only part of the Israeli army was needed to capture it. Two or three thousand men would be enough, they said.

So Joshua sent about three thousand men. But when the men of Ai came out against them, the Israelis suddenly became afraid and ran, and the men of Ai killed about thirty-six of them.

Joshua didn't know what to do. Israel had been defeated! He tore his clothes, and he and the elders of Israel lay on the ground praying until the evening. Joshua cried out to the Lord, saying, "All the people of Canaan will hear how the Israeli army has run away from its enemies; and they will gather around us on every side and kill us, until not one of us is left."

But the Lord said, "Get up! Why

God told Joshua to lead the people of Israel around the city of Jericho in a great procession. They did this every day for six days. On the seventh day they marched around seven times. Finally they all blew their trumpets and shouted—and you can see what happened!

are you lying there? There is sin among the people of Israel; that is why your enemies have defeated you."

Then the Lord told Joshua that one of the men of Israel had kept some silver and gold taken from the city of Jericho. He had taken it for himself instead of putting it into the treasury of the Lord. The Lord said He would not help the people of Israel anymore unless they punished the man who had done this.

God told Joshua to bring all the people before Him, and He would tell Joshua who the thief was. The man who had done this thing must be burned alive in punishment for stealing from the Lord and for not obeying Him. So Joshua got up early in the morning and brought all the people before the Lord, and the Lord showed him the man who was guilty. His name was Achan.

"Tell me what you have done," Joshua demanded.

Achan then admitted that he had seen a beautiful garment and some silver and a piece of gold, and that he had taken them and hidden them in the ground beneath his tent.

Joshua sent messengers who ran to Achan's tent and found the things buried there. They brought them to Joshua and to all the people of Israel and laid them out before the Lord.

Then Joshua and all the people took Achan and the beautiful garment, and the silver and gold, and his sons and daughters, his tent, his cattle, and everything he owned, to a nearby valley. There they were stoned to death and burned. A great heap of stones was piled over Achan's dead body to show where it lay. After that the valley was called the Valley of Achor, which means "The Valley of Trouble."

Then the Lord said to Joshua, "Now you can conquer the city of Ai." And the Lord commanded Joshua to put all the people of Ai to death for their sins. This time, He said, the Israelis could keep the gold and silver they found, instead of putting it into the treasury of the Lord.

So Joshua and all his army attacked Ai. He sent thirty thousand men around behind the city during the night to hide where the people of Ai couldn't see them. The rest of the army attacked from the front.

When the king of Ai saw the Israeli men approaching, he went out with his army to fight them. Then the Israeli soldiers who were hiding on the other side of the city ran in and set the city on fire.

When the men of Ai looked back and saw the smoke rising, they didn't know which way to go. Joshua and his men were in front of them, and those who had set the city on fire were behind them, so they couldn't escape.

Then Joshua killed them all, as the Lord had commanded. But the Israelis kept the gold, silver, and cattle for themselves, for God had said that this time it was all right for them to do this.

Joshua then built an altar of great stones on Mount Ebal and wrote God's law on it, just as Moses had told them to.

QUESTIONS

Why did God let the men of Ai kill some Israelites?

What sin had Achan committed?

What was Achan's punishment?

What happened when the Israelis went again to fight Ai?

61
Joshua Gets Fooled

When the other kings in Canaan heard how Israel had destroyed Ai, they brought all their armies together to fight against Joshua and his people.

But one of the cities, named Gibeon, refused to join the others. The people of Gibeon didn't want to fight, for they knew that the Lord was helping the Israelis and would destroy anyone fighting them. Instead, they sent men to Joshua wearing very old clothes and worn-out shoes and carrying dry and moldy bread, pretending that they had come from another country far away.

They came to Joshua and told him, "We have come from a distant land, for we have heard of your God and of all the great things He has done for you. Our people have sent us to ask you to make a treaty with us and be our friends."

Joshua and the men of Israel didn't ask the Lord what to do, as they should have done; they agreed at once to be friends with the people of Gibeon.

Three days later they learned the truth. These men had not come from a distant country at all, but lived close by, in Canaan, and were among the wicked nations the armies of Israel had been told to destroy.

Then Joshua called for the men of Gibeon and demanded to know why they had lied to him. They said it was because they feared for their lives, for they had heard that God was going to destroy the people living in Canaan and was going to give their land to the Israelis. Joshua couldn't kill them because only three days before he had promised not to. But he said they must be slaves, and work for the priests and the Levites, cutting wood and carrying the water needed at the Tabernacle.

When the king of Jerusalem heard that the people of Gibeon had surrendered to the Israelis, he was very angry. He and four other kings put their armies together and went to Gibeon to fight against it in revenge.

Then the men of Gibeon sent a messenger to Joshua, "Quick! Come and help us," they said, "for the kings from the mountains have come to punish us."

Joshua and his army fought against the five kings attacking Gibeon, and the Lord made them become afraid of the Israelis and run away. But as they ran, the Lord caused great hailstones to fall upon them out of heaven, so that more of them were killed by hailstones than by the Israelis.

As the Israeli army was chasing them, the sun began to set; for it was evening. Joshua was afraid that God's enemies would escape in the darkness, so he commanded the sun not to go down, and he told the moon to stay where it was and not to move farther across the sky.

And the sun stood still and did not go down for many hours after its usual time! That day was longer than any other day has ever been. There was no day like it either before or afterward, for the Lord, at Joshua's request, made the sun and moon stand still in the sky so that the Israelis could keep on chasing and destroying their enemies.

QUESTIONS

How did the men of Gibeon fool Joshua?

Why did the Israeli army protect Gibeon when the other kings attacked it?

What did Joshua tell the sun and moon to do? Did they obey him?

62

The Tabernacle Finds a Home

Joshua and his troops won many, many more battles against many kings, but there was still much land remaining to be conquered.

All the people of Israel went to the city of Shiloh to set up the Tabernacle there. They had carried the Tabernacle all the way from Mount Sinai, taking it down when they travelled and setting it up again when they stopped. But they had come to Canaan to stay—their long journey was ended. The Tabernacle wouldn't have to be moved again.

The priests and Levites brought the Tabernacle to Shiloh, a city near the center of their new country, and set it up permanently as the Lord had told them to.

But although Israel had conquered only part of Canaan, they had grown tired of war and wanted rest and quiet. It seemed as though they did not want all the good land God was willing to give them.

The Lord spoke to Joshua and reminded him that a large part of the land had not yet been taken away from the Canaanites. So Joshua asked all the people how long it would be before they would be ready to continue the war against the heathen nations still living in Canaan. He asked them to choose twenty-one scouts, and Joshua sent them out to inspect the land that was still unconquered. He told them to give him a written report.

The chosen men walked through the land, made maps of it, and brought their report to Joshua in Shiloh. Then Joshua drew straws for the different tribes of Israel so that the Lord could tell them which part of the land each tribe should have. God told them to finish driving out the heathen nations so that they could have the land for their own use. Joshua promised that the Lord would help His people do this.

God said that the priests and Levites were not to own farms like the men of the other tribes, because He wanted them to stay at the Tabernacle and work for God there. But God said they could have cities of their own to live in. The priests and Levites came to Joshua and the leaders of Israel to find out what cities they could have, and they were given forty-eight cities where they could bring their wives and children and have their homes.

QUESTIONS

What was done with the Tabernacle? Where? Why?

Why did the scouts make maps?

Why couldn't the priests and Levites own farms like everyone else?

63

A War Prevented

The men of the tribes living across the Jordan River had stayed with the Israeli army ever since crossing the river and had fought against the heathen nations in Canaan. They received a full share of the cattle, gold, silver, and anything else taken from the enemy.

Joshua called these men to him and thanked them for their help. "You have obeyed me, whatever I told you to do," he said. "You have not let your brothers fight alone, but have stayed with them and helped them. Now go back to your homes on the other side of the Jordan. But be very careful, after you get there, to obey all the commandments Moses gave us, and to love and to serve the Lord your God with all your hearts."

So they started back home. When they came to the Jordan River, they stopped and built a great altar, shaped like God's altar at Shiloh, where the Tabernacle was. But God had told the Israelis not to sacrifice on any other altar but the one at the Tabernacle. When the men of the other tribes heard that they had built another altar, they were angry, and sent their armies to fight them.

Phinehas, the High Priest, and ten Israeli leaders arrived ahead of the army to ask why they had built this altar.

"We want to know," they said, "why you have built another altar to offer sacrifices on, when the Lord said we should have only one altar—the one at Shiloh. Don't you remember how God sent a great plague on us for worshipping the idols of the Midianites and the Moabites? Don't you remember how He punished us when Achan took the silver and gold for himself, in direct disobedience to God?"

The tribes from across the river were very surprised. They said they had never dreamed of using the altar for sacrifices. It was just a monument, in the form of the altar at Shiloh. In years to come, they said, the people on Joshua's side of the Jordan might say that the tribes on their side of the Jordan River weren't really Israelis, because they didn't live in the Promised Land of Canaan. They could then point to the monument as proof that they were truly people of Israel, just like the others. They fully understood, they said, that there must be no sacrificing except at Shiloh.

So then everyone was happy again.

Joshua had become an old man. One day he summoned the leaders of Israel and reminded them of all the Lord had done for them and urged them always to honor God in everything they did. Then the Lord would greatly bless and prosper them, he said.

"The Lord has driven out your enemies and given you cities, fields, vineyards, and a land of your own to live in," Joshua reminded them. "Fear the Lord and worship Him. If you don't want to worship Him, then choose the idols you would rather worship. But as for me and my family, we will worship the Lord."

The people answered, "God forbid that we should leave the Lord to worship idols. For it was He who brought us out of Egypt and gave us this land. We will worship the Lord, for He is our God."

Then Joshua took a great stone and set it up beneath an oak beside the Tabernacle in Shiloh. That stone, he said, would be a witness to remind them of the promises they had made to worship only the Lord.

So Joshua died. This godly man had lived for 110 years; and they buried him on the side of a hill.

During the forty years since they had left Egypt, the Israelis had been carrying Joseph's bones with them. Now at last they buried them at Shechem. (It had been more than four hundred years since Joseph, wearing his coat of many colors, had gone to Shechem to find his brothers.)

QUESTIONS

Why was everyone so angry about the new altar?

Where was the only place that sacrifices could be made?

Whose bones had been brought all the way from Egypt to be buried? How long before this had the boy Joseph looked for his brothers at Shechem?

64
The Faithfulness of God

After Joshua's death, the Israeli army continued to fight the heathen nations as the Lord had told them to; and God helped them and made them victorious. But they stopped fighting before they had driven out all the nations of Canaan; they allowed some of the heathen nations to stay.

Then the Lord said to the people of Israel, "I brought you out of Egypt into this land I promised you. I commanded you to destroy the idols of the nations living here, and I told you never to make peace with them. But you have not obeyed me. Now I will not help you anymore. The rest of the nations shall stay, and they will tempt you to sin and cause you great trouble."

The people of Israel wept when they heard this. But they soon forgot what the Lord had said, for they not only allowed many of the heathen to stay in Canaan, but they treated them as their friends. They even married them; the young men of Israel took heathen girls for their wives, and the Israeli girls were permitted to marry heathen men.

Then the people of Israel began worshipping idols named Baal and Ashtaroth, who were the gods of the people of Canaan. The Lord was very angry about this and sent enemies to fight against His people and to make them their slaves.

But when they turned away from the idols and turned again to the Lord and asked for His help, He helped them by raising up leaders, called judges. These men helped them fight against their masters and win. Yet, as soon as the Lord set the people free, they would forget Him and sin again by worshipping idols and ignoring the Lord. This sinning and repenting continued for more than three hundred years! During that time fifteen judges were their leaders.

The first judge was Othniel; he was the younger brother of Caleb, one of the good spies. Othniel fought against the king of Mesopotamia, who had kept the Israelis as slaves for eight years. And God helped Othniel and the men of Israel conquer their master's army, so they were free again for the next forty years.

But after Othniel was dead the people of Israel began to worship idols again. Then the king of Moab led his army against Israel and enslaved them for eighteen years. But when the people of Israel cried to the Lord for help, the Lord appointed Ehud as their leader. He was a man of the tribe of Benjamin, and was left-handed.

Ehud made a dagger, hid it under his coat, and came to the king of Moab's palace while the king was sitting in his summer parlor.

"I have a secret message from God for you, O king," Ehud said to him. The king sent everybody out of the room so he could hear the secret. Then Ehud pulled out the dagger and killed the king.

Ehud ran out of the house, and shut and locked the doors behind him. When the king's assistants returned, they saw that the doors of his room were locked and said to themselves, "The king must want to be alone; we'd better not go in."

But after they had waited a very long time, they took a key and opened the doors and found the king lying dead on the floor.

By this time Ehud was far away, and they couldn't find him. Ehud went to Mount Ephraim, in the land of Canaan, and blew a trumpet to call the men of Israel to him.

"Follow me," he told them. "The king is dead, and the Lord will help you conquer the army of Moab."

The men of Israel followed him to the Jordan River where they fought and killed ten thousand brave soldiers of Moab; not one escaped. So the Israelis were again free from the Moabites. This freedom continued for the next eighty years.

QUESTIONS

Why didn't God want the Israeli young people to marry non-Jews?

What were the leaders of Israel now called?

Who was the first judge? Who was his brother?

65

Two Brave Women

Shamgar was the next judge of Israel. He led his people against the Philistines; and all by himself, with nothing but a sharp stick and the Lord's help, he killed six hundred of the enemy.

But when the people of Israel began to worship idols again, God let them be conquered again. This time they were slaves for twenty long years. Then the Lord gave them another judge to help them in their troubles. This judge was a woman named Deborah. She lived near Bethel in a house beneath a palm tree.

Deborah sent for a man named Barak and told him that the Lord wanted him to lead ten thousand

Israeli soldiers against Sisera, the captain of the enemy army. But Barak was afraid and wouldn't go unless Deborah went with him. Deborah said she would, but that the honor of the victory would go to a woman!

So Barak and Deborah led the ten thousand men of Israel against Sisera. Sisera called up all his reserves, including nine hundred iron chariots, and came out to fight. But the Lord gave Israel the victory.

Sisera jumped from his chariot and ran away to the tent of a woman named Jael. He didn't know she was a friend of the people of Israel.

"Give me a little water," he begged her, "for I am very thirsty." So she gave him some milk to drink.

"Stand in the door of your tent," he told her, "and if anyone comes by and asks if you have seen me, tell him no."

He was so tired that he lay down and slept. Jael took a sharp tent peg that was used to fasten the tent to the ground, went quietly over to him, and drove it into his head with a hammer, killing him.

Soon afterwards Barak came by looking for Sisera. Jael went out to meet him and said, "Come here, and I will show you the man you are looking for." Then she took him into the tent, and there lay Sisera, dead.

So the Israelis were freed from the king of Canaan that day.

But after forty years of freedom, the people of Israel began worshipping idols again. Then the Midianites came and fought them, and made slaves of them and treated them very cruelly. They drove the Israelis from their homes, making them live in dens and caves in the mountains. They destroyed their crops, leaving little for the Israelis to eat. And they took their oxen, goats, and sheep, so that the people of Israel grew very poor and hungry.

Then, as they had before, the Israelis cried to the Lord to help them. The judge the Lord sent this time was Gideon.

Gideon was threshing wheat one day and trying to hide it from the Midianites, when the Lord came to him in the form of an angel and spoke kindly to him. Then Gideon told the Lord about the troubles the people of Israel were having because of the Midianites.

"You will free the people of Israel from the Midianites!" the Lord told him.

"But, Lord, how can I do that?" Gideon asked.

"That's easy!" the Lord replied, "I will be with you, and you will destroy their whole army as if it were only one man!"

Then Gideon said to the Lord, "Please wait here while I go and get an animal to sacrifice to You."

So Gideon went and killed a young goat, cut it up, put the meat into a basket, and brought it out to the Lord. The Lord told Gideon to lay it on a rock; then He touched the meat with the end of a stick He had in His hand, and fire flamed out of the rock and burned the sacrifice! Then the Lord disappeared.

QUESTIONS

Why did God let His people become slaves again?

What was the name of the first woman to lead and judge Israel?

When Gideon sacrificed the goat, what happened?

66
Gideon and His Wool

Soon a great army of Midianites arrived and camped in the valley of Jezreel. Gideon blew a trumpet and called the men of Israel to go with him and fight them.

Gideon asked God to do a miracle to prove to him that it was really God who had promised to help him when he went to fight against the Midianites. This is the miracle Gideon asked God to do. Gideon said he would leave some wool out on the ground all night. In the morning, if the wool was wet with dew and the ground all around it was dry, this would be a miracle and he would know that the Lord was going to help him in his fight to free the people of Israel.

So Gideon left the wool on the ground all night. Early the next morning he went out and found it full of water. He wrung the dew out of it with his hands and filled a bowl with the water, but the ground all around was dry! Why wasn't the ground wet too? You see, it was a miracle.

Then Gideon asked the Lord for permission to try it again; but this time he asked God to make the ground wet with dew and to let the wool stay dry! God agreed, so Gideon left the wool out another night, and in the morning the wool was perfectly dry, but the ground all around was wet!

Gideon knew by these miracles that the Lord would certainly help him when he went out to fight against the Midianites. Gideon's little army got up early in the morning and started toward the vast army of Midian. But the Lord told Gideon that his little army was too big!

"Send some of your men home," God said. "Tell anyone who is afraid to leave."

When Gideon told his men this, twenty-two thousand of them went home, while ten thousand stayed.

"There are still too many!" the Lord said. "Bring them down to the river, and I will choose the ones I want in the battle."

God told Gideon to send his soldiers home except for three hundred of them who drank from their hands. God would use these three hundred to defeat a vast enemy army.

So Gideon brought them to the river. All the men were thirsty and began to drink. Some lifted the water to their mouths in their hands, and some stooped down and put their mouths into the water. The Lord said that only the ones who drank from their hands (there were three hundred of them) could go with him to the battle!

Gideon was afraid to go with so few, but the Lord told him to take one of his soldiers and creep over to the camp of the enemy through the darkness to listen to what they were saying.

The Midianites were as thick as grasshoppers in the valley below, and they had so many camels it was hard to count them. That night Gideon and another man crept down to their camp and listened outside one of the tents where two Midianite soldiers were talking. One was telling the other about a dream he had.

"In my dream," he said, "I saw a loaf of bread come tumbling into our camp; it struck against a tent and knocked it down flat on the ground!"

And the other man said, "Your dream means that the Lord is going to give Gideon a great victory over us!"

When Gideon heard this he went back to the three hundred men. He told them to get up and come with him, for the Lord would give them the victory. He put them in three different groups and gave each man a trumpet and a pitcher with a lighted lamp inside. He told them that when they came to the camp of the Midianites, they must do exactly as he did. When he blew his trumpet, they must all blow theirs and shout, "The sword of the Lord and of Gideon!"

In the middle of the night he and his three hundred men arrived in the camp of the Midianites. Suddenly he and all of his men blew their trumpets and broke the pitchers and shouted, "The sword of the Lord and of Gideon!"

When the Midianites heard the noise and saw the burning lamps that had been hidden in the pitchers, they yelled in fear and ran for their lives. The Lord made them afraid both of the men of Israel and of each other, too, so that they were killing and fighting one another all over the valley.

Gideon and his men chased them as they fled across the Jordan River. The two kings of the Midianites raced ahead of him with fifteen thousand soldiers. But he caught up with them and overcame them and took the two kings captive.

So the Midianites were driven out of Canaan, and the people of Israel were no longer their slaves.

Gideon was the judge of Israel for forty years. God gave him many sons, and he lived to be an old man.

QUESTIONS

What two miracles did God do with Gideon's wool?

How did the Lord decide which men should be in Gideon's army?

How did Gideon's tiny army defeat the huge Midianite army?

67
The Story of Gideon's Son

As soon as Gideon was dead, the Israelis promptly forgot about the Lord. They turned away from God again, and worshipped the idol Baal.

Gideon's son Abimelech was king of the city of Shechem, but his friends wanted him to be king over all of Israel instead of just one city. They gave him seventy pieces of silver taken from the temple of Baal, and he used the money to hire men to go with him and help him.

First he killed all of his brothers except the youngest, who ran away. Abimelech did this because he was afraid the people might become tired of him and ask one of his brothers to be king instead. So he became the king of all the land of Israel.

After Abimelech had been king for three years, God sent him trouble. Instead of being his friends any longer, the people of Shechem became his enemies. While he was away on a trip, they decided to kill him.

The governor of the city, who was still Abimelech's friend, sent him this secret message: "Be careful. The people of Shechem have rebelled against you. Come in the night with your men, and hide out in the field until morning. As soon as the sun is up, march toward the city; and when the people come out to fight you, you can defeat them."

So Abimelech did this. He brought his men to the city during the night and hid them in the fields near the city. In the morning the people saw him and came out to fight, but he chased them back into the city and killed many of them.

The next morning they came out again. This time Abimelech divided his men into three groups and hid them in the field. As soon as the men of Shechem had gone quite far from the city gate, one of Abimelech's groups ran behind them and stood in front of the gate to prevent the men of Shechem from getting back into their city. Then the two other groups ran toward them from the field and killed them. Abimelech and his men fought against the city all day, until all the people were killed, their houses knocked apart, and the city completely destroyed.

Some of the men of Shechem escaped to the temple of their idol

Baal and barred the heavy gates so that Abimelech couldn't get to them. He led his troops up a mountain and cut off large branches from the trees, then returned to the temple. They piled the branches against the door and set them on fire, burning up the temple and all the people inside.

Then Abimelech went to the city of Thebez, fought against it, and captured it. The people who lived there fled into a strong tower, locked the door, and climbed to its top. Abimelech tried to burn the tower as he had the idol temple in Shechem, but a woman threw down a huge rock from the top of the tower. It hit him on the head, crushing his skull.

When he knew he was dying, he called one of his young men and said to him, "Draw your sword and kill me so it won't be said I was killed by a woman."

The youth thrust his sword through Abimelech, and he died. In this way God punished Abimelech for killing his brothers and also punished the people of Shechem for helping him to do it.

After Abimelech was dead, Tola was the judge of Israel for twenty-three years.

After him, Jair, who lived across the Jordan River in the land of Gilead, was judge for twenty-two years. He had thirty sons, and each of them was the governor of a city in Gilead.

Then the people of Israel turned away from the Lord again and worshipped Baal and Ashtaroth, the same idols their fathers had worshipped. So this time when the Philistines attacked Israel, the Lord didn't help His people. They became slaves again for eighteen years.

In their trouble they cried out to the Lord for help; but He reminded them of how often He had set them free from their enemies, only to see them turn their backs on Him again and worship heathen idols. Let them go to the idols they had chosen, He said, and ask them for help. But the people of Israel confessed their sins and asked God to punish them, but please to set them free from their enemies. They destroyed the idols they had worshipped, and worshipped the Lord again; and He pitied them in their sufferings.

QUESTIONS

Who was Abimelech's father?

Why did God send trouble to Abimelech?

How did Abimelech die?

68
The Story of Jephthah

The Ammonites came to attack Israel again and were camped in the land of Gilead, on the other side of the Jordan River. The Israeli men organized an army, too, but they had no leader; they needed a general to tell them what to do.

One of the Israelis, named Jephthah, was a great and brave soldier, but the men of Israel had been unkind to him, so he had moved away to another country. But when the people wanted a man to lead them against their enemies, they remembered Jephthah. The elders of Israel went to him in the land of Tob, and said, "Come and be the general of our army."

Jephthah answered, "You hated me and sent me away. Why come to me now when you are in trouble?" But the elders promised before the Lord that they would make him their king if he won the war for them. So Jephthah went with them.

He sent messengers to the king of the Ammonites, asking him why he had come to fight. The king answered that hundreds of years before, the Israelis had taken away his land when they came up out of Egypt. "Give me back my land," he said.

But Jephthah sent messengers to say that the land they had taken was given to them by the Lord, and they were going to keep it. Then Jephthah and the men of Israel went out to fight the Ammonite army.

Before the battle, Jephthah made a promise that if the Lord would give him the victory, he would offer up as a burnt offering whatever came out of his door to meet him when he returned home from the battle. Jephthah did wrong in making such a promise, for he had no idea who or what might come to meet him.

When he led his troops against the Ammonites, the Lord gave him the victory, so the Israelis were free from their slavery again. When the battle was over, Jephthah returned to his home. His daughter, his only child, came running out to meet him, full of joy at seeing her father again.

Can you imagine how Jephthah felt? He tore his clothes in his sorrow and finally told her of his promise.

She said, "Father, if you have made

a vow to the Lord, do to me as you have said."

Jephthah should not have kept his wicked promise. God had commanded the Israelis to sacrifice oxen, goats, and lambs as burnt offerings. God had said never to sacrifice their children; this was what heathen nations did and were punished for doing. Jephthah should have repented of his promise and asked God's forgiveness; but instead, he kept his evil promise.

QUESTIONS

How did Jephthah get to be the leader of Israel?

What awful promise did Jephthah make to God?

What happened afterwards?

69

A Visit from an Angel

After this the people of Israel sinned again and displeased the Lord by worshipping idols. Again they became slaves, this time to the Philistines for forty years.

A man named Manoah and his wife were among those who still worshipped the Lord, but they were sad because they had no children. One day the Angel of the Lord came and told Manoah's wife that she and Manoah would have a son. The Angel said their son was set apart for God and must never drink wine or whiskey and must never have his hair cut. The Angel also told them that when their son was grown, he would free Israel from the Philistines.

The woman ran and told her husband that a prophet had spoken to her, for she did not realize he was an angel. Then Manoah prayed, "Lord, let the prophet come again and teach us how to raise the child You are going to give us."

The Lord heard Manoah's prayer, and the Angel came again to the woman as she was out in the field. She ran to her husband and told him the man had come again. Manoah went with his wife and said to him, "Are you the man of God who was talking to my wife?"

"I am," he said.

Then Manoah asked him, "How shall we raise the child you have promised us?"

The Angel answered, "Be sure to do everything I told your wife before."

Manoah begged the Angel to stay and eat with them, for they still didn't know it was an angel. But the Angel said, "Even if I stay I will not eat your food."

Then Manoah said, "Tell us your name so that we can honor you when the child is born as you have promised us."

The Angel answered, "Why do you ask my name? It is a secret."

Then Manoah took a young goat as a burnt offering and sacrificed it upon a rock. The Angel did a wonderful thing as the fire was burning on the rock, its flame going up toward heaven. The Angel of the Lord went up in the flame and disappeared! When Manoah and his wife saw this, they fell flat upon the ground in worship.

Manoah was frightened. "We have seen God," he said, for he believed the Angel was the Lord. "We shall surely die because we have seen Him."

But his wife said to him, "If the Lord had intended to kill us, He wouldn't have accepted our burnt offering nor promised us a son."

A few months later, God gave Manoah and his wife the son He had promised them, and they named him Samson. As the child grew, the Lord was kind to him and blessed him.

QUESTIONS

What happy news did the Angel tell Manoah and his wife?

What would be special about their son?

Who was the Angel?

70
Samson's Riddle

When Samson was grown, he went to a city called Timnath where he fell in love with a Philistine girl. She was not a Jewess, but when he returned home he told his father and mother about her and asked them to get her as his wife. His father and mother told him he should marry an Israeli girl, not a Philistine girl, for the Philistines were enemies of the Israelites. Besides, God had told His people not to marry non-Jews.

But Samson was not willing to give her up. He said to his father, "I want her, so get her for me."

His father and mother went back with him to Timnath. On the way there, a young lion came roaring out at Samson, and the Lord gave him strength to kill the lion with his hands as easily as if it had been a young goat.

When Samson finally met the girl and talked with her, he wanted all the more to marry her. A wedding date was set, and he and his parents went back home. When he returned to marry her, he came to the place where he had killed the lion and went over to look at it. Its body was dried up, and a swarm of bees was living in it, storing honey there. He took some of the honey in his hands and ate it as he walked. Afterwards he gave some to his father and mother, but he didn't tell them he had taken it out of the dead body of the lion.

Samson gave a big party for the young men of the town, for that was one of the marriage customs of those days. Thirty Philistine youths came, and the party lasted seven days. During the party Samson decided to tell them a riddle. He promised to give each of the young men a suit if they found out what his riddle meant before the seven days of the party ended. But if they couldn't find the answer to his riddle, then each of them must give *him* a suit! The Philistine boys agreed to this bet.

"Go ahead," they said, "tell us the riddle."

"All right," Samson replied, "here it is: 'Food came out of the eater, and sweetness came out of the strong!' " (He meant that he had taken honey from a lion, and eaten it. But of course he didn't tell the Philistines the answer because then he would lose the bet!)

For three days they tried to find the answer, but couldn't. Finally the young men went to his bride and told her they would kill her and her whole family unless she found out from Samson the answer to the riddle.

She knew they would kill her, so she asked Samson to tell her, but he wouldn't. Then she started crying and saying he didn't love her or he would tell her.

"I haven't even told my father or my mother," Samson answered; "why should I tell you?"

But she kept on begging and crying, and he finally told her just to keep her quiet. Then of course she went and told the Philistine boys.

They came to Samson on the seventh day, just before the end of the feast, and pretended they had thought up the answer by themselves. "What is sweeter than honey?" they asked. "And what is stronger than a lion?" But Samson knew his wife had told them.

The Lord's time came for Samson to begin punishing the Philistines for their cruelty to the people of Israel. The Lord had told Samson's parents that their son would begin to free the Israelis from their slavery. That was why the Lord had made Samson strong enough to kill the young lion as easily as if it had been a baby goat.

Samson went to a Philistine city called Ashkelon and killed thirty men there. He took their clothes and gave them to the men at the wedding, to fulfill his promise of a suit to each of them if they found the answer to his riddle.

Then he left his wife and returned to his own home, while she stayed with her father in Timnath.

A few months later Samson went to visit her and to take her a present. But her father wouldn't let him in, because he had let another man marry her. Her father thought that Samson had gone away because he had decided he didn't want her. This was why he had given her to someone else.

Samson was very angry and went

out and caught three hundred foxes. He tied burning torches to their tails and let them loose in the fields and vineyards of the Philistines, setting fire to their grain, grape vines and olive trees.

"Who has done this?" the Philistines demanded. When they knew it was Samson, they killed his wife and her father.

Then Samson took revenge by fighting against the Philistines and killing several of them. Afterward he camped on the top of a high rock in the land of Israel. The Philistines went there with an army of several thousand men to capture and kill him. When the men of Israel saw the Philistines coming, they asked what the trouble was and why they had come.

"To get Samson," they answered, "so that we can do to him as he has done to us."

Then three thousand men of Israel climbed to the top of the rock where Samson was to talk to him and to get him to surrender. "Don't you know that we are slaves to the Philistines?" they asked. "Why are you acting like this?"

"I only paid them back for what they did to me," Samson replied. Then the men of Israel told him they had come to get him and to give him to the Philistines. Samson let them bind him with two new ropes and they took him to the Philistines' camp. As he came near them, the Philistines saw him and let out a great shout of joy. But at that moment the Lord gave him such strength that he broke the ropes! Samson picked up the jawbone of a donkey lying by the road and killed a thousand Philistines with it.

Afterward he was so tired he could hardly stand up. He prayed to the Lord, and the Lord opened a spring with water bubbling out; after Samson drank from it, his strength returned to him again.

He went to the city of Gaza and spent the night sleeping with a girl he had met. But this was wrong, for she was not his wife. This was a Philistine city and when the Philistines heard that Samson was there, they shut the city gates and watched all night to capture him when he went out again. But in the middle of the night he decided to leave town. When he found he couldn't leave because the gates were closed, he simply pulled the gate posts out of the ground, picked up the gates, put them on his shoulders, and carried them to the top of a nearby hill!

QUESTIONS

What animal did Samson kill with his hands?

What riddle did Samson tell the boys at his wedding party?

How did they find out the answer to the riddle?

How did Samson light the Philistines' fields on fire? Why?

71
Samson and Delilah

One day Samson decided to visit a Philistine girl friend of his named Delilah. When the kings of the Philistine cities knew he was there, they promised to give Delilah eleven hundred pieces of silver if she would help them capture him. So Delilah begged Samson to tell her the secret of his great strength and how he could be made as weak as other men.

Samson told her a lie. He said that if he were tied with seven ropes made from green flax, then he would be as helpless as any other man.

Delilah told this to the kings of the Philistines, and she tied him with the ropes while he was asleep. He didn't know there were men hiding in the room to grab him.

When she had tied him up she cried out, "The Philistines are here to get you, Samson!" Instantly, Samson woke up and broke the ropes as easily as if they were threads.

Delilah said he had mocked her and told her a lie and begged him to tell her the truth. How could he be tied up so that he couldn't get away? This time Samson said that if he were tied with two new ropes that had never been used before, he would not be able to break them. So she took two new ropes and tied him, while men hid in the room, then called out to him as before that the Philistines were coming to get him. But he broke the new ropes as easily as before.

Delilah scolded him for lying to her again, and again she begged him to tell her how to tie him so he couldn't get away. Samson said that if she would weave his long hair into a loom, his strength would leave him and he would be helpless. So she did this. But when she told him the Philistines were coming, he was as strong as ever.

"How can you say, 'I love you' when all you do is make fun of me and lie to me?" she asked. Day after day she begged him to tell her and would give him no rest. At last he told her the

Samson was so strong that he could break the strongest ropes his enemies tied him with.

R. Hook

truth. He said that he had been a Nazirite since he was born. His hair had never been cut, and if it were, he would no longer be strong, but as weak as other men.

Why did Samson tell her this secret? He was telling her how to take away the strength the Lord had given him to fight against the enemies of Israel. He did it because he had chosen a girl for his friend who didn't care about God, and he listened to her until she persuaded him to do this great sin against God. You and I must be careful not to do wrong things even if people we like want us to and say we should. We must always listen to the Lord instead.

Delilah realized that this time Samson was finally telling her the truth. She sent this message to the kings of the Philistines: "Come once more; this time he has told me the truth!" So they came again and brought her the money they had promised.

Then, while Samson was asleep, a barber came and cut his hair.

Delilah woke Samson up and told him that the Philistines were coming to get him. He thought he could easily get away as he always had before, for he didn't realize that the Lord had let his strength go away. But this time the Philistines caught him, for he could no longer fight against them, and they bound him with bronze chains. They poked out his eyes, making him blind, and shut him up in prison where they made him work very hard turning a millstone to grind their corn.

But while he was in prison, his hair began to grow longer again, and the Lord gave him back his strength.

One day the kings of the Philistines called the people together in their idol's temple to offer a sacrifice to their god Dagon and to rejoice because Samson had been caught. Everyone present praised Dagon (he was an idol), because they thought he had helped them catch Samson! They were all very happy.

"Send for Samson so we can tease him," someone suggested. So they brought blind Samson out of the prison and set him between the two pillars that held up the roof of the temple and made fun of him there.

The temple was packed with people, including all the kings of the Philistines. Many of the people were having a party on the roof, while those inside the temple were laughing at Samson. A boy held him by the hand to lead him because he couldn't see. Samson asked the boy to place his hands on the pillars that held up the temple roof, so he could lean against them. The boy did.

Then Samson prayed, "O Lord, help me, and give me strength only this once." He gave a mighty push against the two pillars as he stood there between them, and said, "Let me die with the Philistines." As he pushed, the pillars moved apart, and the roof fell on the kings of the Philistines and on all the people inside, killing great numbers of them.

Samson died with them, but in his death he killed more of the enemies of

Samson is standing between two pillars and pushing against them with all his might. He has pushed them apart and the building is falling down.

R. Hook

Israel than he had while he was alive. Then his brothers came and took his dead body and buried it.

QUESTIONS
Who was Delilah? What did she want Samson to tell her?
Why was Samson so strong? What happened to him when he finally told Delilah the truth?
What did the Philistines do to Samson? How did he die?

72
The Story of Ruth

During the time judges ruled Israel, a man named Elimelech and his wife, Naomi, moved from Israel to the land of Moab.

His sons married Moabite girls, and they all lived together for about ten years. Then Elimelech and his two sons all died, leaving Naomi alone with her two daughters-in-law.

Naomi decided to go back to her home in the city of Bethlehem in Israel. She asked her daughters-in-law if they would rather stay in Moab, the land where they were born and where all their friends and relatives lived, or whether they wanted to move to Israel with her.

When her daughters-in-law learned of her decision to return to Israel, they cried. One of them, Orpah, decided to stay in Moab; but the other, Ruth, didn't want to leave Naomi.

"I'll go with you," she said, "and live wherever you live. Your friends will be my friends, and your God will be my God."

When Naomi saw how much her daughter-in-law Ruth loved her, she didn't urge her to stay in the land of Moab, but agreed to let her come with her to the land of Israel.

So they came to the city of Bethlehem where Naomi had lived before moving to Moab.

Her neighbors remembered her, of course, and the news of her arrival spread quickly. "Oh, there's Naomi!" they would exclaim. But she would reply, "No, don't call me Naomi anymore, for Naomi means 'pleasant.' Call me Mara, because that means 'bitter.' For the Lord has given me bitter

Naomi is very sad because her husband is dead. Ruth is trying to comfort her.

troubles." She meant that when she left Bethlehem so many years before, her husband and her two sons were with her; but now all three were dead.

One day during harvest time, Ruth said to Naomi, "Let me go out to the harvest fields and pick up grain dropped by the harvesters." She said this because one of God's laws for His people was that poor people must always be allowed to pick up any bits of grain that dropped to the ground at harvest time. Ruth wanted to get some of this grain for them to eat.

Naomi agreed to this. Ruth went to a field belonging to a man named Boaz and began picking up the grains behind his workers.

When Boaz came out to the field later that morning, he asked the foreman in charge of the reapers, "Say, who is that girl over there?"

"She is the one who came with Naomi from the land of Moab," the foreman replied.

Boaz went over and talked to Ruth. He was very pleasant to her and told her to stay with his reapers and not to go to some other field, for he had warned his young men not to bother her. When she was thirsty, he said she should get water from the pitchers placed there for his workers and drink as much and as often as she wished. And he told her to eat lunch with his workers from the food he provided for them.

Ruth thanked him very much and asked him why he was so kind to her since she was only a stranger. Boaz said it was because he knew about her kindness to her mother-in-law: how she had left her father and mother and the land where she was born, and had come to live among the people of Israel. He said he hoped God would bless her because she had done these things. He was glad, he said, that she had left the land of Moab where the people worshipped idols and had come to Canaan to worship the Lord.

Afterwards Boaz told his workers to drop some handfuls of grain on purpose so that she could find the grain and pick it up!

Ruth stayed in his field until evening, then beat out the barley grain she had gathered, and took it to her mother-in-law. When Naomi saw how much Ruth brought, she was glad, and asked the Lord to bless the man who had been so kind to her. She asked who it was, and Ruth said, "The man's name is Boaz." Naomi was surprised and told her he was a close relative of theirs! He was a very rich man, Naomi said.

Ruth said he had asked her to keep coming back to his field until the harvest ended. Naomi, too, said to do this; so Ruth went back day after day until the end of the harvest.

One day Naomi said to Ruth, "Boaz is threshing barley tonight at the threshing floor." In those days the grain was separated from the straw and chaff by throwing it up in the air while the wind was blowing. The wind would blow away the straw because it

Ruth was a young widow who came to Israel from another land. She came with Naomi, her mother-in-law, to take care of her and to love her. Ruth worked hard and God helped her. Do you know who her great-grandson was? King David!

was so light, but the grain was heavier and would fall in a pile on the ground. A threshing floor was a smooth, level piece of ground where this was done. Naomi had heard that Boaz was to divide his barley from the chaff that night, and she had a plan! She told Ruth to go to the threshing floor and find Boaz. Then she told her what to say to him.

Ruth did as her mother-in-law said. Boaz and his workers winnowed his barley that night, and after a hearty supper he lay down for the night beside a stack of sheaves. When it was dark, Ruth went over and lay at his feet! Around midnight he woke up, startled and afraid. "Who's there?" he demanded.

"It's only me, sir," Ruth replied. Then she said what Naomi had told her to say. Because he was a close relative, she wanted him to take care of her and marry her.

The idea pleased him very much. "May the Lord bless you, my child," he replied. He said he would gladly marry her if he could, because all the people of Bethlehem knew what a fine person she was. But first he would need to talk with another man who was an even closer relative of Naomi's, who had the first right to marry her. If he didn't want to, then Boaz would. Boaz said he would talk to the other man that very day. So Ruth slept at his feet all night; and early the next morning before it was light, he gave her a large sack of barley to take home to Naomi. When she told Naomi what Boaz had said and showed her his present, Naomi told Ruth to be patient and see how it would all turn out.

That day Boaz called together ten of the city officials and told them that he wanted to marry Ruth. Soon, the other man who had the first choice of marrying her came by. He said he didn't want to marry Ruth, so Boaz could. Then all the city officials prayed that the Lord would bless Ruth and make Boaz still richer and greater than he was already.

So Boaz married Ruth, and Naomi was very happy. The Lord gave Boaz and Ruth a son, and grandmother Naomi loved the baby very much. They named the little boy Obed.

QUESTIONS

Why did Ruth go to Canaan with Naomi?
Why did Ruth go into the harvest fields?
What kind thing did Boaz tell Ruth?
Who got married in this story?

73
The Story of Job

There was a man in the land of Uz named Job, who worshipped God and was careful to do good at all times. God gave him seven sons and three daughters, as well as a lot of money. He had three thousand camels, seven thousand sheep, one thousand oxen, five hundred donkeys, and many servants; in fact, he was the richest man in that part of the world.

His sons were grown up and had homes of their own. They used to have parties at each other's houses and would invite their three sisters to come too. Afterwards Job would sacrifice burnt offerings to God for each of them, because he feared they might have sinned and displeased God.

After Job had enjoyed this good life for many years, God sent trouble upon him to see whether he would bear it patiently and be willing for his heavenly Father to do what He thought best. God allowed Job's money and children to be taken from him.

One day one of his servants came running to him and said, "While your oxen were plowing in the field and the donkeys were feeding beside them, a band of robbers drove them all away and killed your servants; I am the only one left."

Before this servant finished speaking, another rushed up to Job to say, "A great fire has fallen from the sky and burned up your sheep and the servants who were taking care of them, and I alone am left."

While he was still speaking, another came and said, "Some enemies have taken your camels and killed your servants who were watching them, and only I am left."

At the same time, another messenger came saying, "Your sons and daughters were having a party in their oldest brother's house when a hurricane from the wilderness came, and the house fell on them. They are dead, and only I am left to tell you."

When Job heard these things, he tore his clothes and bowed down to the earth and worshipped, saying, "I had nothing of my own when I was born and I will have nothing when I die. It was God who gave me my children and my riches, and it is God who has taken them all away again. He knows what is best for me, and I thank

Him for all He has done."

So Job did not sin or speak against God, although his grief was so great and had come upon him so suddenly.

After this, to test Job even more, God sent him sickness and pain. He was covered with boils from head to foot, and he sat on the ground beside the city gate in great distress. His wife was angry because God had sent him so much suffering. She came to Job and said, "Why do you still trust God? Speak against Him for treating you like this, even though He kills you for saying it."

Job answered her, "You are talking like a foolish woman. After we have had so many good things from God, shall we not be willing to have evil things too?"

So Job still said nothing that was wrong.

He had three friends who came to talk with him and comfort him. When they saw him, he was so changed that at first they didn't recognize him. Then they tore their clothes and cried and sat beside him on the ground in silence for many days, because they could see that his grief was very great.

These friends thought his troubles had been sent upon him because he had done something bad. After a while they spoke to him and said, "If you have done something bad, don't do it again. You must have sinned. You must have taken something that didn't belong to you. Or perhaps you were cruel to the poor, or you didn't pray. But if you will be sorry for your sins, God will forgive you and make you get well again."

But Job knew he had not done those bad things. He said to them, "You came to comfort me, but what you say doesn't help me at all. I would rather you hadn't come. If you were me, I wouldn't call you bad; I would speak to you kindly and try to help you."

Then Job talked about his troubles. "The Lord has sent great troubles upon me," he cried out. "Oh, that He would put me to death so that I wouldn't need to suffer any more! When I lie down at night, I toss upon my bed in pain and wish it were morning. And if I fall asleep for a little while, nightmares frighten me, so that I would rather die than live. Oh, that I had someone to speak to God for me, for He doesn't listen to my prayers any more. Yet I know that my Saviour is alive, and that after many years He will come to earth, and I shall rise from the grave and see God for myself."

But when Job saw that he could neither die nor get well, but must bear his pain, he grew impatient. He was willing to have these troubles for a little while, but not until God saw best to take them away.

Then he began to find fault and to say that his troubles were too great and that God was being cruel and unfair to him. And his three friends, instead of trying to encourage him, still told him he was bad and had made God angry. They said God didn't punish good people, but only bad people, so Job must have been very, very bad to have so much pain.

This made Job angry at them, and that made them angry at him. They kept on talking back and forth for a long while, and each of them said many things they shouldn't have.

Then they heard the voice of God speaking to them out of a whirlwind. God reminded Job that He had made the earth, the sea, and the sky. It is God who gives the wild animals their food and feeds the young birds when they are hungry. It is God who gives the beautiful tail to the peacock and the feathers to the ostrich. He makes the horse swift and strong and unafraid. He teaches the eagle to build her nest on the high rocks and to fly away to hunt for food for her young ones.

God asked if Job could do things like that, and whether he thought he was wise enough to teach lessons to God.

Then Job saw that he had sinned in finding fault with God. "I am bad," he said, "and have spoken of things that I don't understand; I am sorry for my sin and bow down in the dust before You."

Then God said to Job's three friends, "I am angry with you because you have not spoken what is right to My servant Job in his trouble. Now take seven young bulls and seven rams and sacrifice them as burnt offerings. Then ask Job to pray for you and to ask Me to forgive you, for I will answer his prayers." They did as the Lord commanded, and Job prayed for them and they were forgiven.

After this, the Lord made Job well again. Then all his brothers and sisters and friends came to him and they had a great party at his house. Everyone gave him some money and gold jewelry. The Lord blessed Job twice as much as before and made him twice as rich. Now Job had fourteen thousand sheep, six thousand camels, two thousand oxen, and one thousand donkeys. He also had seven more sons and three more daughters; so now, including those in heaven, he had twice as many children as before; and in all the land there were no girls as beautiful as the daughters of Job.

Job lived 140 years more after all these things had happened to him, and he died when he was a very old man.

QUESTIONS

Was Job a good man or an evil man? Was he rich or poor?

What happened to Job's cattle? His servants? His children?

Why did God send sickness and pain to Job?

Do you think Job's friends were good friends? Are you a good friend? Of whom?

What good things happened to Job after all of his troubles?

74
The Story of Jonah

Long ago Nineveh was one of the greatest cities in the world. In it there were temples and palaces, thousands of homes, beautiful gardens, and green fields for the cattle. Around the city were walls one hundred feet high. These walls were so thick that if there had been a road on top and automobiles in those days, three cars could have been driven along, side by side, on the top of this great wall. Fifteen hundred towers were built above the walls all around the city. These towers were each two hundred feet high. The Assyrian soldiers could shoot arrows from the walls at their enemies when they came to fight against Nineveh.

Nineveh was also a very wicked city.

One day God spoke to the prophet Jonah and said, "Jonah, go to Nineveh, and tell the people about the punishment I am going to send them because of their sins."

But Jonah didn't want to go, so he ran away to Joppa, a city by the sea. There he found a ship headed in a different direction than Nineveh, so Jonah bought a ticket and got on board to try to get away from God.

When the ship had sailed out to sea, the Lord sent a strong wind and a great storm. The ship was in danger of sinking. The sailors were terrified and prayed for help, each one praying to his own god. Then they threw out some of the freight the ship was carrying, to make it lighter and to keep it from sinking. But Jonah didn't know the danger they were in, for he had gone down to the bottom of the ship and lay there fast asleep. The captain found him and woke him up.

"How can you sleep like this?" the captain shouted at him. "Get up and pray to your god; perhaps he may pity us and save us from dying."

Then the sailors talked together and said, "This storm has been sent

Jonah ran away from God. He was in a boat and was thrown overboard by the sailors. Then a giant fish swallowed him. But inside the fish, Jonah finally was sorry; so God told the fish to vomit him out onto the shore. Doesn't Jonah look surprised?

R. Hook

because someone in the ship has been bad. Let's draw straws to find out whose fault it is."

They did, and Jonah drew the short one. They said to him, "Tell us, what wicked thing have you done? What country do you come from?"

Jonah replied, "I am a Hebrew, and I am running away from the God who made the sea and the dry land, because I don't want to obey Him."

Then the men were very much afraid and said, "Why have you done this? What should we do to you so that the storm will stop?"

Jonah told them, "Throw me into the ocean; then it will become calm again. I know it is my fault that this danger has come upon you."

The men didn't want to throw him overboard and rowed hard to bring the ship to land, but they couldn't do it. They prayed to the God Jonah had told them about and cried out to Him, saying, "O Lord, please don't punish us for throwing this man into the ocean, for You have sent the storm because of him."

As soon as they had thrown Jonah in, immediately the sea grew still and calm. The men were amazed and offered a sacrifice to the Lord and promised to serve Him.

The Lord had sent a huge fish to the side of the ship to swallow Jonah as soon as he fell in! Jonah stayed alive in the fish three days and three nights. He prayed to the Lord while he was in the fish and confessed his sin. God heard him and commanded the fish to swim to the shore and vomit him out.

Then the Lord spoke to Jonah a second time. "Go to Nineveh," He said, "and give the people there My message."

So Jonah went to Nineveh. He walked through the city for many hours and finally came to the center and he shouted out God's message: "Forty days from now Nineveh will be destroyed because of the sins of its people."

When the king of Nineveh and the people heard this, they believed God had sent Jonah and they knew what he said would come true. The king took off his beautiful royal robes and wore cheap burlap instead. Then he and his government officials sent a message through the city commanding that no one could eat anything until further notice. "No man or animal," they said, "may eat any food or drink anything, and must wear rough burlap, and must pray with all his heart, and must stop being wicked. For who can tell? Perhaps the Lord will forgive us and take away His great anger from us and not destroy us after all."

God saw how they prayed to Him, and that they had stopped being bad, so He took away His punishment and didn't destroy the city after all.

Jonah was very angry about this. He wanted Nineveh to be destroyed because the people who lived there were enemies of Israel. Also Jonah was afraid that now the people would laugh at him and say he didn't know what he was talking about.

He spoke angrily to the Lord and said, "I knew You wouldn't destroy the city, and that is why I ran away Now please kill me; I would rather die than live." But the Lord spoke pleasantly to Jonah and didn't punish him for talking like that.

Jonah went to a place outside the

city and waited to see whether the city would be destroyed or not. That night the Lord caused a vine to grow, and the next day its thick leaves shaded Jonah's head from the hot sun. He was very glad it was there. But soon God sent a worm that gnawed through the stem of the vine, and the vine died. Then God sent a hot wind on Jonah, and the sun beat down on his head. Since the vine was no longer there to shade him, he grew sick and faint from the heat. Again he became angry.

Then God said, "You are angry because I have destroyed the vine that protected you; and yet you want me to destroy Nineveh, that great city where there are more than 120,000 little children so young that they cannot tell their right hands from their left!"

So God taught Jonah how selfish and wicked he was to wish that Nineveh would be destroyed just because the people were not friends of Israel and because he feared being laughed at for saying something that didn't come true when the people repented.

QUESTIONS

Why was God going to punish the people of Nineveh?

How did Jonah try to run away from God?

Why did the sailors throw Jonah overboard?

What saved Jonah?

What did the people of Nineveh do when Jonah told them God was going to kill them?

What lesson did God teach Jonah with a vine?

75

A Little Boy Named Samuel

There was a man of Israel named Elkanah who lived in the city of Ramah. Every year he took a trip to the Tabernacle in Shiloh to sacrifice to God. His two wives, Hannah and Peninnah, always went with him. Elkanah loved Hannah more than Peninnah and gave her many presents. But Hannah was unhappy because Peninnah had children and she didn't, for the Lord hadn't given her any.

One day Hannah came to the Tabernacle and prayed. She promised the Lord that if He would give her a son, she would give him back to the Lord again, and he would be set apart to serve the Lord all his life at the Tabernacle.

Eli was the High Priest at the time.

Hannah was crying as she prayed. Eli was sitting there and saw her lips moving but couldn't hear her speaking. For some reason he decided that she was drunk and was being silly or muttering to herself. He scolded her for it.

But Hannah told him, "Oh, no, sir, I am not drunk. I am praying in my heart to the Lord."

Then Eli spoke to her in a friendly way and told her he hoped God would give her what she was asking Him for. Then Hannah was glad.

The Lord answered Hannah's prayer and gave her a son. She named him Samuel, which means "Asked of God." She named him this because she had asked God for him and God had given him to her.

Soon after Samuel was born, the time came for his father to go to Shiloh again to sacrifice as he did each year. But Hannah didn't go this time; she wanted to wait until her little boy was older. Then she would take him with her and leave him at the Tabernacle to help God and His priests with their work, for this is what she had promised the Lord.

Finally the time came when he was old enough, and she took him to the Tabernacle.

"Do you remember me?" she asked Eli. "I am the woman who stood here praying to the Lord that time, and you thought I was drunk. I was praying for this child, and the Lord has given me what I asked for. Now I am giving him back to the Lord again; as long as he lives he shall be the Lord's." And so she left little Samuel at the Tabernacle to stay and help Eli.

Eli had two sons whose names were Hophni and Phinehas; they were priests at the Tabernacle. The Lord had said that all His priests must be holy and good because they were God's ministers. But Hophni and Phinehas were not good men. They were very bad. The people didn't even like to come to the Tabernacle with their offerings because of the bad things Hophni and Phinehas did.

But Samuel, although he was only a child, did what was right and pleasing to the Lord. His mother made him a coat each year and brought it to him when she came with her husband to offer their sacrifice. Eli was, of course, very friendly to them and asked the Lord to bless them because they had given Samuel to the Lord.

Eli was very old. He heard about all the bad things his sons were doing and he scolded them, but he didn't punish them or make them stop being priests as he should have done. He let them go on being bad. This was very wrong of him.

One day a prophet came to Eli with a message from the Lord. The Lord asked why he let his sons keep on sinning. Eli cared more about pleasing his sons, the Lord said, than he cared about pleasing God. The Lord declared that He would not let Eli be the High Priest any more, but would choose another man who would do what God wanted him to.

Little Samuel is helping the old priest, Eli. Samuel's mother didn't have any children for a long time, but then she asked God for a baby, and He gave her Samuel. So she gave him back to the Lord by letting him help Eli at the Temple.

And both of Eli's sons, the Lord said, would die the same day.

Samuel helped Eli in any way he could. One night when Samuel had gone to bed, he heard a voice calling him.

"I'm here," he answered and jumped up and ran to Eli. "What do you want?" he asked him.

But Eli said, "No, I didn't call you; go back to bed." So he did.

But then Samuel heard the voice again, so again he ran to Eli and asked him, "Why are you calling me, Eli? What do you want?"

"I didn't call you, my son," Eli said, "Go and lie down again."

But Samuel heard the voice a third time and went to Eli and said, "I'm sure I heard you calling me. What do you want me to do?"

Then Eli knew it was the Lord who had called the child. He said to him, "Go, lie down; and if He calls you again say, 'Speak Lord, I am listening.' "

So Samuel went back to bed. And the Lord came and called as before, "Samuel, Samuel."

Samuel answered, "Yes, Lord, speak, for I am listening." Then the Lord told him He was going to punish Eli and his sons because his sons were so wicked, and Eli hadn't punished them.

When the Lord finished speaking, Samuel lay still until the morning; then he got up and opened the doors of the Tabernacle. He was afraid to tell Eli what the Lord had said.

But Eli called him and said, "You must tell me everything God said. Don't hide it from me. May God punish you if you do."

Then Samuel told him every word and hid nothing from him. When Eli heard it, he said, "It is the Lord. Let Him do whatever He thinks best."

QUESTIONS

Why was Hannah sad? What did she pray for?

Why did Hannah take Samuel to live at the Tabernacle?

Were Eli's sons good or bad? Did Eli try to help them by punishing them? Why?

What did the Lord tell Samuel?

It was nighttime, and Samuel was awakened by God speaking to him. "Samuel, Samuel," God called. Then God told him many things that were going to happen to Eli and his sons.

76

What Happened to the Ark

Everything God said to Samuel came true. One day the men of Israel went out to fight against the Philistines, and four thousand Israeli soldiers died in the battle. The leaders of Israel wondered why the Lord had allowed so many to be killed. They decided to get the Ark from the Tabernacle and take it with them into the next day's battle to see if that would help them. Perhaps they remembered how the Ark was carried around Jericho when the people of Israel captured that city. But then the Lord had told them to do it; this time it was just their own idea.

So they sent messengers to the Tabernacle at Shiloh to ask for the Ark to be brought to them. The two sons of Eli, Hophni and Phinehas, took it out to the army. When the Israeli soldiers saw it, they shouted for joy, and the noise was heard far away on every side. For the Israelis thought that now God would surely bless them.

The Philistines heard the shouting and said, "Why all the noise in the camp of the Hebrews?" When they were told that the Ark had arrived, they were very frightened. "Who can save us now?" they asked. "Let us be strong and fight like men, or we will become slaves of the Hebrews."

That day the Philistines killed thirty thousand Israelis and captured the Ark! And the two sons of Eli, Hophni and Phinehas, were killed. A messenger ran to Shiloh to tell Eli. He sat waiting on a bench by the road, for he was afraid of what might happen to the Ark.

When the messenger arrived in the city and told the people that the Ark had been captured and the army defeated, everyone cried out with fear. Eli was so old that he was almost blind. The messenger ran to him and said, "The men of Israel have run from the Philistines, and a great many of them have been killed. Your two sons Hophni and Phinehas are dead, and the Ark of God has been captured."

When the messenger told about the Ark, Eli fainted and fell backward to the ground, breaking his neck; and so he died. For his grief was greater than he could bear when he heard that the Ark was captured.

The Philistines carried the Ark to Ashdod, one of their cities, and put it in the temple of Dagon, their idol. They set it down by the idol and left it there all night.

When they got up in the morning and came to Dagon's temple, they found that their idol had fallen on its face on the floor in front of the Ark. They set it up again, but the next night the idol fell down again in front of the Ark; and this time its head and hands were cut off!

Soon afterwards a terrible sickness came upon the people of Ashdod, and many of them died. Then those who were left said to each other, "The Ark of the God of Israel must not stay here." So they called together all of the rulers of the Philistines and asked, "What shall we do with the Ark?"

"Let's send it to Gath," they replied. Gath was another city of the Philistines. So they carried it to Gath, but as soon as the Ark arrived there, the people living there began to die. The Philistines kept the Ark for seven months, but all that time the Lord sent great trouble upon them. Then they asked their wise men how to send it back to the land of Israel, for they were afraid to keep it any longer.

There were no automobiles or airplanes in those days, and cows were used for pulling wagons. The wise men told the Philistines to make a new wagon and hitch two cows to pull it, but to take their calves away from them and tie them up at home. Usually cows wouldn't leave their calves unless led away by hand.

"Now put the Ark on the cart," the wise men said, "and let the cows pull it wherever they want to without anyone leading them. If the cows leave their calves behind and take the Ark to the land of Israel, it will show that the Lord is making them go there and that He is angry with us for keeping the Ark, and has sent all these troubles as a punishment. But if the cows turn around and go back to their calves, we will know it was not the Lord who punished us, but our troubles have come upon us just by chance."

The Philistines followed the directions of their wise men. They took two cows and hitched them to a new cart, shutting up their calves at home. Then they put the Ark on the cart and let the cows loose to go wherever they chose. The rulers of the Philistines followed behind to see what the cows would do. As soon as the cows were let loose, they started off straight into the land of Israel, leaving their calves behind.

The Israelis who lived near the border of the country were reaping their wheat harvest in a valley near the city where the cows were headed. When these men looked up and saw the Ark coming, they shouted with joy.

The cows brought it into the field of a man named Joshua and stood still beside a great stone that was there. Then some men of the tribe of Levi carefully took the Ark down from the cart and laid it on the stone. They broke up the wagon for wood, killed the cows for a burnt offering, and sacrificed them to the Lord.

But the men of the city disobeyed God; they wanted to see inside the Ark, so they took off the cover and looked in. God had said never to do this, so many of them died for this sin.

Then the Ark was taken to the city of Kiriath-jearim, into the house of a man named Abinadab. It stayed there for twenty years, and God blessed him.

QUESTIONS

What was the Ark?
Why did the soldiers want to have the Ark with them in the battle?
What happened to the Ark? What happened to Eli's sons?
What happened to the Philistine's idol, Dagon?
How did the Philistines get rid of the Ark?
What happened to the men who looked inside the Ark? Why?

77
The People Demand a King

After Eli was dead, the Lord chose Samuel to be the new judge of Israel. Samuel lived in the city of Ramah where his father Elkanah and his mother Hannah lived.

God had said a long time before that the people of Israel must bring all of their offerings and sacrifices to the altar at Bethel, but Samuel built an altar at Ramah where he lived, and offered sacrifices there.

Then the people of Israel began to sin again, for they worshipped the idols Baal and Ashtaroth. So the Lord sent the Philistines to fight them.

Samuel said to his people, "If you will destroy your idols and obey the Lord, He will save you from the Philistines." So the people knocked down their idols, and then Samuel told them, "Come, all of you, to the city of Mizpeh, and I will pray for you there."

So they came to Mizpeh to confess their wickedness and said, "We have sinned against the Lord."

But when the Philistines heard that the people were at Mizpeh, they went to fight them there. The Israelis were frightened and said to Samuel, "Pray hard that God will save us." Samuel took a young lamb and sacrificed it as a burnt offering, and then prayed to the Lord for the people. And the Lord listened to him. As Samuel was sacrificing the lamb, the Philistine army was coming closer and closer. But God sent a great storm of thunder and lightning upon them, and they ran away in fear.

God wanted to lead His people personally, but they insisted on having a king like the ungodly nations around them. So God let them have their own way.

R. Hook

So the Lord gave the men of Israel the victory. Samuel set up a stone at the place where the Lord helped them. He called it Ebenezer, which means "The Stone of Help."

When he was old, Samuel let his two sons help him rule. But they weren't fair like their father. If two people had an argument and came to his sons to decide which was right, his sons would ask for money and would say that the one was right who would pay them the most. This is taking a bribe and is a very wrong thing to do.

Then all the leaders of Israel came to Samuel at Ramah to tell him he was too old to keep on being their judge and that his sons were bad. They asked him to choose a king for them so that they would be like the other nations around them. It was right for them to tell Samuel that his sons were bad, but it was wrong for them to ask for a king. The Lord was their king, and Samuel was the judge He had set over them. Samuel was displeased when they asked him to choose a king and asked the Lord what he should do.

The Lord said it was not Samuel the Israelis wanted to get rid of, but the Lord Himself. The Lord told Samuel to warn the people what it would be like to have a king, and how cruelly he would treat them. So Samuel told them the king would make their sons work in the fields and make their daughters be cooks and bakers in his kitchen. He would steal the best of their lands and vineyards, their cattle and sheep. They would cry out because of the trouble their king would bring upon them, but the Lord wouldn't listen to them.

But the people insisted. "We must have a king just like all the other nations," they said. "We need him to help us fight our battles." Then the Lord told Samuel to do as they asked and choose a king for them.

There was a young man named Saul, who was good looking and taller than anyone else in Israel. One day some donkeys that belonged to Saul's father ran away and got lost. Saul's father said to him, "Take one of the servants with you, and go look for the donkeys."

Saul started out, but after he had gone a long way and couldn't find them, he said to the servant, "Let's go back; probably by now my father has stopped worrying about the donkeys and is worrying about us!"

By this time they were near the city where Samuel lived. The servant told Saul that a prophet lived there whose words always came true. "Let's go and ask him where to find the donkeys," he suggested.

"That's a good idea," Saul replied. "Come on, let's try it."

As it happened, there was to be a special sacrifice that day in the city, and the people were going to have a celebration afterwards. As Saul and his servant went up the hill to the city, they met some girls going out to draw water and asked them if the prophet was at home.

"Yes," the girls said, "he came today, for there is to be a celebration. You will find him easily as soon as you get into the city." Sure enough, Samuel met them as they were walking along.

The Lord had already told Samuel, "Today I will send you the man who will be the king of Israel." When Samuel saw Saul, the Lord said to him,

"This is the man I told you about."

Saul didn't know Samuel, and he went up to him and asked, "Can you tell us where the prophet's house is?"

"I am the prophet," Samuel answered. Then he told Saul to bring his servant and come to the celebration. As for the donkeys, Samuel said to stop worrying about them—Saul's father had already found them!

Samuel brought Saul and his servant to the celebration and gave them the best places to sit among the guests. Samuel told the cook to bring in the food he had told him to save for an important guest, and the cook brought it and set it before Saul. Samuel told Saul to enjoy it because it had been chosen especially for him. So Saul stayed with Samuel all that day. How surprised he was to receive all this special attention!

QUESTIONS

Who was the new judge of Israel?

When the people of Israel were sorry for worshipping idols, how did God scare away the Philistines?

Why was it wrong for the people to ask for a king?

What did Samuel tell the Israelis that their kings would do to them?

What was Saul out looking for? Did he find them?

78
Samuel's Warnings

Early the next morning as soon as they got up, Samuel had a long talk with Saul. Afterwards he went with him to the gate of the city. As they were walking together, he said to Saul, "Tell your servant to go on ahead, but you stay here so I can show you what the Lord has commanded me to do."

When the servant was gone, Samuel took a bottle of olive oil and poured it on Saul's head. We have read about Moses doing this to Aaron to make him the High Priest. Kings were anointed in the same way. When Samuel poured the oil on Saul's head it meant that God had chosen Saul to be the king of Israel. But no one except Saul and Samuel knew that God had chosen him, for the Lord was not yet ready to announce it to the people.

One day not long afterwards Samuel made a speech to the people and reminded them of the way God had brought them out of Egypt and set them free from their enemies. But they were not satisfied with God's care of them, and now they were asking for a king to rule them instead. Samuel told them to come to the city of

Mizpeh to see their new king. When they came, Samuel announced that Saul was the one. Everyone wanted to see him, but they couldn't find him anywhere. So they asked the Lord where he was, and the Lord answered, "He is hiding," and told them where to look for him!

Then the people ran and brought him out of his hiding place. He was a big, handsome fellow, taller than any of the rest of them. Samuel said, "See, here is the man the Lord has chosen for you; there is no one like him among all the people of Israel." And they all shouted, "God save the king!" Then Samuel told them again how much trouble they would have. He said that Saul would be a very bad king; and Samuel wrote it all down in a book.

After this the Ammonites came up to fight against the Israeli city of Jabesh-gilead. The men of Israel who lived there were afraid and said that if the Ammonites would be kind to them, they would surrender without a fight. But the Ammonites wouldn't promise. Instead, they said they would punch out the right eye of each of them. When the men of Jabesh-gilead heard this, they asked the Ammonites to give them seven days to send messengers to the Israelis in other parts of the land. If by that time no one would come to help them, they promised to surrender and let the Ammonites do as they pleased!

Then the leaders of the city sent messengers to Gibeah, where Saul lived, and told the people what the Ammonites had said. The people cried out in fear. Just then Saul came in from the field with a herd of cattle, and asked what the trouble was.

When he found out, he took two oxen, cut them in pieces, and sent a piece to each part of the land of Israel with this message: "I will do this to the oxen of anyone who doesn't come at once to fight against the Ammonites."

Three hundred thousand came to Saul immediately when they heard this threat. Early one morning he led them out against the Ammonites, and Saul and his army won the battle. The Ammonites who weren't killed in the battle ran away, so the Israelis won a great victory.

After this triumph Samuel made another speech to Israel. He said, "I have given you a king as you asked me to, and your king is here before you. I am old, and my hair is gray; I have been with you from childhood, and you all know what I have been like. Tell me, have I ever stolen an ox or a donkey or anything else belonging to anyone? Or have I ever once been unjust or cruel to anyone, or taken money as a bribe from someone who wanted me to let him do wrong?"

The people answered, "No, you have never done anything like that."

Then Samuel told them that they had done wrong to ask for a king. The Lord was their king, and they shouldn't want another. "Now see what the Lord is going to do," he said. "This is the time of harvest, when we don't have rain, but I will ask the Lord to send a great storm of thunder and rain to make you realize how much you have offended Him."

So the Lord sent a terrible storm of thunder and rain until all the people finally honored the Lord and respected Samuel. And they begged him to pray for them, for they were afraid that they would all be killed by the storm.

Samuel said, "I will never stop praying for you. Only worship the Lord and obey Him with all your hearts, and always remember the great things He has done for you." They had sinned, he said, but now if they would obey the Lord, the Lord would forgive them and take care of them because He had chosen them to be His people. But if instead of obeying Him they kept on being bad, they and their king would be destroyed.

QUESTIONS

How was a person "anointed" to be a king?

Who was the first king of Israel?

What did Saul do to get men to join his army?

79

Prince Jonathan's Victory

Two years after Saul became king, he formed an army of three thousand soldiers. Two thousand of them were under his personal command, and the other thousand were commanded by Saul's son Jonathan.

One day Jonathan went out to fight some Philistines who had invaded the land of Israel. The Philistines gathered together a great army and came with thousands of chariots and horses and so many soldiers that they couldn't be counted. When Saul's little army saw the tremendous forces coming to attack them, they were terrified, and hid in caves and bushes and among the rocks on the mountains, and in holes in the ground. Some of them fled across the Jordan River into the land of Gilead, where the other tribes of Israel lived. Only a few soldiers stayed with Saul, their king, and they were trembling with fear.

Saul came to Gilgal, for Samuel had promised to meet him there to sacrifice burnt offerings and peace offerings and to get God's directions for Israel's battle plans. Saul waited seven days for Samuel, but when he still didn't come, Saul became frantic. "Bring an offering," he commanded—and he himself sacrificed the burnt offering. This was a terrible thing for him to do, for God permitted only the priests to sacrifice offerings.

Just then Samuel arrived in town, and Saul went to meet him. Samuel said at once, "You have done a terrible thing." Saul began to make excuses and said he had been afraid to wait any longer for fear the Philistines would come. But Samuel said it was wrong to disobey the Lord no matter what happened, and the Lord would not let him be king anymore, but would choose someone else in his place. Samuel didn't mean that Saul would stop being king right away, but that the Lord would choose a new king soon.

Saul counted the men who were still with him; there were only six hundred left. And they didn't have any weapons. Not one of the six hundred had either a sword or a spear, except Saul and Jonathan. The reason for this was that the Israelis had been slaves of the Philistines for many years, and the Philistines wouldn't let them have swords or spears for fear they might use them to fight against them.

In those days soldiers wore armor made of iron or bronze, and carried shields made of strong boards covered with the skin of oxen. They held these up in front of them while they were in battle, so that the arrows and darts of their enemies couldn't hit them. Jonathan, Saul's son, had a soldier to carry his shield and spear for him when he wasn't using them. This soldier was called his armorbearer.

The Philistine army was camped nearby and Jonathan asked his armorbearer to go with him to the camp of the Philistines. Jonathan thought the Lord might allow the two of them to defeat all that great army of Philistines! And, of course, it is true that the Lord can give victory to anyone, whether they are many or few. The armorbearer agreed to go with him.

Jonathan told him how they could find out whether the Lord intended to help them or not. They would go and stand where the Philistines could see them. If the Philistines called out to them and told them to wait, they would go no further, for it would mean the Lord was not going to help them. But if the Philistines said, "Come on up and fight!" they would know that the Lord would give them the victory.

So Jonathan and his armorbearer climbed up to where the Philistines were and stood where they could be seen. The Philistines made fun of them and said, "Look, the Hebrews are coming up out of the holes where they were hiding!" And they called out, "Come on up, and we will show you how to fight!"

When Jonathan heard them say this, he told his armorbearer, "The Lord has given us the victory!" Then Jonathan climbed up the rocks to the Philistines' camp, using his hands as well as his feet to climb the steep hill, and his armorbearer climbed after him. When they got to the top, they fought and killed about twenty men.

Then the Lord sent an earthquake. The ground shook, and all the Philistine army trembled with fear and ran away!

Saul and the men who were with him didn't know what Jonathan had done; but when Saul's watchmen looked toward the camp of the Philistines and saw fighting there, they told Saul about it. Saul checked over all his men to find out which of them had gone to fight the Philistines, and he found that Jonathan and his armorbearer were missing. Then when the Philistines started running away, Saul and his men went up to join the battle; and many of Saul's soldiers who had been afraid and had hidden in the mountains came out now and joined him again. The Lord helped the Israelis so that the whole huge Philistine army ran away from them.

The Israeli soldiers were very hungry that night, for Saul had ordered them to eat nothing until evening because he wanted them to go on chasing their enemies. So none of them had tasted any food all day.

They came to a woods where honey was dripping on the ground from a beehive in the trees. But though the men were so hungry, they were afraid to eat the honey for fear King Saul would kill them for disobeying him. But Jonathan didn't know what his father had said, so he reached out the end of a stick he was carrying, dipped it into the honey, and ate it. When Saul heard about this, he was furious at Jonathan for disobeying him. "You must die, Jonathan," he said.

But the people said, "Jonathan must die? He is the one who has given us this great victory!" So they saved Jonathan from being put to death.

QUESTIONS

Why did Saul offer a sacrifice instead of waiting for Samuel?

Was this right or wrong? Why?

How many of Saul's army had weapons to fight with? Why?

How did Jonathan and his armorbearer know whether the Lord would help them?

Why did Saul say Jonathan must die? Was this order carried out? Explain.

80
Saul Disobeys God

After this, Samuel told King Saul that the Lord wanted him to destroy the entire Amalekite nation because the Amalekites had fought the people of Israel when they came out of Egypt hundreds of years before, though the Israelis had done them no harm.

"The Lord says to attack them and destroy them and their cattle, and not to save anything alive," Samuel said.

So Saul got together a great army of more than two hundred thousand men and fought with the Amalekites and defeated them. He killed the people, but he kept their king alive, along with their sheep, oxen, and lambs.

The Lord was angry with Saul for

not destroying everything as God had told him to. "I am sorry that I made Saul king," God told Samuel, "for he has not obeyed My command."

When Samuel heard the bleating of the sheep and the lowing of the oxen Saul had taken from the Amalekites, he said to Saul, "What does this mean—the bleating of the sheep and the mooing of the cows?"

Then Saul began to make excuses. He said that the people had insisted on saving them alive to sacrifice to the Lord. But Samuel asked Saul whether he thought the Lord was better pleased to have sacrifices offered to Him or to have His commands obeyed. Then Samuel told Saul again that because he had disobeyed the Lord, the Lord would not let him continue as king.

God told Samuel to go to Bethlehem, find a man there named Jesse, and anoint one of Jesse's sons as the new king.

But Samuel answered, "How can I? If Saul hears about it he will kill me."

The Lord told Samuel to take a sacrifice with him and to ask Jesse to come to the sacrifice. Then the Lord would show him what to do next.

Samuel did as God commanded. He came to Bethlehem, prepared his sacrifice, and invited Jesse and his sons to come and watch. When they came, Samuel thought that Jesse's oldest son was the one the Lord would choose because he was such a fine-looking young man. But the Lord told him no, he was not the one. Then Jesse called his second son, but the Lord said no. Then he presented in turn his third, fourth, fifth, sixth, and seventh sons. But Samuel said, "The Lord has not chosen any of these. Are these all the sons you have?"

"No," Jesse answered, "there is one other, the youngest, but he is out taking care of the sheep."

"Send for him," Samuel said. So they brought in David.

Then the Lord said to Samuel, "Anoint him, for this is the one." So Samuel took olive oil and poured it over David's head; he anointed him before all his brothers to be the new king of Israel, but not until after Saul was dead.

After David was anointed, the Lord sent His Holy Spirit into David's heart to make him wise and good, but He took His Spirit away from Saul.

We have already read about the angels—those good spirits who serve God. The Bible tells us there are evil spirits, too, who serve Satan. One of these evil spirits went into Saul and troubled him by making him discouraged and angry. Saul's assistants suggested that harp music would chase out the evil spirit whenever it troubled him. So Saul said to his men, "Find me a man who can play well on the harp and bring him to me."

One of Saul's men knew David, and knew that he could play the harp well. So Saul sent messengers to Jesse and told him to send him his son David. Jesse loaded a donkey with bread and wine and a young goat, and he sent them with David as a present to King Saul. But he didn't tell Saul that Sam-

David was a shepherd before he became the king of Israel. See how brave he is.

uel had anointed David to be the new king! So David came to Saul and stayed with him and helped him. Whenever the evil spirit troubled Saul, David played sweet music on a harp to quiet him, and the evil spirit would go away. When David was no longer needed, he returned home; and Saul soon forgot about him.

QUESTIONS
Which is best—to give gifts to God, or to obey Him?
Tell about how Samuel found out whom God had chosen to be the new king.
How did David help Saul when the evil spirit came upon him?

81
David and Goliath

Once again the Philistine army decided to fight Israel, and Saul and the men of Israel got ready for the battle. The camp of the Philistines was on one mountain, and the camp of Israel was on another mountain; the two were separated by a valley between them.

One of the Philistine soldiers was a giant named Goliath. He wore a lot of armor—a bronze helmet to protect his head, an armored coat, and sheets of bronze to cover his legs so that no sword or spear could wound him.

He strutted into the valley between the two armies and yelled to the army of Israel, "I'll fight the best man in your army. If he can kill me, we Philistines will be your slaves; but if I kill him, then you must be our slaves!"

Saul and the men of Israel were frightened; no one in Saul's army was willing to go out and fight with the giant. For forty days he came out every morning and evening to defy the men of Israel.

Meanwhile, David was feeding his father's sheep at Bethlehem, but his three oldest brothers were in Saul's army. One day David's father said to him, "Take this food to your brothers, and take this present of a cheese for their captain, and see how they are getting along."

Early in the morning David started

The giant's name is Goliath. He is an enemy of God and of the Israelis. He laughs at David's sling, but David is using it to shoot a stone that hit Goliath in the forehead, and Goliath fell down dead.

out, leaving the sheep with one of his father's servants. He came to the camp of Israel just as the Israeli soldiers were getting ready for battle, and everyone was shouting and yelling.

David managed to find his brothers, and as he was talking to them, the giant, Goliath, strutted out and gave his usual taunt. When David heard everyone saying that there would be a huge reward for anyone who killed the giant, and he would be given the king's daughter as his wife, he decided to try for these prizes!

"How dare this giant defy the armies of the living God?" David demanded. When the men standing near him heard David say this, they realized that David wanted to fight Goliath. They told Saul, and Saul sent for him.

When David told King Saul that he would like to fight Goliath, King Saul objected.

"You can't possibly do it," he said. "Why, you're only a youngster, while Goliath has been a tough soldier for many years."

"But I can!" David answered. "One day while I was watching my father's sheep, a lion grabbed a lamb and I went after it and struck the lion and he dropped the lamb. Then he came after me, but I caught him by his beard and killed him. Another time I killed a bear with my hands. And I'll do the same to this wicked giant, for he has defied the armies of the living God. The Lord who saved me from the jaws of the lion and the bear will save me from the sword of the giant."

"All right," Saul said, "go and fight him, and the Lord be with you."

Then Saul gave David his own armor—his bronze helmet, his armored coat, and his sword. But David said, "I'm not used to these," and took them off again.

He took his stick with him that he used to protect the sheep, and his slingshot. Choosing five smooth stones from the brook, he put them into his shepherd's bag, and started over toward Goliath. The giant saw him coming and rushed out to fight him. But when he saw David he didn't think he was worth fighting; for David didn't look like a strong, brave soldier, but like a shepherd boy who had never fought before.

"Am I a dog, that you come to me with a stick?" the giant asked angrily. And he called on the idols he worshipped to curse David. "Come over here so I can kill you," he yelled.

But David answered, "You come to me trusting in your sword, your shield, and your spear; but I come to you trusting in the God of Israel. Today He will give you to me, and I will kill you and cut off your head; and the army of the Philistines will be killed, and the birds and wild animals will eat them!"

As Goliath came closer, David ran toward him. Putting his hand into his shepherd's bag, he took out a stone, put it into his sling, and sent it sailing toward Goliath. It struck him square in the forehead, broke his skull, and he fell down dead. So David defeated the giant with a sling and a stone. David ran over to him and used Goliath's own sword to cut off his head.

When the Philistines saw that Goliath was dead they started to run. The army of Israel gave a great shout and started after them, killing many of them. Afterwards the men of Israel came back and went into the Philistines' camp and took all the gold, silver, and clothing from their tents.

David came from the battle with the head of Goliath in his hand. Then Abner, the captain of the army of Israel, took him to Saul.

"Who are you, young man?" Saul asked.

David answered, "I am the son of Jesse of Bethlehem." For some reason Saul didn't realize that this was the same boy who used to play the harp for him.

Saul's son Jonathan was there, and when he saw David and heard him speaking with his father, he loved him as a brother. Prince Jonathan was David's friend in all the troubles that lay ahead, and he and David promised always to be kind to each other.

Then Saul made David a captain in his army.

QUESTIONS

Who was Goliath?

Why did David visit his brothers in the army?

Tell about David's fight with Goliath. Why wasn't David afraid?

Who was Jonathan?

82
David's Friend

After the battle with the Philistines, King Saul and David were travelling together through some of the cities of the land. The women came out with songs and dances to praise them for their victory, but they praised David more then they did Saul! They said that Saul had slain thousands of the Philistines, but David had slain tens of thousands! Saul was very angry about this, and from then on he was jealous of David.

The next day an evil spirit came into Saul's heart and troubled him while David was playing before him on the harp. Saul had a spear in his hand and he threw it at David, intending to pin him to the wall, for he wanted to kill him. But David saw it coming and jumped out of the way just in time.

Saul was afraid of David because he saw that the Lord was with him. The Lord helped David do everything well, and all the people loved him.

One day Saul said to him, "I will let you marry my daughter Merab if you will go out and fight against the Philistines." Saul said this because he hoped the Philistines would kill David.

So David went out and fought with

the Philistines. He won the battle, but Saul didn't keep his promise, for he made Merab marry someone else instead.

One day Saul heard that his younger daughter Michal loved David. He said David could marry her if he would go and kill one hundred Philistines. Saul hoped that this time David would surely be killed.

So David went with his soldiers and fought the Philistines. This time King Saul was true to his word and let Michal marry him.

When Saul realized how much the Lord was helping David, he became more and more jealous and afraid of him. He became his enemy and hated him. He told his son Jonathan and all his friends that they ought to kill David.

But Jonathan loved David and told him what his father had said. "Go and hide for awhile until I talk with my father," Jonathan said, "and I will tell you what he says." So David went away for a few days.

Jonathan begged his father not to harm David, for David had done nothing to hurt him but had only helped him. He had risked his life to kill Goliath the giant, and afterwards the men of Israel had won a great victory. Saul had been happy when these things happened, so why, Jonathan asked, should Saul now be trying to kill David? For David was a good man and had done nothing to deserve to die.

Saul listened to Jonathan and promised before the Lord that David would not be killed. Then Jonathan called David from his hiding place and told him what his father had said. He brought David to Saul, and David stayed at Saul's house as before.

Again there was war in the land, and again David led the army of Israel in its fight against the Philistines, and again he won. But Saul was not pleased, because now the people loved David even more than before.

Once again the evil spirit came into Saul's heart. He sat holding his spear in his hand while David was playing the harp. Again Saul threw the spear at David, and again David jumped away just in time, and the spear went into the wall. Then David ran for his life.

Saul sent soldiers to David's house to stop him from escaping during the night. Michal, David's wife, told him, "It's now or never. If you don't save your life tonight, it will be too late tomorrow." So she let him down by a rope through a second-story window, and he escaped without Saul's men seeing him. Then Michal put something in his bed and covered it up to make it look as if David was still there. When King Saul's men came to get him and take him away to be killed, they saw that he was sick in bed, so they went back to Saul and asked him what to do.

"Bring him to me in his bed!" Saul told them. So they came back again, and discovered that David wasn't there! Saul was very angry with Michal about this.

Meanwhile, David fled to Ramah, where Samuel lived, and told him all that Saul had done. Afterwards he

David and Jonathan were good friends. They had lots of fun together.

went to the town of Naioth. But someone told Saul that David was there, so he sent men to capture him, but the Lord saved him from them. Then he fled from Naioth to the place where Jonathan was and asked him, "What have I done? Why is your father trying to kill me?"

Jonathan hadn't heard that his father was after David again. He promised to do everything he could to help.

The next day was a special religious holiday, and Saul would expect David to eat at his table. But David was afraid to go and begged Jonathan to let him stay away for three days. If Saul asked why he was not at the feast, Jonathan would answer that he had given David permission to go to Bethlehem, where his father lived, to be with his family when they offered their yearly sacrifice. David said that if Saul was angry when he heard this, it would show that King Saul was determined to kill him. But if he wasn't angry, then everything was all right. Jonathan agreed to this plan.

"But how will I find out what your father says when he hears that I have gone?" David asked Jonathan.

"Come out into the field with me and I'll show you what to do." Jonathan replied.

Jonathan showed David a large rock and told David to hide behind it the next day. Then Jonathan would come out into the field and shoot three arrows and send a boy after them to pick them up. If Jonathan called out to the boy, "The arrows are on this side of you," David would know that Saul was not angry with him, and he should return. But if Jonathan called, "The arrows are beyond you," David would know that he must stay away because Saul meant to kill him.

Jonathan suggested this plan because he thought Saul's spies would be watching him, and it would not be safe to go and talk with David.

The next day was the holiday, but David's seat at the table was empty. Saul didn't ask about him, for he thought something had happened to keep him away. But the next day, when David still wasn't there, Saul asked Jonathan, "Where is David? He hasn't been here either yesterday or today."

Jonathan replied, "David asked if he could go to Bethlehem, for his family is having a sacrifice, and his brother commanded him to be there."

Then Saul was very angry with Jonathan for allowing David to go. He said Jonathan would never be king as long as David lived. "Bring David to me," he said, "I'm going to kill him."

"Why? What has he done wrong?" Jonathan demanded. Then Saul, in furious anger, threw his spear at Jonathan. Jonathan jumped up from the table in great anger and wouldn't eat, for he was sad for David because his father had said these things.

The next day was the day when David was to hide in the field behind the rock Jonathan had pointed out to him. Jonathan went there with a boy to chase his arrows. Then he shot an arrow over the boy's head.

"The arrow is beyond you. Hurry, hurry," Jonathan shouted to him. David heard him and knew he must go away, because Saul was planning to kill him.

The boy found the arrows and brought them to Jonathan. Then Jonathan gave his bow and arrows to the boy and told him to take them back to the city.

As soon as he was gone, David came out from his hiding place, and he and Jonathan cried together over what was happening. Jonathan said David must go away and hide from his father. So David became a fugitive, like a person who has done something wrong and has to hide.

QUESTIONS
Why did Saul not like David any more?
Tell about the time Saul tried to kill David.
How did David's wife, Michal, save his life?
What did it mean when Jonathan shot an arrow past the boy?

83
David's Lie and Its Result

David went first to the city of Nob where the Tabernacle was, for it had been moved from Shiloh after the Ark was captured by the Philistines. Ahimelech, the High Priest, was surprised to see David and asked him why he had come. David was afraid to say he was running away, because somebody might send word for Saul to come and capture him.

So he told a lie.

He said King Saul had sent him on a secret errand, but he couldn't tell anyone what it was. This was very wrong of David. The Lord who had saved him from the lion and the bear and from Goliath the giant was able to save him from Saul. He should have spoken the truth and trusted in God. Because he didn't, he got his friends into terrible trouble, as we shall see.

There was a man there at the Tabernacle named Doeg, who was in charge of King Saul's cattle. Doeg told Saul that he had seen David talking with Ahimelech, the High Priest. Then King Saul blamed Ahimelech, and said that he was a traitor for helping David, and Ahimelech must die. But, of course, Ahimelech didn't even know that David was running away. This was very unfair of King Saul.

Meanwhile, David was at the Tabernacle. "Is there a spear or sword here that I can have?" David asked. "I didn't bring my sword with me."

"The sword of Goliath is here, wrapped in a cloth," the High Priest replied. "If you want it, take it, for it is the only one here."

So David took it. "It's the best!" he said.

Then David went to Gath, a city of the Philistines. The leaders of the city brought David to their king and told him, "This is the man the women of Israel sing about, saying he has killed ten thousand of us Philistines."

Then David was afraid and pretended he had lost his senses: he scratched on the doors and acted like an insane person. King Achish said to his men, "Anyone can see the man is out of his mind! Why have you brought him to me? Do I need a madman? Shall such a fellow as this come into my house?" So they chased him away.

He fled from Gath and went into a great cave, called the cave of Adullam, and lived there. When his brothers and his parents heard about it, they came to be with him; and others came too, until there were about four hundred people living with him.

But David's father and mother were old, and he wished they could live in a better place than in a cave. He couldn't send them back to their home in Bethlehem because the Philistines had captured it and wouldn't let them return. So he went to the king of Moab and said to him, "Please let my father and mother live in your land until I find out what God wants me to do." The king said they could, so David brought his father and mother to stay with the king of Moab for as long as he lived in the cave.

One day David got to thinking about the good times he used to have when he lived at Bethlehem, tending his father's sheep. He thought of the well by the gate that he used to drink from as a boy. "How I wish I could have a drink from that well!" he said. Three of his men heard him say it and wanted to please him. They went to Bethlehem and broke through the Philistine guards and got some water from the well and brought it to David. But then David wouldn't drink it! When he realized that his friends had risked their lives to get the water for him, he poured it out on the ground as an offering to the Lord instead.

A prophet named Gad now came to David and said to him, "The Lord has sent me to tell you not to stay here in the cave any longer. You are to go back to the land of Judah." So David went to live in a woods in Judah.

Meanwhile, Saul and his soldiers had gone to Gibeah to search for David there. One day as Saul was resting beneath a tree, with his spear in his hand and his generals standing around him, he began complaining to them that they were not his friends. "If you are my friends, tell me where David is," he begged.

It was then that Doeg the Edomite told Saul he had seen David at the Tabernacle, and that Ahimelech the High Priest had given food to David and had given him the sword of Goliath, the Philistine giant.

The king angrily sent for Ahimelech to come to him with all the other priests who worked at the Tabernacle. Saul asked him why he had helped David. Ahimelech replied that he didn't know David was running away from Saul. Shouldn't he help the king's own son-in-law in any way he could? he asked.

But Saul was very angry. "You must die, Ahimelech," he shouted, "you and all your relatives too." He turned to the soldiers standing there and said, "Kill these priests, because they are on David's side." But the soldiers refused.

Then he said to Doeg, the Edomite, "You do it." And that wicked man killed all eighty-five of them. Then Doeg went to the Tabernacle at the city of Nob, where the priests lived, and killed all their wives and children. But Abiathar, one of Ahimelech's sons, escaped and fled to David to tell him what Saul had done.

David said, "I knew when Doeg saw me at the Tabernacle that he would surely tell Saul. It is my fault that your father and all your relatives have been killed." Then he asked Abiathar to stay with him and promised that no one would ever harm him.

QUESTIONS

What lie did David tell Ahimelech, the High Priest? Why?

How did David act when he was brought before the king of Gath? Why?

How did David take care of his parents?

Why did David and his friends have to hide?

Why did Saul kill Ahimelech and all the priests?

84

King Saul Chases David

After this, someone told David that the Philistines had come into the land of Judah again. They were fighting against the city of Keilah and robbing the people of their grain. David asked the Lord whether he should go and fight against them.

"Yes," the Lord answered, "go and destroy them, and save the city of Keilah."

But the men who were with David were afraid to go. David asked the Lord again, and the Lord told him to go, for He would give him the victory. So David and his men went and fought with the Philistines. They won the battle and saved the people of Keilah.

When King Saul learned that David was at Keilah, he said, "Now I will catch him; I'll surround the city with my soldiers, and he won't be able to escape."

Saul called together his entire army to go down and get David. David asked the Lord whether the people of Keilah, whom he had just saved from the Philistines, would fight against Saul or whether they would let Saul capture him.

The Lord answered, "They will let Saul capture you!"

So David and his men (there were, by this time, about six hundred of them) left Keilah and hid in the woods. Saul searched for him everywhere, but God kept him safe.

One day Prince Jonathan, King

Saul's son, came to see David to renew their friendship. "Don't worry," Jonathan said, "for my father will never find you. You are going to be the next king of Israel." And again they promised always to be friends. Then Jonathan went back home, but David stayed in the woods.

Some people called Ziphites came to King Saul now and said, "We will show you where David is hiding." So Saul and his men went with them. But just as they were closing in on David, a messenger came to Saul, saying, "Hurry back, for the Philistines have invaded your land." So Saul had to return, and the Lord saved David again. Now he went to a new place in the wilderness to hide.

Saul went back to Keilah after fighting the Philistines, but David had escaped. So Saul chose three thousand of his soldiers and took them out into the wilderness to hunt for David among the rocks where the wild goats lived.

Saul went into the same cave where David and his men were hiding! They were lying along the sides of the cave where Saul couldn't see them! Saul didn't know they were there, of course, so he walked into the cave alone to go to the bathroom. David's men wanted to kill Saul, but David wouldn't let them. But David sneaked up behind Saul and cut off a piece of Saul's robe, then hid again.

When Saul had left the cave, David shouted to him, and Saul looked around to see who was calling him. Then David asked Saul why he listened to the wicked men who said that David wanted to harm him. He could easily have killed Saul, he said, and some of his men wanted him to do it, but he had told them he would never kill the man whom the Lord had anointed to be king.

Then David held up the piece of robe he had cut off. "See this piece of your robe!" he exclaimed. "I cut it off but I didn't kill you; now you know that I'm not trying to hurt you. So why are you trying to kill me? Let the Lord judge between us and see which one of us is doing wrong. Let Him punish you for your cruelty to me, but I will never harm you in any way."

When Saul heard David speaking like this, the feeling of hatred went out of his heart, and he started crying. Then he said to David, "You are a better man than I am, for you have done good to me, while I have done wrong to you; even today you have shown me your great kindness, for when I was in your power you didn't kill me. May the Lord reward you for the good you have done. I know very well that some day you will be the king of Israel. Promise me that when you become the new king, you won't kill my children." And David gladly promised.

Then Saul went away to his own home, but David and his men stayed out in the wilderness.

Soon afterwards Samuel died, and all the people of Israel came for his funeral and buried him at Ramah, the city where he had lived.

QUESTIONS

What did David do when King Saul was in the cave?

What did David do afterwards?

Why did King Saul cry?

85
David Gets a Second Wife

David went down to the wilderness of Paran where a very rich farmer lived, who owned three thousand sheep and one thousand goats. His name was Nabal, and his wife's name was Abigail. She was a kind and beautiful woman, but he was a bad, quarrelsome man.

David and his men had their camp near where Nabal kept his flocks. David needed a lot of food for his men, but he never stole a single sheep or goat from Nabal and didn't let anyone else steal them.

When the time came for Nabal to shear his sheep, David told ten of his young men to go and talk with Nabal and ask if he would give David and his men some food in exchange for all their help.

But when they talked to Nabal about it, he laughed at them. "Who is David?" he asked. "There are plenty of men like him nowadays who run away from their masters!"

So David's young men came back and told him what Nabal had said. Then David said to his men, "Get your swords." David took about four hundred men with him and left two hundred to guard the camp. He was very angry and told his men that he had been foolish to work so hard for Nabal by keeping Nabal's flocks safe all the time they were out there in the wilderness. Not a single one of them had been lost, yet when he asked him politely for some food, he wouldn't give him any, but insulted him instead. They would go to Carmel, David said, and punish Nabal. David meant that they would kill Nabal.

So they started out. But before they got there, one of Nabal's young men went to Abigail, Nabal's wife, and told her that David had sent messengers to Nabal, and how unkindly Nabal had treated them. "Yet David's men were very good to us when we were out in the wilderness," the young men said. "They kept us safe night and day, all the time we were there."

Abigail hurriedly took two hundred loaves of bread, two casks of wine, five sheep, five sacks of parched corn, one hundred clusters of raisins, and two hundred cakes of figs. She loaded them on donkeys, and went out to find David. But she didn't tell her husband.

She met David and his men coming toward her house, ready to fight. She got down from her donkey and bowed low before David and told him, "Here is a little present I have brought for your young men." She told David that the Lord would surely bless him and save him from King Saul, and that he would be the new king of Israel. Then she pleaded, "Don't do something you'll be sorry about later on."

David listened to her and thanked the Lord for sending her and for the good advice she had given him, because it had kept him from going on in his anger to kill Nabal. He took the food Abigail brought, spoke to her in a friendly way, and sent her safely away. Then he and his men went back to their camp.

When Abigail came home, Nabal was having a big party and was drunk. So she said nothing to him about David until the next morning. Then, when she told him of the danger he had been in, all his strength left him. He lay paralyzed, motionless as a stone for about ten days, and then died.

When David heard that Nabal was dead, he sent messengers to Abigail to ask her to come and be his wife.

QUESTIONS
What did David's men do to help Nabal?
Was Nabal glad?
What did Nabal's wife, Abigail, send to David?
When Nabal died, what did David do?

86
David Steals Saul's Spear

Some enemies of David came to King Saul and told him where David was hiding in the wilderness. And Saul's bad heart hadn't really changed. Although the hatred had gone for a little while when David spared his life, it soon came back again. Now Saul was as eager as ever to kill David. So when he was told where David was hiding, he took three thousand men to look for him.

David heard about it and sent spies to watch; they soon brought back word that Saul had arrived. Then Da-

King Saul has been trying to catch and kill David. Now David is taking the king's spear, but doesn't try to hurt him.

vid and his nephew Abishai went secretly to Saul's camp at night. Saul lay sleeping with his spear in the ground by his pillow. Abner, the general of Saul's army, and the rest of his soldiers, were sleeping around the king. Abishai begged David to let him go and kill Saul. He would strike the sharp spear through Saul's body into the ground, he said, and Saul would die at once.

But David said no. "Don't do it," he said, "for it is a great sin to kill the king whom God has given us. Perhaps the Lord will kill him, or he will die in battle, but I won't kill him."

Then David had an idea.

"Let's steal his spear and the bottle of water there beside his pillow!" David said. So they crept close and took them, but no one woke up because the Lord had sent a deep sleep upon Saul and his men.

Then David stood on the top of a hill, a safe distance away, and shouted to Saul's men and to Abner. Abner woke up suddenly and jumped to his feet.

"Who is it?" he called.

David shouted back, "Why haven't you kept better watch over the king, so that no one could come and kill him? Where is the king's spear and the bottle of water that was beside his pillow?"

Saul recognized David's voice, and asked, "Is that you, David?"

Then David asked Saul why he was still chasing him and trying to kill him.

Saul said, "I have sinned; I have been wrong. Come back, my son David, for I won't harm you."

David replied, "Here is your spear; let one of the young men come over and get it."

Then David went away into the wilderness again, and Saul went back home.

David didn't believe that Saul would stop trying to kill him, for he had talked that way before and had cried and called him his son, but afterwards he had come out with three thousand men to get him.

"Someday he will finally find me and kill me," David said to himself. "I must go and live in the land of the Philistines. Then Saul will give up looking for me."

So David took his six hundred men to the Philistine city of Gath. Achish, the king of Gath, welcomed David and let them stay in his land and gave them the city of Ziklag to live in. For he hoped to have the help of David and his men in times of war.

When Saul heard that David had fled to the Philistines, he quit searching for him.

QUESTIONS

Tell about the visit of David and his nephew Abishai to King Saul's camp at night.

Tell some of the things that David said to King Saul.

87
King Saul Talks to Samuel

David stayed in the land of the Philistines a year and four months. While he was there, the Philistines declared war on King Saul.

When Saul saw how many Philistines had come to attack him, he trembled with fear. He asked the Lord what to do, but the Lord didn't answer him.

At that time there were people in the land of Israel who could talk with the spirits, and the spirits would tell them what was going to happen in the future. It was a great sin to do this. The Lord had commanded that anyone who did this must be killed, and Saul had chased many of these people out of his land.

But Saul was in great trouble. He had asked the Lord what to do, but the Lord wouldn't answer him. So he said to his men, "Try to find a woman who can talk with the spirits of dead people, so that I can ask Samuel what to do."

"There is a woman at Endor who can do this," his men told him.

Then Saul put on other clothes instead of his royal robes, so that the woman he was going to see wouldn't know who he was. He took two men with him and came to the woman at night. He told her he wanted to talk to a certain man who was dead and asked her to have this dead man's spirit come and talk to him. "Bring me Samuel," he said.

Then Samuel stood before them. Saul fell to the ground before him.

"Why have you disturbed me by bringing me here?" Samuel asked him.

"Because I am in terrible trouble," Saul replied; "for the Philistines are making war against me, and God has gone away from me and won't talk to me. I have called for you so that you can tell me what to do."

"Why ask me, if the Lord has left you and become your enemy?" Samuel asked. "The Lord has done what I told you He would do: He has put you down from being king and has made David king, because you didn't obey God. And He will give the Philistines the victory over Israel tomorrow, and you and your sons will be here with me among the dead."

Saul fell down shaking with fear. When the woman saw his distress she said, "Let me give you some food so you will feel better."

He refused. "No," he said, "I won't eat." But his companions and the woman begged him until he agreed. So he got up off the ground and sat on the bed. The woman owned a fat calf, so she hurried to kill it, and also made some bread, and brought it to Saul and he ate it. Then he went out into the night and returned to his troops.

QUESTIONS
Why did King Saul want to talk to Samuel?
How did he do it?
What did Samuel tell King Saul?

88
The Death of King Saul

The Philistine king brought along David and his six hundred men to help him fight against King Saul. But the Philistine army officers didn't want David. They were angry at their king for bringing him. "Make this fellow go back," they said, "for if he comes with us he might turn and fight against us to win the good will of his master Saul."

Then King Achish called for David and told him, "You'd better go back. I can't fight my generals." So David and his men got up early in the morning and left.

When they got home three days later, they found their houses burned down, for the Amalekites had been there and destroyed the city, and carried off their wives and children. David's men wept until they could weep no more.

David was in serious trouble now, for his men were angry with him for taking them from their homes to go with him. They talked about stoning him, but he trusted in the Lord his God.

David called Abiathar, the High Priest, and told him to ask the Lord whether he should go after the Amalekites.

The Lord answered, "Yes, go after them, and you will get back all they have taken." David took his six hundred men with him, but by the time they reached Besor Brook two hundred of them had to stop and rest because they were so weary and faint that they couldn't keep going. But David went on with the other four hundred.

They found a youth out in a field who was sick and starving. They fed him and when he had eaten he felt better.

"Where are you from?" David asked him.

"From Egypt," he replied. "I am the servant of an Amalekite, and my master abandoned me here three days ago when I became sick."

David asked him, "Can you take us to them?"

"Yes," the young man said, "But promise me first that you won't kill me or give me back to my master."

So David promised and the young man showed them the way the Amalekites had gone. David and his men followed them and found the Amalekites having a big celebration—feasting, drinking, and dancing because of all the booty they had taken from David's city and from the other places they had robbed.

Then David and his men rushed upon them and killed them. Only four hundred escaped on camels.

David's men got back their wives and children and everything the Amalekites had taken, as the Lord had said they would. And they also took the flocks and herds of the Amalekites.

David and his men now returned to Besor Brook. The two hundred men they had left behind came out to meet them.

Then some of David's men who were selfish and wicked said, "These two hundred weren't with us, so we won't give them any of the booty we captured from the Amalekites, but they can have their wives and children back."

But David said no. He told them they must share and share alike—those who were left behind and those who were in the battle should all get the same rewards.

Meanwhile, the battle between King Saul's army and the Philistines had begun. The army of Israel was defeated and many were killed. Then the Philistines began moving in on Saul, and killed Jonathan and two other of Saul's sons. The archers shot at Saul with their arrows, and hit him and he was badly wounded. Then he said to his armorbearer, "Kill me with your sword, because I fear the Philistines will get me and torture me." But his armorbearer was afraid to, and wouldn't do it.

Then Saul took his own sword and stood it on the ground with its point upward; and he purposely fell on it so that it ran into his body and killed him.

When his armorbearer saw that Saul was dead, he also fell on his sword and died. So Saul died, and his three sons and his armorbearer, and great numbers of his men. The Philistines won, as Samuel had told Saul they would.

The next day, when the Philistines returned to the battlefield to get the clothes of the men they had killed, they found Saul and his three sons lying dead on Mount Gilboa. They cut off Saul's head and took his armor, and sent word to all the Philistines that Saul was dead, and that the Israelis had been driven out of their country. They put Saul's armor in the house of their idol, Ashtaroth, and fastened Saul's body to a wall, along with the bodies of his three sons.

But when the Israelis who lived in Jabesh-gilead heard what the Philistines had done to Saul, the brave men of that city travelled all night and took down the bodies of Saul and his sons from the wall, and brought them to Jabesh-gilead; there they burned them, and then took their bones and buried them under a tree. They did this because Saul had been very kind to the people of Jabesh-gilead many years before when he came with an army and saved them from the Ammonites.

QUESTIONS
What did the Amalekites do to David's city?
What did David tell his men about sharing?
How was King Saul killed? What happened to his body?

89
David Becomes the King

Meanwhile, David was still at his home in Ziklag, and didn't know that the Philistines had beaten the Israelis in the battle. But soon a messenger arrived from the battlefield to tell David, "The Israelis have lost the battle and many are dead, and Saul and Jonathan are dead too."

"How do you know Saul and Jonathan are dead?" David demanded.

The young man replied, "I was with Saul when the Philistines surrounded him with their chariots and were ready to kill him. When he saw me he shouted, 'Quick! Come and kill me before they capture and torture me.' So I did, for I was sure he was doomed. And I took the crown from his head, and the bracelet from his arm; here they are, for I have brought them to you."

But the young man was lying to David; for as you know, Saul had killed himself. The young man said this because he thought Saul's death would please David, and David would give him a reward. But David wasn't pleased at all. He tore his clothes in sorrow, and all the men who were with him tore theirs too. And they mourned and wept for Saul, and for his son Jonathan, and for the men of Israel who had died.

David asked the young man why he wasn't afraid to kill the king God had chosen. "You must die for this,"

God told Samuel the prophet to anoint David as the new king. That is what Samuel is doing in this picture.

David told him. And so he was killed instead of getting a reward.

Afterwards, David asked the Lord whether he should go to the land of Israel. And the Lord said yes. Then David asked Him what part of the land of Israel he should go to. And the Lord told him, "To the city of Hebron." Hebron was one of the cities of the tribe of Judah, to which David belonged.

David was now thirty years old. Upon his arrival at Hebron, the leaders of the tribe of Judah asked him to be their king, and he agreed.

But the other tribes of Israel didn't come to him, for they already had a king. His name was Ish-bosheth, a son of Saul. But one day about noon when Ish-bosheth was taking a nap, two of his army captains came into his house pretending they wanted to bring him a gift. But when they came into his room, they killed him.

They cut off his head and brought it to David at Hebron. "Look," they said, "we have brought you the head of Ish-bosheth, the son of Saul your enemy, who wanted to kill you."

But David was very angry. He reminded them that when he was living at Ziklag he had killed a man for killing Saul, and now these two army captains must die, too, for killing Ish-bosheth.

When the other tribes saw that Ish-bosheth their king was dead, they asked David to be their new king. So at last David was king over all twelve of the tribes of Israel.

David now captured the city of Jerusalem and lived there in a strong fort. He became a very great man, for the Lord helped him in everything he did.

King Hiram of Tyre was a good friend of King David's. King Hiram's people were expert construction workers. So Hiram sent builders and carpenters to build David a palace in Jerusalem.

QUESTIONS

Was David happy when he heard about King Saul's death? How do you know?

Did all the tribes of Israel ask David to be their king at first?

What happened to King Ish-bosheth?

Where did David build his palace?

90
The Ark Comes Home

Do you remember that after the Philistines sent back the Ark to the land of Israel, it was carried to the city of Kiriath-jearim, and left there in the house of a man named Abinadab? It had been in Abinadab's house ever since—for more than seventy years—because the people of Israel didn't care anymore and had forgotten all about it. But now King David asked his people to come with him and bring the Ark to Jerusalem. So they set the Ark on a new cart and started off to Jerusalem with it.

Now remember, the Ark was very holy. When it was first brought inside the Tabernacle, God came in a cloud that stood above the Ark, showing His deep interest in it. And when the people of Israel went through the wilderness and took the Ark with them, they were not allowed to put it on a cart, for it had to be lifted up on poles and carried on the shoulders of men called Levites, whom God had chosen for this work. And the Levites were not allowed even to come near it until the priests had covered it with the curtains of the Tabernacle. That is how holy the Ark was.

So when David wanted to bring the Ark to Jerusalem, he should not have put it on a cart. It should have been carried by poles on the Levites' shoulders. But instead he put it on a cart driven by two men whose names were Uzzah and Ahio.

When they came to the threshing floor of Nacon, the oxen pulling the Ark stumbled, and Uzzah, forgetting what the Lord had said about not touching the Ark, put out his hand to steady it. And the Lord killed him instantly for doing this.

David was displeased with the Lord for killing Uzzah. And David was afraid that he, too, would be punished. So he took the Ark no further, but left it in the house of Obed-edom, a Levite.

It stayed there in Obed-edom's house for three months, and the Lord blessed Obed-edom and all his family because of its being there. When David heard how the Lord was blessing Obed-edom, he called the priests and Levites and told them to get ready to bring the Ark to the new Tabernacle he had made for it in Jerusalem.

When the priests and Levites went

to get the Ark, David and the leaders of Israel went too, to show their joy and respect. This time David commanded the Levites to carry the Ark on poles across their shoulders. Do you remember why? It was because God had commanded that it be carried in that way only. David didn't want anything to happen again like what had happened to Uzzah. David was clothed in a robe of white linen, and so were the Levites who carried the Ark, and those who were chosen to sing praises to the Lord as the Ark was being carried along.

So they brought the Ark to Jerusalem with joyful shouts and the music of trumpets, cymbals, and harps. Every time the Levites who carried it went a few steps, David offered up sacrifices to the Lord. He was so glad to be allowed to bring the Ark that he couldn't just walk quietly along, but had to leap and dance for joy. But when Michal, his wife, looked out of a window as he passed his house, and saw him leaping and dancing, she was disgusted. She told him afterwards that he looked silly. But David told her he had done it to please the Lord, and he was willing to look even more foolish than that if it would please the Lord.

So they brought the Ark to Jerusalem and put it into the Tabernacle David had made for it. David then offered up more sacrifices and burnt offerings and peace offerings, and blessed the people and gave them gifts of food.

One day as David was sitting in the beautiful palace he had built for himself at Jerusalem, he got to thinking about the Ark's being out in the Tabernacle, which was really only a great big tent. He felt in his heart that he should build a Temple for it more beautiful than his palace. At that time there was a prophet named Nathan, and David told Nathan what he wanted to do. Nathan said. "Go and do it, for the Lord is with you and will help you."

But that night the Lord spoke to Nathan, and said, "Tell David not to build the Temple." The Lord was glad David wanted to build it, but He said David's son was the one God had chosen for this job. So David stopped his building plans and left it for his son to do, as the Lord had told him to.

QUESTIONS

How long had the Ark been at the house of Abinadab?

Tell about taking the Ark to Jerusalem. Why did God kill Uzzah?

What was the proper way to carry the Ark?

When David decided to build a Temple for the Ark, what did God say?

91
David's Love for Jonathan

David conquered many heathen kings in the countries near Israel, and took away their horses, chariots, gold, and silver. He gave part of the gold and silver to the treasury of the Lord. And the Lord was with him and helped him in all he did; he was a good ruler over his people.

Now that he had become so rich and great, David thought about his dead friend Jonathan, Saul's son, and how he and Jonathan had promised to be kind to each other's children. So David sent for a man named Ziba, who had been a servant of Saul's, and asked him whether any of Jonathan's children were alive. For if they were, he wanted to be kind to them for Jonathan's sake.

Ziba told the king that one of Jonathan's sons was still living, but he was lame. He became lame when he was a small child, on the day his grandfather Saul and his father Jonathan were killed in the war. The little boy's nurse grabbed him and ran before the Philistines could come and get him. But as she was running, she stumbled and he slipped out of her arms and was badly hurt as he fell and had been lame ever since. By now he had grown up and become a man, but he was still crippled. His name was Mephibosheth.

David sent for him. "Mephibosheth, don't be afraid," he said; "I haven't called you here to harm you, but to be kind to you because of my promise to your father. I am giving you all the land that belonged to your grandfather Saul. And I want you to come and eat at my table."

Mephibosheth was surprised. "What am I," he exclaimed, "that you should take any notice of me?"

Then the king called Saul's servant, Ziba, and said to him, "I have given Mephibosheth all the land that belonged to Saul. You and your sons must take care of it for him and bring him all the crops that grow on it. Mephibosheth shall stay with me, and always eat at my table, and be as one of my sons."

So Mephibosheth moved to Jerusalem, and ate at the king's table.

QUESTIONS
Who was Mephibosheth?
Why was David kind to him?

92
David's Sins

Joab was the officer in command of David's army. Once when Joab and his soldiers went to fight against the Ammonites, David stayed in his palace in Jerusalem instead of going with them. It was a warm summer evening, so he went up on the flat roof to walk around and cool off. While he was standing looking out over the city, he could see a beautiful woman taking a bath. Instead of looking the other way, he sent a messenger to find out who she was. The messenger reported that she was Bathsheba, the wife of Uriah the Hittite, who had gone with Joab to fight against the Ammonites.

David sent for her and made her come and sleep with him, even though she was already married to Uriah. This was, of course, a very great sin. Soon afterwards she sent word to David that they were going to have a baby. David sent immediately for her husband Uriah to come back from the army. David wanted everyone to think, when the baby was born, that its father was Uriah instead of David. So David told Uriah to go home to spend the night with his wife. But Uriah didn't do it.

Then David sent Uriah back to the army with a letter to Joab. In the letter David told Joab to put Uriah in the most dangerous spot in the battle, and then for all the other soldiers to run away and leave Uriah by himself against the enemy, so he would be killed. David wanted Uriah dead so that he could marry Bathsheba.

Uriah gave Joab the letter, but didn't know what it said. Joab did what David told him to: he sent Uriah out into the front line of the battle, and he died there. Then David married Bathsheba as soon as Joab notified him that Uriah was dead.

But the Lord was very angry at what David had done. He sent Nathan the prophet to tell David, "A terrible thing has happened. A rich man who has great flocks of sheep has stolen a lamb from a poor man. It was the only lamb the poor man had. It was his children's pet and he himself loved it very much. But a friend came to visit the rich man and he wouldn't use one of his own sheep as meat for dinner, but stole the poor man's lamb and killed and ate it."

When David heard about this he

was furious. "The man who has done this thing deserves to die," he shouted.

Then Nathan said to David, "You are the rich man I am talking about! For the Lord chose you to be king, and gave you many wives and children, and made you rich and great. Yet you murdered Uriah to get his wife." Nathan said the Lord would send a dreadful punishment upon David for doing this.

Suddenly David seemed to realize how wicked he was. "I have sinned against the Lord," he admitted.

When David and Bathsheba's baby was born, David loved him very much. But the Lord sent a sickness upon the little boy. David prayed that the baby wouldn't die, and lay all night on the ground, crying to the Lord. The chief men of the city came and talked to him and tried to get him to eat, but he wouldn't.

Finally, seven days later, the baby died. David's servants were afraid to tell him, for they said, "While the baby was alive, King David was so sad—what will he do now that the child is dead?"

But when David saw them whispering together, he knew what had happened. "Is the child dead?" he asked.

"Yes," they said, "he is."

Then David got up and washed and dressed himself, and went out to the Tabernacle where the Ark was kept, and worshipped the Lord. Afterwards he came back and asked for his dinner. His servants were very surprised, and asked him why he had refused to eat while the child was alive, but now that it was dead, he was willing to eat again.

David answered, "While the baby was alive I fasted and wept because God might be kind to me and let the child live. But now that he is dead, what good does it do to refuse to eat? Can I bring him back again? I will go to him when I die, but he will never return to me."

QUESTIONS

Why did David want Uriah dead?
How did Uriah die?
What story did Nathan tell David? What did the story mean?
What happened to David's and Bathsheba's little baby?

93

David's Son, Absalom

David had other wives besides Bathsheba, and they gave him children too. One of these sons was named Absalom. When he grew up, he was the best looking man in all Israel, and was the best athlete in the entire country. His hair was so thick and long that when he cut it at the end of each year, there were three and one-half pounds of it!

Absalom bought some chariots and horses, and had fifty men running ahead of him wherever he went, so that all the people would notice him and think he was very great. Early each morning he went out to the gate of the city, and when he saw anyone coming to speak with the king, to ask for help, Absalom called to the man and talked with him and said that if only he were king he would give the man everything he wanted. And whenever anyone bowed to him because he was the king's son, Absalom was very friendly and said not to do it. So everyone liked him because he fooled them into thinking he cared about them when he really didn't care at all.

One day he asked his father for permission to go to Hebron to offer a sacrifice. The king said to go ahead. But the real reason Absalom wanted to go was to start a rebellion and to try to get himself made king instead of his father. He sent spies all through the land to persuade the people to come to Hebron and make him their king. The spies told the people that on a certain day when Absalom's friends blew their trumpets long and loud, they should all shout, "Absalom is king in Hebron." Two hundred men from Jerusalem went along to help him.

David finally heard about what was happening and when he realized how many of his people wanted Absalom to be their king, he said to his officials, "Hurry! We must run away before Absalom comes and kills us." So the king and many of his loyal friends fled from Jerusalem, crossed the brook Kidron, and headed toward the wilderness.

The priests and Levites started out with David, carrying the Ark with them. But David told them to take it back into the city again. "Perhaps the Lord will be kind to me and bring me back again," he said, "but if not, then let the Lord do whatever He thinks best." For David knew how wicked he had been to murder Uriah in order to marry his wife. He remembered that the Lord had said that a great punishment would come upon him for doing this. And now it had come, and David knew he deserved it, and was willing to bear it. He climbed barefoot up Mount Olivet, weeping as he went, and all the men with him were weeping too.

When David had gone a little way out of the city, Hushai, one of his friends, came to be with him, for he loved David and didn't want to stay behind. But David told him to go back to Jerusalem and stay there until Absalom came, and to watch and see what he did, and then secretly send messages to David telling him what was happening. So Hushai went back to Jerusalem.

QUESTIONS

Why did everyone like Absalom so much?

Why did David run away from Jerusalem?

94
David Fights His Son

While David was hurrying out of Jerusalem, a man named Shime-i, one of King Saul's relatives, came and cursed David and threw stones at him. Shime-i hated David just because his relative, Saul, had hated David. Abishai, David's nephew, asked, "Why should this dog be allowed to curse my lord the king? Let me go over and cut off his head."

But David said no, probably the Lord had sent Shime-i, and it was all part of the punishment the Lord was sending him. "My own son Absalom is trying to kill me," he said, "so is it any wonder that this man, who is my enemy, would like to do the same?"

Absalom arrived in Jerusalem just after King David left. Absalom asked his friends what to do next. His friend Ahithophel said, "Let me take twelve thousand men with me and start after David tonight. We will catch up with him while he is tired, and all his men will run away, and I will kill him. And when his people see that he is dead, they will come and want you to be their king."

This advice sounded good to Absalom, but first he asked David's friend Hushai what he thought was best. Hushai told him not to go with only twelve thousand men, but to wait until he could get up a great army. Hushai said this because he wanted to give David more time to get away.

As soon as Hushai knew that Absalom had decided to wait, he went to the priests in Jerusalem, who were David's friends, and told them to send a messenger quickly to David and tell him to hurry across the Jordan River before Absalom's army could get there.

There were two young men, sons of the priests, who were hiding from Absalom outside the city, and a woman gave them Hushai's message. They started off to find David, but a boy saw them and told Absalom, and he sent some men chasing after them. The priests' sons ran to a house by the road, with a well in the yard. They climbed down inside and hid there, and a woman spread a covering over the top of the well, and sprinkled corn on the covering so that no one would think of looking inside.

Absalom's men came to the house to look for them, but couldn't find them, so they went back to the city again.

Then the young men came up out of the well, and carried Hushai's message to David. So David and all who were with him crossed the river that night.

After David had crossed Jordan, an old man named Barzillai, who lived there, and some other people too, brought all kinds of food for David and his men to eat.

As soon as Absalom had gathered his army together, he chased after his father.

Meanwhile, David's men went out to fight. David stood by the gate of the city while his men were going out, and as they passed him, he spoke to all the captains, saying, "For my sake deal gently with Absalom."

The battle was in a woods, and God gave David's army the victory.

QUESTIONS

What did Shime-i do to David?

Tell about the two boys who hid in the well.

95
Absalom Hangs by His Hair

After the fighting, Absalom was riding on a mule, and the mule went under the branches of a great oak tree. Absalom's thick hair caught among the branches. Then the mule went away and left him dangling with his feet above the ground.

One of David's soldiers ran to Joab and told him, "I saw Absalom hanging in an oak tree!"

"Why didn't you kill him?" Joab asked. "I would have given you a big reward."

"I wouldn't kill the king's son no matter what you gave me," the man replied. "The king commanded us not to harm him."

"I can't stand here and argue about it," Joab said. Then he took three darts and thrust them into Absalom's body while he was still alive, hanging in the branches of the oak. So Absalom died.

Then Joab blew a trumpet as a signal for his army to come back, for now that Absalom was dead, there was no need for any more fighting. Joab's men threw Absalom's dead body into a pit in the woods and piled a great heap of stones over him.

After the battle was over, one of the priest's sons, whose name was Ahima-az, said to Joab, "Let me run and tell King David how the Lord has punished his enemies."

But Joab said no, and told another man, named Cushi, to go and tell the king.

"Please let me go too," Ahima-az pled.

"What for?" Joab asked him.

But he said again, "Please let me."

So finally Joab let him.

David sat at the gate of the city waiting to hear news from the battle. His watchman on the top of the wall saw a man running toward the city, and shouted this news down to the king. Then the watchman saw another man running too, and he told the king that now two men were coming.

Ahima-az arrived first. He came panting to the king, shouting, "All is well!" Then he threw himself down before the king and exclaimed, "Praise God! He has given us the victory!"

The king asked him, "Is Absalom safe?"

Ahima-az answered, "When Joab sent me, I saw a great commotion, as if something had happened, but I don't know what it was."

Then Cushi, the other messenger arrived. He said, "I have news, my lord king: the Lord has punished all those who rebelled against you."

The king asked, "Is Absalom safe?"

Cushi answered, "May all the king's enemies be as that young man is."

Then David knew that Absalom was dead. He went up into the room above the gate, crying, "O my son Absalom! My son, my son, Absalom! Would that God had let me die instead of you, O Absalom, my son, my son!"

When David's army learned how deeply the king was mourning for Absalom, they were afraid to return to the city. They stole in quietly by another gate, and were like people ashamed of fleeing from a battle, instead of like those who had just won a great victory. But the king kept on mourning. He covered his face, and wept aloud, "O my son Absalom! O Absalom, my son, my son!"

Joab was angry. He came to the king and said. "You have made us all ashamed. We have fought for you and saved your life and the lives of your wives and your children. You seem to love your enemies more than us. I can plainly see that if Absalom had been saved alive and all the rest of us had been killed in the battle, you would have been very happy! If you don't go out and say 'Thank you' to your troops, I am warning you—they will all desert you and you will be worse off than you've ever been from your youth until now."

Then the king went out and talked with his soldiers and thanked them for saving him.

When the people in Jerusalem learned that Absalom was dead, they invited David to return and be their king again. So David started back to Jerusalem.

QUESTIONS

How did Absalom get caught in a tree?

Who killed Absalom?

What news did Ahima-az and Cushi tell David?

Why do you think David was so unhappy?

What did Joab tell David to do?

Absalom's thick hair got caught in the tree branches. As he hung there helpless, his enemy Joab came and killed him.

96
David Is King Again

Shime-i, the man who had cursed David and thrown stones at him, came out to meet the king, and fell down before him, and said, "I was very wicked, but please forgive me."

Then Abishai, David's nephew, said to David, "Shime-i must die because he cursed the king."

But David said no, that none of his enemies would be put to death that day, for it was a day of happiness because he was the king again.

As David went on toward Jerusalem, Barzillai, who had brought him food as he left, came out to meet him. David said to him, "Come with me to Jerusalem and live in my palace and I will take care of you."

But Barzillai said he was an old man now, and hadn't long to live, and he was too old to enjoy being in the king's palace and seeing the beautiful things that were there. He would rather go back to his own city, he said, to die at home, and to be buried in the grave of his father and mother.

Then the king kissed Barzillai and blessed him, and let him go home.

So David returned to Jerusalem, and was the king again, just as he had been before.

But now David sinned against the Lord again. The bad thing he did this time was to tell Joab to count all the men in the land who were old enough to be soldiers. God was displeased with David for doing this, perhaps because David would be proud of his great army instead of being proud of the Lord.

It took Joab and his census-takers more than nine months to count everyone in the land.

Then they came back to Jerusalem, and reported to David that in the tribe of Judah there were 500,000 brave men who could fight with the sword, and in the other tribes there were 800,000.

But afterwards David realized he had sinned. "Please forgive me for what I have done," he pleaded with the Lord.

But God decided to punish David. He sent the prophet Gad to tell David to choose any one of these three punishments: Did he want to have seven years of hunger in the land? Or did he want his enemies to come and fight against him for three months? Or did he prefer three days of deadly sickness among his people?

"I don't know which to choose," David replied. "I guess I would rather the Lord punish us than send our enemies to do it." So David chose the three days of terrible sickness.

Then the Lord sent an angel to bring the sickness to the men of Israel and in three days, 70,000 of them died.

Jerusalem was built on three small hills. On top of one of these hills was a threshing floor belonging to a man named Araunah. The angel of the Lord stood over Araunah's threshing floor, and David saw him standing between the earth and sky, with a sword in his hand stretched out over Jerusalam, as though he would destroy all the people in the city. David and the leaders of Israel fell flat on the ground before Him, and David prayed that the Lord would punish him alone, and spare the people.

Then the prophet Gad told David to build an altar to the Lord at Araunah's threshing floor.

Araunah was threshing his wheat. When he saw the king coming, he came and bowed to him, and asked, "Why have you come, my lord, O king?"

"To buy your threshing floor and build an altar on it, to offer burnt offerings to the Lord," David answered, "so that the sickness will stop."

Araunah said that David could have the threshing floor for nothing, and his oxen, too, to use for a burnt offering.

But David said, "No, I will buy it for the full price; it wouldn't be right to offer a burnt offering to the Lord that has cost me nothing."

So David bought the threshing floor for six hundred pieces of gold and built an altar there and placed an offering upon the altar. Then he prayed to the Lord, and the Lord heard his prayer and sent down fire from heaven that burned up his offering. Now the Lord commanded the Angel, and the sickness ended.

QUESTIONS

Did Barzillai go and live with King David at his palace? Why?

Why do you think it was wrong for David to have the people counted?

David got to choose his punishment: seven years of hunger, three months of fighting, or three days of sickness. Which did he choose?

Which would you have chosen?

How did David get the sickness to stop?

97
King David Gets Old

The years went by and King David was getting old now, and knew he soon would die. He remembered what God had said, that David was not the one to build a beautiful Temple for the Ark, but that his son would do it. So David collected stones and timber and iron—everything his son would need to build the Temple when he became the new king.

David decided the Temple should be built on the top of the hill where Araunah's threshing-floor had been. He put masons to work shaping the foundation stones, and carpenters cut great beams from cedar trees. Other men made iron nails. David bought huge piles of gold and silver and bronze, for large quantities of these would be needed. "My son Solomon is inexperienced," he said, "and isn't able to decide about these things yet, and the Temple must be very, very beautiful, and admired among all nations."

Then David explained to Solomon that many years before, he himself had wanted to build God's Temple, but God had told him not to, because David was a soldier and had killed many people. God had helped him win great victories over the enemies of Israel, but God wanted a man of peace to build His Temple. God had promised that Solomon's reign would be peaceful, and so Solomon could build God's Temple.

But David had another son, Adonijah, who wanted to be king instead of his brother Solomon. And now that his father was old and weak, he thought this would be the best time to try to become the king. So he had a great party for his friends, and persuaded them to let him be their king.

When David heard about it, he commanded his government officials to take his own mule and let Solomon ride on it to a fountain just outside Jerusalem, and to anoint him as king over all the land. "Blow the trumpet," he said, "and shout, 'Solomon is the new king!' Then bring him back here to the palace and let him sit on my throne, and he will be the new king of Israel."

So that is what they did, and that is how Solomon became the new king. Solomon's brother Adonijah and the men who were with him heard all the shouting and asked, "What is all that noise?" Just then someone came and told them that David had said that Solomon was the new king, and all the people were shouting for joy. Then Adonijah was afraid that Solomon would kill him because he had tried to be the new king. But Solomon said that if he would behave himself from then on, no harm would be done to him.

Before King David died, he called together all the leaders of his kingdom and told them that the Lord had chosen Solomon to build the Temple. Then David said to these princes and great men, "You must be very careful to do whatever the Lord tells you to, for then you will always have this good land which God has given us, and you can leave it to your children when you die."

Then David said to Solomon, as all the others listened, "Solomon, my son, obey God and worship Him with all your heart. If you do, He will be your friend, but if you turn away from Him He will destroy you."

Then David gave Solomon the plans and drawings of the Temple and of all the furniture inside. The Lord had given David these plans, and now he was passing them on to Solomon. And David gave Solomon all the gold and silver he had collected. "It is a big job," David said to his son, "but don't be afraid to begin building, for the Lord God will help you all the way until the Temple is finally built."

Then David called together all his people and told them that he had collected much gold and silver, bronze, iron, precious stones, and marble to be used in the beautiful Temple, because he wanted to help build the home of the Lord. Then he asked the people if any of them wanted to give. And they brought gold and silver, bronze and precious stones, and gave them to the Lord.

David thanked the Lord for making him and his people want to give so much to God. But he said that they were only giving back to Him what He had first given to them.

David prayed very earnestly for the people, and for Solomon his son. He asked the Lord to help them keep on loving the Lord and keep on obeying His laws.

David finally died after being king for forty years. All the people loved him and they buried him in the city of Jerusalem.

QUESTIONS

Did David build God's Temple? Why?
Tell about what Adonijah did.
Where did the gold and silver for the Temple come from?
Can you think of some reasons why all the people loved King David so much?

98
God's Temple Is Built

Solomon feared God, and was careful to do what was right. One night God spoke to him in a dream, and told him he could have anything he wanted! What would you have asked for? Solomon finally decided to ask for wisdom! That is, he wanted always to know what was best to do to help his people the most.

God was pleased with Solomon for asking for wisdom, and told him that because he had not asked for money or for a long life or for victory over his enemies, God would give him the wisdom he asked for and all these other things besides! So God made Solomon very rich as well as very wise.

Soon after this, two women came to King Solomon to ask him to decide a serious problem for them. They lived together in the same house, and each of them had a baby. One of the women said, "This other woman's child died in the night, and while I was asleep, she took my baby from beside me, and laid it in her bed, and laid her dead child in my bed. When I woke in the morning to feed my baby, he was dead; but as soon as it was light, I saw that it was not my child."

But the other woman said, "No, the living child is my son, and the dead is yours."

"Bring me a sword!" the king commanded his men. Then he said, "Cut the living child in two, and give half of it to each of these mothers." Then the real mother of the living child said, "Oh, sir, don't kill my baby! Give him to the other woman!"

But the woman who had only pretended to be its mother said, "Yes, cut it in two."

Then the king said to give the baby to the woman who didn't want it killed, because he knew she must be the real mother!

Everyone soon heard about this decision, and was glad to see that God had given Solomon such great wisdom.

These two women are fighting about which one can have the baby. Each one says she is the baby's mother. Finally King Solomon, the wisest king who ever lived, found out which one was telling the truth.

Solomon now got ready to build the Temple. He asked David's friend, King Hiram of Tyre, to send lumbermen into the forests to cut down trees for him to use in the building, because Hiram's men were experts at cutting down trees. Hiram agreed, and sent his men into the forests of Mount Lebanon, where cedar trees grew. Solomon sent many thousands of his own people, too, and they worked together with Hiram's men in cutting down the trees and afterwards bringing them to the sea, which was not far away. There they made them into rafts, and floated them along the shore toward Jerusalem.

Hiram also sent one of his best workmen to Solomon to help make the Temple as beautiful and perfect as possible. This man would make beautiful things from gold, silver, bronze, iron, wood, and from expensive linen cloth.

Now Solomon began to build, carefully following the pattern his father David had given him. The Temple was to be about 100 feet long, 33 feet wide, and 50 feet high. In front of it there was a 200-foot tower, soaring far above the rest of the Temple.

No noise was heard all the time the Temple was being built. Can you guess why?

It was because the foundations of the Temple were built of stone, and each stone was cut into its proper shape before it was brought to the Temple site.

When the walls were up, Solomon covered them on the inside with cedar boards carved with the shapes of flowers, then covered with gold. Even the floor of the Temple was covered with pure gold.

Across the middle of the Temple he hung a curtain colored blue, purple, and crimson, called the veil, to make two rooms just as there were in the Tabernacle. The innermost of these rooms was for the Ark, and was called the most holy place. The inside walls of the most holy place were covered with wood carved into shapes of angels, palm trees, and flowers. These walls and the floor were then covered with gold. In this inner room he made two statues of angels with their wings spread out. The statues were fifteen feet high. They were carved out of the wood of olive trees, then covered with gold. They stood with their faces turned to the wall, and their wings reached from one side of the room to the other.

The doors of the Temple were made from fir boards, with pictures carved on them of angels, palm trees, and open flowers; afterwards the door and all the carvings were covered with gold. Jewels were used in various parts of the Temple to make it more beautiful.

Solomon made two great bronze pillars to stand in front of the Temple, one on the right side and the other on the left. And he made a bronze altar, which was four times as large as the

It took Solomon and all Israel seven years to build this beautiful Temple for the Lord. The people brought lambs and goats and cattle. These were killed, and burned upon the altar to honor the Lord, and He was pleased. Today, we don't need to offer these animals to God, because Christ was killed for us to take away our sins.

K. Hook

one Moses had made for the Tabernacle. There was also a great tank of water that rested on the backs of twelve bronze oxen.

He also made ten huge brass tubs set on wheels, so they could be moved from one place to another. These were to hold water for washing the sacrifices.

Next he made ten gold lampstands to give light inside the Temple.

It took seven years to finish all this work.

QUESTIONS

What did Solomon ask for when God promised to give him anything he wanted? Was God pleased with his wish? What would you ask for if you could have just one wish?

What problem did two women bring to Solomon about a baby? What wise decision did Solomon make?

How did King Hiram help Solomon?

Describe as much as you remember of how the Temple was built. How long did it take to finish building it?

99

Wise King Solomon Sins

Now Solomon summoned all the leaders of the nation to Jerusalem, to be there when the Ark was taken from the Tabernacle to the Temple.

The priests carried the Ark into the most holy place, and set it under the statues of the angels. And when the priests came out again, leaving the Ark behind, a bright cloud of God's glory filled the Temple.

The king stood before the people and publicly thanked God for helping him build the Temple. Then as all the people watched, he knelt down, spreading out his hands toward heaven, and asked the Lord to hear and answer all the prayers the people of Israel would ever pray there. And if their enemies ever conquered them because of their sins, Solomon asked that the Lord would help His people when they came to the Temple and prayed. Or if the Lord had to punish them by not sending rain on their fields, so that their crops wouldn't grow; or if sickness came into the land; or if swarms of locusts and caterpillars came and ate their grain—whatever trouble might come, he asked that the Lord would always help them when they came to the Temple and prayed.

After Solomon had finished this prayer, fire flashed down from heaven and burned up the offering Solomon had placed upon the altar! When the Israelis saw the fire, and the cloud of the glory of the Lord in the Temple, they fell to the pavement, face downward, and worshipped. "God is so good!" they kept exclaiming. "He is always so kind to us!"

Then the king gave many animals to the people to sacrifice—22,500 oxen and more than 100,000 sheep! So the king and all the people dedicated the Temple to the Lord as a place for His Ark, and as a place where sacrifices would always be offered to Him.

Afterwards the people held a great festival for fourteen days. Then Solomon sent the people home again with joyful hearts, thanking the Lord for His kindness to King Solomon and to themselves.

One night soon afterwards the Lord appeared to Solomon and said that He had heard his prayer, and would accept the Temple as His home. He promised that when the Israelis sinned against Him, and He punished them for their sins, He would forgive them and take their punishment away if they would be sorry and would come to the Temple and pray to Him there. And He promised again that if Solomon would obey Him, Solomon could be the king as long as he lived, and his children and children's children would be kings after him.

But if Solomon and his people turned away from God and worshipped other gods, God would no longer bless them but would drive them out of the good land He had given them. And He would no longer stay in the Temple—so glorious and beautiful now—but would destroy it so that all who passed by would be astonished and ask, "Why has the Lord done such terrible things to this land and to His Temple?" And the answer would be, "Because the people disobeyed the Lord God of their fathers who brought them out of Egypt. They chose other gods and worshipped and served them!"

The queen of the far-away country of Sheba heard of Solomon's wisdom and his knowledge of the true God, so she came to visit him. She brought many servants with her, with camels carrying rare and expensive spices, and gold and precious stones. She talked with Solomon and asked him hard questions about many things she wanted to know. Solomon answered them all and explained about everything she asked. When she saw his beautiful palace and the expensive foods on his table, and the number of servants he had, and the Temple, she could hardly believe it. "I heard of your riches when I was in my own land," she exclaimed, "but you are far richer and wiser than I was told!"

Solomon was wiser than all the other kings of the earth, and they came to learn from him.

He made a great throne of ivory and overlaid it with pure gold; there were six steps leading to the top of the throne, and a footstool of gold at the bottom. On the steps were statues of twelve lions, six on one side and six on the other. No other kingdom had such a throne as that one.

All the cups Solomon drank from, and all the dishes, were made of pure gold. His great ships sailed far away and returned every three years bringing gold and silver, ivory, apes, and peacocks.

But Solomon had many wives; he

married many beautiful heathen girls, even though the Lord had told him never to do this because they didn't know or love the Lord. And sure enough, when he grew old his wives persuaded him to worship their idols; so he didn't keep on obeying God as his father, David, had done. He even built beautiful temples for these idols.

The Lord was very angry with him and said that because he had done these things his son could not be king of all the land. Yet for David's sake the Lord didn't take away all the kingdom from Solomon's son; He let him be the king of two of the twelve tribes of Israel, but gave the other ten to someone else. And the Lord raised up enemies to trouble Solomon because of this great sin.

QUESTIONS

When the Temple was finished, where was the Ark placed?

What good things did God promise to Solomon if he always obeyed Him? What if he didn't obey?

Why did kings and queens come to visit Solomon?

How did Solomon sin? What was his punishment?

100
Israel Splits in Two

One day a youth named Jeroboam was leaving Jerusalem, and a prophet came up to him and grabbed hold of the new coat he was wearing and tore it into twelve pieces! Then the prophet gave Jeroboam ten of the pieces! The prophet explained to Jeroboam why he had done this. It was because the Lord was going to let him be king over ten of the tribes of Israel!

When King Solomon heard about this, he tried to kill Jeroboam, but Jeroboam ran away into the land of Egypt where Solomon couldn't hurt him.

Solomon was the king of Israel for forty years, and he died and was buried in Jerusalem. Then Jeroboam's friends sent a message to him in Egypt, telling him to come back home again, and he did. Then he and all the people went to Solomon's son, whose name was Rehoboam, to make him their king.

First, however, they talked with him about the harsh, cruel way his father had ruled them. They wanted to know if Rehoboam planned to treat them better than his father had. If he would promise, then they would let him be their king.

Rehoboam told them to come back

in three days, and he would give them his answer.

After they were gone, Rehoboam went to the old men who had been friends of his father, and asked their advice. They said to speak gently to the people and to promise to rule them with kindness and love. They said that if he did this, the people would gladly choose him as their king for as long as he lived.

But Rehoboam was not satisfied with this good advice from the old men. So he asked the young men who had grown up with him what they thought. The young men told him to speak roughly to the people and to tell them that if they thought his father had been cruel to them, they hadn't seen anything yet! For he would be even more cruel. His father had been a little harsh, but he would be *very* harsh.

When the people came back for his answer three days later, Rehoboam spoke roughly to them, as the young men had advised him to. He shouted, "If you think my father was cruel to you, well, I'll be much crueler; and if you think he was harsh, you'll think it was nothing by the time I get through with you."

Most of the people went away in great anger and said that he couldn't be their king; they wanted Jeroboam instead.

But the tribes of Judah and Benjamin stayed and made Rehoboam their king. The other tribes chose Jeroboam. So Jeroboam was king over ten tribes, as the prophet had said, and Rehoboam was king over only two.

When Rehoboam saw that the ten tribes had left him, he sent a messenger to them, asking them to come back, but they threw stones at the messenger and killed him. Then Rehoboam hastily called together all the soldiers of Judah and Benjamin, 180,000 of them, and formed them into an army to go out and fight against the ten tribes. But God sent a prophet to tell them that his people must not fight against their brothers in the other ten tribes, but to go on back home.

So now there were two kings ruling over the people of Israel. Until this time, one king had ruled over all of them—first Saul, then David, and then Solomon. But now Solomon's son Rehoboam was king over the tribes of Judah and Benjamin, and Jeroboam was king over the other ten tribes.

Rehoboam's kingdom was called the kingdom of Judah; and Jeroboam's, the kingdom of Israel.

QUESTIONS

Into how many pieces did the prophet tear Jeroboam's coat? Why?

Who was Rehoboam's father?

How could Jeroboam and Rehoboam be kings at the same time?

What were their two kingdoms called?

101

A Prophet Is Killed by a Lion

We have read about the way the ten tribes chose King Jeroboam, and deserted King Rehoboam.

One day King Jeroboam said to himself, "If my people go to Jerusalem to offer sacrifices and to worship at the Temple, they will see King Rehoboam, the son of the great King Solomon, and they will want him to be their king instead of me."

So King Jeroboam made two gold statues of calves and placed them in two temples, one at Bethel and the other at Dan, in different parts of his land; and the people went there to worship them. For he said to the people, "It is too far for you to go to Jerusalem to worship God. These gold idols are your gods; worship them, for they brought your fathers out of Egypt." What a wicked thing for Jeroboam to say!

Jeroboam chose wicked men as priests to sacrifice to his calf idols. But he wouldn't allow the priests of the Lord to offer sacrifices to the true God. Because of this, all the good priests and Levites who lived in his land moved to Jerusalem to live; and many other good people who would not worship his calves went with them, and chose Rehoboam as their king.

It was very wrong of Jeroboam to stop his people from going to Jerusalem, where God had commanded them to worship; and it was very wrong of him to tell his people to worship the gold calves. But the people willingly obeyed him and worshipped the calves, and no longer went to Jerusalem to worship the Lord.

One day Jeroboam was standing in his idol's temple beside the incense altar, preparing to burn incense to the gold calf, when a prophet came to him from the land of Judah. This prophet said that a king named Josiah would be born in Judah, and this king would come and wreck Jeroboam's idol! The prophet said this was not going to happen for many years, but to prove that it would surely

King Jeroboam not only disobeyed God himself, but he led the people of Israel to break God's Law by worshipping these gold idols.

R. Hook

happen some day, God would now break Jeroboam's altar, and its ashes would spill to the ground.

Jeroboam was very angry with the prophet for saying such a thing, and tried to grab him, but as he reached for him, the Lord instantly made Jeroboam's arm grow stiff, so that he couldn't draw it back again! And at that moment the altar cracked in two, just as the prophet had said it would, and its ashes were scattered on the ground.

Then Jeroboam begged the prophet to pray that his arm would be all right again. So the prophet prayed for him, and his arm was made well.

Then King Jeroboam said to the prophet, "Come home with me and rest yourself, and I will give you a reward."

But the prophet answered, "If you gave me half the riches in your palace, I wouldn't go with you, nor eat in this place. For the Lord told me not to." Then the prophet started back to the land of Judah.

Now there was another prophet, an old man, living there at Bethel. His sons came and told him about the prophet from Judah, and all he had done to Jeroboam and his altar. The old prophet asked his boys which way the prophet from Judah had gone, for they had seen the road he had taken; and the old man followed after him.

He caught up to him, and found him resting under an oak tree, and said to him, "Are you the prophet from Judah?"

"I am," he replied.

Then the old man said, "Come home with me and eat."

But the prophet from Judah said, "I can't go with you, nor eat or drink in this place, for the Lord has commanded me not to."

Then the old man said to him, "But I too am a prophet, and an angel spoke to me, saying, 'Bring him back with you to your house, to eat with you.' " But the old prophet was lying, and made up the story about the angel.

It was wrong for the prophet from Judah to listen to the old man, for the Lord himself had already told him what to do. But he went home with him and ate with him. The Lord was angry because of this, and while the two men were sitting at the table the Lord made the old man speak to the prophet and tell him that because he had disobeyed the Lord and come back to Bethel and eaten there, he must die.

And sure enough, as he started back to the land of Judah, a lion met him and killed him, and his dead body lay on the road.

Some men came along and saw his body lying in the road, and saw the lion and the prophet's donkey standing there, and they rushed back to Bethel where the old man lived, and told everybody about this strange sight.

When the old man heard about it, he said, "It must be the prophet from Judah who disobeyed the command of the Lord.

"Saddle my donkey," he said to his

Instead of doing exactly what God had told him to do, this old prophet listened to some bad advice. God punished his disobedience by letting a lion kill him.

R. Hook

sons. Then he rode until he found the body of the prophet and saw the donkey and the lion standing there. The lion had not eaten the body nor killed the donkey.

The old man lifted the prophet's body onto the donkey and took it to Bethel, where he buried it in his own grave. Then he said to his sons, "When I am dead, bury me here in this same place; lay my bones beside his bones, for the words that he spoke against the altar in Bethel shall surely come true."

QUESTIONS
What gods did Jeroboam make and worship?
Tell about what happened to Jeroboam's arm when the prophet from Judah visited him.
What happened to the altar?
What was the prophet from Judah not supposed to do in Bethel?
What was the prophet's punishment?
Was the old man nice?

102
A Little Prince Dies

At that time the son of King Jeroboam was sick, and Jeroboam said to his wife, "Take off your fine clothes and put on something old so that no one will recognize you, and go to Shiloh, and visit the prophet who told me I would be king. Take him a present of ten loaves of bread and a bottle of honey, and he will tell you whether the child will get well."

Jeroboam's wife did as he had told her to. She put on a cheap dress instead of her queen's gown, and went to Shiloh, and came to the prophet's house. The prophet was old now, and couldn't see very well, but the Lord had told him that the wife of Jeroboam was coming to ask about her son.

So when he heard the sound of her feet as she came in at the door, he said, "Come in, wife of Jeroboam; why are you pretending to be someone else? I have a sad message to give you. Go and tell Jeroboam, 'The Lord says, I raised you up from among the people, and made you king over ten of the tribes of Israel. I took those ten tribes away from Solomon's son and gave them to you. Yet you have not obeyed my commandments, but have turned away from worshipping me and have worshipped idols instead. Therefore I will destroy you and your family. Not one will be left alive. Dogs will eat those who die in the city, and the birds will eat those who die in the field; for the Lord has told me so.' "

Then he said to Jeroboam's wife, "As you enter the door of your house, your child will die. And all the people shall mourn for him and bury him. He is the only one of Jeroboam's family who will be buried in a grave."

So Jeroboam's wife went home, and as she came in at the door, the child died. And they buried him, and all Israel mourned for him as the prophet had said.

Jeroboam was king for twenty-two years; then he died, and his son Nadab became the new king.

Nadab didn't obey God either, but worshipped the golden calves his father had made. But after two years a man named Baasha rebelled against him and killed him; then Baasha became the king.

The first thing King Baasha did was to kill every one of King Jeroboam's family. So the words of the prophet came true, for he had told Jeroboam's wife that the Lord would bring evil on Jeroboam and his family, until not one of them was left alive.

King Baasha was as wicked as King Jeroboam, and he too worshipped the gold calves. He was king for twenty-four years; then he died and his son Elah became the new king.

Elah was king for only two years. One day he was drinking himself drunk in the house of one of his friends when Zimri, the captain of half of his chariots, came into the house and killed him. Then Zimri said that he was the new king.

The men of Israel were away at the time, fighting against the Philistines, but as soon as they heard what Zimri had done, they said they didn't want him to be their king, so they chose their army general, Omri, to be their new king instead.

Then King Omri and the men of Israel came to the city of Tirzah, where Zimri was, and surrounded it. When Zimri saw that he couldn't prevent them from capturing the city, he committed suicide by going into his palace and setting it on fire; and he died in the flames. So Zimri was king for only seven days.

After Omri became king he bought the hill of Samaria and built a city on it and called it the city of Samaria. King Omri lived in this city, and for nearly two hundred years afterwards the other kings of Israel lived there too.

King Omri sinned as Jeroboam did, for he worshipped the gold calves and encouraged his people to worship them. He was king for twelve years, and died and was buried in Samaria, the city he had built; then his son Ahab became the new king.

QUESTIONS

What did the prophet tell King Jeroboam's wife?

What happened when she went home?

Were any of the kings in this chapter good men who worshipped God?

103
A Dead Boy Lives Again!

Up to this time, six kings had ruled over the ten tribes of Israel, and every one of them had been bad. But the Bible tells us that King Ahab, Omri's son, was worse than any of the others.

He married the daughter of a heathen king. This girl's name was Jezebel, and she worshipped the idol Baal. King Ahab built a temple for this idol in the city of Samaria, and chose bad men as priests to offer sacrifices to the idol. So King Ahab caused the people of Israel to worship Baal just as the heathen nations did.

The Lord was angry with King Ahab and set the prophet Elijah to tell him that as punishment there would not be any more rain in the land of Israel for many years, until Elijah asked God to send it. Ahab was very angry with Elijah because his God had stopped the rain, and he wanted to kill Elijah, so the Lord told Elijah to go and hide.

"Go and hide beside a brook in the wilderness," the Lord said. "You can get drinking water from the brook, and I have commanded the ravens to feed you there!" So Elijah hid by the brook, and the ravens brought him food every morning and evening. But after awhile the brook dried up because there had been no rain, and a great famine came over the land.

Then the Lord said to Elijah, "Go to the city of Zarephath, for I have commanded a widow to feed you there."

When Elijah came to the gate of the city he saw a woman gathering sticks, and he called to her and said, "Please bring me a cup of water to drink." As she was going to get it he called to her again, and said, "And a piece of bread, too!"

But she answered, "As surely as God lives, I have no bread. I have only a handful of meal in a barrel, and a little olive oil in a bottle; and now I am gathering a few sticks to bake a little loaf of bread for me and my son to eat, and then we must die of starvation."

But Elijah told her "No, you won't!

God sent Elijah away to hide. He camped beside a brook and ate the food the ravens brought him in their beaks.

Go and bake the bread, but make a little loaf for me first, and bring it here, and there will be plenty left for you and your son! For the Lord says that although you have only a little flour and olive oil, it will last until the famine ends!"

She did as Elijah said, and sure enough, there was always olive oil left in the bottle and flour in the barrel, no matter how much she used! It was a wonderful miracle! This went on for a whole year until the famine ended.

One day the woman's son became sick and died. Elijah took him out of her arms and carried him up to his own room and laid him on his bed. Elijah pleaded with the Lord and said, "O Lord, why have You brought evil upon this woman in whose house I stay, by slaying her son? Please, O Lord, let the child live again!"

And the Lord heard Elijah's prayer, and the boy came back to life, and Elijah took him down to his mother. What a wonderful miracle!

QUESTIONS

How did Elijah get food and water while he was hiding?

What happened to the woman's flour and olive oil? Why do you think God made this happen?

What did Elijah do when the woman's son died?

104

Elijah Meets Baal's Prophets

There were many other prophets of the Lord besides Elijah in the land of Israel. But Queen Jezebel, the wicked wife of King Ahab, hated them all and tried to kill them.

Obadiah, the manager of Ahab's palace, was a good man who feared the Lord; so he hid a hundred of the Lord's prophets in caves where Jezebel couldn't find them, and sent them supplies of food and water.

After the famine had lasted for more than three years the Lord said to Elijah, "Go to King Ahab, and I will send rain."

King Ahab didn't know Elijah was coming, or that the Lord had promised rain, so King Ahab and Obadiah were out looking everywhere to find grass to save the horses and mules from dying of starvation. They went in different directions so they could finish their work faster.

As Obadiah was walking along, Elijah met him. Obadiah recognized him and said, "Are you Elijah, sir?"

"I am," Elijah replied. "Now go and tell King Ahab that I am here."

But Obadiah was afraid. "King Ahab has looked for you everywhere," he said, "and now as soon as I tell him you are here, the Lord will carry you away and hide you again, and when Ahab comes and can't find you, he will kill me."

But Elijah answered, "As surely as God lives, I will show myself to Ahab today."

So Obadiah found the king and told him, and he came to meet Elijah. When King Ahab saw Elijah he exclaimed, "There you are, you traitor." He said this because he blamed Elijah for the famine.

But Elijah answered, "I am not a traitor, but you and your family are, because you have forsaken the Lord and are worshipping Baal."

Then Elijah told King Ahab to send for all the people to come to Mount Carmel, and to bring with them all 450 of the priests of Ahab's idol, whose name was Baal. So all the people came with the priests.

Elijah asked the people, "How long will it be before you decide whether you will serve God or Baal? If the Lord is God, obey Him; but if Baal is God, then obey him."

The people heard what Elijah said, but didn't answer.

Elijah didn't know there were any other of the Lord's prophets left alive. He told the people that he was the only one in all the land, because all the rest had been killed or had run for their lives; but Baal had 450 prophets.

"Now bring two young bulls," Elijah said, "and let Baal's prophets kill one of them and lay it on Baal's altar, without any fire under it. And I will take the other young bull and kill it and lay it on the Lord's altar, without any fire under it. Then let them pray to Baal to send down fire from heaven to burn up their young bull. And I will pray to the Lord for fire to come from heaven to burn up the young bull on the altar of the Lord. Whichever god sends fire from heaven to burn up his offering, he is the real God." And all the people agreed.

Baal's prophets chose a young bull and killed it, and laid it on the wood on the altar, but put no fire under it. Then they cried out to their idol, Baal, from morning till noon.

"O Baal, hear us!" they shouted, and leaped up and down on their altar. But no voice answered them, and no fire came down from heaven to burn up their offering.

About noon, Elijah mocked them and said, "Call louder, for perhaps your god is talking to someone and isn't listening, or maybe he is away, or is asleep and must be awakened!"

So they yelled and shouted to Baal until evening, and cut themselves with knives until the blood gushed out, hoping it would attract Baal's attention and make him answer them. But no fire came.

Then Elijah gathered all the people around him and used twelve stones to rebuild the altar of the Lord that had long lain in ruins, and dug a trench around it. He put wood on the altar and cut the young bull apart and laid the pieces on the wood.

Then he said to the people, "Fill four barrels with water, and pour it over the sacrifice and over the wood." When they had done this, he said, "Do it a second time." And they did it a second time. "Now do it a third time," he said. And they did. So the water ran down over the sacrifice and over the wood, and filled the trench around the altar.

That evening, at the time when the priests at the Temple used to offer a lamb for a burnt offering, Elijah came near the altar and prayed to the Lord, saying, "Hear me, O Lord, hear me, so that these people will realize that You are the true God."

Then the fire of the Lord fell from heaven upon the altar and burned up the offering and the wood, and even the stones of the altar, and licked up the water in the trench.

When the people saw it, they all fell face downward to the ground, shouting, "The Lord, He is God! The Lord, He is God!"

And Elijah said to them, "Grab the prophets of Baal! Don't let a single one escape!" So the people arrested them and Elijah took them down to Kishon Brook and killed them there; for the Lord had commanded that anyone who told people to forsake God and to worship idols, must be executed.

QUESTIONS

Who was Obadiah and what did he do?

Describe how Baal's prophets tried to get Baal to send down fire to their altar.

Why did Elijah soak the Lord's altar with water? What happened when Elijah prayed?

What did the people do to the prophets of Baal?

105

Elijah's Strange Picnic

Elijah told King Ahab that now he could celebrate, for the rain was coming and the famine would soon be ended. Then Elijah went up to the top of Mount Carmel and kneeled down with his face to the ground, and prayed that God would send the rain. After he had prayed he said to his servant, "Go and look out toward the sea. Are there any clouds yet?"

The servant went and looked, but came back and said, "I couldn't see any."

"Go again seven times," Elijah ordered him.

So the servant went six more times and finally the seventh time he said, "There is one tiny cloud."

Then Elijah knew the Lord was going to send the rain, so he said to his servant, "Go and tell Ahab, 'Quick! Get your chariot ready and get down off the mountain, before the rain stops you!' "

While his servant was going to tell Ahab, the little cloud grew larger and larger until the entire sky was black with clouds, and the wind began to blow, and there was a very heavy rain. Then Ahab rode in his chariot to the city of Jezreel. And the Lord gave Elijah strength to run before the chariot until he came to the gate of the city.

When he got home, King Ahab told his wife, Queen Jezebel, all that had happened, and how Elijah had killed the prophets of Baal. Jezebel was very angry and sent this message to Elijah: "By tomorrow at this time you will be dead, for I will kill you." When Elijah heard this he was badly frightened and ran for his life, and came to the city of Beer-sheba in the land of Judah. There he left his servant, while he himself travelled on for another day and hid in the wilderness.

He sat down under a juniper tree and asked the Lord to let him die. "Now, O Lord, take away my life," he said, for he was very tired of running away from his enemies. But he did wrong in asking to die. God had sent the ravens to feed him, and had saved him from Ahab and from the wicked prophets of Baal. Elijah should have remembered these things and not been afraid; he should have been willing to wait patiently until the Lord was ready to take him to heaven. We shall soon see what glorious things he would have missed if the Lord had let him die as he wanted to, out there in the wilderness.

Finally he fell asleep, and as he lay there under the juniper tree, an angel came and touched him and woke him up. "Get up and eat," the angel said. Elijah looked, and there was a loaf of bread baked on some coals near him, and a bottle of water by his head. So he ate and drank, and lay down and slept again.

Then the angel of the Lord came a second time and touched him and told him to eat, so that he would have strength enough for the journey that lay ahead of him. So he got up and ate again, and the Lord gave him strength from that food to live for forty days and forty nights without eating again, until he came to Mount Horeb, and he lived in a cave on the mountain.

Then the Lord's voice came to him and said, "What are you doing here, Elijah?'

"The people of Israel have broken their promise to obey Your laws," Elijah replied, "and have torn down Your altars, and killed Your prophets, and now I am the only one left, and they are trying to kill me too."

"Come out and stand at the entrance of the cave," the Lord told him. Then the Lord passed by. A terrible wind tore up the earth on the mountain, and even moved the rocks; but the Lord was not in the wind. And after the wind came an earthquake, but the Lord was not in the earthquake. And after the earthquake a fire; but the Lord was not in the fire. After the fire there came a still, small voice. When Elijah heard the voice, he knew that God was there; and he wrapped his face in his scarf, for he was afraid to look upon God.

Then the Lord asked him again, "What are you doing here, Elijah?"

Elijah answered as before, "The

people of Israel have broken their promise to obey Your laws; they have thrown down Your altars and killed Your prophets, and I am the only one left; and they are trying to kill me, too."

But the Lord told Elijah he was not the only one left who worshipped God. "I still have 7,000 others in the land of Israel who have never bowed to an idol!" the Lord told him.

Then the Lord said for Elijah to leave the cave and return to the land of Israel. When he got there he must anoint a man named Elisha, to be the Lord's prophet instead of himself, for the time was coming soon when Elijah must leave the world behind and go to heaven.

So Elijah returned to Israel as the Lord had told him to. As he was walking along, he saw Elisha plowing a field. Elijah went over to him and threw his coat over Elisha's shoulders. Elisha knew that when a prophet did this to someone, it meant that that person should leave his home and become a prophet. So he left the plowing and ran after Elijah.

"Let me go first and say good-bye to my father and mother, and then I will come with you," he said. So Elisha went home to tell his parents, and then he went with Elijah and helped him.

QUESTIONS

Why did Elijah tell King Ahab to be happy?

Tell about Elijah and his servant at the top of the mountain praying for rain.

What made Elijah run away and want to die?

Did God come to Elijah in a wind, an earthquake, a fire, or in a still, small voice? What did He say?

Why did Elijah throw his coat over Elisha's shoulders as he was plowing?

106
Another War

King Ben-hadad of Syria now summoned his army and went to fight against the city of Samaria, where King Ahab of Israel lived. He sent messengers to Ahab to tell him, "Your silver and gold, your wives and children, all are mine."

Ahab was frightened, and said all right, he would give them all to Ben-hadad.

Then Ben-hadad sent another message: "Tomorrow I will send my men to search your castle and bring me anything they choose."

Then Ahab called for all the leaders of Israel and told them what Ben-hadad had said. The leaders told Ahab not to let Ben-hadad walk all over him like that. So Ahab refused to surrender.

When Ben-hadad heard his reply, he sent back a message to Ahab warning him that his great army could easily capture the city.

"Oh?" Ahab replied, "Don't fool yourself!"

This made Ben-hadad very angry, and he sent word to his soldiers: "Get ready for the battle."

But the Lord sent a prophet to Ahab who told him not to be afraid, but to go out and fight the army of Ben-hadad.

Ben-hadad and his captains were having a drinking party in their tents when Ahab and his little army arrived. The huge Syrian army was taken by surprise and ran for their lives in great panic. When Ben-hadad saw what was happening, he jumped on a horse and got away.

Then the prophet came to Ahab again, and told him that Ben-hadad and his army would come back again next year. What the prophet said proved true. For Ben-hadad's advisors persuaded him to gather together another army as great as the first, and they came up and spread over the whole country. In comparison, the tiny Israeli army seemed like two little flocks of baby goats, there were so few of them and they were so helpless and weak.

After seven days the battle began, and the Lord gave Israel another mighty victory, for they destroyed 100,000 of the Syrians. The rest escaped to the city of Aphek, and there a great wall fell down and killed many more. But Ben-hadad fled into the city and hid.

Ben-hadad's men came to him with the suggestion that he throw himself upon the mercy of King Ahab. "We have heard," they said, "that the kings of Israel are merciful; we will dress in burlap to show that we are sorry, and go to the king of Israel and ask him to save your life; perhaps he will let you live."

So they put on clothes made from old sacks. to show their humility, and came to Ahab, and said, "Your servant Ben-hadad begs, 'Please let me live.' "

"Wasn't he killed in the battle?" Ahab asked. When he heard he was still alive, he told them to go and bring him. When Ben-hadad arrived, Ahab let him ride with him in his chariot as though they were friends. Then Ben-hadad promised to give Ahab some of his cities, so Ahab allowed him to return again to his own land.

But God was angry with Ahab for doing this. He had given Ahab the victory over Ben-hadad so that Ahab could put him to death. Now God sent a prophet to Ahab who said, "Because you have let this man go, you must die instead of him."

Soon afterwards Ahab wanted to buy the vineyard of a man named Naboth because it was near his palace. "I'll give you a better vineyard for it," he said, "or else I'll pay you whatever it's worth."

But Naboth didn't want to sell his vineyard. It had belonged to his father and he wanted to keep it. So he refused to sell it.

Ahab returned home angry and unhappy, and lay down and sulked and refused to eat! When Queen Jezebel came home she asked, "What's the trouble? Why so sad?"

"Because Naboth won't sell me his farm," Ahab replied.

"Are you the king of Israel or not?" Jezebel demanded. "Get up and be happy—I will give you the farm!"

Then she wrote letters, and signed them with Ahab's name, and sealed them with his seal, and sent them to the elders of the city of Jezreel where Naboth lived. In the letters she told them to find some bad men who would tell lies about Naboth, and say that they had heard him speak evil of God and the king.

The elders did as Queen Jezebel commanded. They found two men who lied about him. Now the Lord had commanded that anyone who spoke against God should be stoned. Naboth had not done that terrible deed, but the bad men lied and said that he had. So the people took Naboth out of the city and threw stones at him until he died, and the dogs came and licked up his blood. Then they sent a message to Jezebel: "Naboth is dead."

When Jezebel heard it she said to Ahab, "Go and take Naboth's vineyard, for he is dead." So Ahab went down to the vineyard to claim it.

But the Lord told Elijah to go out and meet him at the vineyard and to say to him, "So you have murdered Naboth and taken his vineyard, have you? Well, where the dogs licked up the blood of Naboth, dogs will lick up your blood too."

Then Elijah told Ahab that the Lord would send evil on him and on all his family, and that they would all be destroyed until not one of them was left alive. And of Jezebel his wife, the Lord said, "The dogs shall eat her beside the well of Jezreel."

None of the other kings of Israel were as bad as Ahab, for he tried very hard to disobey God in everything he did. And his wife Jezebel helped him in his sinning. He worshipped idols just like the heathen nations the Lord had driven out of Canaan.

QUESTIONS

Who won the battle between Ahab and Ben-hadad?

How did Ben-hadad escape from being killed?

Tell about what happened to Naboth.

107
Fire from Heaven

One day King Jehosaphat of Judah went to visit King Ahab of Israel. King Ahab asked him to help him fight against King Ben-hadad again. King Jehoshaphat told Ahab to ask God first, and find out whether God wanted them to do this or not.

So King Ahab summoned his 400 false prophets and asked them, "Shall I go to battle or not?"

"Yes," they answered. "for the Lord will be with you." But King Jehoshaphat didn't believe these men, for he knew they were not real prophets at all, but only said whatever they thought would please King Ahab.

"Isn't there a prophet of the Lord around here somewhere?" King Jehoshaphat asked. "Let's ask him, too."

"There is one," Ahab answered, "a man named Micaiah; but I hate him because he doesn't prophesy good things about me, but always something bad."

"Let's ask him anyway," King Jehoshaphat said.

So Ahab sent a messenger to bring Micaiah. Then the two kings put on their royal robes and each sat on a throne by the gate of Samaria. All of King Ahab's false prophets stood before them, telling them to go out to battle, for they would win.

Then the messenger came back, bringing Micaiah. King Ahab asked him, "Shall we go out to battle, or not?"

"Sure," Micaiah said, "go right ahead!"

But the king saw that Micaiah didn't really mean this. "How many times must I tell you not to lie to me?" he demanded.

Then Micaiah answered, "I saw Israel scattered upon the hills like a flock of sheep that is lost and has no shepherd." Micaiah meant that Ahab's army would be scattered like sheep after the battle, without a leader because King Ahab would be dead.

"Didn't I tell you this would happen?" Ahab exclaimed to Jehoshaphat. Then Ahab told his soldiers, "Take Micaiah to prison, and feed him on bread and water and treat him cruelly until I come back safely from the battle."

"If you come back at all, then the Lord has not spoken through me," Micaiah replied.

But despite Micaiah's warning, the king of Israel and the king of Judah went out to the battle. Ahab said to Jehoshaphat, "I'll not wear my royal robes; then no one will know me. But you wear yours and let them see you are a king!"

Before the battle began, King Ben-hadad of Syria had told his captains not to fight with anyone but Ahab. So when King Ben-hadad's soldiers saw Jehoshaphat in his royal robes, they said, "This must be King Ahab," and they surrounded him. Then Jehoshaphat yelled to them that he wasn't Ahab, and so they turned away. It was the Lord who made them do this, because King Jehoshaphat was a good man and the Lord was protecting him.

But just then an arrow hit Ahab between the pieces of armor that covered his chest. No one was aiming at him, for no one knew he was Ahab; the arrow just happened to hit him there.

"Turn around and get me out of here, for I am badly wounded," Ahab said to the soldier driving his chariot. Ahab sat in his chariot all day watching the battle, but that evening he died. So about the time the sun was going down, word was sent throughout the Israeli army to stop fighting and to go home, for their king was dead.

So the men of Israel fled, and King Ahab was killed as the prophet had said, because he had let Ben-hadad get away when the Lord had told him not to.

Ahab's body was taken to Samaria and buried there. And as his chariot was being washed beside a pool of water near the city, the dogs came and licked up his blood, just as Elijah had said they would.

Ahab's son Ahaziah now became king. But he was as bad as his father. One day he fell from an upstairs room in his palace and was hurt seriously. He sent messengers to Baal-zebub, the idol of the Philistines, to ask whether he would get well again. Then the angel of the Lord said to Elijah, "Go to meet King Ahaziah's messengers and ask them, 'Is it because there is no God in Israel that you have to go and ask Baal-zebub, the idol of the Philistines? For doing this, the Lord says that King Ahaziah shall not get well again; he will surely die.' "

Elijah told the messengers what the Lord had said, so they returned to Ahaziah.

"Why have you come back so soon?" he asked.

"A man came to meet us," they told him, "and said for us to return to you and say, 'Is it because there is no God in Israel that you have come to inquire of Baal-zebub, the idol of the Philistines? Therefore you will not get well but will surely die.' "

"What did he look like?" the king asked the messengers.

"He was a hairy man," they said, "with a leather belt."

"It was Elijah!" Ahaziah exclaimed.

The king was angry and sent a captain of his army with fifty soldiers to capture Elijah, and to bring him to the king. They found him sitting on the top of a hill. The captain yelled at him, "Hey, you prophet, the king commands you to come on down."

"If I am a prophet," Elijah answered, "let fire come down from heaven and burn you and your fifty men." And fire came down from heaven, and burned them up.

Then Ahaziah sent another captain

with fifty men, and he came to Elijah and called to him, "Prophet, the king says to come right away."

Elijah answered, "If I am a prophet, let fire come down from heaven and burn you and your fifty men." Then fire came down again from heaven, and burned them up.

Ahaziah sent a third captain with fifty men. But when he came to Elijah, he fell on his knees before him, and said, "O prophet, please save my life and the lives of these fifty men, your servants. Don't let the fire come down from heaven and burn us, as it burned the two captains with their men who were here before."

Then the angel of the Lord said to Elijah, "Go with him, don't be afraid." So Elijah went with him to the king.

Elijah told the king, "The Lord says that because you sent messengers to your god Baal-zebub, the idol of the Philistines, instead of sending them to me, the God of Israel, therefore you shall not get up from this bed, but shall surely die."

So Ahaziah died as Elijah said, and Jehoram his brother became king instead.

QUESTIONS

Was Macaiah a good prophet or a bad prophet? Whom did he come to visit? What did he say would happen?

When King Ahaziah got hurt, why was he angry with Elijah?

What happened to the soldiers who went to capture Elijah?

108
A Chariot Ride to Heaven

The day soon arrived when the Lord was ready to take Elijah up to heaven. Elijah wanted to be alone when the Lord took him, so he said to Elisha, "Stay here, please, for the Lord has sent me on to Bethel."

But Elisha said, "I'll not leave you." So they went to Bethel together.

The young men from the school for prophets there came over to Elisha and asked him, "Do you know that the Lord will take away your master from you today?"

"Yes," he said, "I know."

Then Elijah said to Elisha, "Stay here at Bethel, please, for the Lord has sent me to Jericho."

But Elisha said, "I'll not leave you." So they came to Jericho.

The young men who were in the

school for prophets there at Jericho came to Elisha and asked him, "Do you know that the Lord will take away your master from you today?"

"Yes, I know," he replied.

Then Elijah said to Elisha, "Stay here, please, at Jericho, for the Lord has sent me to the Jordan River."

But Elisha answered, "I'll not leave you." So they went on together. Fifty young men from the school of the prophets followed them, to watch and see what would happen.

Elijah and Elisha stood at the edge of the river, and Elijah struck the water with his coat, and the river divided before them so that they went over on dry ground!

When they were on the other side, Elijah said to Elisha, "Tell me what you want me to do for you before I am taken away."

Elisha asked to have even more of God's Spirit upon him than Elijah had.

"You have asked a hard thing," Elijah answered, "but if you see me when I am taken from you, you shall have what you are asking for; but if not, you will not get it."

As they walked along and talked together, suddenly a chariot of fire, with horses of fire, swept between them and snatched Elijah away from Elisha, and took him up to heaven in the chariot. Elisha saw it, and cried out, "My father, my father, the chariot and horsemen of Israel!"

Elisha never saw Elijah again on earth. He picked up Elijah's coat that had fallen on the ground, and with it he struck the river, and the water divided before him as it had for Elijah, and Elisha went over on dry ground!

The fifty young men from the school of the prophets, who were watching from a distance, came to meet him and bowed low before him. They said to Elisha, "Let us go and look for your master; perhaps the Lord has taken him up on some mountain, or into some valley, and left him there."

"Don't go!" Elisha said. "He isn't there."

But they kept telling him he should let them search, until Elisha was ashamed to refuse any longer. "All right," he said, "go ahead and look for him."

So they searched three days without success. Then they came back to Jericho and told Elisha that they couldn't find Elijah anywhere. "I told you it wouldn't do any good," Elisha said.

Then the men of Jericho came to Elisha and told him, "Our city is pleasant to live in except that the water is no good. It ruins the ground so that nothing will grow here."

"Bring me a water jar and put some salt in it," Elisha told them. So they brought it to him. He went to the spring where the city got its water and threw the salt in and said, "The Lord says, 'I have made these waters pure; they shall never again cause the people to be sick, or ruin the

God took Elijah to heaven in a fiery chariot. As he left, he gave his coat to Elisha. This showed that Elisha was to be the new prophet.

R. Hook

ground.' " So the water was pure from that day on.

Elisha now went from Jericho to Bethel. As he was going, little children came out of the city and mocked him and yelled after him, "Go away, bald head! Go away! Go away!" So they made fun of him for being bald. Elisha asked the Lord to punish them for their sin. Then two bears came out of the woods and killed forty-two of them.

QUESTIONS
What did the students tell Elisha?
How was Elijah taken to heaven?
Why couldn't the seminary students find Elijah's body?
What did Elisha do to the water of Jericho?

109
Elisha Helps a Widow

After this, King Jehoram of Israel gathered his army together to fight against the Moabites. He asked King Jehoshaphat of Judah to help him.

"All right," Jehoshaphat said, "I'll go with you."

The king of Edom went with them too. So these three kings took their armies with them and marched for seven days, and in all that time they found no water to drink. Then the king of Israel was frightened; for he knew that his soldiers were so thirsty they couldn't fight.

King Jehoram of Israel worshipped idols, but King Jehoshaphat worshipped the Lord. So Jehoshaphat asked, "Isn't there a prophet here who can find out from the Lord what we should do?"

One of the king of Israel's officers said, "Elisha is here; he was Elijah's assistant.

"Let's ask him," Jehoshaphat said. So the three kings went to visit Elisha.

Elisha was angry and disgusted when he saw the king of Israel. "Why have you come to me?" he asked. "Go to the false prophets of your father Ahab, and of your mother Jezebel; let them help you!"

Elisha said this to him because the king didn't ever obey God except when he was in trouble. Then Elisha said to him, "If it weren't for King Jehoshaphat of Judah's being with you, I wouldn't even listen to you."

The Lord told Elisha to tell the kings to command their soldiers to dig many ditches in the valley where their camp was. The Lord said there would be no wind or rain, but the ditches would be filled with water! Then all the soldiers could drink as much as they wished.

"You will destroy the cities of the Moabites," Elisha said, "and will cut down their trees, and fill up their wells, and spoil the best of their land."

Elisha's words all came true the next morning, for the Lord caused water to flow along the ground and fill the ditches, and so everyone had plenty of water to drink. And when the enemy soldiers from Moab looked across the valley to the camp of Israel, the sun shone on the water in the ditches and made it look red. When the Moabites saw the redness, they thought the armies from Israel had been fighting and killing each other, and that the red water was blood!

"We've defeated them," they shouted. "Let's go and see what we can loot from their tents."

So they ran to the Israeli camp. But suddenly they realized that their enemy was still there! Now they fled back in disorder.

The men of Israel ran after them, and chased them all the way back to their own country. Then the Israelis cut down their trees and destroyed their cities, filled up the wells, and scattered stones and boulders on every piece of ground, just as Elisha had said they would. Afterwards the men of Israel returned to their own land.

One day the wife of one of the seminary students came to Elisha with a serious problem: "My husband is dead," she said, "and you know that he loved the Lord. But he owed some money and I can't pay it back, and now the man I owe it to has come to take away my two sons and make them his slaves."

Elisha asked her, "What do you have that you can sell?"

"Nothing," she answered, "except one jar of olive oil!"

"Well," he said, "I'll tell you what to do. Go and borrow empty jars from all of your neighbors, and take them into your house and shut the door. Then take your jar of olive oil and begin pouring it into the jars you borrow."

So she borrowed empty jars and pots, and took them into her house and shut the door. Then as her sons brought the empty jars to her, she poured olive oil into them from her one little jar, and the oil kept coming until all the jars were full! Finally, when she said to her son, "Bring me another jar!" he answered, "There is not another empty one left!"

She came and told Elisha, and he said, "Go and sell the olive oil and pay the man what your husband owed him, and take the money that is left to buy food for yourself and the children."

QUESTIONS

How did God provide water for the thirsty army?

What did the widow tell Elisha?

What did Elisha tell her to do? Then what happened?

110

Elisha Does Great Miracles

After these things, as Elisha was travelling around through the land, he came to the city of Shunem, where a rich woman lived, and she invited him to stop at her house for dinner. And always after that, whenever he passed that way, he stopped for a meal.

One day she said to her husband, "I'm sure this man is a prophet of the Lord. Let's give him a little guest room and whenever he comes to visit us, it will be ready for him." So that is what they did.

Once when Elisha was there with his servant, whose name was Gehazi, he said to him, "Call this woman."

When she came, Elisha told Gehazi to say to her, "You have been very kind to us; what shall we do for you in return? Is there anything you want me to ask the king to give you?" But she replied that she needed nothing.

After she was gone Elisha said to Gehazi, "Can you think of anything we can do for her?"

"Yes," Gehazi said, "she has no child."

"Call her again," Elisha said. So Gehazi called her and she came again and stood at the door. Then Elisha told her that the Lord would give her a son. And Elisha's words came true the following year.

When the child was old enough, he went out one day to the field with his father, to watch the reapers. While he was there he became sick, and cried out to his father, "My head! Oh, my head!"

His father said to one of the young men, "Carry him to his mother." So the child sat in her lap until noon, and then died.

She took him up to Elisha's room and laid him on the bed, and shut the door and left him there. Then she sent a message out to the field to her husband asking him to send one of the young men and one of the donkeys so she could hurry to the

This mother had waited many years to have a little boy. When he suddenly died, her heart was sad. The prophet Elisha brought him back to life, and once more there was joy in their home.

prophet and come right back again. She didn't tell him that their boy was dead, and so he said to her, "Why to-day? There isn't any special meeting today!"

"I need to go today," was all she would say.

So he told her to go ahead. "Drive hard," she said to the servant. "Hurry, don't stop for anything." So she came to Elisha at Mount Carmel.

Elisha saw her in the distance and said to Gehazi, "Look, here comes that Shunammite woman. Run to meet her and ask, 'Is everything all right? Is your husband well? How is your child?' "

Gehazi ran and asked her and she replied, "Everything is fine." When she came to Elisha, she knelt down and caught him by the feet, and Gehazi came to push her away.

But Elisha said, "Let her alone, for she is in some sort of trouble, and the Lord hasn't told me what it is."

Then the woman said to Elisha, "Why have you told God to give me a son, and then take him away?" So then he knew that her boy was dead.

"Hurry," he said to Gehazi, "take my staff and go to the child. If you meet any one along the way, don't talk with him, and if any one speaks to you, don't stop to answer him. Lay my staff upon the face of the child."

Then the woman said to Elisha, "I'll not return without you," so Elisha went too. Gehazi had gone on ahead of them, and came to the woman's house and went up into the prophet's room and laid the staff on the child's face. But the child didn't stir.

Gehazi went back to meet Elisha and said, "The child didn't wake up."

When Elisha came into the house the boy was still dead, lying there upon the bed. So Elisha went in and shut the door and prayed. Then he lay upon the child, and put his mouth upon the child's mouth, and his eyes upon the child's eyes, and his hands upon the child's hands; and the child's flesh grew warm!

Elisha came out of the room, and walked back and forth for a while in the house. Then he went up and stretched himself upon the child again; and the child sneezed seven times, and opened his eyes and came to life again!

Then Elisha said to Gehazi, "Call her!" So Gehazi did.

"Take your son!" Elisha said to her as she came into the room!

Oh, how thankful that mother was!

One day Elisha went to Gilgal to visit the school of the prophets.

Upon arrival he told the cooks to set the great pot on the fire, and to cook a special dinner for the students that night.

One of them went out into the field to gather vegetables to boil in the pot. He took some from a poisonous plant, not realizing, of course, that it was poisonous. He cut up the pieces and added them to what was in the pot, and when it was cooked, he poured it out into bowls for the men to eat. But as they were eating, something tasted funny, and they realized that there was that poisonous vegetable in it.

"O prophet," they screamed, "there is poison in the pot!"

"Well, bring me some flour," Elisha told them calmly. And he threw it into the pot. Then he said, "Go ahead and eat it, for it won't hurt you!" So they ate it, and it didn't harm them!

One day a man gave a present to Elisha of twenty loaves of bread and some ears of corn. Elisha sent them to the students at the seminary, for there was a famine in the land, and food was hard to get.

But his servant objected. "What?" he asked. "Shall I take such a little bit of food to a hundred hungry men?"

"Yes, set it before them," Elisha answered, "for the Lord says they will all have enough, and some will be left over!"

And sure enough, as the food was divided up among the students, the Lord caused the twenty loaves of bread and the ears of corn to become more, so that there was enough for all of them! And after they had finished eating, there was some left over!

QUESTIONS

What did the rich woman do for Elisha?

What did the woman do when her son got sick?

How did Elisha make the dead child well?

Why did Elisha throw flour in the pot?

III

A Little Girl Helps Naaman

The king of Syria liked Naaman, the general of his army, because he had won so many battles against his enemies. But Naaman was a leper. A leper is a person with a sickness which affects the skin, and finally makes the nose and fingers and toes rot away.

Now it so happened that when the Syrians conquered the land of Israel, they brought back with them a little Israeli girl who became the slave of Naaman's wife.

One day she said to her mistress, "I wish my master could go and see God's prophet in Samaria, for he would cure him of his leprosy."

Someone told the king what the little girl had said, so he told Naaman to go to Samaria and be healed.

Naaman took a fortune in silver and gold with him, and ten sets of new clothing. All this was a present for the prophet if he would heal him. He went to the city of Samaria with a letter from the king of Syria addressed to King Jehoram of Israel. The letter said, "This man is General Naaman. Cure him of his leprosy."

When the king of Israel read the letter he tore his clothes and said to his government officials, "Am I God? How can I cure this man of his leprosy? See, the king of Syria is looking for an excuse to declare war on us again."

But when Elisha heard about it, he

sent this message to the king: "Why have you torn your clothes? Send the man to me and he will find out that there is indeed a prophet in Israel who can heal him."

So the king told Naaman to go see Elisha. Naaman came in his chariot, and stood at the door of Elisha's house. Elisha didn't even go out to meet him but just sent this message to him: "Go and wash yourself seven times in the Jordan River and you will be healed of your leprosy."

But Naaman was angry. "Do you mean to tell me the prophet isn't even going to come out here and pray to the Lord his God for me, and put his hand on me and make me well?" he demanded. "Aren't the rivers in my own country better than all the rivers in the land of Israel?" So he turned around and went away in a rage.

But then some of his men came to him and said, "Sir, if the prophet had told you to do some hard thing to make you well, wouldn't you have done it? So when he tells you just to go and wash, and you will be healed—why don't you at least try it and see?"

So Naaman went down to the Jordan River and dipped seven times, and suddenly his skin became as new and fresh as a little child's, and he was healed of his leprosy. He went back to the house of Elisha and said, "Now I know that there is no other God in all the earth except the God of Israel."

He wanted to give Elisha a present, but Elisha said, "No, I won't accept it." Naaman begged him, but Elisha wouldn't take it.

Then Naaman asked for two mule-loads of earth from the land of Israel to take home with him, and he would make an altar from it, for he never again would offer a burnt offering to any other god but the Lord.

Naaman started home to his own country, but when he had gone just a little way, Elisha's servant Gehazi said to himself, "It's a shame my master wouldn't accept the present Naaman wanted to give him. I'll run after him and ask for something for myself."

When Naaman saw Gehazi running after him, he stopped his chariot and stepped down to meet him, and said, "Is everything all right?"

"Yes," Gehazi answered, "but my master has changed his mind. He sent me to tell you that after you left, two young men, prophets' sons, came to visit him. He asks you to give them a wedge of silver and two sets of clothing."

"I'll give *two* wedges of silver!" Naaman replied.

So Naaman gave Gehazi two wedges of silver and two sets of clothing, and sent two servants to help Gehazi carry them, for the silver was very heavy. But when they were near Elisha's house, Gehazi took the silver from the servants and sent them back to Naaman again. Then Gehazi hid the silver and clothing for he didn't want Elisha to know about it. But the Lord had already told Elisha. So when Ge-

General Naaman had a serious disease called leprosy. His servant girl, who was one of the captives the Syrian army took from Israel, told Naaman that the prophet Elisha could cure him by God's power. After he was healed, Naaman believed in the one true God.

hazi came and stood before him, Elisha asked him, "Where have you been, Gehazi?"

"Nowhere," Gehazi said.

Elisha replied, "Didn't I know it when Naaman stepped down from his chariot to meet you? Is this a time for us to take money and clothes? And now, because you have done this, Naaman's leprosy shall be on you and on your children forever." And as Elisha spoke, the leprosy covered Gehazi, and he went out with white splotches of leprosy all over his body.

One day the seminary students complained to Elisha that their dormitory was too small. "We want to build an addition," they said. "We are going down to the river to chop down trees and cut them into boards. Will you come with us?"

"All right," Elisha said, "I will." So he went along.

As one of the students was chopping down a tree beside the river, the head of his ax flew off the handle and fell into the water. The young fellow came to Elisha in a panic. "What shall I do, sir?" he pleaded. "The ax was borrowed."

"Where did it fall?" Elisha asked. When the young man showed him the place, Elisha cut a branch from a tree and threw it into the river where the ax-head had sunk, and the iron ax-head rose to the top and floated, and the boy reached out and grabbed it!

QUESTIONS

What good news did the little Israeli slave girl tell her mistress?

What did Elisha tell Naaman to do to be cured of his leprosy?

What lie did Elisha's servant tell Naaman? What was his punishment?

How did Elisha recover an ax-head from the river?

112
Four Lepers Find Food

Later on, King Ben-hadad of Syria declared war on Israel and tried to capture their king. But when Ben-hadad's soldiers arrived where the king of Israel had been, he was always gone, for Elisha had warned him that the Syrians were coming. This same thing happened again and again. King Ben-hadad was very angry. He thought one of his men was a traitor, and was telling the king of Israel about his plans. He called his men together. "Which one of you is a traitor?" he demanded.

"No," they said, "we aren't the ones who give away your secrets. It's Elisha the prophet who tells your plans to the king of Israel. Elisha knows it when you even whisper in your bedroom!"

"Then we'll capture Elisha first," the king of Syria said. "Find out where he is, and go and get him."

The king's spies reported that Elisha was in the city of Dothan. So Ben-hadad sent horses and chariots and soldiers by night to Dothan, and they surrounded the city.

Early the next morning when Elisha's servant went out of the house, there were soldiers wherever he looked. He rushed back to Elisha, shouting, "Alas, my master, what shall we do?"

"Don't be afraid," Elisha replied, "for we have more on our side than the king of Syria has on his!"

Then Elisha prayed that the Lord would help the young man to see better! And the Lord did, and now he saw that the enemy army was surrounded by horses and chariots of fire, sent by the Lord to take care of Elisha.

When the Syrian soldiers marched into the city to capture him, Elisha prayed that the Lord would make all of them blind. Then Elisha went out to them and said, "Follow me, and I will take you to the man you are looking for!" But he led them to the city of Samaria, where the king of Israel lived! Now he prayed that the Lord would open their eyes again. And the Lord did, and they saw where they were.

King Jehoram of Israel shouted excitedly to Elisha, "Shall I kill them? Shall I kill them?"

"No!" Elisha answered. "Feed them and send them back to their own land!"

So Jehoram did as Elisha said, and

they returned to their master, King Ben-hadad of Syria.

Not long after this, Ben-hadad mobilized his army again and returned to Samaria to attack it. His soldiers surrounded the city to keep anyone from getting in or out. No one could take any food to the people inside, so there was a great famine. As the king of Israel walked among his soldiers on the top of the city wall, a woman called to him for help.

"What's the matter?" he asked.

She answered, "Another woman here suggested to me that we should eat my little son one day and her son the next day. So we killed my son and ate him, but the next day when it was time to kill her son, she hid him."

When King Jehoram heard this, he tore his clothes in anguish over the dreadful famine raging through the city, and that such a thing had been done among his people. But Jehoram was as wicked a man as his father Ahab, and that is why God sent these terrible troubles upon them. Jehoram should have repented and asked God to help him. Instead, he blamed the troubles on Elisha and said the prophet would be put to death that very day.

Elisha knew the king was planning to kill him, so when the executioner arrived at his house, Elisha told those with him to lock the door and keep the man out.

Afterwards the king himself came to Elisha's house with one of his assistants. Elisha told them that the famine would end the next day, and there would be plenty of food, for the Lord had told him this. But the king's assistant wouldn't believe it. Elisha told him that because he didn't believe the words of the Lord, he would see the food, but wouldn't taste one bite of it. Soon we shall see how Elisha's words came true.

That night four lepers were sitting outside the city walls. They said to each other, "Why sit here until we starve? If we go into the city we'll die from the famine. If we sit here, we have nothing to eat, and will die. Come on, let's go out to the army of the Syrians. If they don't kill us, we will live; if they kill us, we will only die like we're going to anyway."

So they went across the field to where the Syrian army was camped—but no one was there! For the Lord had made the Syrians hear the noise of a great army coming out against them. They fled in the night, leaving their tents and horses and everything else. But really there was no one attacking them at all!

When the lepers had walked through the entire camp and found no one, they went into one of the tents and ate the food they found there, and took money and clothing, and hid them. Then they went into another tent, and carried away more silver and gold, and hid it too. But then they stopped and looked at each other.

"This isn't right," they said. "We have good news for our people, and yet we aren't telling them. If we stay

God frightened the Syrian army away. Four lepers found food in the deserted Syrian camp. They shared it with all the other starving Israelites.

R. Hook

here until morning, God will punish us. Come on, let's go and tell the king of Israel."

So they returned to the city that night and shouted to the guards on the wall, "We have been to the camp of the Syrians and no one is there! The horses are tied, and the tents are standing there, but no one is around!"

The guards rushed over and told the king. "It's a trick," he said. "The Syrians know we are starving and so they are hiding outside the camp. When we go over, they will rush back and capture us."

One of the king's assistants said, "We still have a few horses. Let's ride over and see."

So the king sent a few of his men over to the Syrian camp and sure enough, no one was there. They searched as far as the Jordan River, and all along the road there were clothes and equipment thrown away by the Syrians as they ran. Then the men returned to Samaria and reported to the king.

When the news reached the people, everyone rushed out to the camp of the Syrians and brought back huge supplies of flour and grain left by the Syrians when they fled. So the famine was suddenly ended, and now there was plenty of food. The king sent his assistant—the one who wouldn't believe Elisha—to stand at the gate and keep the people in order. But he fell beneath the surging crowd and was trampled and killed. So it happened to him as Elisha had said: he saw the food but never tasted it.

QUESTIONS

How did King Jehoram of Israel know when King Ben-hadad of Syria would try to capture him?

What did Elisha's servant see when he went outside? What did he see when Elisha prayed for God to open his eyes?

What happened to King Ben-hadad's army?

What did the lepers find at the Syrian camp? Where were the Syrians?

113
The Sick King Is Murdered

One day Elisha said to the woman whose son he had brought to life again, "Move to some other country for awhile, for the Lord is going to send another seven years of famine to the land of Israel."

So she took her family to the land of the Philistines, and lived there for seven years. Then she returned to Israel, but found that while she was gone, someone had moved into her house and claimed her fields.

Taking her son with her she went to see King Jehoram, to plead for her right to her farm again. When she arrived at the palace, Gehazi, the servant of Elisha, was there and the king was talking with him.

"Tell me about some of the wonderful things Elisha has done," the king said. Gehazi was just telling him how Elisha had brought a boy back to life, when that boy and his mother came in to speak with the king!

Gehazi said, "My lord, O king, this is the woman I was just talking about, and this is her son who came back to life again!" When the king asked her whether it was true, she told him it was. Then the king told one of his assistants to see to it that she got back her house and land; and to pay her for any fruit and grain that her fields had produced while she was in the land of the Philistines.

Elisha now went to Damascus, where King Ben-hadad of Syria lived. Ben-hadad was sick at the time, so he said to Hazael, one of his assistants, "Take a present to Elisha the prophet, and tell him to ask God whether I will get well again." So Hazael went to visit Elisha, and took a present to him—forty camel loads of the good things of Damascus.

He said to Elisha, "The king of Syria has sent me to ask you whether or not he will get well again."

Elisha answered, "Go and tell him he can get well. But the Lord has shown me he will die."

Elisha stared silently at Hazael, as though reading his thoughts, until Hazael was embarrassed; then Elisha started crying.

"Sir, why are you weeping?" Hazael asked.

Elisha answered, "Because I know the horrible things you will do to the people over in Israel; you will set their cities on fire, and kill their young men, their women, and their little children."

Hazael was astonished. "Am I such a dog as that?" he asked.

And Elisha replied, "The Lord has shown me that you will be the king of Syria."

So Hazael went back to King Ben-hadad.

"What did Elisha say?" the king asked.

"He told me you'll get well," Hazael lied.

But the next day Hazael took a thick, wet cloth and spread it over the king's face as he lay sick and helpless, so that he couldn't breathe. Thus King Ben-hadad was murdered and Hazael declared himself king.

QUESTIONS

Tell about when the woman came to ask the king for her land.

Did King Ben-hadad die from his sickness?

114
Jezebel's Terrible Death

At this time Elisha summoned one of the students at the seminary and said to him, "Get some anointing oil and go to the city of Ramoth-gilead and look for Jehu, who is a captain in the king of Israel's army. When you have found him, take him into a room alone, and pour the oil on his head, and say, 'The Lord has anointed you to be the king of Israel.' Then open the door and run."

So the young man went to Ramoth-gilead, and found the captains of the army sitting around, with Jehu among them. The young man went up to him and said, "I have a message for you, sir."

"For which one of us?" Jehu asked him.

"For you," the young man replied.

Jehu took him into a room in the barracks and the young man poured the olive oil on his head, and said to him, "The Lord says, 'I have anointed you to be the king of Israel! And after you become king, you must punish Ahab for killing my prophets by putting to death all who are left of his family. Dogs shall eat Queen Jezebel in the city of Jezreel, and no one will bury her because of all the people she has murdered."

Then the young man opened the door and ran.

When Jehu rejoined the other captains, one of them asked him, "What did that crazy fellow want?"

"I'm sure you know," Jehu replied mysteriously.

"Of course we don't," they said.

"Well," Jehu told them, "He said the Lord has appointed me as the king of Israel."

Then the captains blew a trumpet and shouted, "Jehu is king!" So, backed by the army, Jehu became king instead of Jehoram.

"Don't let anyone go to Jezreel to tell King Jehoram what we have done," Jehu said to the captains. "I will go there myself."

So Jehu rode to Jezreel in his chariot. As he came near the city, the watchman who stood in the tower over the gate saw him coming, and told King Jehoram.

Jehoram commanded, "Send out a man on horseback to ask whether he is friend or foe."

So a man rode out and demanded, "Is it peace or war?" But Jehu wouldn't reply and told the man to follow behind his chariot.

Then Jehoram sent out another man to ask the same question. But Jehu wouldn't answer him, either, and gave him the same command, to follow behind his chariot. When Jehoram saw that the men didn't come back, he jumped into his chariot, and rode out himself to meet Jehu. "Is it peace, Jehu?" he demanded.

Jehu answered, "How can there be peace with your sinful mother, Jezebel, still around?" When Jehoram heard this, he tried to get away, for he saw that Jehu had come to fight. But Jehu drew a bow with all his might, and shot an arrow at Jehoram, and it went into his heart, and he fell down dead in his chariot. Then Jehu commanded his captain to throw Jehoram's dead body out onto the ground. And the place where he threw it was in the vineyard that his father Ahab had stolen from Naboth.

As Jehu arrived in the city, Queen Jezebel, Jehoram's mother, heard the commotion and put on her ornaments and makeup, and looked out from a window. As Jehu came in at the gate she called down to him.

He looked up at the window and shouted to the men in the house with her, "Who is on my side?" Two or three people stuck their heads out and said they were.

"Then throw her down," Jehu instructed them. So they threw her out the window, and her blood was sprinkled on the wall, and the horses of Jehu's chariot trampled her. Then Jehu went into the palace and had a celebration feast. Afterwards he said to his assistants, "Go out and get the body of that wicked woman and bury it, for she was a king's daughter." But they could only find her skull, feet, and the palms of her hands, for the dogs had eaten her.

Then Jehu killed off all of Ahab's family. So the words of Elijah came true, spoken fifteen years before at the time when Ahab stole Naboth's vineyard. Elijah had warned Ahab then that the Lord would send evil upon him and upon his family, too, until not one of them would be left alive. And of Jezebel, Elijah had said, "The dogs shall eat Jezebel by the wall of Jezreel."

Jehu reigned for twenty-eight years in all, and was a very bad king. Then his son Jehoahaz became the new king.

After seventeen years, King Jehoahaz died, and his son Jehoash followed him upon the throne.

One day Elisha became sick and realized he soon would die. King Jehoash of Israel came to see him, and stood beside his bed with tears running down his cheeks. Elisha said to him, "Get a bow and some arrows. Now put an arrow in the bow and aim it through the open window." As the king did this, Elisha placed his hands over the king's hands. "Now shoot!" Elisha said, and the king did. Then Elisha told him what that arrow meant; it meant that the people of Israel would defeat the Syrians, and be free.

Next Elisha told the king to take some arrows and strike them against the ground. The king struck the ground three times and stopped. Elisha was angry, and said, "You should have struck five or six times, for then you would have struck the Syrians until they were all destroyed; but now you will win against them only three times."

So Elisha died, but even after he was dead he caused another miracle! For as some people were carrying out a dead man to bury him, they saw some bandits coming toward them. In their haste and fright they quickly placed the dead man in Elisha's tomb, and when the dead body touched the bones of Elisha, the man came back to life again!

QUESTIONS

How did Jehu become the new king of Israel?

What happened to King Jehoram?

What happened to wicked Queen Jezebel?

Tell about Elisha helping King Jehoash shoot his bow and arrow.

What miracle did Elisha cause after he was dead?

115
A Nation Dies

After the death of Elisha, King Jehoash of Israel mobilized his army against the Syrians and defeated them three times, just as Elisha had said he would. Jehoash was king for sixteen years, then died and was buried in the city of Samaria; and his son Jeroboam II became king instead.

The Lord was kind to Jeroboam and the people of Israel, for He pitied them for all they had suffered from their enemies. So He helped Jeroboam defeat the Syrians, and conquer two of their cities, Damascus and Hamath. But the people of Israel didn't thank God for His kindness. Although He helped them in their trouble, and saved them from their enemies, they still worshipped the statues of the gold calves instead of worshipping God.

The Lord sent Amos the prophet to talk to them about this. Amos told them that although the Lord had chosen them to be His very own, yet, instead of worshipping God they were worshipping idols, and were not obeying God's laws at all. For they were cruel to the poor, and they cheated and robbed one another when they sold corn and wheat, and they were selfish and lazy, and took bribes, and hated those who did right and told the truth.

The Lord had seen all of their sins, Amos told them, and so He had kept back the rain from their fields, and had sent famine and disease and hunger to show them He was angry. But still they hadn't turned from their evil ways, so an even greater punishment would now be sent upon them. There would be crying in their streets and on their farms; for an enemy would come and defeat them and treat them cruelly, and they would be carried away as slaves to other lands, and their king would be killed. But Amos told them that if they would only repent and obey the Lord, the Lord would even now forgive them, and these terrible things wouldn't happen to them.

Amaziah, who was the head priest at the idol temple at Bethel, was furious when he heard Amos tell the people these things. He reported to King Jeroboam that Amos was talking against the king, and saying that the king would be killed and the people taken away as slaves. Amaziah told Amos to run for his life and get out of the country.

This was Amos' reply to Amaziah: "I am a herdsman, not a prophet; I am from an unknown family at Tekoa. But as I was leading my sheep out to pasture the Lord said to me, 'Go and prophesy to the people of Israel.' So I did. Now you tell me not to warn the people about what God is going to do to them. Well, the Lord will punish you for this. Your wife will leave you and your sons and daughters will be killed, and you yourself will die in a far-off heathen land."

The prophet Hosea, too, came and warned the people, telling them about the great punishment the Lord would send upon them. He too begged them to repent so that the Lord could forgive them. But they wouldn't listen. Finally, after being king of Israel forty one years, Jeroboam died, and his son Zachariah became the new king.

But Zachariah was the king for only six months. Then a man named Shallum rebelled against him and killed him, and became king. But Shallum reigned only one month! For a man named Menahem killed him, and became the king!

Menahem ruled for ten long and evil years. Finally King Pul of Assyria declared war on him and came with his armies to fight against Israel. Menahem was frightened and promised to pay King Pul a thousand pieces of silver if he would go away. King Pul agreed to this, so King Menahem forced the rich men of his kingdom to give him the money to pay King Pul.

Then King Pul took the money and went away. Menahem died soon after this, and his son Pekahiah became the new king.

But Pekahiah was as great a sinner as King Jeroboam was. Jeroboam, you remember, was the king who first set up the images of gold calves and told the people to worship them. And now King Pekahiah didn't destroy these idols as he should have, but worshipped them himself and taught the people to do this too, instead of worshipping God. He had been king for two years when one day a man named Pekah, the son of one of his army officers, came into the palace and killed him. Then Pekah became the new king.

From these true stories about the evil kings of Israel you can see how very wicked the people of Israel were. Instead of doing as God had taught them, they chose to worship idols, just as the heathen nations living around them did. Those nations refused to worship God, because God demanded that the people who worshipped Him must live pure, good lives. But the people didn't want to be good, so they worshipped false gods, who, they said, would let them do anything they wanted to, no matter how bad.

So the people of Israel burned incense and sacrificed to the idols worshipped by the heathen nations. They even burned alive their little sons and daughters as sacrifices to the idols.

God was very angry with the people of Israel for doing such things. Yet He waited patiently for them to stop doing wrong. He sent famine and disease and war into their land to show them He was angry. And when they continued to disobey Him, then He sent his prophets to warn them again and again. These prophets preached to the people, telling them of the terrible punishment ahead, and begging them to stop doing wrong so that God could forgive them and keep them as His children. But they wouldn't listen. So at last God did as the prophets had warned and sent an enemy to conquer them and take them far away to another country to live as slaves, and they never saw their own country again.

So the kingdom of Israel was finished. It had lasted 254 years, ever since the ten tribes chose Jeroboam as their king. Nineteen wicked kings had ruled over them during that time. Now the king of Assyria sent people from his land to live in the cities of Israel. We do not know what happened to the ten tribes. They never returned to their own country again, and nothing more is said about them in the Bible or in any other history book.

That is the end of the story of the kingdom of Israel, so now we will go back 254 years and begin the story of the kingdom of Judah.

QUESTIONS

What did Amos tell the people of Israel?

Why did God punish His people?

What finally happened to the people of Israel because they would not obey God?

116
The Little Kingdom Grows

We have already read about what happened after King Solomon died. His son Rehoboam became the king of the two tribes of Judah and Benjamin, but the other ten tribes didn't want him as their king and got someone else instead. Rehoboam lived at Jerusalem near the Temple built by his father, King Solomon. For three years Rehoboam and his people did what was right and obeyed the Lord.

But when he grew rich and strong, and no longer feared that his kingdom would be taken from him, he stopped obeying the Lord. He and all the people of Judah began to worship idols. Then the Lord sent the king of Egypt with 1,200 chariots and 60,000 cavalry and a vast army of regular soldiers to attack Jerusalem. King Rehoboam and the people were very frightened.

But a prophet came and said to them, "The Lord says, 'You have stopped worshipping Me, so I will not help you against the king of Egypt.' " When Rehoboam and the princes heard this, they bowed their heads, and confessed that it was right for the Lord to punish them. This pleased the Lord and so He sent His prophet back to them again to say that because they had admitted their sins, God wouldn't let the king of Egypt kill them, but would only take away their money. So the king of Egypt conquered Jerusalem, and took away the treasures from the Temple and from the king's palace, then returned to his own land.

Rehoboam was forty-one years old when he became king of Judah, and he reigned seventeen years. Then he died and was buried in Jerusalem, and his son Abijah became king instead.

Soon there was war again between the armies of Judah and Israel. The army of Judah had 400,000 men in it, but the army of Israel had 800,000. Before the battle began, King Abijah of Judah stood on a mountain and shouted down to King Jeroboam and the men of Israel, "Don't you know that God has said that only the sons of King David should be your kings? Your king Jeroboam isn't a son of David. Yet he has declared himself to be Israel's king. This is wrong. And you have twice as large an army as we do, but you worship the gold calves made for you by Jeroboam; he says they are your gods. We worship only the Lord, and He is with us, and is our captain. O men of Israel, do not fight against the Lord, for you can never win against Him."

But while Abijah was speaking, Jeroboam led the army of Israel into action against him and the battle began. Then the men of Judah cried out to the Lord for help, and the priests who were with them blew on their trumpets. Then the men of Judah gave a great shout, and as they did, God helped them, and Jeroboam and his army ran away. So the men of Judah won the victory because they trusted in God.

King Abijah reigned for three years, then died, and his son Asa became the new king of Judah.

Asa was a good king who tried to please the Lord, so the Lord gave His people rest from war. Then King Asa said to them, "Let us build more cities in our land, with walls, towers, and gates, so that our enemies can't conquer us." So the kingdom of Judah grew strong and prosperous.

The army of Judah now had 300,000 men in it from the tribe of Judah, and 280,000 from the tribe of Benjamin. The soldiers of the tribe of Judah were experts with spears and shields, while the men of Benjamin were experts with bows and arrows. All were brave soldiers. The king of Ethiopia made war against them with an army much greater than theirs. But King Asa cried out to the Lord and said to Him, "You can help us easily, even though our army is so small. Oh, help us, our God, for we are trusting you. O Lord, don't let us be defeated by this great army that has come to fight against us." So the Lord helped them and gave them the victory.

Then the Lord sent a prophet who said, "Listen to me, King Asa, and all you men of Judah and Benjamin: The Lord will be with you and help you as long as you obey Him. But if you forget about Him He will forget about you. So don't be afraid always to obey Him and He will reward you."

When Asa heard this, he felt brave enough to knock down the idols the people were worshipping all over the land, and to repair the Lord's altar of burnt offering that stood in the court of the Temple; for it was no longer being used. Then he called a meeting of all of his people at Jerusalem and offered many sacrifices to God—700 oxen and 7,000 sheep taken from the Ethiopians. And the people made a treaty with the Lord and promised to worship Him wholeheartedly. They said that anyone, no matter who—rich or poor, man or woman—who would not worship God must die.

Thirty-five years after Asa became the king of Judah, King Baasha of Israel declared war against him. But this time instead of praying to the Lord for help, King Asa took the silver and gold from the Temple and from his palace and sent it to the king of Syria, to hire him to come and help him fight the king of Israel. The king of Syria did as Asa asked and sent his army to attack some of the cities of Israel. So King Baasha returned to defend his country, ending the war against Asa.

But the Lord sent a prophet to rebuke Asa for asking help from the king of Syria instead of from God. "Didn't God defend you against the mighty army of Ethiopians?" the prophet asked. "God did this for you because you trusted Him. For the eyes of the Lord are looking everywhere around the world to find those who love him, so that He can help them. You have done foolishly because you trusted the king of Syria instead of trusting God. From now on your enemies shall conquer you."

Asa was angry with the prophet for saying this and put him in jail.

Three years later Asa became ill with a disease of the feet. His trouble grew worse and worse, yet in his sickness he didn't ask the Lord to heal him, but trusted only in his doctors. After three years of illness he finally died. The government officials of Judah laid him in a bed perfumed with sweet-smelling spices, and then buried him in a grave he had made for himself in Jerusalem. And his son Jehoshaphat became the new king.

QUESTIONS

How many tribes were in the kingdom of Judah? Who was their first king?

What did King Asa do that shows he didn't trust in God?

When King Asa was sick, did he trust in God or in his doctors?

117
A Good King

The Lord was with Jehoshaphat because from the time he was made king he did what was right. All his people brought him gifts, and he had riches and honor. In the third year of his reign he sent teachers all through the cities of Judah, with the book of God's laws as their textbook, to teach God's will to the people. And the Lord made the heathen nations afraid to fight against Jehoshaphat's army. Even the Philistines brought him presents and tribute money; and the Arabs brought him flocks of thousands of sheep. So he became very great and had a great army. He built many castles, and great cities to keep his treasures in.

One day he went down to the city of Samaria to visit King Ahab of Israel. King Ahab prepared a great party for him, and then persuaded him to go with him to fight against the king of Syria. One of the stories in this book has already told us how Jehoshaphat put on his royal robes and went into the battle, and how the Syrians thought he was Ahab, and tried to kill him. But when he cried out, then they saw their mistake and quit following him, because God would not let them kill him. When the battle was over Jehoshaphat came back to Jerusalem.

The Lord sent a prophet to ask him, "Was it right for you to help a wicked man like Ahab, and to be a partner with a man who hates the Lord? The Lord is angry with you. But you have done well in other things: you have taken away the altars where the people worshipped idols, and you have been anxious to serve God." So Jehoshaphat stayed at home in Jerusalem after that. When he travelled, it was only to visit his people in various parts of Judah, and to command them to destroy their idols. He appointed judges in all the cities of Judah to punish those who did wrong, and to save the innocent from harm. He said to the judges, "Be careful that you act justly, for you must give account to the Lord, not to me, and the Lord sees all you do."

Once the Moabites, the Ammonites, and the Edomites came up to fight against King Jehoshaphat. When he heard that they were coming, he sent word to all his people, asking them not to eat for a few days but to pray hard asking for God's help. People came from all over Judah to the Temple at Jerusalem to pray.

Then King Jehoshaphat stood up before them and prayed, "O Lord, are You not our God who drove out the heathen from this land, and gave it to Your people? And we have built this Temple where we worship You and pray to You. But now the Ammonites, the Moabites, and the Edomites are coming to drive us from the land You have given us. Will You let them do this? For we are not able to fight against this great army they are bringing. We don't know what to do. But we are looking up to You for help."

As Jehoshaphat prayed this prayer, all the people were standing there before the Lord, with their wives, children, and little babies.

Then the Lord sent a prophet to tell King Jehoshaphat and the people, "Don't be afraid of this vast army. Tomorrow go out and face them. You will find them by the brook in the wilderness. But you will not need to fight with them! Just stand still when you get there, and you shall see how the Lord will save you. O men of Judah and Jerusalem, don't be afraid, for the Lord will help you."

Then King Jehoshaphat fell flat on the ground with his face in the dust, worshipping God. And all the people of Judah and Jerusalem did the same.

Early the next morning they went out to meet their enemies. As they were going, King Jehoshaphat said to his soldiers, "Trust in the Lord and believe what His prophet has said; then you will be victorious." And Jehoshaphat placed a choir at the head of the army to sing praises to God!

As the choir began to sing, God helped the men of Judah: for the Moabites, the Ammonites, and the Edomites began fighting and killing each other! When the men of Judah arrived, they saw their enemies lying dead on the ground. Then they went among the slain, and gathered from their dead bodies gold and silver and precious jewels, more than they could carry away. It took three days for them to get it all, there was so much of it. On the fourth day they met together in a nearby valley and blessed and thanked the Lord for giving them the victory. And always after that the valley was called Berachah Valley, which means, "The Valley of Blessing." Then King Jehoshaphat and the Judean army returned to Jerusalem, led by a band and orchestra of harpists and trumpeters, and went to the Temple to express their thanks to God.

The heathen nations feared to fight him after that, and God gave him and his people rest from war.

But afterwards King Jehoshaphat did wrong again, for he joined with the wicked king of Israel to send ships to a land called Ophir, to bring back gold. A prophet came and told him that because he had done this, his ships would be wrecked. And what the prophet said came true, for his ships were broken and wrecked at Ezion-geber, where they were built, so that they could not go to that far-off land.

King Jehoshaphat was king for twenty-five years, and, for the most part he did what was right and was pleasing to the Lord. Then he died and was buried in Jerusalem.

QUESTIONS

Can you remember some good things that King Jehoshaphat did?

Why did King Jehoshaphat ask his people not to eat for a few days, but only to pray?

What happened when King Jehoshaphat sent ships to bring gold from Ophir?

118

God Makes a Bad King Sick

Jehoshaphat had seven sons. At his death he left part of his treasures to each of them, and put them in charge of some of the cities of Judah; but he appointed his oldest son Jehoram to be the next king.

Jehoram wasn't like his father, though, for he didn't worship God. And he was afraid his brothers might lead a revolt and take the kingdom away from him, so he had them murdered.

While Jehoram was king, the Edomites, who had been his slaves, rebelled against him and chose a king of their own. Then Jehoram went out to fight them with all of his war chariots, but he lost the battle, so he couldn't make them obey him anymore. The Lord refused to help him.

King Jehoram also sinned by building altars in the mountains where the people went to worship idols.

King Jehoram's reason for doing all these wrong things was that he had married the daughter of Ahab, the wicked king of Israel, and she encouraged him to worship idols instead of worshipping God.

One day a letter came to King Jehoram from the prophet Elijah, and this is what it said: "The Lord says, 'Because you have not obeyed Me as your father Jehoshaphat did, but have been wicked and have made the people wicked, and have killed your brothers who were better than you are, I will send many troubles upon you. You will become sick with a terrible sickness.' "

Then the Lord sent the Philistine and Arab armies to attack King Jehoram and his people. They came to Jerusalem and plundered his palace of its riches and took away his wives and his sons as captives, so that not one of his sons was left except Ahaziah, the youngest. After all this, the Lord sent a dreadful disease upon him, just as Elijah had said. He was sick for two years, and grew worse and worse, for he couldn't be cured. Finally he died in the eighth year of his reign. But the people didn't mourn for him. He was buried in Jerusalem, but not where the other kings of Judah were buried. Then his son Ahaziah became king instead.

Ahaziah reigned only one year. Like his father, he was a very bad man; for his mother, who was the daughter of wicked King Ahab, taught him to sin.

One day King Ahaziah went to visit King Jehoram of Israel, at Jezreel. While he was there, Jehu attacked King Jehoram and killed him. We have already read about this, how Jehu drew a bow with all his might, and shot an arrow at King Jehoram that went into his heart, and the king fell down dead. King Ahaziah tried to help King Jehoram, and so Jehu told his men to kill him, too, and they did. Afterwards, the servants of King Ahaziah brought his body in a chariot to Jerusalem, and buried him there, in the graves of the kings.

QUESTIONS

What happened to King Jehoram because he didn't love God?

What happened when King Ahaziah went to visit King Jehoram of Israel?

119

A Little Boy Becomes a King

When Ahaziah's evil mother, Athaliah, heard that her son was dead, she killed his sons (who were her own grandchildren), so that she could be the queen. But one of his sons, a little boy named Joash, was hidden from her in the Temple, along with his nurse, for six years. Jehoiada the High Priest, and his wife, who was the little boy's aunt, took care of him, and in all that time Queen Athaliah never found out that he was still alive. But after six years Jehoiada showed the little prince to the Levites, and said that it was time to crown him as the king of Judah.

They talked it over secretly and made their plans. There were in the Temple some spears and shields that had belonged to King David. The priests gave these to the Levites. And when the agreed-upon day arrived, the Levites came to the Temple and kept guard all around it with these spears in their hands, to keep everyone out who might make trouble. Then they brought out little Joash, who was now seven years old, from the room where he had been kept hidden, and they anointed him as king of Judah by pouring olive oil upon his head, and then crowning him. Then they all clapped and shouted, "God save the king!"

When the queen heard all the noise and shouting, she ran to the Temple to see what was happening, and saw the little king standing there by a pillar with the crown on his head. The leaders of the nation stood beside him and all the people rejoiced and blew trumpets, and the singers in the Temple sang, accompanied by the royal band and orchestra. The queen ran in shrieking, "Treason! treason!" The High Priest told the Levites to take her outside, for she must not be killed in the house of the Lord. So they dragged and pushed her over to the stable of the king's palace, and killed her there.

Afterwards, the High Priest made an agreement with King Joash and all the people that they would obey the Lord. For the queen had worshipped an idol called Baal, and had built a temple with images of the idol in it, but she had let the Temple of the Lord fall into ruin and decay. She had stolen the sacred vessels of gold and silver from the Temple of the Lord and had put them into the temple of Baal. But now that the queen was dead, all the people went to Baal's temple and tore it down, and broke the altars and idols, and killed the priests of Baal. Then Jehoiada directed the priests of the Lord and the Levites to go to the Temple of God and to begin worshipping God again. He put guards at the gates so that no one could go in to rob or wreck it.

When Joash grew older he decided to repair the Temple of the Lord, for it was in very poor condition. He called the priests and Levites and said, "Go into all the cities of Judah and collect money from the people to repair the Temple of the Lord. And see that you hurry." But the Levites didn't get started on this project for a long time. Finally the king sent for Jehoiada the High Priest and asked him, "Why don't the Levites collect the money and repair the house of the Lord?"

Then Jehoiada took a chest and bored a hole in its lid and set it at the door of the Temple. Word was sent throughout the nation that everyone coming to the Temple should bring some money as an offering to the Lord. Everyone was happy to do this and brought the money willingly and dropped it into the chest. Whenever the chest was full, the High Priest and the king's treasurer came and emptied it out and counted it, and put it in bags, and gave it to the men who were in charge of the carpenters, masons, and builders.

After all the repairs were finished, the money left over was brought to the king and to Jehoiada. They used it to make gold and silver spoons and bowls for the Temple, replacing those that had been taken to the heathen temple by Athaliah.

Jehoiada arranged for sacrifices to be offered at the Temple every day, and persuaded the king to obey the Lord. For although Joash had wanted to repair the Temple, he didn't really love God in his heart. Yet as long as Jehoiada lived to advise him, he did what was right. But Jehoiada finally died at the age of 130 and was buried in Jerusalem in the graves of the kings, because he had done so much good for the nation. He had not only obeyed the Lord himself, but had taught the people to obey Him, too.

But the nation's leaders were wicked men; for although they had worshipped at the Temple while Jehoiada was alive, it was only because Jehoiada had persuaded the king to worship there, and they had to go to the Temple with him. But as soon as Jehoiada was dead they told the king they didn't want to worship God anymore, and the king, whose own heart was wicked, gave them permission to stay away from the Temple. Then they went and worshipped idols instead.

QUESTIONS

Why was Joash hidden in the Temple for six years?
How old was Joash when he became the king?
How did Jehoiada collect money to repair the Temple?
Who encouraged Joash to obey the Lord?
What happened when Jehoiada died?

Queen Athaliah murdered her own grandchildren so she could rule Judah. Only little Joash escaped and was hidden by the High Priest until he was old enough to be king. Then the wicked queen was executed.

R. Hook

120
God's Temple Is Robbed

When Zechariah the priest, Jehoiada's son, saw the wickedness of the people and their leaders, he spoke up to them. "Why do you disobey the commandments of the Lord?" he demanded. "You will bring great trouble upon the land. For you cannot prosper when you disobey God."

King Joash was angry with Zechariah for saying this, and issued orders to kill him. So he was killed with large stones being thrown upon him in the court of the Temple. Joash forgot about the kindness of Zechariah's father, who had protected him as a child and made him the king.

As Zechariah was dying, he said to the people, "The Lord will see what you have done, and will punish you for it."

What Zechariah said came true; for at the end of the year the Syrians attacked Judah. They came into Jerusalem, killed the political leaders, and took their silver and gold and sent it to their king at Damascus. He had sent only a small part of his army against Jerusalem, but the Lord gave them the victory over the huge army of Judah because the men of Judah had stopped obeying God. So the Lord punished King Joash and the people for their sins. A terrible sickness now came upon King Joash, and after the Syrians were gone, his own people rebelled against him and killed him as he lay in his bed. He was buried in Jerusalem, but not in the graves of the kings. He had reigned forty years at the time of his death. Then his son Amaziah became the new king.

Amaziah mobilized a vast army of 300,000, all armed with spears and shields, and hired 100,000 other brave, strong soldiers from the kingdom of Israel, to join his men in a war against the Edomites.

But a prophet came to him and said, "O king, don't let the men from Israel go with you to the battle, for the Lord is not with them. If they go with you, God will not help you; for God has power to help you against your enemies or to give them the victory instead."

Amaziah said to the prophet, "But I have already paid them $200,000!"

"The Lord is able to give you back much more than this, if you will trust in Him," the prophet replied. Then

Amaziah obeyed the command of the Lord, and sent the men of Israel back to their homes. They left in great anger because they couldn't go to war with the men of Judah and Benjamin.

Amaziah now led his army against the Edomites, and the Lord gave him the victory. But when he came back from the battle he brought with him the idols of the men of Edom, and set them up to be his gods! The Lord again sent a prophet to him. "Did those idols help the Edomites when you fought against them?" the prophet demanded.

But Amaziah was angry with the prophet, and said to him, "Who are you to interfere and tell me what to do? Be quiet or you'll be sorry."

Then the prophet said, "I know that God has determined to destroy you because you have done this wicked thing, and because you will not stop despite His warning."

King Amaziah of Judah now sent this message to the king of Israel: "Come with your army and let us fight each other."

But the king of Israel said, "Just because you have beaten the Edomites, don't be so proud and ready to boast. Stay at home. Why should you meddle with me, and bring trouble on yourself and all the people of Judah?"

But Amaziah wouldn't listen, because the Lord meant to punish him and the people of Judah for worshipping the idols of Edom.

So King Amaziah went with his army to attack Israel, and the king of Israel came out to stop him. But then King Amaziah's army panicked and ran away! The king of Israel captured King Amaziah and took him back to Jerusalem where he broke down the walls of the city. Then he went into the Temple and took the gold and silver bowls that were there, and the treasures from the king's palace, and carried away some of the people as captives to his own city of Samaria. Later the people of Jerusalem rebelled against King Amaziah and killed him as he tried to escape from them. They brought his body to Jerusalem, and buried him there. He had been the king of Judah for twenty-nine years.

QUESTIONS

Why did King Joash have Zechariah killed?

How did God punish Judah for its sins this time?

121
Isaiah Tells the Future

After King Amaziah's death his 16-year-old son, Uzziah, became the new king. At first he did what was right; for he had a good and wise counsellor named Zechariah whose advice he followed, and as long as he did right the Lord caused him to prosper. He owned a great many cattle, and many wells. He loved to sow grain and plant vineyards, and he had many farmers working his fields for him.

There were 370,000 men in his army, all armed with shields, spears, helmets, bows, and slings. He built war machines to shoot arrows and stones from the walls against his ememies. These "cannons" were mounted on the walls of the city of Jerusalem. And God helped him in fighting against the Philistines so that he conquered many of their cities. The Ammonites brought him gifts, and his name was known and feared in many nations.

But that made him proud, and he began to disobey the Lord; for he went into the Temple where only the priests were allowed to go, and took a censer in his hand to burn incense on the golden altar. Then Azariah the High Priest and eighty other priests went in after him, and told him "Get out! You have no right to burn incense to the Lord; only the priests, the descendants of Aaron, may do that. Leave at once, for you have sinned! The Lord may punish you for doing this."

But instead of being afraid and hurrying outside, Uzziah was angry with the priests for talking to him like that. Then, suddenly the dread disease of leprosy appeared upon his forehead; and the priests saw it there as he stood beside the gold altar. Then they took hold of him and pushed him out of the Temple. Now he himself hurried to get away because the Lord had sent this punishment upon him.

The king never got well, but was a leper until his death. He had to live in a house by himself because God had said that no leper should live with the rest of the people. His son Jotham ruled the land in his place. King Uzziah died at the age of fifty-two and was buried in Jerusalem. Then Jotham became the king.

Jotham was twenty-five years old when he began to reign, and he reigned sixteen years, in Jerusalem. He built cities in the mountains of Judah, and built castles and towers in the forests. He fought the Ammonites, and made them his servants. Each year they paid him thousands of dollars in money, wheat, and barley. And he became very great because he always tried to please the Lord.

But though he himself worshipped the Lord, his people were wicked; so God sent Isaiah the prophet to warn them. Isaiah came and told them that they were more stupid than animals, for animals appreciate their owners who feed and care for them, but the people of Israel didn't pay any attention to the Lord, even though He gave them every good thing they had. The land was full of idols, and the people worshipped them idols the people had made with their own hands from pieces of wood! The Lord asked them why they bothered to offer Him sacrifices at the Temple when they worshipped idols afterwards, thus disobeying all of God's commands? He didn't want their sacrifices any longer, He said. And when they prayed to Him, He wouldn't listen to their prayers. But if they would only stop doing wrong and learn to do good, then He would forgive them and bless them.

But the people didn't pay any attention, for their religious and political leaders were mostly wicked men. The Lord was very angry with them because of their sins, Isaiah said, so He would call their enemies from far-off countries to come and conquer them. These enemies would be fierce as lions, and no one could stop them. The people of Judah would be taken away to distant lands as captives. Their land would be left lonely and desolate, covered with briars and thorns, their cities empty and deserted, with Jerusalem and the Temple destroyed. But after many years, Isaiah said, the cities would be rebuilt, for the Lord would raise up a great king, named Cyrus, who would command that the city and the Temple should be built again.

Isaiah told the people many other things about the future. He said that Jesus would be born in the family line of King David, and that He would grow up to have sorrow and suffering and afterwards be put to death for the people's sins. Isaiah told about these things 700 years before they happened, for he was a prophet and God told him about future events. He told about John the Baptist, too, saying that someone else would come before the Saviour did, to preach out in the wilderness, telling everyone to get ready to receive the Saviour by turning from sin.

But the people of Judah wouldn't listen to the preaching of Isaiah, so God took away their good king from them when Jotham died. Then his son Ahaz became their king instead.

QUESTIONS

Where did King Uzziah go that he shouldn't have?

What disease did Uzziah get as a punishment? Where did he have to live?

Who was Isaiah?

Can you remember some of the important things Isaiah told the people of Judah about the future?

122

King Ahaz Closes the Temple

Ahaz was twenty years old when he began to reign. But he didn't obey God as his father had done, but worshipped idols instead. He even sacrificed his little sons as burnt offerings to the idols, just as the heathens did to their children. So the Lord sent the kings of Syria and Israel against him.

They came and attacked Jerusalem and took away many of the people as captives to the city of Damascus.

The king of Israel now fought against Judah, too, and killed 120,000 of the army of Judah in one day. He sent great numbers of women and children far away to another land.

But it was not only the kings of Syria and Israel who declared war against Judah, but the Edomites and Philistines too. Then the king of Judah took some of the silver and gold from the Temple and some of the treasures from his own palace, and sent them to Tiglath, king of Assyria, to hire his army to fight against the enemies of Judah. King Tiglath accepted the present and did as King Ahaz asked him to: he fought against the Syrians, and took the city of Damascus from them. But it did Ahaz little good, for the Lord was against him because he had sacrificed his sons to the idols.

King Ahaz went to Damascus to congratulate King Tiglath on his victory. While there, Ahaz saw an idol altar that greatly pleased him because of its unusual design. He sent its pattern to the High Priest in Jerusalem, commanding him to make one just like it. The High Priest did, and put the altar in the court of the Temple of the Lord. When Ahaz returned to Jerusalem, he went there to the Temple to offer sacrifices on it. He even took away the altar of the Lord from its place in the court to make room for the idol altar.

After this Ahaz became even more wicked. For he broke up and destroyed the Temple wash tanks, placed there by King Solomon hundreds of years before, and took down the great

King Ahaz led the people of Judah away from God. He even closed up the Temple so that the worship of God would stop.

R. Hook

brass basin resting on the backs of the twelve oxen, and set it on the pavement of the court instead. He also cut apart the sacred bowls of gold and silver, and boarded up the Temple so that no one could go there to worship. But he placed idols all over Jerusalem, and not only in Jerusalem but in every city throughout the land. So the Lord was very angry with Ahaz and the people of Judah because of all their wickedness.

Ahaz was king for sixteen years, then died and was buried in Jerusalem, but not in the graves of the kings. Then his son Hezekiah became king instead.

Hezekiah did what was right and followed the Lord. As soon as he became king he reopened the Temple, which his father Ahaz had closed, and called back the priests and Levites, who had been sent away from the Temple by his father. He ordered them to put everything back in order so that the people could come and worship God again.

"It was wrong for my father to close the Temple," he said. "That is why the Lord has been angry with us and has sent us all the trouble and shame that have come upon us. Our men have been killed by our enemies and our sons and daughters have been led away as slaves by our enemies because of all the wicked things we have done. But now I want to make a promise to the Lord that I will obey Him, so that He will not be angry with us any more. You priests and Levites, hurry and get the Temple of the Lord ready for use."

Then the priests went to work and after fifteen days of hard labor they came back and reported to the king, "It's all finished! All the cleaning has been done, the altar is ready for use, and we have brought back the gold and silver bowls taken away by Ahaz. Everything is ready."

Then King Hezekiah got up early the next morning, and went up to the Temple with the leaders of Jerusalem. They took with them seven young bulls, seven rams, seven lambs and seven goats. Hezekiah commanded the priests to kill and burn them on the altar as a sacrifice to God for all their sins. He also organized a great choir and orchestra from among the priests and Levites to sing praises to the Lord. As the offering began to burn on the altar, the people began to sing praise to God, accompanied by music from the cymbals, harps, and trumpets. So all the people worshipped, and the singers sang, and the trumpets sounded, until the burnt offering was finished.

After the king and the leaders had sacrificed, King Hezekiah invited the people to bring their offerings. They brought 70 young bulls, 100 rams, and 200 lambs, and the priests offered these for the people's sins. The king was glad, and so were all the people, because the Lord had caused everyone to want to bring offerings to God, and because the Temple was open again and the Lord was being worshipped.

QUESTIONS

Did King Ahaz respect God's Temple? What did he do to it?

Was King Hezekiah like his father?

What good thing did King Hezekiah do?

123
A Holiday in Judah

King Hezekiah now wrote a letter to all of his people in Judah, and also to the people of the land of Israel, asking them to come to Jerusalem and to celebrate the feast of the Passover. For it had been many years since the people had celebrated it as the Lord wanted them to. So messengers went out among the people carrying this letter from the king:

"My dear people: You have been disobeying the Lord, but return now to Him and obey Him. Then He will return to you and bless you. Don't be like your fathers and your brothers who went on sinning against God and were taken away as captives because of their sins. But obey His commandments and come to His Temple and worship Him so that He will stop being angry with you. If you do this, then God will be kind to those who have been taken captive, and will make their enemies kind to them, and allow them to come back to us again."

The messengers carried the king's letters throughout the whole country of Judah and Benjamin, but when they came to the land of Israel, the men of the ten tribes wouldn't listen to them, but mocked and laughed at them. However a few confessed their sins and were sorry for them, and came to Jerusalem.

But in the land of Judah, the Lord made all the people want to come. So there was a great crowd in Jerusalem to celebrate the feast. Before beginning it, they fanned out through the city and knocked down all the idol altars and threw them into Kidron Brook.

Then the Passover festival began. Each father brought a lamb to the Temple, where it was killed before the altar. Afterwards, he took it home to roast it, and he and his family ate it that night as the people of Israel did on the night they came out of Egypt. The Lord wanted the people to remember that night in Egypt, and how He had saved them from Pharaoh and the cruel Egyptians. That is why He had commanded them to celebrate this Passover festival each year. But they had stopped doing this long before. That is why Hezekiah called them to come to Jerusalem to begin to obey the Lord again, so that He would be pleased with them and bless them.

They celebrated happily for seven days. The priests and Levites sang praises to God every day, playing on harps and trumpets. And the Levites went out among the people and taught them the law of the Lord so that they would know what He wanted them to do.

At the end of those seven days of celebrating, they all agreed on seven more days of praising God. King Hezekiah and the leaders gave them a vast number of cattle for sacrifices—2,000 young bulls, and 17,000 sheep. So all the people of Judah, with the priests and Levites and the men who had come from Israel, were filled with joy. Since the times of Solomon there had never been such a wonderful time in Jerusalem.

When the celebration finally ended, the people went out to the cities of Israel and Judah and broke up all the idols, and destroyed the altars where the idols were worshipped.

Afterwards, King Hezekiah set up a schedule for the different groups of priests and Levites to take turns in assisting the people to worship the Lord at the Temple. He organized morning and evening sacrifices, and special sacrifices on the Sabbath and on feast days. The king told the people to bring to the Temple a tenth of all their crops so that the priests and Levites would have enough to eat, just as Moses had commanded; for the people had not done this for a long time. Now they obeyed the king, and so did many who lived in the land of Israel, bringing their gifts to the priests.

When the king and the leaders came to the Temple and saw the great heaps of food brought in by the people, they thanked the Lord for making them want to bring so much.

QUESTIONS

What was the Passover? Can you remember about the first Passover when the Israelis left Egypt? Tell about it.

After the celebration, what happened to the idols?

Why was everybody so happy?

124
God's Angel and the Enemy

The king of Assyria and his army now invaded the land of Judah again, and conquered some of its cities. When King Hezekiah of Judah learned that the invading army was on its way toward Jerusalem, he quickly repaired the walls of the city and set the people to work making huge quantities of shields and darts. He told his army, "Be strong and brave. Don't be afraid of the king of Assyria or his mighty army, for there are more on our side than on his! For we have God fighting for us!"

But for all his brave words, King Hezekiah was badly frightened, and sent great quantities of gold and silver to the invading Assyrian king, hoping he would accept these gifts and go away.

And that is just what happened. The king of Assyria took the gold and silver and returned to his own land. But afterwards, he came back!

On the way back he stopped at a city called Lachish to attack it, but sent some of his officers to Jerusalem to tell the people he was coming to destroy it. His messengers shouted up to the people watching from the top of the Jerusalem wall, "The king of Assyria says, 'Don't listen to King Hezekiah when he tells you he is able to fight against me, and that the Lord will save you from my power. Pay me more money and come and be my slaves. If you do, then I won't hurt you, but if you don't. . . ."

When Hezekiah heard what the messengers were saying, he tore his clothes and put on sackcloth, and went up to the Temple to pray to the Lord. And he sent messengers to Isaiah the prophet telling him what the king of Assyria had said, and asking him to pray for the people.

Then the prophet Isaiah sent back this message to King Hezekiah: "The Lord says, 'Don't be afraid of the words spoken against Me by the king of Assyria. For I will send a great punishment upon him, and he shall turn and go back to his own land, and there I will cause him to die.' "

So King Hezekiah refused to give up the city to the king of Assyria. But the king of Assyria sent his officers back again, this time with a letter to Hezekiah that said, "Don't let your god fool you into believing that I can't conquer Jerusalem. You know how the kings of Assyria have destroyed other nations. Their gods were not able to save them. Why do you think your god can do any better?"

When Hezekiah read the letter he was very much afraid. He took the letter to the Temple and spread it open there before the Lord. Then Hezekiah prayed and said, "O Lord, You are the only God. You made the heaven and the earth. Lord, look and see and hear the words spoken against You by the king of Assyria. What he says is true, that he has destroyed many another nation, and tossed their gods into the fire, for those gods were only lifeless idols made of wood and stone; so of course he was able to destroy them. But now, O Lord, he is planning to destroy Jerusalem. Please save us from him, so that all the kingdoms of the world will know that You are not like the idols of the heathen nations, but that You are the Lord, and that there is no other God besides You."

The Lord listened to this prayer of Hezekiah, and then told Isaiah the prophet to take this message to him: "The Lord says, 'I have heard your prayer and I will do as you asked. The king of Assyria shall not come here or build forts around this city, or shoot an arrow into it! He will go home! For I will save Jerusalem!' "

And what Isaiah said came true. That night the Lord sent His destroying angel into the camp of the Assyrians and killed 185,000 of them.

So the king of Assyria went back in shame to his own land. And while he was worshipping there in the house of his idol, two of his sons killed him. That is how the Lord saved Hezekiah and the people of Judah from the king of Assyria, and from all their enemies.

QUESTIONS

Why did King Hezekiah repair the walls?
What did he do with the letter?
Why did the prophet Isaiah tell King Hezekiah not to be afraid?
Did Hezekiah have to fight the Assyrians? What happened?

125
The Saviour Will Come!

In those days King Hezekiah became very sick from an infected boil, and the prophet Isaiah said to him, "The Lord says to get ready to die."

Then Hezekiah turned his face sadly to the wall and prayed, "O Lord, remember how I have tried to please You in all I do." Then he broke down and cried.

So the Lord told Isaiah to return to Hezekiah, and to tell him, "The Lord says, 'I have heard your prayer, and seen your tears, and I will make you well again. Three days from now you will be well enough to go to the Temple, and I will add fifteen years to your life!' " So Isaiah told this to the king. And he said to the king's assistants, "Take a lump of figs and lay it on the boil." And they did, and he was soon well again!

King Hezekiah became very rich and famous. He had great flocks, and herds of cattle, horses, and sheep. For the Lord helped him so that he prospered in everything he did.

But strange as it seems, Hezekiah did not stay humble and thankful to God for his blessings. He grew proud of his riches and power as though he had gotten these things by himself. Then the king of Babylon heard of his greatness, and sent messengers with letters and a present for him. When the messengers came to Jerusalem, Hezekiah was proud to have them visit him because they represented a great king, and he boasted to them about his great wealth and showed them his silver and gold, and his horses and armor, and all the wealth of his kingdom.

Then Isaiah the prophet came to Hezekiah and said, "What did these men say? And where did they come from?"

"They came from Babylon," Hezekiah replied.

"What have they seen in your palace?" Isaiah asked.

And Hezekiah answered, "Everything! There is nothing among my treasures that I haven't shown them."

Then Isaiah said, "Hear what the Lord says to you. 'After you die, all your wealth shall be carried to Babylon; nothing shall be left.' "

Hezekiah answered, "Whatever God does is right. At least there will be peace while I'm alive."

King Hezekiah had persuaded the people to put away their idols and to worship the Lord, but soon they began praying to idols again. God sent the prophet Micah to speak to them about this. He asked what God had done to them to make them weary of obeying Him? He had rescued them from being slaves to Pharoah, and had sent Moses and Aaron to guide them through the wilderness. And afterwards, when the king of Moab asked Balaam to curse them, God had made him bless them instead. Was it hard to serve the Lord? Is that why they didn't want Him any more? Hard in what way?

"All God requires," Micah said, "is for the people of Israel to be just and kind and merciful to each other, and to be humble and obedient to the Lord!"

But they refused to obey these simple rules. Their rich men were cruel to those who were poor. Their judges, instead of punishing the wicked, were wicked themselves. Scarcely any good men were left in the land. All were ready to rob and kill. Even friends couldn't trust each other any more. Brothers and sisters and even fathers and mothers were often enemies.

Micah told them that the Lord would send a great punishment upon them because of all this evil. It would be the terrible punishment of exile. That is, they would be sent far away as slaves to a distant country. And Jerusalem, their beautiful city, would be destroyed, leaving only heaps of stone. The Temple would be torn down and taken away, and the place where it stood would be plowed like a field.

Micah, like Isaiah, prophesied of the Saviour, telling where He would be born—it would be in the city of Bethlehem. (Not only Micah and Isaiah, but almost all the prophets told about Him hundreds of years before He was born. Because they predicted this, we who are living today can know the Saviour is the Son of God, just as the prophets said, and that God sent Him.)

Hezekiah was the king of Judah for twenty-nine years, then he died and was buried in Jerusalem in the best of the graves of the kings. His son Manasseh became the new king.

Manasseh was twelve years old when he became king. But he was a bad king and did many wicked things. For instance, he worshipped the sun, the moon, and the stars. And he built the idol altars again which his father Hezekiah had destroyed, and even set up an idol in the Temple of the Lord. He gave his little children as offerings to be burned up before his idols, and he talked with evil spirits although the Lord had strictly commanded the people of Israel never to do this. And he killed many innocent people who had done no wrong. So he was more wicked than the heathen nations of Canaan who lived there before the people of Israel arrived.

The Lord sent prophets to warn

King Hezekiah foolishly showed off his treasures to visitors from Babylon, and bragged about his wealth. Years later the visitors came back with an army and stole all the treasure and carried it away to Babylon.

Manasseh and his people to stop sinning, but they wouldn't listen. So the Lord sent the Assyrian army to capture King Manasseh, and they caught him as he was trying to hide from them in some bushes. They bound him with chains and took him to Babylon. When he was there far from home and in great sorrow, then he thought about his sins and finally was sorry for them. He prayed with all his heart to the Lord; and the Lord heard him and was kind to him and brought him back to Jerusalem.

Then Manasseh knew that the Lord was the only true God, and he took away the idol he had set up in the Temple, and tore down all the altars he had built in the courts around the Temple and threw them out of the city. He also repaired the altar of the Lord and presented sacrifices to God upon it.

Manasseh was king over Judah for fifty-three years, then died, and was buried in the garden of his palace in Jerusalem; and his son Ammon became king instead.

Ammon was twenty-two years old when he began to reign. But he was a bad king; for he offered sacrifices to all the gods his father Manasseh had worshipped. And he wasn't sorry afterwards and didn't destroy them as his father had, but went on sinning more and more. After he had been king for two years his people rebelled against him and killed him, and chose his son Josiah as their new king.

QUESTIONS

What was Hezekiah's prayer? How did God answer it?

Where did Micah say the Saviour would be born? Did this happen?

What made King Manasseh finally turn to God?

Was Manasseh's son, Ammon, a good king or a bad king?

126

Little King Josiah

Josiah was eight years old when he became king. He reigned thirty-one years and did what was right; for while he was yet a boy he began to serve the Lord. He went all through the land of Judah and destroyed the altars of Baal wherever he found them, and tore down the idols. He also travelled out among his people who were living in the land of Israel (for the ten tribes who had been living there were gone, having been captured and driven away), and did the same thing there. Then he returned to Jerusalem and set his men to work repairing the Temple, for it had fallen into disrepair. The people brought gifts of money to pay the workmen.

One day Josiah sent one of his officers to the High Priest to tell him to count the money the people brought, and then to give it to the carpenters, builders, and masons for repairing the Temple. As the officer was talking with the High Priest about these matters, the High Priest happened to remark to him, "I've found the book of Moses' laws! It was here in the Temple!"

Hundreds of years before this, Moses had written down the laws God had given him. He commanded that these laws must be read out loud to all the people every seven years. But the wicked kings and people of Judah hadn't cared to hear God's laws, and had let the book be lost and forgotten, so Josiah had never seen it before. But now while the Temple was being repaired the High Priest had found it again. He gave it to the king's officer, who took it to Josiah and read it to the king.

When King Josiah heard the words of God's laws, and learned about the punishments God said He would send on the people for not obeying, he tore his clothes and wept. He told the High Priest, "Go and ask the Lord whether He is going to punish us for our sins. For He must be very angry because we and our fathers have not obeyed the commands written in this book."

The High Priest went to a woman named Huldah, who was a prophetess, and asked her the king's question. "Yes," she replied, "the Lord says, 'I will send upon you all the punishments written in the book because you have turned away from worshipping Me and have worshipped other gods. But as for King Josiah who sent you, go and tell him, "Because you were grieved for the sins of the people, and have humbled yourself and wept before Me, I will not send the punishments now while you are living. You will not see all the evil that is going to come upon Jerusalem." ' "

Josiah immediately summoned to the Temple all the priests, the Levites, and the people, and read the book to them. Then the king made a covenant with the Lord and promised to obey His commandments with all his heart and soul. The people promised, too, that they would obey God's laws.

The wicked kings of Judah who lived before Josiah had made spoons, forks, and dishes to be used in offering sacrifices to Baal, and these were in the Temple of the Lord. An idol had even been placed inside the court of the Temple, and priests burned incense to it, and gave offerings to it. But now Josiah fired these bad priests and replaced them with the priests of the Lord and told them to clean out the Temple and to get rid of all the things used in worshipping idols, and to take them outside the city and burn them. Josiah punished all who talked with evil spirits, and tore down the idol Molech in the valley of Hinnom where the people used to burn children as sacrifices.

Then Josiah went to Bethel where, 300 years before, King Jeroboam of Israel had placed one of the gold calf-idols he had made. King Jeroboam had been burning incense to his calf-idol when a prophet came and told him that a king would be born in

Judah, named Josiah, who would defile his altar by burning men's bones on it. It had been more than 300 years since the prophet spoke those words, and of course Jeroboam had long been dead, yet now the prophet's words came true. For while King Josiah was at Bethel breaking the ancient idol-altar which was still there, he looked around and noticed burial caves nearby in the mountain. So he took some men's bones from the caves and burned them on the altar, just as the prophet had said.

We have already read about King Hezekiah's great celebration of the Passover after many, many years of neglect. But after he died, the Passover was again forgotten for a long, long time. But now Josiah called everyone to Jerusalem to celebrate it again. He gave the people 30,000 lambs and young goats, and 3,000 young bulls, so that everyone would have a sacrifice to offer. But although the people obeyed the command of the king and came to celebrate the feast, they didn't truly love God or sincerely worship Him, for in their hearts they still trusted in their idols.

The prophet Jeremiah reminded them of how God had brought them from slavery in Egypt and had given them this good land He had promised their fathers; but they hadn't thanked God nor obeyed His commandments. God had seen their wickedness and was angry with them, Jeremiah said. Yet if they would turn from their evil ways He would forgive them and not punish them. But the people wouldn't listen to Jeremiah. They weren't at all sorry for their wickedness, but sinned more and more. Even while Jeremiah was speaking to them they said, "Let's kill him." But God saved him from them.

Then the king of Egypt came with his army, and Josiah went out to fight him. But the Egyptian king sent a message that he was merely passing through on his way to make war against the king of Assyria, and he told Josiah to let him alone. But Josiah wouldn't turn back. He took off his royal robes and put on others so that no one would recognize him and went into the battle. There an arrow struck him.

"Get me out of here, for I am badly wounded," he said to his servant; and then he died.

They brought him in a chariot to Jerusalem and buried him in the graves of the kings, and everyone was sad. His son Jehoahaz now became the king of Judah instead.

QUESTIONS

How old was Josiah when he became king?
Where was the book of Moses' laws found? Who found it?
What did Josiah do when he heard the laws?
Could Josiah make his people love God?
How was Josiah killed?

127
Slavery!

Jehoahaz was twenty-two years old when he became the king, but he reigned only three months. He didn't do right as his father had, and the people disobeyed God. So Pharaoh, king of Egypt, came and attacked him and took him in chains to Egypt. There he remained until his death.

Pharaoh appointed Jehoiakim, the brother of Jehoahaz, to be the new king. Then he forced Jehoiakim and the people of Judah to pay him thousands of dollars in silver and gold. Afterwards, when Pharoah had gone away with all the money, the people of Judah faced a new danger. For now King Nebuchadnezzar of Babylon arrived to attack them. Nebuchadnezzar took some of the sacred vessels from the Temple and carried them to Babylon, and put them in the Temple of his idol there.

In the fourth year of Jehoiakim's reign, the Lord told the prophet Jeremiah to write down all the punishments that were still going to come upon the people of Israel. The Lord said that when the people heard about those punishments, perhaps they would turn to God so He could forgive them. Jeremiah dictated God's message to a good man named Baruch, and Baruch read it to the people at the Temple, and to the king and his officers. The king was sitting beside the fireplace, for it was winter. As soon as his officers read to him three or four pages of God's message, the king would use his penknife to slash the pages and throw them into the fire. Some of his men begged him not to do this, but he wouldn't listen; he wasn't afraid of God's punishments, he said. He was very angry with Jeremiah and Baruch for writing these messages, so he sent his guards to arrest them, but the Lord hid them.

Then the Lord said that because the king had burned up God's messages, Jeremiah must dictate it all again. So Baruch wrote it all down once more, and a lot more besides.

The people hated Jeremiah for telling them about their sins, and he complained to the Lord about it. "I have done them no harm," he said, "yet they all curse me."

Then the Lord promised that when the enemies of Jerusalem arrived to capture the city, they would not harm

Jeremiah. "I will make them treat you well," the Lord said.

Jehoiakim reigned eleven years, then died, and Jehoiachin his son became king instead.

Jehoiachin was eighteen years old at the time, but he reigned only three months, for King Nebuchadnezzar of Babylon came and defeated him. Nebuchadnezzar took away more of the golden bowls made by Solomon, and took away the treasures from the king's palace, and captured the king, his mother, his wives, the leaders of Judah, the builders, smiths, carpenters, and all the soldiers. He drove them all before him to far-off Babylon.

After they were gone the prophet Jeremiah wrote a letter to them, telling them to build houses and plant gardens and be content in that distant land of Babylon, because the Lord said they must stay there seventy years and serve the king of Babylon. But when the seventy years ended, and they had repented of their sins and prayed to be forgiven, then the Lord would bring them back again to their own land.

QUESTIONS

Why were the people of Judah punished so much?

What did Jeremiah and Baruch do?

What did the king do to Jeremiah's message?

How long did Jeremiah say the people would have to live in Babylon?

128

Jerusalem Is Burned

Nebuchadnezzar appointed Zedekiah, the brother of Jehoiakim, as the king of the people he left in the land of Israel. Zedekiah had to promise to obey Nebuchadnezzar, but after Nebuchadnezzar had gone back to Babylon, Zedekiah rebelled against him. So Nebuchadnezzar came back again with all of his army and made forts around Jerusalem, from which darts and arrows were shot at the men defending the walls, and everyone was kept from going in or out of the city.

Jeremiah was inside Jerusalem with the rest of the people. King Zedekiah begged him to pray that Jerusalem

When the Babylonian army conquered Judah, Nebuchadnezzar ordered his soldiers to burn the city of Jerusalem and the beautiful Temple of God.

would be saved. But the Lord told Jeremiah to tell the king that Nebuchadnezzar would capture the city and burn it. If the people would accept the punishment the Lord was sending upon them and would surrender to Nebuchadnezzar without fighting and be his slaves, they would not be killed. But if they refused to surrender they would die.

The Lord told Jeremiah to act out this message by wearing a wooden yoke on his shoulders. A yoke stands for service or slavery, so when the people saw Jeremiah wearing it, they understood that God was going to make them serve Nebuchadnezzar.

"Jerusalem will certainly be captured and burned," the Lord said. "This will punish the people for their sins."

Some of the leaders of Judah went to King Zedekiah and demanded that Jeremiah be killed for saying such things, because it discouraged and frightened the people.

"He says the Lord will send famine and plagues upon us, and will give the city to the king of Babylon," they told Zedekiah.

He told them to do as they liked with Jeremiah, so they put him into prison, and let him down by ropes into a deep well that was filled with mud at the bottom.

But one of the king's assistants went to the king and said, "My lord the king, these men are wicked to put Jeremiah into the dungeon, for he may die of hunger there."

Then the king told his assistant to take thirty men with him and get Jeremiah out. They took some pieces of old clothes and rags, and let these down into the dungeon on ropes. The king's assistant called down to Jeremiah and told him to put the rags beneath his arms, under the ropes, so that the ropes wouldn't hurt him when they pulled him up.

So they took him out of the well but they didn't set him free; he was still kept in another part of the prison.

Then King Zedekiah sent for Jeremiah again. He was brought to the Temple where he and the king could talk secretly. The king said, "I want to ask you a question; don't hide the truth from me."

Jeremiah answered, "If I tell you the truth will you promise not to have me killed?"

"Yes," the king replied, "I promise."

Then Jeremiah told him, "The Lord says, 'If you will surrender to the king of Babylon and be his slave, you and your family will be saved alive, and Jerusalem won't be burned.' "

The king replied, "I'm afraid that if I surrender to Nebuchadnezzar, he will give me to the men of Judah who have turned against me, and they will torture me."

"No," Jeremiah told him, "he won't do that. Don't be afraid, but obey the command of the Lord and all will be well, and you will be saved. But if you refuse to surrender to the king of Babylon, you and your wives and children will be captured by Nebuchadnezzar's army, and Jerusa-

Here is the prophet Jeremiah walking around wearing a heavy wooden yoke. This was God's way of teaching His people that they must surrender to Babylon and become Nebuchadnezzar's slaves.

lem will be burned."

But King Zedekiah wouldn't obey the command of the Lord to surrender. So King Nebuchadnezzar's army attacked Jerusalem for eighteen months. By that time the food was all gone; there was nothing left to eat.

One night Zedekiah fled from the city with his army, but he was caught and brought to the king of Babylon for trial. That cruel king killed Zedekiah's two sons before his eyes, then put out Zedekiah's eyes and bound him with chains and took him to Babylon, where he was kept in prison until he died.

Nebuchadnezzar's army burned the Temple and the palace and all the homes, and broke down the walls all around the city. They carried away to Babylon the two bronze pillars standing before the Temple, which Solomon had made; also the bronze tank that stood on the backs of the twelve bronze oxen in the court of the Temple; and the gold and silver bowls and other things. He took the people away as slaves, except some of the poorest who were left to work in the fields and vineyards. Gedaliah was chosen as their governor.

So the kingdom of Judah ended as the kingdom of Israel ended, because of the sins of the people. It had lasted 388 years—ever since Rehoboam was made king over the tribes of Judah and Benjamin. Nineteen kings and one queen had ruled over the people during that time. Of these, fifteen were wicked, and five obeyed the Lord. But even when there were good kings, the people often worshipped idols. And though the Lord waited long, and gave them time to repent, and sent His prophets to warn and persuade them, they wouldn't obey Him. So at last He sent them into exile far away to Babylon, as He had already done to the other ten tribes.

QUESTIONS

Did Jeremiah tell King Zedekiah to fight?

Tell about King Zedekiah's secret conversation with Jeremiah?

What happened to King Zedekiah? What happened to the kingdom of Judah?

The angry leaders of Judah put Jeremiah down into this deep well because he told them the truth about their sins. Later the king decided to rescue him from that dangerous place, and he was pulled up with a rope.

R. Hook

129
Judah Is Deserted

The Lord had promised that Jeremiah would be treated well when Nebuchadnezzar conquered Jerusalem. Now the Lord made this promise come true, for after the city was captured, the king of Babylon told the commander-in-chief of his army to be good to Jeremiah. "Don't harm him," he said, "and give him anything he wants."

So the commander took Jeremiah out of prison, where the men of Judah had left him, and told him, "If you want to come with me to Babylon, fine; I will take care of you; but if you would rather stay here, that will be all right. Do whatever you like—live anywhere you want to, come and go as you please."

The commander gave Jeremiah money and food. He decided to live with Gedaliah, the new governor of Judah, because he wanted to stay in the land.

Some of the Jews had escaped to other countries when Nebuchadnezzar captured Jerusalem. When they heard that Nebuchadnezzar had left some of the people in the land and had appointed Gedaliah as governor, they came back to the land of Judah to the city of Mizpeh, where Gedaliah lived. He couldn't live in Jerusalem, of course, because it had been destroyed.

Gedaliah encouraged them and said, "Don't be afraid to come back and live in your own land. If you will stay here and sow your fields and harvest your grain and serve the king of Babylon, you will be happy and all will go well with you." So the people came back and lived in the land.

Then some men came to Gedaliah and said, "The king of the Ammonites has sent Ishmael, one of the princes of Judah, to kill you."

One of these men spoke secretly to Gedaliah and said, "Let me go and kill Ishmael, and no one will know who did it! Why let him kill you and cause all the people left in the land to be scattered and destroyed?"

But Gedaliah wouldn't believe what the man said. "No," he said, "Leave him alone. I'm sure what you are telling me isn't true."

But it *was* true. A man named Ishmael came to Gedaliah's house, with ten other men pretending to be his friends. But after dinner they jumped up and killed him. Then Ishmael fled away into the land of the Ammonites.

All the people were afraid that the king of Babylon would come and punish them because Gedaliah had been killed. So they came to Jeremiah and begged him to ask the Lord to show them where to go and what to do.

"Yes," Jeremiah said, "I will pray for you, and whatever the Lord tells me, I will tell you; I will hide nothing from you."

Then they said to Jeremiah, "All that the Lord commands us, we will do, no matter whether we like what He says or not; we will obey the Lord."

So Jeremiah prayed and asked the Lord, and after ten days the Lord answered him, and told him what to say to the people. Then Jeremiah called the people together and told them, "The Lord says, 'If you stay here I will bless you. Don't be afraid of the king of Babylon, for I am with you and I will save you from harm; and I will make him kind to you. He will let you live here in your own land and won't take you far away to Babylon. But if you disobey Me and refuse to stay here, but go to Egypt to find food and peace, then the war and the famine you fear will follow you and kill you in Egypt. You will never again see your own land.' "

Then all the proud and wicked men among them answered Jeremiah, "You lie! The Lord didn't say for us to stay here and not to go to Egypt! You just want us to stay here so Nebuchadnezzar can come and kill us or take us away as captives to Babylon."

So they wouldn't obey the commandment of the Lord, but went to Egypt and forced Jeremiah to go with them.

Then the words came true that the prophet Isaiah had spoken more than a hundred years before: "The land of Judah shall be left lonely and desolate, overgrown with briars and thorns, and filled with abandoned houses."

Even after the Jews had been taken away to Babylon as captives, they refused to obey the Lord. Jeremiah the prophet wrote them a letter telling them to be loyal citizens of Babylon, and to be content, because they would stay there for seventy years. But instead of doing as Jeremiah told them, they complained and wanted to come back home to Jerusalem.

QUESTIONS

Did Jeremiah go to Babylon or stay in the land of Judah?

What happened to Gedaliah, the governor of Judah?

Did the people believe Jeremiah when he told them not to go to Egypt? What did they do?

130
Ezekiel's Strange Visions

Among the Jews taken away to Babylon, before Jerusalem was finally destroyed, was a priest named Ezekiel. One day Ezekiel had a strange vision or dream. He saw a whirlwind and a cloud, and in the cloud were four angels beneath God's throne in heaven. On the throne was what looked like a man made of fire, surrounded by bright colors like a rainbow. It was the glory of the Lord that Ezekiel saw, and he fell face downward to the ground in worship.

Then the Lord told him to warn the other Jews who were with him in captivity, to obey God. "Give them My messages whether or not they will listen," the Lord told him. "Don't be afraid of them even though they seem as dangerous as poisonous snakes! I will make you strong and brave when you stand before them, so that you can tell them everything I want you to."

Then the Lord told Ezekiel to prepare an object lesson for the people still living in Jerusalem, to show them what was going to happen to their city. "Get a flat tile and draw a map of Jerusalem on it," God told him, "and put this tile on the ground with an iron pan in front of it to protect it like a wall. In front of the pan build a little fort. Now lie down on the ground on your side, facing the map, and stay there many, many days without moving. Eat only a little coarse bread each day, and drink only a little water."

Ezekiel was showing what would happen to Jerusalem: Nebuchadnezzar would attack it with his army and build forts around it, and besiege it for many days. When the people saw Ezekiel eating only a little coarse bread every day, and drinking only a little water, they would know that the Jews in Jerusalem were going to suffer from famine. They would have hardly enough food and water to keep them from starving because the army of Nebuchadnezzar would be fighting against them.

After this the Lord commanded Ezekiel to take a razor and shave off all of his hair and his beard. Then he was to weigh the hair into three equal parts. One part was to be burned, one part cut into small pieces with a knife, and one part to be held in his hand until the wind blew it away.

The Lord told Ezekiel that this

was an illustration of how the nation of Israel would be destroyed. The Lord had chosen Israel as His people, yet they had sinned against Him more than any other nation in the world. Now He was going to punish them as He had never punished any other nation before. A third of them, like the hair Ezekiel burned, would die from sickness and famine; a third, like the hair he cut to pieces with a knife, would be killed by their enemies outside the city; and a third, like the hair Ezekiel held out in his hand for the wind to blow away, would be carried away from their own land and scattered over all the earth.

Then Ezekiel had another vision. He seemed to see the Lord sitting on a throne in a cloud, and a hand seemed to reach out and take hold of his hair and lift him into the sky, and carry him away to the gate of the Temple in Jerusalem. There the Lord said, "Look north!" Ezekiel looked, and saw an idol near the altar of burnt offering at the Temple. And the Lord asked him, "Do you see what the people of Israel have done, even putting an idol in this holy place? This sin against Me has caused Me to leave My Temple."

Then the Lord showed Ezekiel something worse yet. He brought him out to the court of the Temple, and when he looked, he saw a hole in the wall. The Lord said to him, "Dig into the wall." When Ezekiel had done this, he saw a door leading into a darkened room. The Lord said, "Go into the room and see the things that are done there."

So Ezekiel went in, and there on the walls around him he saw pictures of all the idols the people of Israel worshipped. Before these pictures stood the seventy elders of Israel burning incense to the idols. The Lord said to Ezekiel, "Do you see what the elders of Israel are doing? They are worshipping idols here in this darkened room. For they say, 'The Lord doesn't see us, He has gone away.' "

Then the Lord said to Ezekiel, "Now I will show you more of their sins." So He brought him to the inner court of the Temple, and there Ezekiel saw about twenty-five men bowing down to the sun and worshipping it.

And the Lord said to Ezekiel, "Do you see them? Is it a little thing for the men of Judah to do all the evil they are doing here? For they have filled the whole land with wickedness, and now they have come back to the Temple to sin against Me and make Me angry. Now I will punish them in My anger, and will not pity them; and though they cry out to Me in their suffering, I won't listen."

Then Ezekiel was again, in his vision, lifted into the sky and taken back to Babylon, the land of his captivity. He told the captives all he had seen in the vision, but they didn't believe what he told them; they still chose to believe the false prophets who said that the people in Jerusalem would not be punished, and that their city would not be destroyed by king Nebuchadnezzar.

QUESTIONS

Whom did God choose to be his messenger in Babylon?

What did it mean when Ezekiel ate and drank only a little each day?

Why did God tell Ezekiel to shave off all his hair and beard?

Where did God take Ezekiel in his vision? What did he see at the Temple?

131
God's Messages

Now the Lord told Ezekiel to act out what was going to happen to the people of Jerusalem. He was to pretend that he was moving out of his home in the darkness of the night. He was to dig a hole through the back wall of his house, and to go out through the opening, carrying his things on his shoulder. He was to cover his face as if he didn't want anyone to recognize him.

So Ezekiel did. As the people watched, he packed his things and carried part of them out of his house and left them in another place. In the evening he dug through the wall and brought out more of his things, with his face covered.

The next morning the Lord said to him, "If anyone asks you what this means, tell them that terrible things will happen to King Zedekiah and his people in the land of Israel. When you moved things out of your house to another place, it was a picture of their being taken away as captives to other lands. King Zedekiah's officers will break through the wall of the city so that he can flee away in the night, carrying what he can on his shoulder, and he will cover his face to keep the enemy from recognizing him. But he will not escape; I will see to it that he is brought here to Babylon as a prisoner, to die here; but he won't see Babylon!"

The Lord meant that King Zedekiah wouldn't see the land of Babylon because King Nebuchadnezzer would blind him by gouging out his eyes before taking him there.

Then the Lord told Ezekiel to eat some bread and drink some water, trembling as he did it, like a person who was afraid of his enemies. For the people in Jerusalem and the land of Israel would tremble when their enemies came. Some of the Jewish captives came to Ezekiel and asked him, "Is there any way to be forgiven for our sins? Is there any way to keep from being punished?"

Ezekiel answered them, "Yes, be sorry about the wrong things you have done and stop being bad. For the Lord says, 'I certainly have no pleasure in punishing the wicked. I only want them to turn from their badness and live. Turn, turn from your evil ways; for why will you die, O people of Israel?' "

Then one day the Lord told Ezekiel

to mark that day on his calendar. "Today," He said, "the king of Babylon has begun his attack on Jerusalem." Ezekiel was hundreds of miles away from Jerusalem and there were no newspapers or TV in those days, but Ezekiel knew what was happening that day far away in Jerusalem, because God told him.

Three years later Jerusalem surrendered. A man who escaped brought word of its fall to the Jews in Babylon. Then everyone knew that Ezekiel had told them the truth when he said the Lord had abandoned Jerusalem; and everyone now realized that the false prophets had lied when they kept saying that Israel would not be punished for its sins, and that Jerusalem would not be conquered by the king of Babylon. The king of Babylon not only conquered Jerusalem, but broke down its walls, burned the houses, the palace, and the Temple, and took away King Zedekiah and put out his eyes, and brought him and his people to Babylon. The whole land was left lonely and desolate.

And yet, although the Lord had sent all these troubles upon the people of Israel, His purpose wasn't to destroy them, but only to punish them so that they would be sorry for their sins and begin to worship Him again. Then He could bless them. He told Ezekiel to tell His people that the day was coming when He would search for them in every land where they were captives, just as a shepherd searches for his lost sheep, and that He would bring them back again to their own land.

QUESTIONS

Why did Ezekiel pretend that he was moving out of his home?

What did it mean when Ezekiel trembled?

How did Ezekiel, far away in Babylon, know when Nebuchadnezzar attacked Jerusalem for the second time?

Why did God have to keep on punishing the people of Israel?

132

Bones Become a Living Army

And now once more the Lord showed Ezekiel a vision. Ezekiel seemed to be out in a valley where the ground was covered with dead men's bones, old and dried. The Lord asked him, "Can these bones live again?"

Then the Lord told Ezekiel to say to the bones: "O dry bones, listen to the command of the Lord: flesh shall come upon you, and breath shall come into you, and you shall live!"

As soon as Ezekiel said this, a strange, rattling noise began as the bones moved and came together to form their skeletons. Then flesh grew upon them, and skin, until the bones were bodies again. But there was no breath in them; they were still dead.

Then the Lord told Ezekiel to say to the winds, "Come, O winds, and blow upon these dead bodies so that they will have breath and be alive." And when Ezekiel did this, the wind blew over the dead bodies and breath came into them; they breathed and were alive, and stood up, and were a great army!

Then the Lord explained to Ezekiel why he had shown him this vision, and what it meant. He told him that all the people of Israel complained because of their punishment and their trouble. They said they were like bones that were dry and dead, and that they had lost all hope of ever being happy, or of seeing their own land again. But the Lord said He would raise them up out of their troubles, as He had raised those dry bones to life, and that He would bring them back to their own land. When He had saved them from their misery and put His Spirit into their hearts and had brought them back to their own land again, then the people of Israel would know that it was the Lord who had given him this vision and made his words come true.

After this the Lord told Ezekiel to get two sticks and give each of them a name; one was to be named for the kingdom of Israel, and the other for the kingdom of Judah. He told Ezekiel to hold the two sticks close together, and they would grow into one stick in his hand.

When the people saw this strange miracle and asked him what it meant, Ezekiel answered them, "The Lord says, 'I will bring back the people of Israel to their own land, and they will not be divided into the two nations of Israel and Judah any more, but I will make them one nation. Neither shall they worship idols any more or be wicked; for I will put My Spirit into their hearts and make them holy, and they will be My people and I will be their God. They will live in the land where their fathers lived, and their children and their children's children will live there always. And I will be kind to them and give them a good king who will rule over them forever.' "

Jeremiah had told the people that they must stay as slaves in Babylon for seventy years, and then at last they could go back to Jerusalem. And this came true. After seventy years the Jews returned to their own country. But there they sinned more than ever, and made God more angry with them than ever before, because they crucified His Son. So He sent them out of Canaan again, and scattered them among all the nations as they are today. But some of them have now returned to the land of Israel, for God has let them come back home again once more.

Ezekiel told them that the time will come when they will want to worship God and will believe Him and obey Him and accept Him as their Saviour.

QUESTIONS

In Ezekiel's vision what happened to some old, dry bones?

What did this strange vision mean?

What happened after seventy years of exile in Babylon?

133
Daniel and a Dream

King Nebuchadnezzar of Babylon decided that he needed some new advisors, so he started a school to train some of the Israeli boys who had been captured at Jerusalem. He said that all the students at the school must be handsome, quick to learn, and in perfect health. He wanted them to learn everything there was to know. They would attend his school for three years, and then would work for the king as his advisors and government officials.

Among those chosen to go to school were four Jewish boys whose names were Daniel, Shadrach, Meshach, and Abednego. These young men had a problem: they loved God and wanted to obey Him, but the king didn't want them to. The king said that they should pray to idols before every meal and thank them for the food. But God said no. So what should they do?

Daniel and his three friends decided to ask the king for permission to eat other food, instead of food for which the idols had been thanked.

Daniel talked to one of his teachers about it. This man liked Daniel a lot, but he didn't dare give permission. "I'm afraid it will make the king angry," he said. "If he notices that you look paler and thinner than the young men who eat the food blessed by the idols, he will be angry with me and kill me."

"Please let us try it for just ten days," Daniel begged. "Give us only vegetables and water, and after ten days see if we don't look as well as the fellows who eat the other food. If we don't, then we will go ahead and eat the same as the others do."

The teacher finally agreed, and they were fed vegetables and water for ten days. At the end of that time they looked better and healthier than any of the others! So from then on they could eat whatever they wanted to. God helped them become wise, and he made Daniel able to understand the meaning of dreams.

At the end of their three years' training, the teachers brought them to the palace. There King Nebuchadnezzar talked with them and soon realized that these four Jewish boys were the best students of all! They always knew the right answers when the king was puzzled, and the king discovered that they were ten times smarter than the wisest men in his kingdom.

One night King Nebuchadnezzar

wakened from a dream and couldn't get back to sleep. So he summoned all his wise men, and they came and stood before him. "I had a dream that worries me," he said.

"Well," the wise men replied, "tell us the dream and we will tell you what it means."

But the king said, "I can't remember it! And if you won't tell me what I was dreaming about, and what it means, you will be killed and your houses torn down and made into piles of ruins. But if you tell me my dream and what it means, you'll be the richest, most honored men in the kingdom."

"But you have to tell us the dream before we can tell you what it means!" they protested. "Why, there isn't a man on earth who can tell a person what he dreamed about, and no king or ruler would even think of asking such a thing. Only the gods could tell you, and they don't live on earth."

Then the king was very angry and ordered all of them killed because they hadn't told him his dream!

Daniel and his three friends hadn't been summoned before the king, but they were among the wise men, so the king's death order for all the wise men meant that they would be killed too. But when a soldier came to kill them, Daniel asked what it was all about, and when he found out, he said to quit killing people and he would tell the king what he had dreamed!

Then Daniel went home and told his three friends to pray and ask God to show him what the king's dream was, so that they wouldn't be killed. And that night, in a vision, God showed the dream to Daniel.

Then Daniel praised God, and said, "I thank You and praise You, O God of my fathers, because You have heard our prayer, and have told me what the king wants to know."

Then Daniel went to the captain of the king's bodyguard and said to him, "Don't kill the wise men of Babylon, but take me to the king and I will tell him the meaning of his dream."

So the captain rushed Daniel before the king, and the king said to him, "Can you tell me my dream and its meaning?"

Daniel replied, "The wisest man on earth can't tell it to the king; but there is a God in heaven who tells secrets: and God has told me what your dream was, not because I am wiser than anyone else, but so that you will know that He is the true God. He has told you in your dream what will happen in the future."

Then Daniel told King Nebuchadnezzar his dream: "You saw a great statue of a cruel king, gleaming in the sunlight.

"Its head was made of gold, its chest and arms of silver, the rest of its body of brass; its legs were iron, and its feet were part iron and part clay. As you watched, a stone cut without hands from a mountain cliff struck the feet of the statue and shattered them. Then the statue crashed to the ground and the iron, the brass, the silver, the gold, and the clay were all broken small as dust, and the wind blew it all away. Afterwards, the stone that had broken the statue grew to be a great mountain and filled all the earth. That was your dream."

Then Daniel told the king what the dream meant:

The gold, silver, brass, iron, and clay meant different kingdoms. The head of gold meant Nebuchadnezzar himself, because God had given him the greatest of the kingdoms, making him greater than any other king in all the earth. But after he died, new world powers would rise, represented by the silver, brass, iron, and clay. And last of all, the Lord would set up one more kingdom which would never be destroyed. It would smash all the other kingdoms just as the stone cut from the mountain had broken the statue in Nebuchadnezzar's dream. This stone meant the kingdom of Christ that would someday come upon all the earth.

After Daniel told the king the dream and its meaning, the king threw himself to the ground in front of Daniel to show him deep respect, and said to him, "Your God is a God of gods and a King of kings and can tell secrets, for He has told you this dream."

Then the king made Daniel a great man and gave him many gifts and appointed him ruler over the province of Babylon, and he became the head of the wise men. And at Daniel's request, his three friends became rulers too.

QUESTIONS

Who were Daniel, Shadrach, Meshach, and Abednego?

Why didn't they want to eat the king's food?

What was King Nebuchadnezzar's dream? What did it mean?

How did the king honor Daniel and his friends?

134
Three Boys in a Furnace

King Nebuchadnezzar of Babylon now made a huge statue of gold and set it on a plain in the province of Babylon. Then he sent for all of his princes, governors, captains, judges, and all the other rulers of his kingdom to come and worship it. One of the king's assistants told them, "It is commanded that as soon as the band begins to play, you must fall down and worship Nebuchadnezzar's gold statue. If anyone refuses, he shall be thrown into a flaming furnace."

Then the king commanded the band to begin to play and instantly everyone fell down and worshipped the gold statue.

Daniel's three friends refused to do it, because they knew it was wrong to worship a statue. Then some of the Babylonians went to the king and complained to him about them.

"Didn't you make a law that everyone must fall down and worship the statue when the band begins to play, and that if anyone refuses, he will be tossed into a white-hot furnace?" they asked him. "Well, there are some Jews holding high political positions in your empire, and these men haven't

obeyed you; they don't worship your gods, and they refuse to bow to your gold statue. They are Shadrach, Meshach, and Abednego."

King Nebuchadnezzar was furious. He commanded that the three young men be arrested at once and brought to him. "Is it true, O Shadrach, Meshach, and Abednego," he shouted, "that you do not worship my gods, and refuse to bow to my gold statue? I'll give you one more chance. When you hear the band begin to play, *fall down and worship the statue,* or you will be thrown at once into a flaming furnace; and who is the god who will be able to save you from my anger?"

Then Shadrach, Meshach, and Abednego said to the king, "We won't do it! If you throw us into the furnace, our God is able to save us, and He will. But even if He doesn't, we will not worship your gods, sir, nor bow to your gold statue."

Nebuchadnezzar's fury became more fierce. "Heat the furnace seven times hotter than ever before!" he commanded his men. Then he called for the biggest soldiers in his army to tie up Shadrach, Meshach, and Abednego and throw them in. The furnace was so hot that the flames killed the soldiers, but after Shadrach, Meshach, and Abednego had fallen down into the fire inside the furnace, they got up again and walked around in the flames! For God wouldn't let them be burned. The only things that burned were the ropes they were tied with; these burned from their wrists!

King Nebuchadnezzar was surprised beyond belief when he saw the three boys walking around in the fire! "Didn't we throw three men into the fire, tied tightly with ropes?" he exclaimed. "And now there are four of them, loose and walking around in the fire! And the fourth looks like the Son of God!"

Nebuchadnezzar got as near as he could to the mouth of the furnace and shouted to them, "Shadrach, Meshach, and Abednego, you servants of the Most High God, come out!"

So out they came. The princes, governors, and captains crowded around them and could see that the fire hadn't hurt them a bit; not a hair of their heads was even singed, and they didn't even smell of smoke!

Then Nebuchadnezzar said, "Blessed be the God of Shadrach, Meshach, and Abednego, who has sent His angel and saved these young men who trusted in Him. Therefore I now make a law that anyone who says anything bad about the God of Shadrach, Meshach, and Abednego shall be destroyed, and his house shall be torn down and made into a heap, for there is no other God that can rescue people as their God can!" Then the king made Shadrach, Meshach, and Abednego even greater than they had been before.

QUESTIONS

What was Nebuchadnezzar's command?

What happened to Shadrach, Meshach, and Abednego in the furnace?

Who was the fourth person walking in the fire?

God is taking care of these three young men. They refused to bow down and worship the king's huge gold statue, because God told them not to. So the king tied them up and threw them into this fire. But who is the fourth man in there with them? It is an angel, or perhaps it is Jesus. He has come to help these brave men who were willing to die rather than disobey God.

135
The King Who Ate Grass

Babylon was a huge city with the Euphrates River running through the middle of it. Part of the city was on one side of the river, and part on the other. The walls of the city were sixty miles around, with 100 bronze gates and many high towers. King Nebuchadnezzar's palace was very large, and was ornamented with many statues of men and animals. It was filled with objects made from gold and silver, and with all sorts of beautiful things stolen from the nations he had conquered.

Near his palace were large gardens, called the Hanging Gardens. These were terraces on the sides of a hill, and were filled with lovely flower beds. Nebuchadnezzar made these gardens to please his wife, who had lived in a hilly country when she was young. But Babylon stood on a wide, level plain, and she longed for hills and woods like those in the land where she was born. So Nebuchadnezzar made this great hill for her! It was 400 feet high and was planted with trees, ornamental shrubs, and flowers. Steps led to the top, and water was pumped from the river to water the gardens. From a distance it looked like a mountain covered with woods.

Nebuchadnezzar was a mighty king, and his men flattered him by praising everything he did; so he soon forgot about God and thought only of his own riches and power. God was displeased with him because of this and sent a strange punishment upon him.

After it was all over, he told his people about it. This is what he said to them:

"I had conquered all my enemies and was enjoying life in my palace, with no worries at all. Then I had a dream that made me afraid. So I called together all the wise men of Babylon and told them the dream, but they couldn't tell me what it meant. At last I called for Daniel, who has the spirit of the holy gods with him; and I told him my dream. I said to him, 'I saw a very high tree standing in the center of a wide plain. The tree grew taller and taller until it reached to heaven, and its branches spread out to the ends of the earth. Its leaves were green, and it was filled with fruit. The animals rested beneath its shade, and birds nested in its branches, and everything that lived came to it for food.

" 'Then, in my dream, I saw an angel come down from heaven. "Chop down the tree," he shouted, "and cut off its branches; shake off its leaves and scatter its fruit. Let the animals get away from beneath it, and the birds from its branches. Yet leave the stump of the tree in the ground where the dew shall fall upon it for seven years." O Daniel, what does my dream mean?'

"At first Daniel was afraid to tell me, but I insisted, so finally Daniel told me:

" 'The giant tree you saw, with the animals resting in its shade and the birds nesting in its branches—that tree means you, O king. You have grown great and powerful, and your kingdom reaches to the ends of the earth. And you saw a holy angel coming down from heaven, saying, "Cut down the tree and destroy it, yet leave its stump in the ground, and let it be wet with dew. Let him wander with the wild animals of the field for seven years." This is what your vision means, O king: You will no longer be in your palace to be waited on by your servants, for they shall chase you out to live among the wild animals. You will eat grass like a cow, and sleep on the ground, and be wet with the dew, until you have learned that God rules over all the nations of the earth, and makes anyone He wishes be the king.'

"Everything came true just as Daniel said it would. Twelve months after this dream I was walking on the roof of my palace, and as I looked out upon the great city of Babylon with its high walls, temples, palaces, and gardens, my heart was filled with pride. I forgot that it was God who let me be the king, and I said, 'Is not this great Babylon that I have built by my own power and for my own honor and majesty?' While the words were still in my mouth, there came a voice from heaven, saying, 'O King Nebuchadnezzar, to you it is spoken—the kingdom is taken from you. You will be chased away from human society and will live with the wild animals and eat grass like a cow for seven years, until you know that God rules over all the nations of the earth and makes anyone He wants, to be the king.'

"That very hour I became insane, so that I was no longer fit to rule my kingdom. I was chased out into the fields to live, and ate grass like a cow and slept on the bare ground, and my body was wet with the dew until my hair grew long as eagles' feathers, and my nails were like birds' claws.

"But at the end of the seven years I looked up to heaven, and my reason came back to me. And now I praise God and honor Him who lives forever, and whose kingdom shall have no end. He does whatever He wills, in heaven and on earth, and no man can hold back His hand, or ask why He does anything. And when my reason came back to me, so did my honor and my kingdom. For the rulers and governors sought for me and I was made the king again, and all my greatness was given back to me. Now I, Nebuchadnezzar, praise and honor God, the King of heaven, who does only what is just and true; and He is able to bring down the proud to the dust."

QUESTIONS

What present did King Nebuchadnezzar give to his wife?

What was the king's dream about a tree? What did the dream mean?

What happened to Nebuchadnezzar when he became insane?

When he was well did Nebuchadnezzar believe in God? Why do you think so?

136
Handwriting on the Wall

After King Nebuchadnezzar died, King Belshazzar became the new ruler of Babylon.

One day Belshazzar invited a thousand of his political officers to a great party, where they all drank a great deal of wine. Then he commanded his servants to bring him the gold and silver bowls and dishes which his father Nebuchadnezzar had taken from the Temple in Jerusalem. When they were brought in, the king and his princes and his wives drank from them, and praised his idols.

Suddenly a hand appeared, writing words on the wall. But no one could read the writing, for it was in a different language. The king's face grew white with fear, and his knees trembled.

He screamed to his assistants to bring in the wise men, and said to them, "If you can read that writing on the wall and tell me what it means, I'll pay you a fortune." But none of the wise men could read or understand it.

The king was *really* worried by now, and his assistants didn't know what to do. But when the queen heard what was happening she came in before him and said, "O king, don't let this mystery trouble you. For there is a man in your kingdom who has within him the spirit of the holy gods. Your father Nebuchadnezzar discovered him and made him master of all the wise men of Babylon; for he has great knowledge and knows how to interpret dreams and predict the future. Call for this man, Daniel, and he will tell you what the writing says."

So Daniel was brought in before the king. "Are you the Daniel who was brought as a captive from the land of Judah?" the king asked him. "I have heard that the spirit of the gods is in you, and that you are very wise. My wise men can't read the writing over there on the wall, and I must know what it means. If you can tell me what it says, I'll make you very rich."

"Keep your gifts," Daniel replied, "but I will read it for you and tell you what it means. O king, the most high God gave your father Nebuchadnezzar a kingdom and glory and honor. And because God made him so great, all nations trembled and feared before him. He killed or kept alive anyone he wanted to.

"But when he became proud and forgot God, God made him come down from his throne and his greatness was taken from him. He was driven from his palace and became like an animal, and lived with the wild donkeys. He ate grass like the cows and his body was wet with dew, until he learned that God rules over the nations of the earth, and that God alone decides who shall rule in Babylon.

"But you, his son, have not humbled your heart, though you knew all this. You have been proud and have sinned against God. And you have sent for the bowls from the Temple of God, and you and your lords and your wives have drunk wine from them, while praising your idols that can't see, hear, or know anything at all. And you haven't praised the true God who lets you live, and gives you all you have. So, God has written these words: MENE, MENE, TEKEL, UPHARSIN. This is what the words mean: Your kingdom is ended; God has taken it from you. He tried you out as king, but you didn't obey Him. He has given your kingdom to the Medes and the Persians."

Then Belshazzar commanded his assistants to clothe Daniel with royal scarlet, and put a gold chain around his neck; and he appointed Daniel as the third ruler in the kingdom. But that same night the army of the Medes and Persians entered the city and killed King Belshazzar and took over the empire. Darius, the Mede, became the new emperor.

QUESTIONS

Tell about the frightening thing that happened at the king's party?
What did the words on the wall mean?
Did the words come true? What happened?

137
Daniel in the Lions' Den

Darius decided to divide the empire into 120 states ruled by 120 governors. Over these governors were three presidents, with Daniel as their chief because of the wise and good spirit that was in him. Darius was planning to make Daniel ruler over the entire empire. But when the other presidents and governors heard about it, they were jealous and tried to find something bad to say about him to the king. But they couldn't find a thing, for he was faithful to his duties and they couldn't point out a single fault.

Finally they decided, "We'll never be able to complain about Daniel to the king except possibly about his religion."

So they came to the king, and said, "King Darius, live forever! All the presidents and governors of your kingdom want a law made that any person who prays to anyone but you for the next thirty days shall be thrown into a den of lions. O king, make this law and sign it, so that even you can't change it." And King Darius signed the law.

When Daniel knew that the law was signed, he went home, opened the windows of his room toward Jerusalem, knelt, and prayed and gave thanks to God three times a day, just as he always had done before. Then the other presidents and governors got together and went over to Daniel's house and found him praying, and rushed back to the king and said, "Didn't you make a law that any person praying to anyone but you for thirty days must be thrown into the den of lions?"

"Yes," the king said, "I certainly did. It is now a law of the Medes and Persians which can never change."

Then they said, "That fellow Daniel isn't obeying you, O king, for he prays to his God three times a day!"

The king was crushed! Oh, why had he signed that law? He didn't want to punish Daniel. He tried every way he could to save him. But the presidents and the governors said to him, "You know perfectly well, O king, that no law the king has signed can be changed!"

So at last King Darius gave up, and Daniel was thrown into the den of lions. But first the king said to him, "O Daniel, your God whom you serve so faithfully will save you."

Then, after Daniel was thrown in, a great stone was rolled across the mouth of the lions' den so that no one could get Daniel out.

The king went home to his palace and refused to eat, and sent away the orchestra that played for him each evening. He was up very early the next morning and hurried out to the lions' den, and called sadly to Daniel: "O Daniel, servant of the living God, was this God of yours able to deliver you from the lions?"

Then Daniel called to the king, "O king, my God has sent His angel to shut the lions' mouths so that they haven't even scratched me!"

The king was overcome with joy and excitement and commanded that Daniel be taken out at once. So Daniel was unhurt because he trusted in his God.

And now the king ordered the men who accused Daniel to be thrown into the den of lions along with their children and their wives—and the lions leaped on them and killed them as soon as they fell to the bottom of the den.

Then King Darius wrote this letter to his people in all the nations of his empire: "I make a decree that in every part of my kingdom men tremble and

Daniel's enemies said that if he prayed to God, they would kill him by throwing him to the lions. But Daniel didn't care. He prayed anyway. And God closed the lions' fierce jaws and made them friendly!

fear before the God of Daniel. For He is the living God; His kingdom is the one that shall never be destroyed, and His power shall never end. He is the God who can save from danger—He saved Daniel from the lions."

So Daniel prospered in the reign of Darius, and also in the reign of Cyrus, who became king after Darius was dead.

While Daniel was in Babylon he read the book written by Jeremiah the prophet, and learned from it that the Jews would go back to their own land after seventy years of exile and captivity in Babylon where Daniel was living. Well, those seventy years were nearly ended! So Daniel fasted and prayed to the Lord asking that his people, the Jews, might return to the city of Jerusalem and build it again.

"O Lord," he said, "we have disobeyed Your laws and wouldn't listen to Your prophets when they told us of our sins. We and our kings and our leaders and all the people of Israel have disobeyed You. That is why this punishment of slavery came upon us. And now, O Lord who brought Your people out of Egypt long ago, please don't be angry with us anymore. O Lord, forgive us; hurry and help us. We don't ask this because we deserve to be forgiven, but because You are merciful."

Three weeks later, as Daniel was continuing to pray this prayer, the angel Gabriel arrived from God's presence in heaven. It was in the evening, about the time when the priests had offered a lamb for a burnt offering at the Temple in Jerusalem.

"O Daniel," the angel said, "I am here to tell you about the future. Three weeks ago at the beginning of your special prayers for Jerusalem, I was commanded to come to you, for you are greatly loved of God. Now listen carefully."

Then the angel told Daniel that the Jews would soon go back to their own land and rebuild Jerusalem, and that in 484 years the Saviour would be born! But, the angel said, the Saviour will be killed and his enemies will come again and destroy Jerusalem and the Temple.

QUESTIONS

Why did King Darius decide to make Daniel the ruler of his empire?

What law did Daniel refuse to obey?

Was Daniel hurt in the lions' den? Why not?

What did Daniel learn from reading Jeremiah's book? What more did the angel Gabriel tell him?

138
Many Jews Return to Israel

At long last the seventy years of captivity in Babylon ended, and the time came for the Jews to go back to their own land. Cyrus was king of the Babylonian empire at that time, and God made him willing to let the Jews go home again to Jerusalem. Then the words came true that were written long before by the prophet Isaiah, that God would raise up a great king named Cyrus who would send the Jews back to rebuild Jerusalem and the Temple again. It had been nearly 200 years since the prophet Isaiah had said this! Cyrus had not even been born when the prophet told what he would do! And the Jews were still in their own land and didn't think anyone would ever capture them. But God knew all that was going to happen, and He told His prophet to tell about these things long before they happened.

So King Cyrus made a law and sent this message all through his empire: "The Lord commanded me to rebuild His Temple in Jerusalem. Who among the captives from Judah wish to go back to their own land? Let them go now and rebuild the Temple of the Lord; and let those who don't go help those who do by giving them silver and gold and cattle and clothing to take with them."

Then the Jewish leaders, the priests, the Levites, and all those the Lord made willing, prepared to start off on their journey to Jerusalem, rich with all the gifts given them by those who didn't want to go. King Cyrus gave them the golden bowls taken from the Temple by Nebuchadnezzar long before. In all, there were 5,400 of these gold and silver bowls and goblets. King Cyrus entrusted them to Zerubbabel to take them safely to Jerusalem.

Of the people of Israel, 42,360 returned to Jerusalem at that time, along with their 7,337 servants. They had with them 736 horses, 245 mules, 435 camels, and 6,720 donkeys.

Upon their arrival at Jerusalem they found it in ruins, for the army of Nebuchadnezzar had demolished it seventy years before, and no one had touched it since. Jerusalem's walls and houses, and the Temple, had been broken down or burned.

The first thing the people did was

to rebuild the altar of the Lord in the court of the Temple, so that they could use it to worship God and to ask for His help; for they were afraid of the nations around them. They used the altar to offer burnt offerings to God every day—a lamb in the morning, and a lamb in the evening, just as the people of Israel used to do before they were taken away to Babylon as slaves.

Then they got ready to rebuild the Temple. They hired workmen from Tyre, as King Solomon had done hundreds of years before, to cut down cedar trees on Mount Lebanon, making rafts of them and floating them down the Mediterranean Sea to the shore near Jerusalem.

When the very first stones of the foundation of the new Temple were laid, the priests and Levites were so happy that they played on trumpets and cymbals and sang songs of praise to the Lord. Everyone was glad, and shouted with a great shout, because the rebuilding of the Temple had begun. But many of the old men, who remembered the beauty of the Temple that stood there before, couldn't keep back the tears of disappointment, because the new Temple wouldn't be nearly as nice. So the shouting and the crying mingled together, and were heard far away.

QUESTIONS

What did King Cyrus tell the captive Jews in his land to do? Why?

What did they find when they got to Jerusalem?

What did they rebuild first? Why?

Why were some people happy and some people sad when the new Temple was begun?

139
God's Temple Is Rebuilt

Do you remember that after the king of Assyria carried away the ten tribes of Israel as captives, he sent people from his own land to live in Israeli cities? These people, the Samaritans, worshipped idols, though they pretended to serve God. But now when they heard that the people of Judah had come back to their own land, and were rebuilding the Temple, they came to Zerubbabel and to the other Jewish leaders and said, "We want to help you, for we are servants of God just as you are; we have offered sacrifices to Him ever since the king of Assyria sent us to live here in the land of Israel."

But Zerubbabel, and Joshua the High Priest, and the Israeli leaders said, "No! We will build it ourselves, as Cyrus, king of Persia, has commanded us."

This made the Samaritans angry, and they did all they could to stop the Jews, and paid some men to tell the king of Persia that the Jews were disobeying him. Artaxerxes was now king of Persia, for King Cyrus had died.

They wrote this letter to him: "We want you to know, O king, that the Jews who came from Babylon are rebuilding the wicked city of Jerusalem. You should know that once they get the walls rebuilt, they will stop paying taxes to you, and will rebel against you. We don't want this to happen, so we suggest that you read up on the history of the city of Jerusalem, and see for yourself that it has always been a rebellious city, and has given much trouble to the kings who were before you; in fact, that is why Jerusalem was destroyed."

The king did as the Samaritans asked him to, and sent them this reply: "Thank you for your letter. I have checked into the matter and find that Jerusalem is, as you say, a very rebellious city that has always given us trouble. So tell the men of Judah to stop building the Temple until I give them permission."

Then the Samaritans hurried to Jerusalem and made the people stop building. So the work ended during the entire time Artaxerxes was king.

After Artaxerxes' death, Darius II became king. But although the Jews knew there was another king in Babylon, they didn't ask him for permission to start building the Temple again. For ever since the Samaritans had stopped them from building God's house, they had been building houses for themselves, and had become more interested in this than in finishing the Temple.

The Lord was displeased with them, and sent Haggai the prophet to tell them, "You say, 'It isn't yet time to rebuild the Temple!' Well, is it time for you to be living in beautiful houses while My Temple lies in ruins? It is because you have left it unbuilt, and have all hurried to build your own houses, that I have not blessed you; that is why you have not prospered and been happy. Go up to the mountains and cut timber and build the Temple, and I will be pleased with it."

Then the people obeyed the command of the Lord, and began to build it. But when the Samaritans heard about this, they came again to Zerubbabel and Joshua the High Priest, and said to them, "Who has commanded you to begin building the Temple again?"

Zerubbabel and Joshua answered them, "King Cyrus did. He sent us here with specific instructions to do this. And he gave us the gold and silver bowls which Nebuchadnezzar had taken out of the Temple. 'Carry them to Jerusalem,' King Cyrus told us, 'and build the Temple.' "

Then the Samaritans wrote a letter to King Darius II at Babylon, and told him what the people of Judah had said. And they asked the king to find out whether it was true that Cyrus had commanded them to build the Temple. When Darius read the letter, he told his aides to search in the books where all the decrees of the kings of Babylon were written down. And sure enough, one of the books had this note in it. "In the first year of the reign of King Cyrus, he made this decree: 'Let the people of the Lord rebuild the Temple at Jerusalem. Lay strong foundations. Get money from the king's treasury to buy whatever materials you need. And take to Jerusalem the gold and silver bowls which Nebuchadnezzar took from the Temple; place them in the new Temple when it is built.' "

As soon as King Darius II found this decree which Cyrus had made many years before, he sent word to the Samaritans to let the men of Judah build the Temple of the Lord, and not to disturb them.

And Darius said, "I make a decree that some of the taxes from the Samaritans shall be paid to the Jews so that they may go on building the Temple: and that young bulls, rams, and lambs be given them for burnt offerings; also wheat, salt, wine, oil and whatever else the priests need. Let these things be given them day after day without fail, so that they will pray for the king and his sons." Then King Darius added this: "Anyone who changes this law that I have made shall have the timber pulled out of his house and a gallows built from it, and he shall be hanged on the gallows. Then his house shall be torn down and made into heaps!"

When the Samaritans and their leaders heard this decree, they were frightened and stopped bothering the Jews, and gave them young bulls, rams, and lambs for burnt offerings, and also wheat, salt, wine, and oil, as the king commanded. So the men of Judah went on building the Temple until it was finished.

Then they dedicated it to the Lord and presented sacrifices to Him—100 young bulls, 200 rams, 400 lambs, and 12 goats. The people celebrated the feast of the Passover for seven days, rejoicing because the Lord had been so kind to them and because he had caused the king of Persia to help them finish the Temple.

QUESTIONS

Why did Artaxerxes make the Jews stop building the Temple?

What message did Haggai bring from God?

How did King Darius II help the Jews to finish rebuilding their Temple?

140
The King Helps Ezra

While Artaxerxes was the king of Persia, there was a Jew named Ezra who lived in Babylon with the other exiles from Jerusalem. Ezra was a good man who loved his people, and was very anxious for them to obey God so that He would give them His blessings. He asked King Artaxerxes to let him go to Jerusalem to teach God's laws to the Jews who were there, and to see that they obeyed them.

Artaxerxes gave Ezra permission to go, and gave him presents of gold and silver to take with him as gifts to God. And the king gave Ezra a letter which said, "I make a law that all the people of Israel who are still in Persia, and who want to go to Jerusalem, may go with Ezra. He is going to Jerusalem to find out whether the laws of God are being obeyed there, and to take the silver and gold which the king and his princes and the people of Babylon are donating to the God of Israel."

"And if you need more money," the king told Ezra, "get it out of my treasury. And I, Artaxerxes the king, command all the treasurers who have the care of my money in the provinces where Ezra is going, to give him, whenever he asks for it, as much as $200,000 plus 1,100 bushels of wheat, 900 gallons of wine, and as much salt as he wants. Help in every way possible to get God's Temple built so that God won't be angry with me and send some disaster upon my kingdom."

Then he said to Ezra, "When you get to Jerusalem, select mayors and other public officials to rule the people. Be sure that the men you choose know the laws of God, so that they can teach the people who don't. Anyone refusing to obey God's laws and my commandments is to be punished with whatever punishment he deserves—death, exile, heavy fines, or prison."

Ezra thanked God for the king's kind attitude toward him. Then he called together some of the leaders of the Jews in Babylon, and some of the priests and Levites, for a meeting on the shore of the Ahava River. They brought their tents and camped there three days. They ate nothing during the entire time, for they spent their time praying to the Lord and asking Him to direct their trip to Jerusalem and to protect them and their children and their money. Ezra was ashamed to ask the king to send soldiers with them to guard them, for he had told the king that the Lord Himself guards all those who obey Him, and punishes those who sin against Him.

Then Ezra called twelve of the priests and counted out to them the money and the gold and silver bowls and dishes the king had given to the Temple. "This silver and gold is an offering to the Lord," he told the priests, "so guard it carefully. Count it again when you arrive to be sure you have it all, and then give it to the priests and Levites at the Temple."

So Ezra and all those returning with him to Jerusalem gathered at the Ahava River campground toward the end of April, and left from there on the long trip of many weeks' travel to Jerusalem. They had to go through wild desert country, full of bandits waiting to rob them. But the Lord watched over them and wouldn't allow their enemies to harm them, and in about four months they reached Jerusalem safely. There they rested for three days and then went up to the Temple, and counted the money and the golden bowls again, to see that none had been lost. Then they gave them to the priests and Levites at the Temple. And how they thanked God for giving them a safe trip through the land of their enemies!

Ezra gave the letters from the king to the governors who ruled over the provinces in that part of the kingdom. And of course the governors obeyed the king and gave Ezra and the people with him everything the king had told them to.

QUESTIONS
Why did Ezra want to go to Jerusalem?
What did Ezra take with him?
How much was stolen from them during the long, dangerous trip to Jerusalem?

141
Many Sinful Marriages

One day some of the leaders of the Jews came to Ezra and told him that the people of Jerusalem had disobeyed the Lord by marrying women from the surrounding heathen nations. Even some of the priests and Levites were guilty of this. In fact, the leaders were the worst offenders! When Ezra heard this he was filled with sorrow. He tore his clothes and yanked out some of his hair to show his anger, and sat on the ground in great distress. Then all the people who wanted to obey God came to Ezra, for they were afraid that God would punish them for their wickedness. But Ezra still sat on the ground in his grief and stayed there all day until the time when the evening sacrifice of a lamb was being offered at the Temple.

Then he got down on his knees and spread out his hands toward heaven and prayed. "O my God," he said, "I am ashamed even to look up toward You because the sins of the people of Israel are higher than the mountains. All our lives we have been sinning against You, and because of our sins You have let the heathen nations gain the victory over us, and they have killed our people, and made us their captives.

"But our God, You have had pity upon us, and You have made the kings of Persia kind to us so that they let us come back here to our own land, to rebuild the Temple. Yet after all this, we have disobeyed Your laws against marrying heathen women. O Lord, You are good to us, for You have not destroyed us for this. And now we are here before You covered with guilt and shame, for we have no excuse."

When Ezra had prayed and confessed to God how bad his people were, great numbers of men, women, and children came to him weeping because of these sins.

Then one of the men—his name was Shecaniah—said to Ezra, "We have sinned against God by marrying girls from heathen nations. But now we promise to send away these heathen wives, as you have said we should, so that God will forgive us. Ezra, make us obey you! Go ahead and do whatever needs to be done."

Then Ezra sent a message through all the land of Judah that everyone who had married a non-Jewish wife must come to Jerusalem; anyone not there within three days would have his money, property, and cattle taken away from him and he would no longer be counted as one of the people of Israel. So all of them came within three days and gathered in the street near the Temple, afraid and trembling on account of their sin, and also because of the heavy rains and cold.

Then Ezra stood up and spoke to them. "You have disobeyed God," he said, "by marrying non-Jewish wives, and have brought great guilt upon the people of Israel. Now confess your guilt to God and do what will please Him. Don't be friends any longer with the wicked nations surrounding us, and divorce your heathen wives."

Then all the people answered, "We will do as you have commanded. But we cannot stand out here in the rain; and it will take a long time to settle the matter of our wives, for so many of us are guilty. So do this: Let our judges meet together, and let all those who have married non-Jewish wives come before them to be judged. The judges will decide what each one must do, and the anger of our Lord will be turned away from us."

So Ezra and the judges talked to all who had married heathen wives. It took Ezra and the other leaders three months to question them all and to hear what they had to say, and to decide what should be done in each case.

QUESTIONS

What sin of the people of Jerusalem made Ezra so unhappy? Why was it wrong for the people to do this?

How long did it take the judges to decide about all the people who had married non-Jews?

142
Beautiful Esther

Not all the Jews went back to Jerusalem with Zerubbabel and Ezra; many of them still lived in the land of Persia. King Ahasuerus was now the Persian emperor. In the third year of his reign he prepared a great party for his officers in the garden court of his palace, in the city of Shushan where the kings of Persia lived during the winter. The courtyard of the palace was decorated with white, green, and blue curtains. The benches in the courtyard were made of gold and silver, and the pavement was red, blue, white, and black marble. Those invited to the party drank from cups of gold, and there was plenty of wine for everyone to drink as much as he wanted.

Queen Vashti held a party at the same time for the women who lived and worked in the palace of King Ahasuerus. On the seventh day of the king's party, when he was drunk, he sent for Queen Vashti, to show everyone her beauty. In Persia the women lived in a separate part of the house, by themselves, and never came out before men unless they wore veils. So when King Ahasuerus sent for Queen Vashti to come before all the princes and people with her face unveiled, she refused knowing that this would be quite wrong.

But the king was so angry at her refusal that he called in his advisors and asked them, "What shall I do to Queen Vashti? How shall she be punished for not obeying me?"

One of the men replied, "Vashti has done wrong not only to you but to all the people of your kingdom. All the women of Persia will stop obeying their husbands when they hear that you commanded Queen Vashti to come and she refused. Let the king make a decree, and let it be written among the laws of the Medes and Persians which cannot be changed, that Queen Vashti shall never see the king again; and let the king choose someone else for his queen. Then, when this becomes known, wives everywhere will be afraid not to obey their husbands."

The king and his aides thought this was a good idea. So he sent letters through all the different provinces of his kingdom, commanding every husband to make his wives obey him.

Then the king's advisors said to him, "Let's have a national beauty contest to discover the most beautiful girls in Persia. Bring them all here to the palace to become your wives, and the one you decide you like best will be the new queen instead of Vashti." So that is what they did.

Among the government officials at the palace there was a Jew named Mordecai who had a young cousin named Esther. She was a Jewess. Her father and mother had died, so Mordecai adopted Esther as his daughter and brought her up in his house. She was very beautiful, so she was selected to be one of the king's new wives. But would she be the one selected as his queen? Everyone liked Esther very much and hoped she would be the one he would choose. She was given seven young girls to wait on her and was given a nice apartment in the harem, the place where the king kept his wives.

But Esther didn't tell anyone she was a Jewess, for Mordecai had advised her not to.

Sure enough, King Ahasuerus loved Esther more than any of the other girls who were brought to him, so he placed the royal crown upon her head and made her queen instead of Vashti. Then the king celebrated with a big party and gave gifts to all his servants.

QUESTIONS

What did Queen Vashti do to displease King Ahasuerus? Had she done right or wrong?

What was her punishment?

How did the king choose a new queen?

Who became the new queen? Did anyone know she was a Jewess?

143

Evil Haman Makes a Law

It so happened that two of the king's officers were angry with the king and wanted to kill him. Mordecai heard them talking and discussing their plans. He sent a message to Esther, telling her about the danger the king was in, and Esther told the king. The men were arrested and executed by being hanged on a gallows. Mordecai's deed in saving the king's life was written down in a book that told about all the main things that happened while he was king.

There was a man at the palace named Haman who was very great, for he was in charge of all the king's assistants. They all bowed to him, for the king had told them to. But Mordecai wouldn't do it. They asked Mordecai, "Why don't you obey the king and bow to Haman?" They kept asking him about this for several days, but he wouldn't listen to them, so they finally told Haman about it.

When Haman realized that Mordecai wasn't bowing to him, he was very angry and determined to punish him. But he wasn't satisfied to punish Mordecai alone; he decided that since Mordecai was a Jew, he would punish all the Jews of Persia.

So Haman said to King Ahasuerus, "There are people called Jews scattered all through your kingdom, and they have laws of their own which are different from our laws; and they don't obey the king's laws. It is not good to let such people live. If the king will make a law to have them all killed, I will pay a hundred thousand dollars into the king's treasury."

King Ahasuerus agreed to this. He told Haman to make any law he wanted to against the Jews, and he would sign it.

Then Haman wrote a law declaring that on the thirteenth day of February the people of Persia were to kill all the Jews in the kingdom, both young and old—women and children as well as men and boys. Whoever killed a Jew could have that Jew's house and money for himself. Haman sealed the decree with the king's ring, and copies of it were sent by messengers to the governors and rulers of all the provinces, so that all the people of Persia would know about it.

When Mordecai heard about the law Haman had made, he was filled with horror; he tore his clothes, and put on sackcloth and went out into the streets of the city and cried with a loud and bitter cry. And in every province where the messengers brought the decree, there was great mourning among the Jews, and going without food, and weeping.

Queen Esther hadn't heard about this new law, but her maids came and told her that Mordecai was clothed in sackcloth, and crying out in the street. This made Esther sad, and she sent new clothes to him, but he wouldn't take them. So Esther called one of the king's assistants and sent him to ask Mordecai what the trouble was. Mordecai told him all that had happened, and about the money Haman had promised to pay into the king's treasury if the king would let him kill the Jews. Mordecai gave him a copy of Haman's law to show to Esther; and he asked him to tell the queen to go to the king and beg him to spare the lives of the Jews.

When he told Esther what Mordecai said, Esther sent back this message: "Everyone knows that anyone going to the king without being sent for will be killed instantly unless the king holds out his golden sceptre. And he hasn't sent for me to come to him during the last four weeks. How can I go and speak with him?"

But Mordecai returned this message to Esther: "Don't think that our enemies will spare you just because you are the queen, when they kill all the other Jews. If you don't try to save your people now, someone else will do it, but you and I and all your relatives will die. And who knows, perhaps God made you queen for just this purpose, to help the Jews at this particular time?"

Then Esther sent word to Mordecai, "Gather together all the Jews in this city, and tell them to go without food and pray for me. Do not eat or drink for three days, night or day; I and my maidens will do the same. Then I will try to go in and speak with the king. And if I die, I die."

So Mordecai called all the Jews together, and they did as Esther commanded.

QUESTIONS
How did Mordecai help the king?
What made Haman so angry at Mordecai?
What law did Haman make?
What did Mordecai ask Esther to do?

144

Brave Esther Saves the Jews

Three days later Queen Esther dressed herself in her royal robes and went into the inner part of the king's palace and stood before the king as he sat upon his throne. And God was with her, for the king held out his golden sceptre to her. So she came to him, and touched the top of the sceptre.

Then the king asked her, "What is it you wish, Queen Esther? Whatever it is I will give it to you, even if it is half of my kingdom."

Esther answered, "Please come today with Haman to a banquet I have prepared for you!"

Then the king said to his aides, "Tell Haman to hurry and get ready."

So the king and Haman came to the banquet. The king knew Esther wanted to ask some favor from him, and so as they sat at the banquet he asked her again, "What is it you wish? I will give it to you, even if it is half of my kingdom."

Esther answered, "Please come with Haman to another banquet I will prepare for you tomorrow, and then I will tell you what it is I want to ask of you."

Haman was thrilled and proud to be invited—he and no one else except the king himself—but as he was leaving the palace he noticed Mordecai sitting at the gate refusing to bow to him. He was very angry, but said nothing.

When he arrived home, he called for his friends and for his wife, and boasted to them of his riches and greatness, and told them how the king had honored him above all the princes, and above all the king's other aides.

"Yes," he said, "and Queen Esther

invited no one else but me and the king to come to her banquet. And tomorrow I am invited again, with the king! Yet I can't be happy while I see Mordecai the Jew sitting there refusing to bow to me."

Then his wife and all his friends said, "Make a gallows seventy-five feet high, and tomorrow ask the king for permission to hang Mordecai on it; then you can be happy at the queen's banquet."

Haman was pleased with this advice, and he had the gallows made that very afternoon.

That night the king couldn't sleep. He told his servants to bring him the history book recounting the principal events of his reign. So the book was brought to him and as he was reading from it he noticed the item about how Mordecai had saved his life. For Mordecai had told him about the plot against his life.

King Ahasuerus asked his aides, "What reward or honor was given to Mordecai for this?"

"Nothing, sir," they replied.

While the king was talking about this, Haman arrived at the palace to ask the king for permission to hang Mordecai on the gallows. When the king was told that Haman was outside and wanted to see him, he said, "Yes, tell him to come in."

So Haman came in, and before he had a chance to tell the king his errand, the king said to him, "Haman, what is the highest honor I can give to a man who has helped me?"

Haman said to himself, "The king must mean me: I am the one he wants to honor."

So he said, "Let the man wear the king's robes, and his crown, and let him ride upon the king's horse; and let one of the king's most noble princes lead the horse through the streets of the city and shout to all the people, 'See how the king is honoring this man!' "

"Good!" the king said to Haman. "Take these robes of mine and get my personal horse, and take the crown, and do as you have said, to Mordecai the Jew."

Well, Haman had no choice but to obey the king, so he took the king's robes, his horse, and his crown, and brought them to Mordecai, and led him on horseback through the streets of the city, shouting out to all the people, "This man is being honored by the king!"

Afterwards Mordecai returned quietly to his duties at the king's gate, while Haman hurried home, full of shame, hiding his face so that no one would recognize him. As he was telling his wife and friends what had happened, the king's messenger arrived to take him to Queen Esther's banquet.

There at the banquet the king asked Esther again, "What is your wish, Queen Esther? What is your request? For it shall be given you, even to the half of my kingdom."

Esther answered, "If the king is pleased with me, this is my request,

Queen Esther was afraid to go in to see the king because it was against the law unless he asked her to. But she went anyway in order to save her people, and God made the king happy to see her.

that the king will save my life and the lives of all the Jews. For we face death. I and all my people are to be killed; every one of us must die."

"Who would dare to touch you and your relatives?" King Ahasuerus roared.

Esther answered, "This wicked Haman is our enemy."

Haman turned pale with fright as the king rose from the table in great fury and stalked out into the palace garden. When he came in again, Haman had fallen down beside the queen to beg for his life. But the king had decided to kill him.

"Why not hang him on the gallows made for Mordecai?" someone suggested.

And the king said, "Yes, hang him there." So that is the way Haman died.

King Ahasuerus gave Haman's palace to Queen Esther, and Mordecai was called in before the king (for Esther now told the king that Mordecai was her cousin, and how kind he had been to her) and the king appointed him as his prime minister, the job Haman had had before.

Then Esther went to the king again, though he had not called for her, and fell down crying at his feet. The king held out the golden sceptre toward her and she stood before him and begged that Haman's law dooming all the Jews be changed. "For how can I bear to see my people die?" she wept.

But even the king couldn't change it, for no law of the Medes and Persians could ever be changed, not even by the king himself. Then King Ahasuerus had an idea! He told Esther and Mordecai to make another law giving the Jews permission to fight back against anyone who tried to harm them!

Mordecai sent copies of this new law to all the provinces of the kingdom. The message went by swift messengers on horseback, mules, camels, and young dromedaries.

So on the thirteenth day of February the Jews gathered together in every city, armed to fight for their lives; and they destroyed all their enemies. So God saved Esther and her people from those who had tried to destroy them. Then Esther and Mordecai sent letters to all the Jews telling them to hold an annual celebration of their victory, with parties and presents for each other and for the poor.

QUESTIONS

Why was Esther afraid to go to the king?
Why did she have a banquet?
What did Haman suggest that the king do to honor someone?
What happened to Haman?

145
The Jews Rebuild Jerusalem

It had now been ninety years since the exiles had returned to Jerusalem from Babylon. Artaxerxes was now the Persian king, and Nehemiah, a Jew, was one of his trusted government officials. One day Nehemiah met some men from Judah and asked them how things were going in Jerusalem.

"Not very well," the men told him.

They said the walls of Jerusalem were still in ruins, and the gates of the city had never been rebuilt at all.

Nehemiah cried when he heard this. Then he began going without food as he prayed for the Jews, asking God to make King Artaxerxes willing to help them. For Nehemiah had decided to ask the king to send him to Jerusalem to rebuild the city walls.

As King Artaxerxes was sitting one day in his palace, and Nehemiah was there with him, the king noticed that Nehemiah seemed very depressed.

"Why so sad today?" the king asked him. "Are you sick?"

"No," Nehemiah replied, "but how can I help being sad while my city of Jerusalem stands without walls?"

"Well, what do you want me to do about it?" the king asked. At first Nehemiah didn't answer, but silently, in his heart, he prayed again that God would make the king willing to help.

Finally he said, "Would you send me to Jerusalem to rebuild its walls?"

"How long will it take?" the king asked. "How soon could you return?"

And after they had talked about it for awhile, the king told him to go!

Nehemiah then asked the king for letters to carry with him, addressed to the governors of the provinces he would pass through, telling them to help him; also a letter to the keeper of the king's forest near Jerusalem, saying to give him timber to make beams for the city walls and gates. So the king gave him the letters, and also sent soldiers to go with him and guard him.

But there were two wicked men named Sanballat and Tobiah living near Jerusalem, who were enemies of the Jews. When they heard that the king had sent someone to help the Jews in Jerusalem, they didn't like it at all.

Nehemiah arrived safely in Jerusalem, and after he had been there three days, he went out secretly at night, so that his enemies wouldn't see him, and examined the ruined walls of the city.

The next morning he called a meeting of all the people and told them, "You see the danger we are in, with no walls to guard us. Come, let us rebuild the walls as a protection against our enemies." Then he told them about the king's instructions to him.

"Yes, let's get started; let's build the walls," they said to one another.

Everyone helped—the priests, the Levites, the people, and even some of the women.

But Sanballat was angry when he heard about it. "What are these weak Jews trying to do?" he mocked. "Do they think they can build a wall clear around Jerusalem? Where will they find enough stones among the heaps of rubbish left by their enemies?"

And Tobiah, who was with him, said, "If a fox walked on their wall it would fall down!"

But the Jews went on with their work until they had built the wall to half its height all around the city.

Then Sanballat and Tobiah and all the enemies of the Jews decided to attack suddenly and kill them before they had a chance to escape. But the Jews were told of the plot, so Nehemiah instructed the men of Israel to carry their weapons at all times.

"Don't be afraid," he said. "Remember, the Lord will help us. Fight for your wives, your children, and your homes."

But when their enemies heard that the Jews were prepared to fight them, they changed their plans and didn't come.

After that scare, half the men of Israel worked on the walls while the other half guarded. And even those at work carried their swords with them. Nehemiah kept a trumpeter near him in case of enemy attack, for it was a long way around the city, and the workmen were widely separated.

"If you hear the trumpet," he told them, "hurry to help."

So all the people worked hard from morning till evening. They didn't even take off their clothes, day or night, except for washing.

QUESTIONS

Why did Nehemiah want to go to Jerusalem?

Why was it dangerous for the men who worked on the walls?

What did the sound of the trumpet mean?

146
Troublemakers!

But now the Jews began to have trouble among themselves. Some of them were poor and complained against the rich. "We have had to borrow money from them to pay our taxes and buy food, and we have even sold our children to them as slaves to get enough money to live on. And now these rich men are demanding their money back, and because we can't pay them, they have taken our lands and our vineyards, and we have nothing left, and can't buy back our children from them. Yet we are all Jews, just the same as these rich men are, and we love our children as much as they love theirs."

When Nehemiah heard about this he was very angry with the rich men. He summoned all the people and spoke to their rich leaders: "You are wicked, cruel men to act like this against your brothers," he said. "Give them back their children, houses, vineyards, money, corn, wine, and olive oil."

"All right, sir," these men replied. Then Nehemiah called for the priests and made the leaders vow before the Lord that they would do what they promised.

When Sanballat and Tobiah heard that Nehemiah and the men of Israel were still at work on the wall, and that it was half built already, they were afraid to go into Jerusalem. So they sent word to Nehemiah to come down to one of the villages on the plain and meet them there. But Nehemiah knew they wanted to harm him, so he sent messengers to tell them, "I am doing a great work, and I cannot come down. Should I stop the work just so I can talk with you?"

They sent him the same message four times, but each time he gave them the same answer.

Then Sanballat sent a messenger to Nehemiah with this letter: "I am told that you Jews in Jerusalem are going to rebel against the king of Persia. I am told you are plotting to be their king; that is why you are building the wall around the city. Come and talk with me, or I will tell the king what you are planning."

But Nehemiah sent back this reply: "It isn't true, and you know it."

Then Nehemiah prayed to the Lord to help him, and prayed that the work on the wall would not be stopped by these enemies.

When Sanballat and Tobiah found that they couldn't persuade Nehemiah to leave Jerusalem, they hired a man in the city named Shemaiah to try to frighten him. He locked himself in his house and pretended that the Lord was giving him a message for Nehemiah. Then he came out and told Nehemiah, "Run to the Temple and hide, for your enemies are coming to kill you."

But Nehemiah said, "Should a man doing the Lord's work leave it unfinished and run? If a man is doing right, why should he hide in the Temple to save his life? I won't go in." Nehemiah could tell that the Lord had not spoken to Shemaiah at all, but that Sanballat and Tobiah had paid him to tell a lie. Then Nehemiah prayed to the Lord and asked Him not to let Sanballat and Tobiah stop him from his work.

So Nehemiah and the people kept on working on the wall and finished it in fifty-two days. Then they held a great celebration. The priests, Levites, and the people walked along the top of the wall in two groups, going in opposite directions, with trumpets blaring and harps playing, singing praises to God as they walked around the city until the two groups met. Then they came down from the wall and marched together to the Temple, and offered sacrifices to God with joy and gladness. So the wall was dedicated to the Lord to guard His Temple and His people from their enemies.

Nehemiah now appointed ward leaders throughout the city and told them, "Shut the gates at night, and don't open them in the morning until the sun has risen high in the heavens. And each of you must take his turn at guard duty on the walls, to watch for our enemies."

QUESTIONS

Why were the poor Jews angry with the rich Jews?

How long did it take to repair the walls of Jerusalem?

Tell about walking on the wall.

147
A Time to Celebrate

Now it was the time for the annual Festival of Trumpets, which was a sort of Thanksgiving Day. The people met together that day to worship. They asked Ezra the priest to bring from the Temple the book of laws proclaimed by Moses. Ezra brought out the book and stood outside the Temple on a pulpit where all the people could see him. Then he opened the book and read out of it from morning until noon as everyone listened—men, women and even the children. And the priests and Levites explained what he read.

When the people heard God's laws and remembered how often they had disobeyed them, they began crying. But the Levites said to them, "Don't weep, for this is a day of happiness. Go home and eat and drink of the good things God has given you, and send presents to the poor." So all the people went home to have a big dinner and to send gifts to the poor. They were glad because the Lord had been so good to them, and because they had understood the words that were read to them out of God's law.

The next day they came to Ezra again so that he could read more of God's laws to them. This time he read to them from the part of the book commanding them to celebrate the Festival of Tabernacles each year. "Go up to the mountains," the book said, "and cut down olive, pine, and myrtle branches, and make huts and live in them all week." So the people went up and cut branches from the trees, and built huts on the flat roofs of their houses or in their yards, and in the courts of the Temple, and even in the streets. Then they moved out of their houses and lived in the huts for the seven days of the celebration. And there was great joy among them. There hadn't been such a celebration in Jerusalem for hundreds of years.

They remembered how often they had disobeyed God. So on the twenty-fourth day of the month they met in sorrow to go without food and to confess their sins to God; and they wore sackcloth to show their grief.

Then some of the Levites stood and prayed: "O Lord, remember all the troubles that have come upon us since we were taken away as captives until this very day. Yet it was right for You to punish us, for we have been wicked. That is why You have given our lands to the Assyrians, and they rule over us and do with us as they please, and we are in great distress. But now we want to be Your servants. We promise to obey You."

Their leaders then wrote out their promise to obey God; then Nehemiah the governor and some of the priests and many of the chief men of Israel signed the agreement. The people promised to obey all of God's commandments; and not to make friends with the heathen nations, nor to marry wives from among them; and to keep the Sabbath day holy; and to give the Lord a tenth of all their crops; and to bring the first of their grain and their fruits to the Temple each year as an offering to the Lord.

Nehemiah went back to Babylon after this, for he had promised the king he would. We are not told how long he stayed there, but when he returned to Jerusalem again he found that the people had already forgotten their promise to obey God's law. They had again made friends with the heathen nations around them, and had intermarried with them. And the people of Israel had stopped giving the priests and Levites a tenth of their fruit and grain; so the Levites had left the Temple to work in the fields to raise food for themselves. Nehemiah was grieved, and called the priests and Levites back to the Temple. "Why is the Temple of God forsaken?" he asked.

Nehemiah saw the people loading their donkeys and bringing their grain in from the fields on the Sabbath. He rebuked their leaders. "Why are you so wicked?" he demanded. "Didn't God punish our fathers by destroying this city for doing these very same things?"

On the evening before the Sabbath, when it began to grow dark, Nehemiah commanded that the gates of the city must be shut and not opened again until the Sabbath ended. And he stationed guards to prevent any traders from coming into the city to buy and sell on the Sabbath day. Then those who came with fish and other goods to sell on the Sabbath found the gates shut, so they lay down outside the walls and slept there all night. The next Sabbath they did the same thing. Then Nehemiah said to them, "Why do you keep coming? If you do it again I will have you arrested." So they stopped coming on the Sabbath.

Then he spoke to the men who had married heathen women and said, "Wasn't Solomon a great and wise king? Yet when he married foreign wives he fell into the sin of worshipping their idols. Should we listen to you, then, when you want us to disobey God by doing this same wicked thing?

QUESTIONS
Why did the people cry?
How did the Jews celebrate the Festival of Tabernacles? What is a hut?
What promise did the leaders sign?
Did they keep their promise?
How did Nehemiah make others keep the Sabbath day holy?

(This ends the Old Testament stories of the Bible.)

148
Hardship and Cruelty

The last chapter completed the stories of the Old Testament. The Bible tells us nothing more about the Jews until Jesus came more than 400 years later. We can find out from our history books at school what happened during those 400 years. They tell us that the Jews continued to be servants of the king of Persia for 100 years after Nehemiah returned from Babylon. Then Alexander, a great Greek general, went to war with Persia; he captured Jerusalem, and the Jews served him for nine years.

After Alexander's death the Jews were servants to the kings of Egypt for more than 100 years. Some of these kings treated them well, but others didn't. When one of these kings came to Jerusalem and saw the beautiful Temple, he demanded to go in where the priests alone were allowed to enter.

The priests begged him not to disobey God by doing this, and the people cried out with horror when they saw him go in. But when he came to the holy place, God struck him with great terror and weakness so that he had to be carried out like one almost dead. He was very angry because he couldn't do whatever he wanted to, so he treated the Jews cruelly, making slaves of some and killing many others.

But afterwards the Jews rebelled against Egypt and agreed to serve the king of Syria if he would come and help them. This king was good to them as long as he lived, but after he died, the Jews rebelled against Syria, too. When Antiochus, the new king of Syria, learned of their rebellion against him, he came with his army and conquered Jerusalem, putting old and young to death. In three days 40,000 were killed, and as many more were sold as slaves. The king then went into the Temple and took away the gold altar, the gold table, the gold lampstand and all the treasures that were kept there.

And God let him do it.

Two years afterwards he sent Apollonius, one of his generals, with 22,000 soldiers to further destroy Jerusalem. Apollonius waited until the Sabbath day when he knew the Jews wouldn't fight. On that day he told his soldiers to kill all the men, to take away all the women and children as slaves, to rob the houses, and to break down the city walls. The soldiers killed so many Jews that day that the streets of the city and the courts of the Temple ran red with their blood.

But not satisfied with what he had already done to show his fury against them, the king of Syria later made a law forbidding the Jews from offering sacrifices to God. They must not obey God's laws or keep the Sabbath day, he said. He drove them away from the Temple and made it a place in which to worship idols. Heathen altars were set up in every city of the land, and the Jews who would not sacrifice upon them were punished. One of their elders, an old man named Eleazar, was forced by the king's soldiers to take pig's meat into his mouth. (The Lord had commanded the Jews not to eat pork). When he spat it out, he was beaten to death.

Seven brothers and their mother were whipped by the king to try to get them to eat some pork, but the oldest brother said to the king, "We won't eat it; we would rather die than disobey the laws of God." Then in great anger the king commanded that his tongue be cut out and parts of his feet and hands cut off, and afterwards he was burned slowly over a fire until he was dead. Then the other brothers were asked whether they would obey the king. They too refused and one by one they were tortured and put to death. When the mother had seen her seven sons die, she also was killed.

QUESTIONS

How much time was there between the last story in the Old Testament and the first story in the New Testament?

Why were the mother and her seven sons tortured to death?

Tell some of the things that happened to the Jews during this time.

A heathen king would not let the Jews obey God's laws. These soldiers are forcing an old Jewish man to eat some forbidden pork.

R. Hook

149
God's Temple Rebuilt

There was at this time a Jewish family called the Maccabees. The father was a priest, and had five sons. He loved to worship God and hated the worship of idols. He killed one of the king's assistants for setting up an idol's altar in the city where he lived. Then he fled with his sons to the mountains. Many of the Jews came to him there until he had gathered a little army around him to fight against their enemies.

But being an old man he couldn't bear the hardships of war, and feeling that the time of his death was near, he called for his sons, to give them his blessing. He told them not to fear the Syrians but to be brave and to trust in God.

His sons drove the Syrians from the Temple and destroyed the idol altar they had erected. Then they cleansed the Temple and began to worship God in it again. They won other victories over their enemies too, until Jerusalem was free again. After that the family of the Maccabees ruled the land of Israel for nearly 100 years.

But now when God had freed the Jews again, they forgot about Him, and instead of obeying His command to love one another they grew proud and selfish, and had wars and battles among themselves. Finally, while two brothers were quarrelling about which of them should be the king, the Romans came and captured Jerusalem and broke down its walls again. So now the Jews became servants to the Romans as they had been to the Egyptians and the Syrians.

The Romans sent General Herod to be their new king. He was not a Jew, but he pretended to believe in their religion and to worship God as they did. He was really a fierce, cruel man who cared only for himself. He put many to death, including his wife and two of his sons.

After he had been king for eighteen years the Jews still hated him for his wickedness so he decided to try to

King Herod tried to make the Jews like him by rebuilding the Temple. It took 18,000 men nine years to finish it. It was one of the world's most beautiful buildings.

R. Hook

please them by rebuilding their Temple. The Temple had been built by the Jews who returned from exile in Babylon 500 years before, and it was broken and decayed. Herod took it down a section at a time, and built it again with great stones of white marble. He covered some of these stones with silver and gold. The building was very splendid, and shone so brightly under the morning sun that it dazzled the eyes.

Inside, the Temple was divided into two rooms as before, by the curtain called the veil. One room was the holy place where the gold altar, the gold table, and the gold lampstand stood. The other was the most holy place where the Ark had stood; but the Ark had been lost long before when the Jews were exiled to Babylon on account of their sins. They had no Ark now to bring into the most holy place, and we are told that it was empty except for a stone that lay on the spot where the Ark should have been.

Outside the Temple was the Court of the Priests, where the altar of burnt offering and the washstand for the priests stood. Outside of this court was another called the Court of Israel, where only the men of Israel could come. Beyond this was a third court called the Court of the Women, because the Jewish women could go there. A very large court called the Court of the Gentiles surrounded the others; the Gentiles, that is, people of other nations, were allowed to go in there.

Nine large, splendid gates opened into these courts. One, more splendid than the rest, was called the Beautiful Gate. It was seventy-five feet high, covered with Corinthian bronze, which at that time was more costly than silver or gold. Walls were built around the different courts. The one around the court of the Gentiles was twenty-five feet high. On the inside of this wall were wide porches with flat roofs built on marble pillars so large that three men with their arms stretched out could hardly reach around one of them. The floor of the porches was paved with different colored marble. One of the porches was called Solomon's, because it stood over a very high wall which Solomon had built up from the valley below. These porches made a beautiful covered walk in hot or stormy weather. In pleasant weather people enjoyed going up to the flat roofs where they could see the city and the mountains surrounding Jerusalem.

The Jews didn't go into the Temple itself to worship; only the priests were allowed to enter there. The people worshipped in the courts of the Temple, and when they said they were going to the Temple, they meant they were going up to its courts. The way up to these, on the top of Mount Moriah, was by long flights of steps.

Herod had 18,000 men at work on the Temple and its courts, and it took nine years to finish rebuilding it.

QUESTIONS

Tell about the Maccabees.
Who rebuilt the Temple for the Jews? Why?
Can you describe the new Temple?

150
God's Special Messenger

Now the time came for the Saviour to arrive on earth. And how the world needed Him, for everyone was selfish and unhappy! No one was pleasing to God. All the people in the world were sinners, just as Adam and Eve had been. When Adam and Eve sinned in the Garden of Eden, God promised them that a Saviour would come someday to take away their sins. The prophets too had often told the people of Israel that this wonderful Saviour was going to come.

The prophets said that someone else would come before the Saviour did, to tell the people to get ready for His arrival by turning away from their sins. This was John the Baptist. Here is the story of his birth:

While Herod was king of Judea, an old priest named Zacharias worked at the Temple, helping the people to worship God. His wife's name was Elizabeth. They were both careful to obey all of God's commandments, but God had never given them a child.

The priests at the Temple began their work early every morning before it was light. Some of them cleaned the altar where the offerings were burned, taking away the ashes from the day before. Others piled fresh wood on the fire, which was never allowed to go out. Still others trimmed the lamps on the gold lampstand and cleaned the gold incense altar.

At nine o'clock in the morning and again at three o'clock in the afternoon, one of the priests sacrificed a lamb on the altar of burnt offering, while another burned incense on the golden altar. In this way they were asking God to forgive the sins of the people of Israel who trusted God, and He did. At these times the people stood outside in the court, praying.

Each day before the priests began their work, they drew straws or threw dice to decide what part of the work each priest would do.

When it was Zacharias' turn to burn the incense on the gold altar, he stood in the holy place at the hour of prayer. Suddenly he saw an angel standing beside the altar! He was terribly frightened.

But the angel said, "Don't be afraid, Zacharias. God will give you and Elizabeth a son, and you are to name him John. He must never drink wine or any other alcoholic beverage; and he will be filled with God's Holy Spirit from the time he is born. He will tell the people of Israel about the Saviour who is coming; and he will persuade many of them to turn from their sins and obey Him."

Zacharias was amazed! "How can I be sure you are telling the truth?" he asked the angel.

"I am the angel Gabriel," he replied. "I live in heaven and stand before God, doing whatever He commands me. He has sent me to tell you this good news. And now because you haven't believed me, you will be punished by being unable to speak until all that I have told you comes true."

Meanwhile the people were waiting for Zacharias to come out. "What could be keeping him so long?" they wondered. When he finally came, he was unable to speak! But he made them understand by his gestures that he had seen a vision.

Zacharias' wife Elizabeth had a young cousin named Mary. She was in the royal line of Israel, for she was a relative of King David who had lived hundreds of years before.

Six months after the angel appeared to Zacharias in the Temple, God sent His angel to Mary. She was frightened, for she had never seen an angel before. But Gabriel said, "Don't be afraid, Mary! God has greatly blessed you. You are going to have a baby and His name will be JESUS. He will have no human father, for He will be the Son of God. And God is giving a baby to Zacharias and your cousin Elizabeth.

Mary didn't understand how she would have a baby, for she was a virgin, that is, she wasn't married and so she had never slept with a man. But the angel explained that this wasn't necessary, for God would do a special miracle to make her pregnant while she was a virgin. No other baby has ever been born without a human father. Jesus was different. How excited and happy Mary was at this wonderful news that she would be the mother of the Saviour of the world!

She was engaged to be married to a kind man named Joseph, who was a carpenter. But when he heard that Mary was going to have a baby, he was sad. He thought she had sinned and that some other man was the baby's father. He said that now he wouldn't marry her. But God talked to him about it and explained that God was the baby's father, so it was all right for him to marry her after all; so he did. But he didn't sleep with her until after the baby was born.

Meanwhile, God gave Zacharias and Elizabeth the son He had promised them. When the baby was eight days old, their neighbors and relatives came to dedicate him to the Lord and to decide on his name. They wanted to call him Zacharias, because that was his father's name. But his mother said, "No, we will name him John."

"Oh, no," they said to her, "none of your relatives have that name." Then they motioned to Zacharias, asking him what he wanted to name the baby. He couldn't speak yet, and

An angel explained to Mary that she would have a baby even though she was a virgin, for God would place the baby in her womb. He would be God's Son and His name would be Jesus.

couldn't hear, so he took a sheet of paper and wrote, "His name is John." They were all very surprised, for Zacharias hadn't told them about the angel giving him this name in the Temple.

As soon as Zacharias had written this, he could speak again! And how he praised God! All the people in that part of the country heard about the angel and about Zacharias' not being able to speak, and they said, "What strange things! What sort of a child is this going to be?"

Little John grew, and the Lord blessed him. When he was older he lived out in the lonely wilderness away from the rest of the people until the time came for him to preach to the Jews and tell them about Jesus. For this child God had given to Zacharias and Elizabeth was John the Baptist, the one who came to prepare the way for Christ.

QUESTIONS
What did the angel tell Zacharias?
What did the angel tell Mary?
What did Zacharias and Elizabeth name their baby?
When did Zacharias get his speech back?

151
The Birth of God's Son

In those days the Jews were under the rule of the Romans; they had to do whatever the emperor of Rome and his assistants told them to. Now he made a law that the name and address of every Jew must be written down. He instructed everyone to go to the city where his ancestors had lived, so that the Roman officers could record their names. Ancestors means relatives who lived hundreds of years before. So Joseph and Mary went to Bethlehem where King David used to live, because they were relatives of his, though he had lived hundreds of years before they were born.

But when they arrived at Bethlehem there was no room for them at the little hotel; it was already full. So they went out to the stable where the

What a happy time it was for old Zacharias and his wife Elizabeth! She was much too old to have a baby, but God gave her one anyway. His name was John and he was a cousin of Jesus.

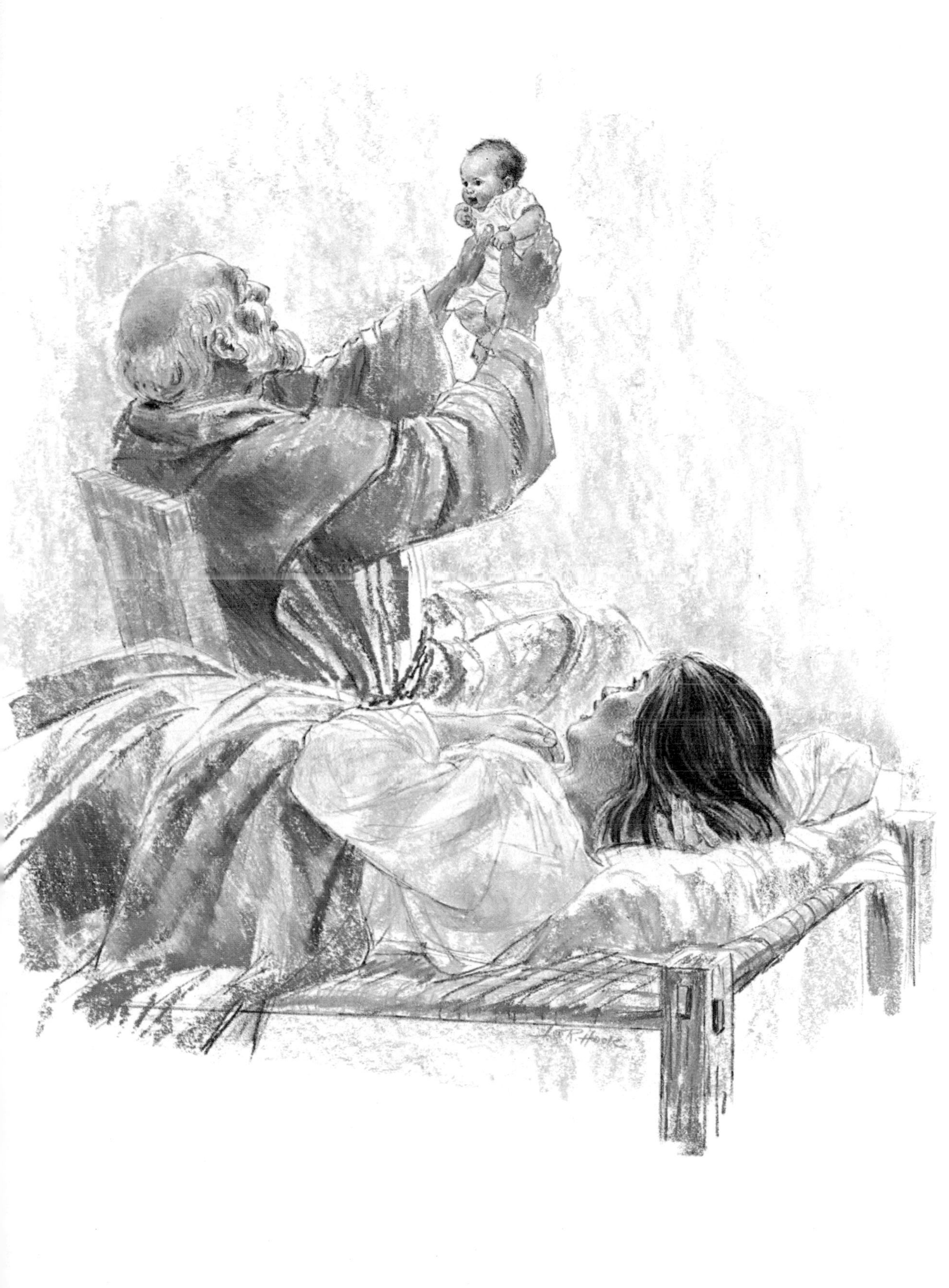

donkeys and camels were kept, to sleep in the straw on the floor. And while they were resting in the stable, Mary's baby was born. He was the little son that the angel Gabriel had told her about. Yes, Jesus was born out there in the stable; and Mary dressed Him in some baby clothes she had brought, and wrapped Him up in a blanket, and laid Him in a manger.

That same night some shepherds in the fields outside the town were watching their sheep to protect them from wild animals. Suddenly an angel surrounded by a bright light appeared to them. They were very frightened. But the angel said, "Don't be afraid; for I have good news for you, and for all the world! Tonight, in Bethlehem, your Saviour was born! His name is Christ the Lord.

"And this is how you will know Him: you will find Him wrapped in baby clothes and lying in a manger!"

Then suddenly many, many other angels appeared, praising God and saying, "Glory to God! Peace on earth between God and men!"

After the angels returned to heaven the shepherds said to each other, "Let's hurry to Bethlehem and find the baby!" So they ran into the village and soon found Mary and Joseph, and the baby lying in a manger! Afterwards the shepherds returned to their flocks again, praising God for what the angel Gabriel had told them to. they had seen the Saviour.

When the baby was eight days old, his parents named Him Jesus, just as the angel Gabriel had told them to. And they dedicated Him to the Lord, for He was the Son of God.

Then Joseph and Mary took Him from His home in Bethlehem to the Temple at Jerusalem, and sacrificed young pigeons as the law required for the oldest boy in every Jewish family. And there he was circumcised. Circumcision is a tiny operation of cutting away the loose skin around the tip of the penis. God had commanded this to be done to all Jewish baby boys.

There was a wonderful old man named Simeon there at the Temple that day who loved God very much, and had been waiting many years to see the Saviour whom God had promised to send. The Holy Spirit had promised Simeon that he would not die before seeing Jesus. So, on the day Jesus' parents took Him to the Temple, the Holy Spirit told Simeon to go there, and when Joseph and Mary brought in their baby, Simeon took Him in his arms and said, "Now, Lord, Your promise has come true: I have seen the Saviour. Now I can die in peace."

Also at the Temple that day was a very old woman named Anna. She was a prophetess, that is, God sometimes told her about things that would happen in the future. She was a widow, and for many years had lived near the Temple so that she could worship there at any time, day and night. While Simeon has holding the baby Jesus in his arms and talking to

The hotel was full — "no rooms," the sign said. And there was no hospital where Mary could go for Jesus to be born. So Joseph took her to the stable and made a bed of hay. That is where Jesus, God's Son, was born.

Mary and Joseph, Anna came in and saw them there, and began thanking God for letting her see God's Son.

Not long afterwards some men who study the stars came to Jerusalem from a distant eastern land. "Where is the baby who will become king of the Jews?" they asked. "For we have seen His star and have come to worship Him." They knew in some way from seeing the star that Jesus had been born. So they came to Jerusalem looking for Him, but they didn't know just where to search.

When King Herod heard them asking about a new king, he was worried, for he was the king and he didn't want anyone else to have his job! He told the men to find Jesus, and then to come and tell him where He was so that he could worship Jesus too! But what he really intended was to kill Jesus.

King Herod now summoned some priests who had spent their lives studying the Scriptures, and asked them whether the Bible said where the new king would be born.

"Yes," they replied, "in the city of Bethlehem; that is what one of the prophets said."

So Herod sent the astrologers to Bethlehem. "Go to Bethlehem and search for the child," he said, "and when you have found him, come and tell me so that I can worship him too!"

So the men went to Bethlehem. And as they went, the star they had seen appeared to them again, and seemed to stand right over one certain house. They went in and saw the baby there with His mother Mary, and they bowed low before Him, worshipping Him. Then they gave presents to the new king—precious gifts of gold and spices. Afterwards they returned to their own country, but they didn't go through Jerusalem, for in a dream God warned them not to tell Herod where Jesus was.

When Herod discovered that the astrologers had disobeyed him, he was very angry and sent his soldiers to Bethlehem to kill all the little children two years old or less. Since he didn't know which baby was the little king, he killed them all. But before the soldiers arrived, the angel of the Lord told Joseph to hurry to Egypt with the baby and His mother. So Joseph wakened them in the night and they fled to Egypt and stayed there until King Herod was dead. Then the angel spoke to Joseph again and told him, "Go back to the land of Israel, for King Herod is dead."

Joseph did as the angel commanded, and he and Mary and Jesus came and lived in the city of Nazareth.

QUESTIONS

Why did Mary and Joseph go to Bethlehem?
What did the angels tell the shepherds?
Did Simeon and Anna recognize that the baby Jesus was the promised Saviour? How did they know?
Where did the astrologers go to find Jesus?
What terrible thing did Herod do? Why?

Shepherds were taking care of their sheep one night near Bethlehem, when suddenly the skies were filled with angels telling them of Jesus' birth. In this picture the angels have just gone back again into heaven, and the shepherds are watching them go.

152
Jesus Grows Up

Joseph and Mary went to Jerusalem every year to celebrate the Passover. When Jesus was twelve years old, he went with them. After the celebration ended, they started walking back to their home in Nazareth, along with many other people. For friends and neighbors travelled together to the celebrations at Jerusalem. Some rode on mules and horses, but many of them walked. Joseph and Mary noticed that Jesus wasn't with them, but thought He was with some of their friends, so they didn't worry. But when they didn't see Him all day, and evening came and still He wasn't back, they began looking for Him and worrying, and asking everyone if they had seen Him. But no one had. By this time they were *very* worried and started back to Jerusalem to search for Him there. It took them a day to return and it was another day before they finally found Him. He was at the Temple talking with the great teachers there, listening to them and asking them questions!

These men were greatly surprised at how much Jesus knew, for He was only twelve years old, while they were college professors.

"Son!" His mother exclaimed, "why have You treated us like this? Your father and I have been searching for You everywhere."

Jesus was surprised. "Didn't you know I would be here at the Temple?" He asked.

Joseph and Mary didn't understand what He meant, but His mother always remembered what He had said and often thought about it. Afterwards she understood—He was the Son of God and naturally would want to be at His Father's house, which was the Temple.

Then Jesus returned home to Nazareth with His parents and did all

One day God told His old friend Simeon to go to the Temple right away if he wanted to see the Messiah—the great King of the Jews whom God promised to send. The King is Jesus, and in this picture you see Simeon holding Him in his arms.

that they told Him to do. And as He grew, God blessed Him; and everyone loved Him.

The next we are told about Jesus, He was a man thirty years old. But very few knew that He was the Son of God, for John the Baptist hadn't yet begun to tell them about Him.

Meanwhile John was living out in the wilderness. His clothes were woven of coarse camel hair, fastened around his waist by a leather belt. He ate locusts for his food—they were plentiful out there in the wilderness —and honey from the wild bees.

But now the time had come for John to preach to the people, telling them to get ready for the Saviour by turning from their sins. He began his preaching beside the Jordan River, and great crowds came there to hear him. He told them that the Saviour would soon be coming to save them and to destroy the wicked. John said that they mustn't think their sins would be forgiven just because they were descended from a good man like Abraham! No, they themselves must obey God. Many who heard John preach turned from their sins and were baptized by him in the river.

Then Jesus came to John and asked to be baptized. John didn't want to do it. "*I* need to be baptized by *You,*" John told Him; "why do You come to me?" Jesus had no sins to be washed away; why then should He be baptized? It was because He had come to earth to obey all of God's commandments for us.

Jesus told John to baptize Him anyway, even though he didn't understand why, for it was necessary. So John agreed. Then, as Jesus was coming up out of the water after being baptized, the sky above Him opened and what looked like a dove came down from heaven and lighted upon Him. It was the Holy Spirit. At the same time God's voice spoke from heaven saying, "This is My beloved Son. I am very pleased with Him."

Afterwards Jesus went out into the wilderness alone for forty days and forty nights. All that time He ate nothing, but fasted and prayed to God; and afterwards He was hungry.

Do you remember how Satan tempted Eve to disobey God? And when she did, it caused all the rest of us to have wicked hearts? Well, when Satan saw that Jesus had come to give us new, pure hearts, and to make us good, he thought he would try to stop Him. So he went out into the wilderness to tempt Jesus, as he had tempted Eve in the Garden of Eden.

He came to Him and said, "If you are the Son of God, change these stones into bread, so that you will have food, for you are very hungry."

But Jesus knew why Satan had come, and He refused to turn the stones into bread. He told Satan, "It is written in the Bible that it is better to be hungry than to obey Satan."

Then Satan took Jesus into Jerusalem to a very high part of the Temple. "If you are the Son of God," he said to Him, "throw Yourself down,

Men far away in a distant land learned from the stars that a new king of the Jews had been born. They travelled many weeks to bring their gifts to Jesus.

for it is written in the Bible that the angels will keep You from hurting Yourself."

But Jesus said it was also written in the Bible that we must not put ourselves in danger just to find out whether God will help us.

Then Satan tried again. He took Jesus up on a high mountain and showed Him all the kingdoms of the world at the same time, with their beautiful cities, their mighty armies, and their great riches: and he said to Him, "I will give You all of these if You will only kneel down and worship me." For that is what Satan wanted most of all—to get Jesus to worship and obey him.

But Jesus said, "Get out of here, Satan, for it is written in the Bible, 'You shall worship only the Lord your God, and serve Him alone.' "

Then, when Satan saw that he couldn't make Jesus obey him, he went away; and angels came and cared for Jesus.

Then Jesus returned to the Jordan River where John was baptizing. When John saw Him coming, he said, "Look! There is the Lamb of God!" He called Jesus the Lamb of God because Jesus would die as a sacrifice just as lambs were sacrificed at the Temple. Two of John's disciples heard him say this, and immediately followed Jesus wherever He went. He talked with them, and invited them to His home. Then one of them, Andrew, went to get his brother Peter. The next day two others, Philip and Nathaniel, decided to go with Him. So now Jesus had five disciples.

QUESTIONS

Did Jesus get lost in Jerusalem? What happened? How old was He?

What did John preach about?

What did Satan suggest to Jesus?

Why did John call Jesus the Lamb of God?

One night God talked to Joseph in a dream and said to go away to Egypt, because some enemies would try to kill Jesus. Here in this picture you can see the baby Jesus, His mother Mary, and Joseph as they quickly obeyed God.

R+F. Hook

153
Jesus Turns Water into Wine

One day Jesus went to the city of Cana to attend a wedding. His mother and His disciples were there too. During the wedding supper something unfortunate happened: the host ran out of wine and the guests would be disappointed. Jesus' mother told Him about it, expecting Him to somehow get some more. Then she told the servants to be sure to do whatever He told them to.

There were six large, stone water jars there in the house, used to store water, for there were no faucets in those days as we have in our homes now.

Jesus told the servants to fill the water jars with water, and they filled them to the brim. Then He said, "Take some to the master of ceremonies." And when they did, the water had become wine!

The master of ceremonies didn't know that Jesus had changed it (but the servants did) so when he had tasted it, it was so good that he called the bridegroom over. "I've never heard of anyone's saving the best wine to the last!" he exclaimed. "Everyone else serves the best first, and after everyone has had enough, then they serve the wine that isn't so good!"

This was Jesus' first miracle. When His disciples saw what had happened, they believed that He was the Son of God.

Now it was time for Jesus to go to Jerusalem for the annual Passover celebration. This was a holiday week to remind everyone about the time when God used Moses to rescue the people of Israel from Egypt.

After arriving in Jerusalem, Jesus went to the Temple and saw that it was being used as a market to sell oxen, sheep, and doves to people who wanted to bring sacrifices. Jesus was angry to find that the holy Temple of God had become a market, so He made a whip of small cords and drove out all the merchants, along with their sheep and oxen. Then He poured out their money on the ground and turned over their tables, and said to those who

Jesus grew from a baby to a little boy, then a big boy, then a man. And everyone loved Him.

sold doves, "Take them away; My Father's house is a place for prayer, not a place for buying and selling."

Then many others believed on Him when they saw what He did at the Passover celebration.

Nicodemus was one of the political leaders of the Jews. After dark one night he came to Jesus and remarked, "Sir, we know God has sent You, for no one could do the miracles You do unless God were with Him."

Jesus replied, "Unless you are born again, you cannot be one of God's children!"

"What?" Nicodemus asked in surprise. "How can a person be born a second time? Can he enter into his mother's body again as a tiny baby and be born again?"

Then Jesus explained to him that by being born again He meant becoming eager to do God's will, and asking Jesus to take away one's sins so that God gives him new, eternal life.

And then Jesus said something else that seems very strange at first. He said, "As Moses lifted up the serpent in the wilderness, so must I be lifted up." What did He mean? Well, do you remember the time when the people of Israel were in the wilderness and God punished them by sending fiery serpents into the camp to bite and kill them? But then God told Moses to make a bronze statue of a serpent and put it on a pole and lift up the pole so that everyone who had been bitten could look at it; and when they did, they got well.

So now Jesus said to Nicodemus, "As Moses lifted up the serpent in the wilderness, so must I be lifted up." Jesus meant that He was to be lifted up on the cross so that we might look to Him and be forgiven of all our sins. That is, we can thank Him for dying for us.

Jesus also told Nicodemus, "God loves the people of the world so much that He sent His only Son into the world to die for them, so that whoever looks up to Him in faith will not be punished for his sins, but is forgiven and goes to heaven when he dies."

By this time King Herod was dead. His son—his name was Herod too—was now the governor of Galilee. Like his father, he was a wicked man. He had married his brother's wife, Herodias, even though she was married to his brother. When John the Baptist told Herod this was wrong, Herodias became very angry and tried to get Herod to kill John for saying such a thing. But Herod wouldn't do it. Herod was afraid to kill him because he had heard him preach and knew he was a holy man. Yet, to please Herodias, he arrested John and put him in chains, and shut him up in prison.

While John was in prison, Herod's birthday came around and there was a big birthday party with all his government officials invited. During the party, Salome, the daughter of Herodias, came in and danced. Herod en-

If you were twelve years old, would you be able to talk intelligently with these old, wise men? Probably not, but Jesus did. He had a high I.Q., but most important of all, He was God's Son and so He already knew as much as they did about God, or even more.

R. Hook

joyed her number very much and said to her, "Ask me for anything and I'll give it to you, even if it is half of my kingdom!"

So Salome ran to her mother and asked, "What shall I ask him for?"

"Ask him for John the Baptist's head!" she replied.

So Salome ran back to the king and said, "Please give me the head of John the Baptist on a tray."

Then Herod was very sorry for his promise, but everyone had heard him say it, so he didn't dare refuse. He sent one of his soldiers who cut off John's head in the prison. He brought it to Salome, and she gave it to her mother.

When John's disciples heard about it, they came and took away his body and laid it in a tomb, and went and told Jesus.

QUESTIONS
What was Jesus' first miracle?
What were the people doing at the Temple that made Jesus angry?
Did Jesus already know how He would die? How do you know?
What happened at Herod's birthday party?

154

A Little Sick Boy Is Healed

One day Jesus and His disciples came to the village of Sychar. Just outside the city was a well, called Jacob's Well, where the people came to get water. It was hot, and Jesus was tired from the journey. He sat down by the well while His disciples went into the city to buy food.

A woman came from the city, carrying her empty pitcher to get some water from the well. This woman didn't love God in her heart, and had done many things to displease Him. Jesus knew this, for He sees all our hearts and knows everything we do. He talked with the woman and told her some of the things she had done that displeased God. She was surprised and said, "Sir, I see You are a prophet." She meant that He must be a person to whom God told things that other people didn't know. "I

The first miracle Jesus did was to turn water into wine at a wedding in the city of Cana.

know that the Saviour is coming into the world," she said to Jesus, "and when He comes He will tell us everything."

Then Jesus told her, "I am the Saviour!"

The woman left her pitcher and hurried back to the village and said to the people, "Come and see a man who told me everything I have ever done! Could this be the Saviour?"

The people rushed out to see Jesus and begged Him to visit their city. So He stayed with them three days, and they listened carefully to what He taught them. Then they said to the woman, "We, too, believe He is the Saviour, but not just because of what you told us about Him; for we have heard Him for ourselves, and we know now that He is the Saviour from heaven."

From that time on, Jesus began to tell the people that the judgment day was coming, and that they must turn away from their sins and trust Him to save them.

He now returned to the village of Cana where He had changed the water into wine. While He was there a rich man from another city came to Him and begged Him to heal his son who was very, very sick. "Come quickly before my child dies," he pleaded.

But Jesus replied, "Go home, your son is already well again!"

The man believed Jesus, so he started back home. But before he arrived, his servants met him and said, "Your son is well!" He asked them what time the child had begun to get better and they replied, "Yesterday at about one o'clock in the afternoon, the fever left him!"

Then the man realized it was the same time that Jesus had said to him, "Your son is well!" So he and all his family believed in Jesus as the Son of God.

The Jews only offered their sacrifices at the Temple of Jerusalem, but they had churches called synagogues in every city. When Jesus returned to Nazareth, where He had been brought up, He went into the local synagogue on the Sabbath day. He was asked to read aloud to the people from the book of the prophet Isaiah. So He read from the part where Isaiah told the people of Israel about the Saviour who was coming into the world. After he had finished reading and had sat down, everyone in the synagogue was staring at Him. So then He stood up again and preached to them. He told them that what He had just read had come true that very day, right before their eyes. He said that He Himself was the Saviour, the Son of God, whom Isaiah was writing about in the part of the Bible He had just been reading to them.

But when He said this, all the men in the synagogue, or Jewish church, became very angry, for they didn't believe He was telling the truth when He said He was the Saviour. They jumped up and grabbed Him and led Him out to the top of a steep hill on which their city was built, to throw

One dark night Nicodemus came to talk to Jesus about how to get to heaven when he died. Jesus told him, "God loves you so much that I was sent from heaven to die for your sins. Believe this and do what is right."

Him off a cliff and kill Him. For they thought it was very wrong for Him to say He was the Son of God. But Jesus walked away from them, and they couldn't seem to stop Him! This was, of course, another miracle.

QUESTIONS
Who did the lady at the well think Jesus was?
Who did Jesus say He was?
Did Jesus have to go to the sick boy to make him well?
Why were men in the Jewish church angry with Jesus?

155

Jesus Helps Some Fishermen

Jesus now came to Capernaum, a city beside the Sea of Galilee, and great crowds came down to the beach to hear Him preach. There were so many people that Jesus was almost crowded into the water. So when He noticed two fishing boats pulled up along the shore, with the fishermen mending their nets, Jesus stepped into one of the boats—it belonged to Peter—and asked him to push it out a little way into the water. Then He sat down and taught the people from the boat.

When He had finished, He said to Peter and his brother Andrew, "Now go out into the lake and let down your nets."

Peter answered, "Sir, we fished all night and didn't catch a thing; but if You say so, I'll try it again." And to their surprise, in just a little while they caught so many fish that their net broke! Then they shouted to their partners, James and John, who were in the other boat on the beach, to come and help them, and they filled both boats with fish until they almost sank!

When Peter saw the miracle Jesus had done, he knelt before Him and worshipped. Then Jesus said to Peter and Andrew, "Come with Me." And they left their boats, nets, and everything else, and went with Him everywhere, for now they were His disciples.

On the Sabbath day when Jesus

This woman is talking to Jesus beside a well where she has come to get some water. Jesus tells her how to have eternal life and love and joy. Can you see how surprised and interested she is? You can have eternal life from Jesus, too.

went into the synagogue to teach the people, there was a man there who had an evil spirit in him. The evil spirit screamed at Jesus, "Let us alone; what have we to do with You, Jesus of Nazareth? Have You come to destroy us? I know You—You are the Son of God."

Jesus told the evil spirit, "Be still, and come out of him."

Then the spirit yelled and threw the man down on the ground, and finally came out of him. All the people in the synagogue were astonished and said among themselves, "What kind of a man is this that even the wicked spirits obey Him?"

When they left the synagogue, Jesus went to the home of Andrew and Peter. James and John were there, too; and Peter's mother-in-law, but she was sick, and had a fever. They all begged Jesus to heal her. So He went in and stood beside her bed and commanded the fever to leave. Instantly she was well, and got up and cooked dinner for them!

In the evening, at sunset, a great crowd gathered in front of the house, bringing Him many sick people to be healed, and those with evil spirits. And He healed them all, and made the evil spirits come out and go away.

In the morning, getting up long before it was light, Jesus went out to a lonely place in the wilderness to pray. Although He was God's Son, yet He was on the earth as a man who felt pain and hunger, joy and sorrow, and needed to pray for God's help just as the rest of us do. That is why He went out into the desert that morning to pray.

While He was away, many people came to Peter's house looking for Jesus. So Peter and the other disciples went out to find Him, and told Him to come back because everyone was asking where He was. But Jesus replied, "I must go and preach the gospel in other cities, too."

Then He travelled all through Galilee, teaching the Good News in the synagogues and on the beaches. What Good News was it that Jesus preached? It was this: That He had come into the world to be punished for our sins, so that if we turn away from those sins and believe His promise to save us, we won't be punished at the Judgment Day, but God forgives us and takes us to heaven when we die, and we will be happy there forever.

A man with leprosy now came to Jesus and knelt before Him. "Lord, You can heal me if You want to," he pleaded.

Jesus pitied him and put out His hand and touched him. "I want to!" Jesus told him. "Be healed!"

The leprosy left him instantly and he was well again! Jesus told him not to tell anyone who it was who had healed him, but to go to the priest at the Temple and offer a sacrifice, as Moses had commanded those who were cured of leprosy. But as soon as Jesus was gone, the man told everyone what He had done for him!

One special group of Jews were

Some of Jesus' disciples had been fishing all night, but didn't catch a thing. Then Jesus called to them from the shore and told them where to place their nets. See what happened! There are almost too many fish to get them all ashore!

called scribes, and another special group was called the Pharisees. They pretended to be very good, and told the people to obey all the laws in the Scriptures, but they themselves didn't bother with them. They obeyed some of God's commandments, like not working on the Sabbath, but they didn't obey such commandments as being kind and fair. They were hypocrites, that is, they pretended to be good but in their hearts they really weren't at all. So when Jesus told them to turn away from their sins and to obey God, they hated Him and did all they could to keep the people from believing Him.

QUESTIONS

Tell about Peter and Andrew and all the fish.

What happened when Jesus told evil spirits to come out? Tell about this.

What was the Good News Jesus preached?

What does the word hypocrite mean? Are you a hypocrite?

Why did Jesus go out into the desert?

156
Jesus' Twelve Disciples

Now Jesus came again to the city of Capernaum, and great crowds came to the house where He was staying, and He preached to them. The house was a one-story building with a flat roof. Among those who came to Him were four men carrying a sick friend on a stretcher. But there was such a crowd that they couldn't get inside. So they went up on the roof and took off some tiles, and used ropes to let the stretcher down carefully, with their friend on it, right into the room where Jesus was! In fact, the sick man landed right in front of Jesus!

When Jesus saw how much faith they had, He said to the sick man, "Your sins are forgiven!"

But some of the scribes and Pharisees who were sitting there said to themselves, "Who does this man think he is, forgiving sins as though he were God?"

Jesus knew their thoughts and asked them, "Why do you think such sinful thoughts? Is it any harder for Me to forgive this man's sins than to cure him of his sickness? Now I will make him well." Then He said to the sick man, "Stand up and go on home!"

Instantly the man jumped up, stood there for a moment, then picked up the stretcher he had been lying on, and disappeared through the crowd! The people who saw it happen just couldn't get over it. "We've never seen anything like this before," they exclaimed.

In those days the Jews had to pay taxes to the Romans. The taxes were collected by other Jews called publicans and everyone hated them, because most of these tax collectors were unfair—they cheated by collecting extra money for themselves. As Jesus walked along He saw a publican named Matthew sitting at his tax collection booth. Jesus told him, "Follow Me." And Matthew did. He left everything and followed Jesus, and from that time on he was one of Jesus' disciples.

Soon afterwards, Jesus went to Jerusalem to attend the celebration of one of the Jewish holidays, and passed the pool of Bethesda on the way. This pool had five porches around it, all filled with sick, blind, and lame people. Jesus saw a man there who had been sick for thirty-eight years. How Jesus pitied him! This man and all the other sick people had been waiting there because every once in awhile the water moved as if someone had stirred it, and the first person in the water after it stirred was healed of whatever disease he had!

"Do you want to be healed?" Jesus asked him.

"Of course!" the man replied, "But I have no one to help me into the pool after the water stirs; while I am trying to get down into it, someone else steps in ahead of me and I'm too late."

Jesus told him, "Pick up your sleeping mat and start walking!" And immediately the man was well!

But Jesus did this on the Sabbath, the day each week when no work was permitted, so the Jewish leaders scolded the man for "working" by carrying his sleeping mat that day!

"But the man who cured me told me to!" he answered.

"Who said that?" they demanded. He told them it was Jesus. Then the Jews tried to kill Jesus for not obeying their law.

Jesus said that the miracles He did proved that God had sent Him. He told them He was the Son of God and had power to raise the dead—a power only God has. He said the time would come when all who are dead will hear His voice and rise again, and He will judge them. Those who have done good will be rewarded for their obedience, and those who have done evil will be punished for their sins. For His Father has made Him the Judge of all, so that all must worship and obey Jesus just as they worship and obey God.

Another time, again on the Sabbath, Jesus and His disciples were walking through some grain fields. The disciples were hungry, so they picked some grain, rubbed it in their hands to get rid of the husks, and ate the kernels. When the Jewish leaders saw them doing this they again said that the disciples were working on the Sabbath, but Jesus told them it was all right, for God had put Him in charge of the Sabbath, so He knew best about what work could be done on the Sabbath.

On another Sabbath day He went into the Jewish church, or synagogue, and saw a man there with a shrunken hand. The Pharisees watched to see whether Jesus would work on the Sabbath by healing the man! But Jesus knew their thoughts and said to them, "If one of your sheep fell into a well on the Sabbath, wouldn't you pull it out? And if it is right to help a sheep on the Sabbath, how much more a man?"

Then He said to the man, "Reach out your hand!" And when he did, it was healed!

This made the Jewish leaders very angry, and they began to talk about killing Jesus. So He and His disciples left that place and went away to the Sea of Galilee. Many people from Jerusalem and Judea and from countries far away came to see Him when they heard of the wonderful things He did. The sick people crowded around Him to touch Him, for when they did, they got well!

After this He went alone into the desert and stayed there all night, praying to God. When it was morning, He called His disciples and chose twelve of them to be with Him, and to preach, and do miracles, and to heal the sick and cast out devils. These twelve were called "apostles," or "messengers." These were their names:

Peter,
Andrew (Peter's brother),
James,
John (James' brother),
Phillip,
Bartholomew,
Thomas,
Matthew (the publican),
James,
Thaddeus,
Simon,
Judas Iscariot.

QUESTIONS

Tell about the paralyzed man and his four friends.

What was Matthew's job before he followed Jesus?

Why did sick people come to the Pool of Bethesda?

How many of the twelve apostles can you name?

Jesus is telling his friends that they must be kind and good. If they are harmed because they don't fight back, He will give them some special blessings.

157
Jesus Talks to the Crowds

When Jesus saw the crowds coming to Him He climbed a hill and sat there with His disciples, teaching them. These are some of the things He told them:

"Blessed are the humble, for the kingdom of heaven belongs to humble people. They are the truly happy ones.

"Blessed are those who mourn, for they shall be comforted.

"Blessed are the meek, for they shall inherit the earth.

"Blessed are those who are anxious to do right and to please God, for they shall be satisfied.

"Blessed are those who are merciful to others, for they shall have mercy shown to them.

"Blessed are the pure in heart, for they shall see God.

"Blessed are the peacemakers (that is those who will not quarrel and who try to keep others from anger and fighting), for they shall be called the children of God."

Jesus told His disciples that when they were treated cruelly because they were His followers, they should be glad, for they would get a big reward in heaven!

He also told them that they must not be afraid to let others know that they loved and obeyed God. Their example would help others to love and obey Him too.

If we do the things God commands, and teach others to do them, we will be great in the kingdom of heaven.

He told His disciples that before they worshipped God and prayed to Him, they must try to remember and set right the wrongs they had done. If they had taken something that didn't belong to them, they must give it back, or if they had told a lie they must confess it and try to catch the lie before it got away any farther. For God won't accept our worship while there is sin in our hearts that we refuse to confess.

Jesus also told His disciples that they must always be pure and good in thought and action; they (and we) must not even think bad thoughts.

And when others are unkind to us, and do us harm, we must not try to pay them back. Instead we must do good to them and pray for them and love them; for then we will truly be the children of our Father in Heaven. We will be like Him, for He is kind even to those who don't obey Him or love Him.

Jesus told His disciples not to just pretend to be nice so that others would praise them for it, but to please God by being *really* nice to others. And when we give help to the poor we must not go around bragging about it.

Jesus said we must not want to be rich, but must send our money on ahead to heaven. How do we do this? By giving our money to the church and Sunday school, and to the missionaries, and to the poor. And then in heaven we will have more things to make us happy than all the money in the world can buy.

This is something else that Jesus said to the people at this time: "You can't obey both God and Satan. For if you obey God you will do what is right, but if you obey Satan you will do what is wrong. So you can't do both—you must choose one or the other.

He told His disciples to stop arguing and blaming each other. This is important for us, too. The person we blame may not have done the thing we blame him for; and if he did, he may not have meant any harm. We can't see his heart and know how he felt while he was doing it; only God knows that, and perhaps God doesn't blame him. And how often we ourselves do the very things we blame others for! Jesus said for us to stop doing wrong before we try to tell others about their faults!

He said that we should treat others as we want them to treat us. If we want them to be kind to us, we must be kind to them.

"Work hard to enter the narrow gate of heaven," Jesus told His disciples, "for the road to hell is wide and smooth." He meant that we must choose the road we will travel along through life. The road to heaven is narrow and rough, where few bother to walk. The road to hell is broad, well-paved, and popular, and stands wide open before us, welcoming us.

Jesus said that not everyone who calls Him Lord and Master will get to heaven, but only those who obey His Father in heaven. Many will come to Him at the Judgment Day and call him "Lord" and will say they have worked for Him and taught others about Him. But He will tell them they have never truly been His disciples. And He will send them away with all the other wicked people because they only pretended to be His disciples but didn't really do what He told them to.

One day Jesus told His disciples an important story about two men who built two houses. One of them chose solid rock to build his house on. When he had finished it, a great storm came up, but the rain and wind could do no harm because the house had such a solid foundation.

The other man built his house on sand, and when the storm came, the rain washed the sand away from beneath his house, and the wind blew against it, and it fell down in a great heap and washed away.

Jesus said that we are either like the wise or foolish man. If we listen to His teaching and do what He tells us to do, then we are like the wise man who built his house on the rock. But those who listen to Him but don't do what He tells them to are like the foolish man who built his house on the sand. Those who do what He tells them to will be saved, but those who disobey Him will be lost, for the storm means the Judgment Day.

QUESTIONS

What did Jesus say we should do before we pray to God?

What did Jesus say to do if someone hurts us?

How did Jesus say we should use our money?

Since we want other people to be nice to us, how should we treat them?

Can you tell the story about the wise man and foolish man who built houses? What does the story mean?

Jesus talked to John and Peter on the beach. Their fishing boat is on the lake behind them. Both of them decided to become Jesus' disciples. "Come with Me and fish for men!" Jesus invited them.

R. Hook

158
Jesus Defeats Death

In the city of Capernaum there lived a Roman army officer who had a servant he dearly loved, but the servant was very sick and ready to die. When the officer heard that Jesus had come to his city, he asked some of the Jewish leaders to go and find Jesus and beg him to come to the officer's house and heal his servant. So they went and found Jesus and pleaded with Him for help. "This officer is a Roman, not a Jew," they explained, "but he has a deep love for the Jews and has been very kind to us and has even built us a church with his own money."

Jesus started off with them to the officer's house. But before they got there, the officer sent Him this message: "Please don't come! For I'm not good enough to have You in my house. Instead, stop where You are and just say that my servant must get well, and he will! I'm sure the sickness will obey Your orders and go away, just as my soldiers obey me and do whatever I tell them to!"

Jesus was very greatly surprised. "I've never before met even a Jew with this much faith!" He exclaimed. "And I tell you, at the Judgment Day many people of other nations who have faith in Me will be in heaven, while many of the Jews won't, because they don't believe."

So Jesus didn't go to the man's house, but healed the servant while he was far away. And when the officer returned home, he found that the servant was well again!

The next day Jesus went to the city of Nain. Just as He was entering the city gate, He met some people carrying out a dead boy to bury him. He was the only son of his mother, and she was a widow, that is—his father was dead. Many of her friends were with her.

When Jesus saw her, He pitied her. "Don't cry!" He said. Then He stopped the funeral procession and went over to the dead boy and said, "Young man, get up!" And the boy sat up, alive! And Jesus gave him back to his mother!

Everyone was frightened by this amazing miracle, and how they praised God! "Jesus must be a very great prophet indeed to be able to bring someone back to life again," they exclaimed.

One day a man named Simon asked Jesus to come to his home for dinner. But as they were eating, a prostitute* came with an expensive bottle of perfume and knelt at Jesus' feet, crying because she was sorry for her sins and wanted to be forgiven. Her tears fell on Jesus' feet and she wiped them with her long hair and kissed them and poured the perfume over them.

Simon knew this woman was a sinner, and he said to himself, "If Jesus were really God's Son, He would know who this woman is, and how bad she is, and He would send her away."

Jesus knew what the man was thinking and said to him, "Simon, I have something to say to you: Two people owed a man some money. One owed him a lot, and the other owed him only a little. But neither of them had any money to pay him back, so he told them they could forget about it and they didn't have to give him back the money. Tell me now, which of these two men do you suppose will like him best for being so kind to them?"

Simon replied, "I suppose the one who owed him the most."

"Yes," Jesus said, "that is correct." Then He turned to the woman and said to Simon, "Do you see this woman? When I came into your house, you didn't give Me any water to wash My feet, but she has washed My feet with her tears, and wiped them with her hair. You didn't give Me the customary kiss of greeting on my cheek, but this woman has kissed My feet again and again. And so her many sins are forgiven, for she loves Me so much. But those who have little to be forgiven for will love Me only a little."

Then Jesus turned to the woman and said, "Your sins are forgiven; go home in peace!"

After this Jesus went through the entire country, preaching the Good News in every city and village; and the twelve apostles were with Him.

Jesus was very poor, though He could have been very rich if he had wanted to be, for the world was His. Yet He chose to be poor and to suffer for us so that He could save us from being punished for our sins. And because He was so poor, some of the women He had healed gave Him the things He needed. One of them was named Mary Magdalene, another Joanna, and another Susanna, and there were many others.

QUESTIONS

Why was Jesus surprised when the Roman officer believed Him?
Did He go and heal his servant?
Tell about Jesus making a dead boy live.
Did Jesus send the prostitute away because He knew she was bad? Why not?
Was Jesus rich or poor? Why?

*Definition for younger readers: "A woman who goes to bed with men she isn't married to." This is strictly against God's laws.

159
Some Parables

Jesus often told the people stories which contained lessons. These stories are called parables. One of His stories made them see how foolish and wicked it was for them to put their trust in money. Here is the story:

"There was a rich man with many farms and orchards. When harvest time came, his crops were so large that his barns wouldn't hold them all. Then he said to himself, 'What shall I do? I haven't enough space to store my harvest. I know! I'll tear down my barns and build larger ones. Then I can eat, drink, and be merry, for I'll be rich enough to live for many years without ever working again.'

"But God said to him, 'Fool! Tonight you die! Then who will get all your wealth?'

"All those who live to get rich are like that foolish man. For death often comes when they are least expecting it, and they must leave their money for others, and go away to a world where nothing but sorrow has been stored up for them."

Jesus told His disciples not to be afraid of being poor. "Be like the birds," He said. "They don't plant seeds in the fields, or reap grain, yet they have enough to eat because God feeds them. And God cares more about you than He does about the birds! And look at the flowers! They don't need to work hard to get clothes for themselves, and yet they are more beautifully clothed and have brighter colors than Solomon the king of Israel! So if God gives such beautiful clothing to the flowers, which are of so little value that one day they are growing in the field and the next are cut down and burned, He will surely give you all the clothes you need. So don't be afraid to trust Him. Your heavenly Father knows what you need. The most important thing for you to do is

Jesus told a story about a man who planted his field by throwing handfuls of seed across the ground. That is the way farmers used to do before they had machinery as we do today. Can you explain what Jesus' story meant? Here is a hint: the seeds are God's words.

R. Hook

to obey Him and to be His child. Then He will give you everything you need."

Great crowds surrounded Jesus as He walked along the shore of the lake, so He got into a boat and taught the people from there. He told them this story:

"A farmer went out into the field to sow grain. Some of the seed fell on the hard ground of a path that ran along beside the edge of the field, and the birds flew down and ate it. Some of the seed fell on stony places where there wasn't enough earth on top of the rocks to make strong roots, so in a few days the little plants withered away. And some of the seed fell where briars and weeds were growing; the seeds began to grow but the weeds were tall and thick and shut out the sunshine and used up the rain, so the little plants soon died. But the rest of the seed fell on good ground—plowed and harrowed and ready to receive it. The rain watered it, and the sun shone down upon it, and it soon grew; and after a few months there was a harvest of grain—a hundred times as much as the farmer had planted."

When Jesus was alone with His disciples, they asked Him to explain this parable to them. He told them that the seed meant His words. Some of His words are heard by people with hard hearts who refuse to believe Him. Satan comes and takes God's words away from them by making them think of other things, just as the birds ate the seed that fell on the hard pathway. Other people to whom Jesus speaks try for awhile to obey Him, but it is only for a little while. As soon as they have trouble, or are laughed at by others, they turn away from Him. This is like the seed that falls on the stony ground; at first it grows quickly, but in a few days it withers away.

Other people hear Jesus preach and are glad, but afterwards they begin to care more for their homes, their money and their pleasures than they do for the things of God. This is the seed that fell among thorns, and the thorns grew up and choked it.

But there are some people who listen carefully to everything Jesus says, and remember it, and try every day to obey whatever He tells them to. They are like the good soil where the seeds grew well and there was a crop of a hundred times as much seed as the farmer had planted.

Then Jesus told them a story about a mustard seed. It is among the smallest of seeds, but when it is planted it becomes a very large bush. So it is with our trust in God. At first it seems very small. But if we are truly His children, our faith will grow stronger and greater until we trust Him more and more, and try to please Him in everything we do.

Jesus also told the people about a jeweler looking for pearls to buy at a bargain. He went to everyone who had any to sell, and at last he found a pearl that was larger and more beautiful than any he had ever seen before. But although it was priced at far less than its real value, he still didn't have nearly enough money to buy it. So he sold everything he owned and came back and bought that one precious pearl. This is the way people feel who want their sins forgiven. They cannot be happy until it is done, and they are willing to give up every sinful pleasure, and everything that offends God, so that they may come to Him and ask Him to forgive their sins.

Then Jesus talked about fishermen and their nets. The fisherman takes his net out in his boat and throws it into the water, and then pulls it slowly to shore, and finds many fish in it. But the fish are of many different kinds. Some are good to eat and some aren't. The good ones are gathered into baskets to keep; those not good are thrown away. Jesus told His disciples it will be like that at the end of the world; angels will come and separate the good people from the bad, and send away the bad people to be punished.

One of the Jewish leaders came to Jesus and said, "Master, I want to be with You wherever You go."

Jesus replied, "The foxes have dens to live in, and the birds have nests, but I have nowhere to lay My head." Jesus meant that He was poorer than the foxes and the birds, for they had homes of their own, but He had nowhere to go when He was weary.

QUESTIONS

What is a parable?

Why did Jesus say it was foolish to worry about earning lots of money?

In what way should people be like the birds and flowers?

Can you tell the story Jesus told about a farmer planting seed? What did the seed mean, in the story?

160
Miracles!

That evening Jesus and His disciples got into a boat to sail over to the other side of the Sea of Galilee. But suddenly it began to be windy, and soon there was a great storm, and the waves dashed into the boat and began to fill it with water so that it was beginning to sink. But Jesus was asleep.

"Master!" they shouted to Him, "Save us! We'll all be drowned!"

Then Jesus stood up and spoke to the winds and the sea, and said to them, "Peace! Be still!"

The wind stopped blowing, and the sea became very still and calm. Then He said to His disciples, "Why were you afraid? How is it that you have so little faith?"

So they went on to the other side of the lake, and when Jesus got out of the boat, there was a man there with an evil spirit in him. The man had torn off his clothes and was naked and very fierce, so that no one could go by him without getting hurt. His friends had often tied him with chains to keep him at home, but he broke the chains and went out and lived in a graveyard, crying out and cutting himself with stones.

While Jesus was still far out on the lake, the man saw Him and ran to Him as He stepped ashore and fell down at His feet and worshipped Him. The evil spirits in the man were frightened when they saw Jesus, for they knew He could make them go away. They begged Him to let them enter a herd of pigs feeding nearby, and Jesus told them they could. So the evil spirits came out of the man and went into the herd of pigs. Then the whole herd (there were about two thousand of them) ran over to a cliff and tumbled off into the sea, and were drowned.

The men who had been taking care of the pigs ran into the nearby city and told everyone what had happened. So all the people came rushing out to see Jesus. When they saw the wild man sitting there quietly—clothed, and in his right mind—they were afraid, and asked Jesus to go away from their country.

So He got back into the boat to leave. The man begged to go with Him, but Jesus said, "No, go home to your friends and tell them what great things the Lord has done for you." So the man began telling everyone how Jesus had made him well.

QUESTIONS

What does it mean to have faith like a mustard seed?

Tell about how the wind and the sea obeyed Jesus.

When Jesus sent away the evil spirits from the man, where did they go? What happened to the man?

A terrible storm threatened to sink the disciples' little boat. Jesus was asleep, but they screamed to him to wake up and save them all from drowning. So Jesus stood up and told the storm to calm down, and suddenly the wind died away, the waves disappeared, and the storm ended. Then at last the disciples believed that Jesus really was the Son of God.

R. Hook

161

Sick People Get Well

As soon as Jesus returned to Capernaum, one of the leaders of the local Jewish church came and knelt at His feet and told Him, "My little daughter is very sick and I'm afraid she is going to die. Oh, please come and put your hands on her head, so that she will get well again."

Jesus went with him, and so did His disciples, followed by a great crowd. In the crowd was a woman who had suffered for twelve years from a disease no doctor could cure; she had given them all the money she had, but was no better—in fact, she was worse. But when she heard that Jesus was in town she said to herself, 'If I can only touch Him, I'll get well.' So she pushed her way through the crowd and touched Him; and as soon as she did, her sickness was cured.

Immediately Jesus turned around to the crowd and asked, "Who touched Me?"

The disciples were disgusted with Him. "Why ask such a foolish question?" they said. "The whole crowd is pushing and touching You!" But He still kept looking around to see who had done it. When the woman saw that He knew what she had done, she came trembling and fell at His feet, and told all the people why she had touched Him, and how in a moment she was well.

"Daughter, don't be afraid," Jesus said to her. "Because of your faith in Me you are healed."

While He was still talking to the woman, a messenger arrived to tell the little girl's father, "Your child is dead. It's no use for the Master to come now."

But Jesus told the father, "Only have faith and she will come back to life!"

When they arrived at the house, Jesus saw the people weeping and wailing and said to them, "Why weep? The child isn't dead, she is only

Jairus was the pastor of a Jewish church. One day his little girl became sick, so he went to find Jesus to make her well again. But she died while he was away. Then Jesus came and took her by the hand and told her to get well again. How happy everyone is now!

asleep!" He meant that she would soon be alive again, like one wakened from sleep. But they didn't believe Him, and laughed at Him. Then Jesus told all of them to leave, and took three of His disciples—Peter, James, and John—and the father and the mother of the dead child, and went into the room where she lay. Then He took her by the hand and said, "Get up, little girl!" And the little girl—she was twelve years old—jumped up and started walking! Then Jesus said to give her something to eat!

As Jesus left her home, two blind men followed Him, calling, "Oh, son of David, have mercy on us." They called Jesus this because He was a relative of King David's, and this was a title of honor and respect among the Jews.

"Do you believe that I am able to make you well?" Jesus asked them.

"Oh, yes, Lord!" they replied. Then He touched their eyes, and immediately they could see.

"Don't tell anyone what I have done for you," Jesus told them, but they told everyone!

Now a man was brought to Him who couldn't talk because of an evil spirit in him. So Jesus told the evil spirit to go away, and it did. Then the man could talk again! "What wonderful things are happening today," all the people exclaimed.

But the Jewish leaders were jealous of Jesus and hated Him. They told the people that He was able to cast out devils only because Satan, the prince of the devils, was inside Him. What a wicked thing to say!

Jesus now returned to Nazareth where He had been brought up, and went into the Jewish church on the Sabbath day and taught the people. They were amazed at His wonderful sermon. "Where did this man get such great wisdom and power to do such wonderful miracles?" they asked. "Isn't He the son of Joseph the carpenter, and of Mary? And aren't His brothers and sisters here with us?"

So they refused to believe He was anything special, because He seemed so common to them. And because they didn't believe, He did few miracles among them except to put His hands on a few sick people to heal them.

QUESTIONS

Jesus said, "Because of your faith in Me you are healed." What is faith? Do you have faith in Jesus?

What did the blind men call Jesus? Why?

Why didn't Jesus do a lot of miracles in his home town?

162
Power for Jesus' Disciples

Jesus now sent His twelve disciples all through the land to preach the Good News. But He told them to go only to the Jews, for they were God's chosen people, and God wanted the Good News preached to them first.

Jesus gave the disciples power to do miracles so that everyone would believe what they preached. "Wherever you go," He told them, "heal the sick, make the lepers well, raise the dead, and tell everyone that Christ has come to save all who believe on Him. But don't expect them to be kind to you! They will treat you as they have treated Me. They will take you before their judges and whip you because you preach to them about Me. But don't fear them, for they can only kill your bodies. Fear God who is able to destroy both soul and body in hell."

Jesus told them not to take any money or food with them on their trip, for God would give them all they needed. "God even cares about the sparrows and feeds them," Jesus said, "and not one of them dies without God's knowing about it. So don't be afraid that He won't take care of you! For you are much more valuable to Him than the sparrows are! He remembers the smallest thing about you, and knows even the number of hairs on your head. And He will notice everyone who treats you well. When anyone is kind to you, he is being kind to Me, and whoever gives you even a drink of cold water because you are My disciples will be rewarded for doing it."

When Jesus had finished talking to them, they went out to the cities and towns preaching to the people and healing those who were sick.

Afterwards, when they returned, they told Him all they had done. "Let's get away to some quiet place where you can rest awhile," He said. There were so many people coming and going that they scarcely had time to eat. So they all got into a boat and sailed across to the other side of the Sea of Galilee where they could be alone. But when the people saw where they were headed, they followed on foot, walking around the lake to the other side where Jesus was.

As soon as they arrived across the lake the people recognized Him and ran to get those who were sick, so that He could heal them. And wherever He went, in villages or cities, sick people were laid in the streets and all who touched Him became perfectly well!

In the evening His apostles came to Him and said, "Send the people away to the villages to buy food, for it will soon be dark."

"They don't need to go away," Jesus said; "you feed them!"

"What?" the disciples exclaimed, "Feed all this crowd?"

"How many loaves of bread do you have?" Jesus asked them. "Go and see."

When they knew, they said, "Five, and two small fish."

He told them to tell all the people to sit down in groups on the green grass. Then He took the five loaves and two fish, looked up to heaven and thanked God for them; then broke the loaves in pieces, and gave them to the apostles; also the two fish. Then the disciples passed them out to the people. And the strangest thing happened! As the disciples broke off pieces of bread, the loaves were still the same size as before, so there was enough for everyone! And it was the same with the fish.

QUESTIONS

To whom did Jesus give power to do miracles? Why?

How can thinking about sparrows remind us of how much God cares for us?

What happened to the five loaves and two fish?

Jesus is feeding 5,000 hungry boys and girls and mothers and fathers! He borrowed a little boy's lunch of five buns and two fish, and broke them into pieces and gave them to His twelve disciples, and they passed them out to the people sitting on the ground. No matter how much they gave them, there was still enough left for everyone. Twelve basketfuls were left over!

F+R. Hook

163

A Miracle at a Picnic

Jesus now returned to Capernaum again, and went into the Jewish church to teach the people about God.

"What should we do to please God?" the people asked Him.

"Believe that I am the Saviour!" He replied.

But the Jews were expecting a Saviour who would be a great soldier and set them free from the Romans, so that they could have their own king. But Jesus was a poor man, not some great hero. He didn't promise to make them rich, but told them they were sinners. Many people didn't like Him for this, and refused to believe that He was the Saviour, and went away and left Him.

Then He said to the twelve disciples, "Are you too going to leave Me?"

Peter replied, "Lord, where else can we go? For no one else but You can save us."

Then Jesus told them, "I have chosen you twelve to be My apostles, and one of you is My enemy." He meant Judas Iscariot, who was going to help the chief priests and elders of the Jews put Him to death. They hated Jesus and did all they could to keep the people from believing Him.

Jesus then left the country of Israel and went to Tyre and Sidon. The people who lived in those cities were not Jews, but Gentiles. While He was there a woman begged Him to get rid of an evil spirit that was in her daughter. At first He turned away as if unwilling to hear her because she wasn't a Jew, but He did this only to find out whether she truly believed in Him. Then she begged Him more earnestly, and fell at His feet and worshipped Him. "Lord, help me," she begged.

Then Jesus told her, "Because of your faith in Me, your daughter is healed." And when she got home, the evil spirit had gone out of her daughter and she was perfectly well.

Jesus now returned to Israel. A deaf man who could hardly speak was brought to Him to be healed. Jesus led him away from the crowd and put His fingers into the man's ears, and touched his tongue with spit, and looking up to heaven, said, "Be opened!" And immediately the man was well and could both hear and speak!

Soon many sick people who were lame and blind, or couldn't speak, were brought to Him and laid before him so that He could heal them. And He healed them all. The people marvelled as they saw the lame walking, and the blind seeing. And how they thanked God!

The crowd soon became very large, and once again Jesus fed them with only a few loaves of bread, and a few fish. The people had been with Him for three days and had nothing left to eat, for they had eaten all the food they had brought with them.

Then Jesus said to them, "If I send these people away to their homes without food, they will faint along the road, for many of them have come from far away. How many loaves of bread do you have with you?"

"Seven!" they replied, "and a few small fish!"

Then He told the 4,000 people to sit on the ground, and He took the seven loaves and the fish and thanked God for them, and gave them to His disciples to give to the people. And everyone ate until full. Afterwards, seven basketfuls of scraps were picked up off the ground!

He went next to the city of Bethsaida, where a blind man was brought to Him, and the people begged Jesus to touch and heal him. Jesus took him by the hand and led him out of the town; then Jesus touched the man's eyes with spit and placed His hands on him.

Jesus asked him if he could see. "Yes," the blind man said, "I see some men, but they look like trees walking around."

Then Jesus put His hands on the man's eyes again, and told him to look up, and now the man could see everything clearly

QUESTIONS

What kind of Saviour were the Jews expecting? Was Jesus this sort of person?

Did Jesus know that one of His twelve apostles was His enemy? What is a traitor?

How did Jesus feed the huge crowd that came to Him?

164
Who Is Jesus?

As Jesus was going to the city of Caesarea with His twelve disciples, He asked them, "Who do the people think I am?"

"Some say You are John the Baptist, risen from the dead," they answered. "Others say You are the prophet Elijah, come back to earth again."

Then Jesus asked, "Who do you think I am?"

Peter replied, "You are the Christ, the Son of God." In other words, Peter was telling Jesus that he believed He was the Saviour. But Peter and the other disciples were looking for a Saviour who would save them from being ruled by Rome. They knew He was poor, but they expected Him to become rich and great, and believed that He would make them great, too. Like the rest of the Jews, they had not yet learned that He had come to rule in their hearts. Instead of fighting battles for them as a king, He was going to die on the cross for their sins.

Now Jesus began to tell his disciples what was going to happen to Him when He arrived in Jerusalem: He would be cruelly treated by the chief priests and other leaders of the Jews. In fact, they would kill Him, but He would come back to life again three days afterwards.

When Peter heard this he exclaimed, "No, these things will never happen to You." But it was for this very reason—to suffer these things—that Jesus came into the world. So when Peter said they would not happen to Him, Jesus was displeased and called Peter His enemy. For Peter didn't want Him to do what would please God, but what would please Peter.

One day Jesus took Peter, James, and John up on a high mountain to pray. As He prayed His face began to shine like the sun and His clothing glistened and became as white as snow. Suddenly two men were standing beside Him, talking with Him. They were Moses and Elijah, who had died many hundreds of years before. Now they had returned to this world to talk with Jesus about His being crucified at Jerusalem.

The disciples recognized these two men—we don't know how—and were too excited and frightened to know what to think. Finally Peter exclaimed, "Master, this is great! Would You like us to get three tents—one for You, one for Moses, and one for Elijah?"

But just then a bright cloud came across the sky and God's voice spoke from the cloud. "This is My beloved Son," God called to them. "Listen carefully to everything He tells you."

The disciples fell face downward to the ground in awful fear, but Jesus came and touched them and said, "Get up, don't be afraid." When they stood up and looked around, Moses and Elijah were gone; and no one was there except Jesus. Then Jesus told them, "Don't tell anyone what you have seen until after I have died and become alive again." But they didn't understand what He meant when He spoke of becoming alive again.

When they came down from the mountain the next day, many people were waiting to see Jesus. A man came and knelt before Him and pleaded, "Master, please help my son, my only child. An evil spirit has gotten into him, and it tried to kill him by making him fall into the fire and into the water. I took him to Your disciples, but they couldn't heal him. Oh, please, help me."

"Bring him here," Jesus told him. But as the father was bringing his boy, the evil spirit in the boy threw him to the ground, foaming at the mouth. Jesus asked his father, "How long has he been this way?"

"From the time he was just a little child," the father replied.

Then Jesus said to the evil spirit, "I command you to come out of this boy and never enter him again!"

Instantly the spirit began shrieking and then came out as the boy lay on the ground, apparently dead. "The evil spirit killed him," everyone said. But Jesus took the boy by the hand and pulled him to his feet, and he was well!

When Jesus and the disciples went back to Capernaum, the tax collectors asked Peter whether or not Jesus was going to pay the Temple tax. Jesus knew the men were talking to Peter about this, so when Peter came back into the room Jesus said to him, "Go to the Sea of Galilee and throw in a hook and a fishing line. Open the mouth of the first fish you catch, and you will find a piece of money in it! Give it to these men as the tax for both of us." So Peter did as Jesus said, and found the piece of money and gave it to the men!

QUESTIONS

Who did Peter believe that Jesus was?

What two men came back to life to talk to Jesus? Do you remember reading about them earlier in this book? Tell something about them.

Why did the little boy fall into fires and into water?

What did Peter find in the fish's mouth? What did Jesus say to use it for?

165

One Leper Says, "Thank You"

Now although Jesus had plainly told the disciples what was going to happen to Him—that He would be treated cruelly and put to death at Jerusalem—still they never seemed to understand. They thought that even if He had to suffer, soon afterwards He would be crowned the king of Israel and become very great, and then they would be great too!

One day as they were walking along, the disciples began to argue with each other about which of them would be the greatest in Jesus' kingdom. When they arrived at the house where they were going, He asked them, "What were you arguing about out there on the road?" But they didn't answer, for they were ashamed to tell Him. Then He called a little child over to Him and gathered His disciples around. He told them that unless they put away their pride and became like the little child—humble and willing to obey—they could not even get into the kingdom, let alone be the greatest in it.

Another time He said, "If your hand or foot causes you to do wrong, cut it off." He meant that it is far better to turn away from the most enjoyable sin and go to heaven than to keep on sinning and find oneself in hell.

Jesus also told His disciples that whenever they met to worship Him, even though only two or three were there, His Spirit would be right there with them. And if one of them did something wrong and afterwards confessed it and was sorry about it, the person he had wronged must forgive him.

Peter asked, "How many times must we forgive him—as many as seven times?"

"No!" Jesus answered, "not only seven times, but seventy times seven!" He meant that we must *always* be ready to forgive each other.

Then He told them another story: "There was a king," He said, "and a man who owed the king $1,000,000. But the man couldn't pay it back. So the king ordered him and his wife and his children to be sold as slaves, so that the money they were sold for could be paid to the king for the debt. That was the custom in those days. Then the man fell down on his knees before the king and begged him to be patient until he could repay the money and the king was sorry for him, and was kind—he forgave him the entire debt!

"But that same man went out and found another man who owed him only a few dollars. He caught him by the throat and said, 'Pay me what you owe me!' The man fell down at his feet and begged, 'Have patience with me and I will pay back everything I owe you.' But the first man wouldn't wait; he had him arrested and thrown into jail, to be kept there until he paid.

"When the king heard about this, he summoned the first man. 'How low can a man get?' he demanded. 'I forgave you all that huge debt just because you asked me to, and shouldn't you have pitied that other fellow just as I pitied you?' And the angry king sent him away to be punished until he paid back all he owed."

In this story, the king means God, and the man who owed so much means us, because we have sinned so often against God. And God will punish us if we don't forgive others, just as the king in the story punished the man who wouldn't forgive.

As Jesus and His disciples travelled to Jerusalem, He sent two of them on ahead to get hotel reservations. They came to a village and asked where they could stay that night, but the men of the village told them to go away, for they hated all Jews.

When James and John heard what had happened they were very angry, and asked Jesus to let them ask God to send down fire from heaven to destroy the entire city. Jesus wasn't at all happy with James and John for talking like that. "I didn't come to destroy lives, but to save them," He said. So He and His disciples went on to another village.

As they were walking along, ten lepers came to meet Jesus. They stood at a distance and shouted, "Jesus, Master, have mercy on us."

When Jesus heard them shouting to Him, He called back to them. "Go and show yourselves to the priest." For if lepers got well, they went to the priest to examine them, to say they were healed.

And as these ten men were going to the priest's house, they were healed. But only one of them came back to thank Jesus for making him well.

QUESTIONS

What did the disciples argue about?

How many times did Jesus say we must forgive someone?

In the story Jesus told, what did the man do after the king forgave him his debt?

Of the ten lepers Jesus healed, how many returned to thank Him?

166
The Good Samaritan

When Jesus arrived in Jerusalem, He went to the Temple to teach the people about God. "Soon I'll be going back to My Father," He told them, "and then you will look for me but won't be able to find Me. And you can't go where I am going because you refuse to believe that I am the Son of God. So you will die without having your sins forgiven. But if anyone believes Me, he will never really die."

Jesus meant that those who trust Him will have eternal life after death. But the Jews thought He was saying that they would never die at all. "Abraham died," they said, "and the prophets died, and yet you say that if a man believes You, he will never die! Are you greater than Abraham and the prophets?"

Jesus replied that Abraham knew about Him and His coming to earth, and believed and trusted Him.

"Of course!" the Jewish leaders sneered. "Why, you aren't even fifty years old—how could you have known Abraham?"

Jesus told them that He had been alive in heaven before Abraham was born. This made them so angry that they picked up stones to throw at Him and kill Him, but He just walked away.

Another day while He was teaching the people, a lawyer asked Him this question: "Master, what must I do to be saved?"

"What does God's law say?" Jesus asked him.

The lawyer replied that the Bible said for him to love God and his neighbors.

"Right!" Jesus replied, "Do that and you will be saved!"

"But who is my neighbor?" the lawyer asked.

Jesus answered by telling him this story: "A man was travelling from Jerusalem to Jericho, but some robbers stopped him and stole his cloth-

Jesus told a story about an Israeli who was beaten up by robbers and left for dead. The Jewish priests wouldn't stop to help him, but an Arab did. He took him to the hospital and paid all of his expenses. That, Jesus said, is the kind of love that all of us should have for our enemies.

R. Hook

ing and beat him up. He was seriously wounded, and the robbers left him half dead beside the road. While he lay there on the ground, too weak to get up, a Jewish priest went by. He was a minister and a teacher of God's law, but instead of being kind to the wounded man, he crossed over to the other side of the road and went on, pretending he didn't see the man lying there. Next, a Levite came along (Levites were the men who helped people worship at the Temple) but when he saw the man, he too went right on without trying to help him.

But then, a Samaritan came by. The Jews hated the Samaritans so it wouldn't be surprising if this Samaritan had refused to help the wounded Jew. But when he saw him he pitied him, and pulling out his first aid kit, bandaged up his wounds, and put medicine on them. Then he helped him onto the back of his donkey, and took him to a hospital, and paid the man's bill.

"Which of these three men was a neighbor to the wounded man?" Jesus asked the lawyer.

"The one who helped him," the lawyer replied.

Then Jesus told him, "Go and do the same to everyone who needs your help." Jesus meant that people who say they love God must prove it by being kind to others.

Jesus now went out to the village of Bethany, a little way from Jerusalem, to visit two sisters named Martha and Mary and their brother Lazarus. When Jesus arrived, Mary sat at His feet to listen to Him tell about the way to heaven. But Martha kept on working in the kitchen and was angry with her sister for not helping. She said to Jesus, "Sir, don't You even care that Mary has lcft all the work for me to do? Tell her to come and help me."

But Jesus said, "Martha, Martha, you get upset so easily. Only one thing is important and Mary has chosen it. And I don't think I should tell her not to." Mary had chosen to listen to Jesus, the very most important thing that any of us can ever do.

Jesus now taught His disciples how to pray, giving them this sample prayer: "Our Father in Heaven, may Your name be reverenced by everyone. May Your kingdom come soon. May Your will be done on earth as it is in heaven. Give us this day our daily bread, and forgive us our sins just as we forgive those who sin against us. And lead us not into temptation but deliver us from evil. For Yours is the kingdom, and the power, and the glory forever, Amen."

QUESTIONS

Jesus said, "If anyone believes Me, he will never really die." What did the Jews think He meant? What *did* He mean?

Can you tell the story of the good Samaritan? What does it teach us?

What did Martha do when Jesus came to visit? What did Mary do?

Jesus taught His disciples how to pray. Do you know how? Do you pray regularly? When?

Martha is mad! She wants Mary to come and help her instead of just sitting there talking to Jesus! But Mary was wise. Do you ever talk to Jesus?

167

A Man Born Blind

Now Jesus chose seventy more disciples besides the first twelve, and sent them out two by two into every city and town where He Himself expected to follow later. He told them to heal the sick and to preach the Good News to people everywhere.

Afterwards they returned to Him full of joy because they had been able to do wonderful miracles in His name. But He told them not to be glad just because they had power to do miracles, but because their names are written down among those whose sins are forgiven, and who will go to heaven when they die.

As He left the Temple, He saw a man who had been blind ever since he was born. Jesus spat on the ground and made clay of the spittle, and put it on the eyes of the blind man and said to him, "Go and wash in the pool of Siloam."

He did, and when he came back, he could see! Then his neighbors and many others who knew him when he was blind, asked, "Isn't this the blind beggar?"

Some said, "Yes," and others "No, he just looks like him."

But the man said, "Yes, I'm the blind beggar, but now I can see!"

"Wonderful!" they exclaimed. "Whatever happened?"

"A man called Jesus made clay and put it on my eyes, and told me to go and wash it off in the pool of Siloam, and I did, and suddenly I could see," he explained.

"Where is Jesus?" the neighbors asked.

"I don't know," the man replied.

Then they brought the man to the Jewish leaders. They, too, wanted to know how he had been healed.

"Jesus put clay on my eyes, and I washed it off and now I can see," he explained.

Then some of the leaders said, "The man who cured you can't be a good man, because he did it on the Sabbath day!" They meant that God had told His people not to work on the Sabbath, and they were calling healing, work! Then they asked the man what he thought of Jesus.

"I think He must be a prophet," he told them.

But these Jewish leaders wouldn't believe he had been blind. Finally they called in his parents and asked them, "Is this your son? Was he born blind? Then how can he see now?"

"Yes," they said, "he's our son, and was born blind, but we don't know what happened. He's old enough to speak for himself, so ask him." The parents were afraid to say that it was Jesus who had cured their son, because the Jewish leaders had threatened to hurt anyone who said Jesus was the Saviour.

Then the leaders talked to the man again and told him, "God healed you, not that fellow who put clay on your eyes, for we know he is a sinner."

"I don't know whether He is a sinner or not," the man replied, *"but one thing I do know: I used to be blind, and now I see!"*

"What did he do to you?" they asked him again.

Then the man got mad. "I told you once," he snapped. "Why don't you listen? Why do you want to hear it again? Do you want to be His disciples too?"

They were furious. "You are his disciple, but we are Moses' disciples. We know that God sent Moses, but as for this fellow, we don't know who sent him," they sneered.

"How very strange!" the man replied. "Here's a man who can cure blind people, and yet you don't know who He is! Since the beginning of the world such a thing has never been heard of before, that a man born blind can see. If God didn't send this man, He couldn't have cured me."

"You dirty bum," they snarled. "Are you trying to teach *us*?" And they threw him out of their church, the Jewish synagogue, and told him never to come back again.

When Jesus heard what had happened, He found the man and asked him, "Do you believe on the Son of God?"

"I want to," the man answered, "Who is He?"

"He is the person talking with you!" Jesus replied.

"Lord, I believe," the man said, and worshipped Him.

QUESTIONS

How did Jesus make the blind man see? How long had he been blind?

Did the Jewish leaders want to believe that Jesus healed him? Why not?

168
Another Victory over Death

Another time Jesus said to His disciples, "I am the good shepherd and I know My sheep." He meant that He was like a shepherd to His disciples, and they were like His flock of sheep. In that country the shepherd walked ahead of his sheep, and they followed him. Each sheep had its own name and knew its own shepherd's voice, and came when he called it. The shepherd stayed with his sheep night and day to keep them from being lost, and to guard them from wild animals. Yes, Jesus is our shepherd and is always with us to guard us from Satan and to show us the way to heaven.

Jesus now went again to the Temple, and the Jewish leaders crowded around Him and demanded, "If You are the Son of God, why don't you say so?"

Jesus replied, "I have, but you wouldn't believe Me because you are not My sheep. My sheep listen to My voice and follow Me, and I give them eternal life. They will never be lost —no one can ever take them away from Me. My Father gave them to Me, and no one can kidnap them. My Father and I are One." Jesus meant that He is God—not God the Father, but God the Son. He is as good and as great as God the Father, and He is to be loved and worshipped as such.

Then the Jewish leaders picked up stones to hurl at Him and kill Him because He said He was God, but He escaped from them, left Jerusalem, and went out beyond the Jordan River to the place where John had baptized Him. Crowds came to listen to Him there, and many of them believed Him.

About that time Lazarus, Mary and Martha's brother, became ill. His sisters sent a message to Jesus to tell Him about it. Jesus loved Lazarus, Martha, and Mary very much, but when He heard of Lazarus' serious sickness, He didn't go at once to help them, but

The Good Shepherd is willing to go anywhere to rescue His sheep. He gave His life to save and help all those who belong to Him. Have you asked Him to be your Shepherd? If you have, you have everything you need.

R. Hook

stayed where He was for two more days.

Then He said to His disciples, "Now, let's go to Bethany, for Lazarus is asleep and I will go and waken him." Jesus meant that Lazarus was dead, and that He was going to bring him back to life again. But His disciples thought He meant Lazarus was resting.

Then Jesus told them plainly, "Lazarus is dead."

Bethany is about two miles away from Jerusalem, and many of the Jewish leaders had gone there to be with Martha and Mary, to try to comfort them in their sorrow. When Martha heard that Jesus had arrived, she went out to meet Him, but Mary stayed in the house.

Martha said to Him, "Sir, if You had been here, my brother wouldn't have died. But I know that even now whatever You ask of God will be given to You."

Jesus said to her, "Your brother will live again."

"Yes, of course," Martha replied, "—at the Judgment Day."

Then Martha went back to the house and told Mary that Jesus had arrived and wanted to see her. So Mary ran out to where He was, and knelt down at His feet and said, "Lord, if You had been here, my brother wouldn't have died."

When Jesus saw her crying, and the Jewish leaders crying too, He was angry because they didn't think He could help them. "Where have you buried Lazarus?" Jesus asked them.

"Sir, come and see," they replied.

Then Jesus wept.

"See how He loved him," the Jews said. And some of them asked, "Couldn't this man who opens the eyes of blind men have saved Lazarus from dying?"

Lazarus' body had been placed in a cave with a stone rolled across in front of it, to seal it.

"Take away the stone," Jesus said.

But Martha objected. "By this time his body has begun to decay," she protested, "for he has been dead four days. The smell will be terrible."

"Didn't I tell you that if you would only believe in Me, you would see how great God's power is?" Jesus asked.

Then they took away the stone and Jesus shouted, "Lazarus, come out!" And he came out, wrapped up in the sheet he had been buried in. "Unwrap him," Jesus told them, and they did.

When the Jewish leaders who had come to visit Martha and Mary saw this great miracle, many of them finally believed on Jesus. But some went to the Pharisees and told them what they had seen.

The Pharisees and chief priests were terribly disturbed and called a meeting to discuss it. "What shall we do?" they said. "There is no arguing with the fact that this man Jesus does wonderful miracles. But if we let him alone, everyone will believe he is God's Son and make him their king;

Do you know why Lazarus is so happy and smiling? It is because he was dead, and was buried in that cave for four days, but now is alive again. Jesus stood outside and told him to come back to life, and he did!

R. Hook

and then the Romans will be angry, and come and destroy our government."

So from then on the Jewish leaders began plotting how to get rid of Him by killing Him.

QUESTIONS
How is Jesus like a good shepherd?
Tell about Jesus raising Lazarus from the dead.
Why weren't the Jewish leaders happy because Jesus did such wonderful miracles?

169
The Runaway Boy

One Sabbath day when Jesus was teaching in one of the Jewish churches, a woman was there who had been bent over for eighteen years, and couldn't straighten herself up. When Jesus saw her He called her over to Him and said to her, "Ma'am, you are healed!" Then He laid His hands on her, and immediately she straightened up. How she praised God, for she was well!

But the pastor of the church was angry because Jesus had healed her on the Sabbath day. He said that this was wrong because people shouldn't work on the Sabbath, and healing someone was work. He said to the people, "There are six days for working; if any of you want to be healed, come some other day than on the Sabbath."

Jesus was angry. "You hypocrite," He told the man, "don't you feed and water your donkeys and cows on the Sabbath? If it is right to care for animals on the Sabbath, isn't it right to heal a woman on the Sabbath who has been suffering for eighteen years?"

Then the Jewish leader was ashamed, and the people were glad because of the miracles Jesus did.

On another Sabbath Jesus went into the house of one of the leaders and told a story about a man who invited a lot of friends to a big party. When everything was ready, the man sent his helpers to those who were invited, to tell them that dinner was ready and it was time to come. But they began to make excuses for not coming!

The first said, "Please excuse me but I have bought a piece of ground, and I must go and see it."

Another said, "I have bought some oxen, and I must go and see how they work; please have me excused."

And another said, "I have just been married so I can't come."

The servant returned to his master with their excuses. The master was very angry and told him to go out into the streets and bring in the poor, the lame, and the blind. So the servant did, and came back and told his master, "There is still room for more."

"Go out again, all though the streets and alleys of the city," his master said, "and bring in more people until there are enough guests to fill every place at the table. For none of those who were first invited shall taste of my supper."

In this story the master means God; the dinner means the Good News that God forgives our sins. The servant means God's ministers who tell the Good News to others. And the men who were first invited and wouldn't come were the Jews; for the Good News was preached to them first, but many of them wouldn't believe it. The men who were invited afterwards are the people of other nations —all who have heard the Good News since that time and have believed it. And the command to go out and get people from the streets and alleys means that not only the rich, but also the poor and despised are invited to come and be saved.

Great crowds came to hear Jesus. But He said that even though people come and listen to Him, they can't be His disciples unless they care more for Him than for money and popularity, and unless they refuse to do things that are wrong.

When some tax collectors, who cheated people whenever they could, came to hear Him, the Jewish leaders were disgusted. "Why does Jesus act nice to these bad men, and even eat with them?" they asked.

This was Jesus' reply: "If you have a hundred sheep and lose one of them, don't you leave all the others and hunt for the one that is lost? And when you find it, you take it on your shoulders and carry it home rejoicing. And when you get home, you tell all your neighbors and friends, and they rejoice with you, for you have found your lost sheep. Well, that's the way it is with these cheaters. I have come to save them too—I haven't come just to save good people." Their wickedness is not a good reason for sending them away. Instead, they should be encouraged to come to Jesus so that He can teach them to repent. Then they will no longer be lost, and even the angels in heaven will be glad to see these wicked men begin to obey God.

Then He told them this story: "A man had two sons. The younger one said to him, 'Father, give me my share of the money you are planning to divide up among your sons.' So his father did, and soon afterwards this younger son took the money and went away to a distant country, and spent it all doing all sorts of bad things.

"When the money was gone, there was a great famine in that land, and he began to be very hungry. Then he hired himself out to a man who sent him into his fields to feed pigs. He was so hungry he wanted to eat the husks the pigs ate, but of course he couldn't digest them, so he went hungry instead.

"Finally he said to himself, 'At home even the servants have plenty to eat, while I am here starving. I'll go to my father and tell him, "Father,

I have sinned against God and you, and don't deserve to be called your son anymore; just let me be one of your hired servants." '

"So he returned to his father. And while he was still far away, his father saw him and ran out to meet him and threw his arms around him and kissed him. Then his son began his speech: 'Father,' he said, 'I have sinned against God and you, and don't deserve to be called your son any more . . .'

"But his father said to the servants, 'Bring out my best suit for him, and get him some shoes, and go get the finest calf and kill it and let's have a party; for this son of mine was lost and is found.' So they had a big dinner to celebrate his son's return.

"When the older son returned home that evening from working out in the fields, he heard the music and dancing and called one of the servants, and asked him what was going on.

" 'Your brother's back!' the servant told him, 'and your father has killed the best calf for a big party because he is back safe and sound.'

"But the older son was angry and wouldn't go in. His father came out and begged him.

" 'Look,' he told his father, 'I've worked hard for you all my life, and in all that time I've never disobeyed your instructions, yet you never once gave a party for me and my friends. But as soon as this son returns after throwing away your money and doing all sorts of bad things, you kill the best calf on the farm for him.'

"The father replied, 'My son, I've always loved you dearly, and everything I have is yours. But it is right that we should be happy, for this brother of yours left us and has come home again; he was lost and is found.' "

By using this story Jesus was telling the proud Jewish leaders—who hated Him for preaching to sinners—that God loved those sinners and was willing to forgive them, and was willing to have them as His children if they would only stop being bad and start obeying Him.

QUESTIONS

Tell the story about the man who invited many guests to dinner. What does the story mean?

Why was Jesus kind even to bad men?

What happened when the runaway son finally came back to his father?

Why did the older brother object to the party?

Another story Jesus told was about a boy who ran away from home and was very bad, but when he finally came home, his father loved him anyway.

F+R. Hook

170
Jesus Blesses the Children

Another time He told a story to those who love money and spend their time enjoying themselves instead of obeying God.

"There was a rich man," He said, "who dressed in beautiful clothes, and ate only the best foods. And there was a beggar named Lazarus, who was sick and covered with sores. Because he was so poor he had very little to eat, and his friends carried him to the rich man's gate and left him there to beg for the scraps from the rich man's table. Even the dogs seemed to pity him, for they came and licked his sores.

"The beggar died, and was carried to heaven by the angels. He wasn't poor there, for he ate with Abraham! Then the rich man died too, but he went where the bad people go. There, being punished for his sins, he looked up and saw Abraham and Lazarus far away. 'Father Abraham!' he shouted, 'Have pity on me and send Lazarus to dip the tip of his finger in water to cool my tongue; for I am tormented in these flames.'

"But Abraham said to him, 'Remember that in your lifetime you had everything and Lazarus had nothing, but now he is happy and you are sad. And besides there is a great gulf between us, so no one can come and help you, and you can't come to us.'

"Then the rich man said, 'Then please send Lazarus to my five brothers at home, to tell them to repent and obey God, so that when they die they won't come to this dreadful place.'

"Abraham replied, 'The Bible already tells them that.'

"But the rich man said, 'No, Father Abraham, that isn't enough. But if someone returns from the dead and tells them, then they will surely repent.'

"Abraham replied, 'If they won't listen to what God says to them in the Bible, they won't obey Him even

"Love" is the best title for this picture. Jesus especially loves little children because they will let Him. Sometimes adults, who need Jesus' love so badly, turn away from Him and don't want Him for their friend.

if someone rises from the dead.' (Afterwards Jesus rose from the dead, but even so, few people listened to Him.)

Jesus told still another story to teach His disciples that they should continue to pray, and not be discouraged when prayers aren't answered right away:

"Once there was a wicked judge who feared neither God nor man, and was very unfair. A poor widow lived in his city, and she kept coming to him and asking him to punish a man who had hurt her. For a while the judge wouldn't listen to her, but afterward he said to himself, 'It's not that I fear God, but this woman bothers me, so I'll do what she asks.'

Then Jesus said, "If that unfair judge did what the widow asked because she asked so often, won't God, who is holy and who loves His children, eventually give them what they pray for, even though it seems for a while as though He isn't listening to them?"

Then Jesus told a story to those who thought themselves better than others. He said, "Two men went up to the Temple to pray. One was a proud Jewish leader and the other was a cheating tax collector. The Jewish leader stood where everyone would see him and prayed, 'God, thank You that I am better than other men, and especially that I am better than that bad tax collector over there. For I fast twice each week, and give the church a tenth of all I earn.'

"But the tax collector, who knew how bad he was, and was sorry for it, stood where he hoped no one would notice him, and bowed his head and beat upon his breast in great sadness, saying, 'God, be merciful to me, a sinner.' "

Then Jesus said a surprising thing about the two men. He said that the cheating tax collector went home forgiven, while the Jewish leader didn't! "Everyone who is proud will be brought low," Jesus said, "but those who are humble and confess their sins will be honored."

Once when some mothers brought their little children to Jesus so he could put His hands on them and bless them, His disciples shooed them away. But Jesus didn't like this. "Let the little children come to Me," He said. "Don't tell them not to, for little children are in the kingdom of heaven." He meant that only those who are humble and loving like little children, will ever get into His kingdom. Then He took the children in His arms and placed His hands on them, and blessed them.

One day He took the twelve disciples aside and told them that the time had come to go to Jerusalem, and when they got there everything the prophets had said about Him would happen: He would be laughed at, and whipped, and spat upon, and nailed to a cross, and killed; and the third day He would come back to life again.

But the disciples expected Him to be crowned king of the Jews soon, so they couldn't understand what He was talking about.

QUESTIONS

What happened to the beggar Lazarus when he died?

What happened to the rich man?

Should we be discouraged if our prayers aren't answered right away? Tell the story Jesus told about this.

How was Jesus different from the disciples, in what He said about the little children?

171

Jesus Rides a Colt

When Jesus arrived in the city of Jericho, on the way to Jerusalem, the usual crowds pushed along behind Him. A blind man, Bartimaeus, was sitting beside the road, begging, and when he heard the commotion he asked what was happening—what was all the noise and excitement about?

"Jesus of Nazareth is coming," someone told him.

As soon as he heard this he began to shout, "Jesus, son of David, have mercy on me!"

"Quit making such a racket," everyone told him.

But he just shouted louder, "Son of David, have mercy on me!"

Jesus stopped in the road and said for Bartimaeus to come to Him.

"He's calling for you!" the blind man was told. So he jumped up, tossed aside his old coat and went over toward where Jesus was waiting.

Jesus asked him, "What do you want me to do for you?"

"Sir, I want to see," the blind man answered.

"All right," Jesus told him, "because you have faith, you are well!" And immediately he could see! Then he followed Jesus down the road, praising God for the mighty miracle that had been done to him.

In Jericho there was a man named Zacchaeus who was in charge of collecting taxes in that city, and because he cheated so much, he was very rich. As Jesus passed through the streets of the city, Zacchaeus tried to see Him, but couldn't because of the crowd, for he was too short. So he ran on ahead, climbed up into a sycamore tree, and waited for Jesus to pass by.

When Jesus came along the road past the tree, He stopped and looked up into the branches and saw Zacchaeus sitting there. "Come on down, Zacchaeus," Jesus told him, "for I am going to your house for dinner!" So Zacchaeus happily took Jesus with him.

As I have already said, Zacchaeus and the other tax collectors were unfair, cruel men. They forced the people to give them more money than was right. But when Jesus came to Zacchaeus' home, Zacchaeus became very sorry for what he had done. He stood up before all the people and told Jesus that he would stop being unfair, and from then on he would be kind to the poor and would give them half of his money. And if he ever took more money than he should, he would give back four times as much as he had taken.

When Jesus saw that Zacchaeus was sorry and was ready to do whatever Jesus told him to, He said that all of Zacchaeus' sins were forgiven. But the Jewish leaders said Jesus shouldn't eat with a tax collector because he was a sinner. Jesus replied that He had come into the world on purpose to be among sinners, to teach them to repent and to save them from being punished for their sins.

Passover was now near (it was a happy time, a little bit like Christmas is to us) and many of the people went to Jerusalem to celebrate it. Everyone wanted to see Jesus, and as they stood around in the courts of the Temple they asked each other, "Do you think He will come?" For the Jewish leaders were saying that if anyone knew where Jesus was, he must tell them so they could have Him arrested and killed.

Six days before the Passover, Jesus came to Bethany where Lazarus lived. Lazarus, you remember, was the man Jesus had brought back to life again after he was dead. People from all over the country knew about Lazarus, and knew that he lived in Bethany, two miles from Jerusalem. So great crowds went there to see him. Then the chief priests decided to arrest and kill Lazarus too, because so many people believed on Jesus after visiting Lazarus; for he told them about his experience of dying, and being brought back to life again by Jesus.

Then Jesus left Bethany to go to Jerusalem. When He had come as far as the Mount of Olives He sent two of His disciples to a nearby village.

"You'll see a colt tied there that has never been ridden," He said. (A colt is a baby horse.) "Untie him, and bring him to me. If anyone asks why you are taking the colt, just say, 'Because the Lord needs him,' and they will let you have him."

The two disciples found the colt just as Jesus had said. And as they were untying him, the owners asked, "What are you doing there, untying that colt?"

"The Lord needs him," the disciples replied. Then the owners let them have the colt for Jesus to ride on. They brought him to Jesus, and the disciples threw their coats across his back and Jesus sat on him.

As He rode the colt toward Jerusalem, a great crowd spread their coats on the road in front of Him, while others cut down branches from the trees and made a green carpet for Him to ride over. They did this to honor Him, for that is what people used to do when a king rode through their streets. Then the crowd surrounding Him began shouting, "Praise God for sending us a king!"

But Jesus knew they didn't really love Him, and that in a few days they would be shouting, "Crucify Him!"

Zacchaeus was a kind of robber, but he wanted to see Jesus. He was too short to see over the crowd, so he climbed a tree to watch from there. Jesus went home with him to eat supper, but the crowd didn't like it, because Zacchaeus was bad.

As He neared Jerusalem He began crying as He thought of all the city's wickedness, and of the sufferings that were coming upon His people. He told His disciples that the enemies of the Jews would come with a great army and besiege the city and destroy it. Every house would be knocked down, so that not one stone would be left standing upon another. All this tragedy would come upon the people of Jerusalem as punishment for killing their Saviour who had come all the way from heaven to help them in His own wonderful way.

Upon His arrival in Jerusalem, Jesus went up to the Temple and began healing the blind and the lame who were brought to Him there. But the Jewish leaders were angry and jealous because some school children who were visiting the Temple began praising Jesus for His wonderful miracles.

That evening He went out to Bethany and slept there. In the morning as He returned to Jerusalem, He was hungry, and noticing a fig tree along the road, He went over to see if there were any figs on it; but there were only leaves. Then He said to the fig tree, "You will never bear fruit."

The next day, as Jesus and His disciples were passing that way again, they saw that the fig tree was dead!

QUESTIONS

What wonderful thing did Jesus do for Bartimaeus?

Tell the story of Zacchaeus.

How did the crowds honor Jesus as He rode into Jerusalem? Why did Jesus cry instead of being happy when this happened?

What happened to the fig tree that Jesus scolded?

This is a picture of the first Palm Sunday. Jesus is riding to Jerusalem on a donkey colt, and everyone is celebrating. All the people are waving branches and making a green carpet of leaves on the road ahead of Him. They think He will soon be their king.

172
More of Jesus' Stories

Jesus told the people this story: "There was a farmer who planted a vineyard and built a wall around it and built a guard tower to protect it from robbers. He leased it to a man who promised to give him part of the grapes when they were ripe. Then the owner went away to a distant country.

"When the grapes were ripe he sent someone to collect his share of the crop. But the man who was leasing the farm beat him up and scared him away. Then the owner sent someone else to collect his share, but the man on the farm threw stones at him and wounded him in the head, seriously injuring him. Afterwards the owner sent still other men to collect the rent for him, but some were beaten up and others killed. The owner sent his only son, for he thought, 'They won't dare harm my son.'

"But when the tenant saw the owner's son coming, he said to his friends, 'That boy is going to own the vineyard someday; come on, let's kill him and then it will all be ours!' So they caught him and dragged him out of the vineyard and killed him."

Jesus asked, "When the owner of the vineyard returns, what will he do to those men?"

The people answered, "He will kill them and lease his vineyard to someone who will give him his proper share of the grapes."

In this story the owner of the vineyard means God, and the wicked man leasing the farm means the Jewish leaders. God chose them to be His people, and He gave them the land of Canaan. He taught them His laws, and they promised to obey Him. But afterwards they turned against God and persecuted and killed His prophets whom He sent to warn and persuade them. Then at last God sent His only son, Jesus. And now in a few days they were going to kill Him just as the wicked farmers had killed the son of the owner of the vineyard.

When the Jewish leaders heard this

Jesus is healing a blind man. His name Bartimaeus. He cannot see the trees and flowers, but now his friend Jesus is helping him so that he can.

story, they knew that Jesus was talking about them; and they were very angry and wanted all the more to kill Him.

Then Jesus told the people another story. "A king's son was getting married," He said, "and there was a big party to celebrate the happy occasion. But the people he invited to the party wouldn't come. So he sent for them again. 'My dinner is ready,' he said. 'Come to the marriage.'

"But some turned away and wouldn't listen, and others tortured and killed his messengers. When the king heard about it he was very angry, and sent his soldiers to destroy those murderers and burn up their city.

"Then the king said to his friends, 'The wedding dinner is ready, but I won't let those I first invited come. Go out into the streets and lanes and invite everyone you see to come to the marriage.' So the messengers brought as many people as they could.

"The king gave a gift to each guest—a new outfit of clothes! And he required that the guests wear these clothes at the wedding dinner. But when the king went into the banquet room where the dinner was being served, he noticed a man who wasn't following instructions, for he had on his regular clothing.

" 'Friend,' the king asked, 'why no wedding clothes?' And the man was silent, for he had refused to take them when they were offered to him.

"Then the king was angry and said to his servants, 'Bind him hand and foot and take him away, and throw him into the dark dungeon where people are kept who will not obey me.' "

In this story, the king means God, and the king's son means Jesus. Those who were first invited to the party and wouldn't come were the Jews, because they were the first to be asked to believe in Jesus, but many of them wouldn't do it. The people who were invited to the dinner afterwards are the people of other nations who believe Jesus. The man without the wedding clothes is anyone who pretends to believe and to accept God's invitation, but won't obey Him. Such people may seem to obey God's Word, and might fool others, but God sees their hearts. We cannot hide our hearts from Him, even for a moment.

One of the Jewish religion teachers now came to Jesus and asked Him this question: "Master, which is the greatest of God's commandments?"

Jesus answered, "You must deeply love the Lord your God. This is the first and greatest commandment. And the next most important commandment is, you must love your neighbor as yourself." Jesus said that all the other commandments in the Bible came from these two. If we obey these two great laws of God, we will be obeying all the other laws too; we will be doing everything the Bible tells us to.

Jesus said the Jewish leaders were hypocrites, that is, they pretended to be good when they really weren't at all. They stood on the street corners and prayed long prayers in public so that people would respect and praise them for their earnestness. But really they weren't good and earnest men at all, for they were unfair and cruel to the poor. Jesus said they would be punished at the Judgment Day.

Then He went into the court of the Temple, where the offering boxes were, and sat down and watched as people threw in the money they were giving to God. He noticed that many rich men gave much, but a poor widow gave only one penny! Then Jesus called His disciples and told them that her penny meant more to God than all the bags of money given by the rich men! For they kept all but a little of their money for themselves, but the poor widow kept nothing—she had given every penny she had.

QUESTIONS

In the story of the vineyard, what happened to the owner's son?

Who does the story mean?

What did Jesus say were the two most important commandments? Talk about what they mean.

Why was God more pleased with receiving one penny from the widow than lots of money from rich people?

173
Two Important Stories

Although the Jews had seen Jesus do many miracles, most of them still wouldn't believe that He was the Saviour, for they didn't like Him. Others believed but were afraid to say so, for fear the Jewish leaders wouldn't let them come to church anymore. They were more concerned about being well thought of than they were about pleasing God.

The Temple was made of white marble and was one of the largest and most splendid buildings in all the world. As Jesus was leaving the Temple, one of His disciples remarked, "Master, look at the huge stones in this beautiful building!"

"Yes," Jesus told him, "but the day is coming when this beautiful building will be knocked down so that not one stone will be left upon another!" For Jesus knew that the Jews were going to crucify Him, and afterwards God was going to punish them by sending their enemies to destroy the Temple and the entire city.

Jesus said always to be ready for the Judgment Day because no one knew when it would come. Then He told a story about ten girls at a wedding reception. In that country when a man was married, he brought his bride home after supper, and his friends would go out with their lamps to meet them and welcome them to their new home. That is what these ten girls planned to do. They lit their lamps and were ready, but because the bridegroom and the bride didn't come right away, the girls sat down to wait, and fell asleep. Five of them had been wise enough to bring extra oil so that if their lamps went out, they could fill them again. But five were foolish, and didn't have any extra oil.

Around midnight there was a shout, "Here comes the bridegroom! Go out and meet him." Then the girls woke up, but the lamps of five of them had gone out—the five who hadn't brought extra oil along. They said to the other girls, "Please give us some of your oil."

But the others replied, "We don't have enough. Some of the shops are still open—go and buy some."

While they were gone, the bridegroom came, and all those who were ready went in with him to the reception and the door was locked. When the other girls came back they knocked loudly at the door, "Sir, open to us," they called. But the bridegroom refused to let them in.

In this parable the bridegroom means Jesus coming back to earth. The ten girls mean all of us who call ourselves His disciples, and who want to meet Him. Will we be ready? Do we really love Him and obey Him? Or have we forgotten to be ready when He comes?

Jesus then told his disciples another story, this time about a man who was preparing for a trip to a distant country. Before he went, he gave money to his servants and told them to use it to earn more for him while he was away. He gave $5,000 to one servant, $2,000 to another, and only $1,000 to the third.

The servant who had the $5,000 used it to buy things, and then he sold them for more than they cost him. He kept buying and selling like that until finally he had twice as much money as he started with! The servant with $2,000 did the same, until he had earned $2,000 more. But the servant with the $1,000 didn't use it. He hid it instead.

After a long time the master came back, and called in his servants to find out how much they had earned with his money.

The servant with the $5,000 said, "See, I have earned $5,000 more." His master was pleased and paid him well for his fine service.

Then the servant with the $2,000 came and reported, "See, I have earned $2,000 more." And the master was pleased and gave him a good reward.

Then the servant with the $1,000 came. "Master," he said, "I know how unfair you are and that you take what isn't yours. I knew you would take away all the money I earned, so I didn't earn any! Here is your money again, just what you gave me."

The master was angry. "You disobedient, lazy fellow," he said, "if I take all your profits, that is no excuse for your being idle while I was gone."

Then he said to his other servants, as he took back the $1,000, "He doesn't get even a tiny reward!"

In this story, the master means

One of these girls brought enough oil for her lamp, but the other one didn't. Now she doesn't know what to do. Can you tell which one didn't bring enough?

Christ. He has gone to heaven to stay for a while—we don't know how long—but He is coming back. The servants are all of us left here in this world to work for Him. The money means whatever He has given us to work with. Some of us have many abilities and opportunities and some of us have few, but each of us has some ability God can use. When Jesus comes again, He will reward those who have used their talents well, but He will punish those who have not used them, or who have used them for themselves.

QUESTIONS

What did Jesus say would happen to the beautiful Temple?

Why did some of the girls in Jesus' story miss the wedding reception?

What were the servants supposed to do with the money they were given?

What happened to the servant who didn't use his money, but hid it? What can we learn from this story?

174

Mary Shows Her Love

One day Jesus talked to His disciples about what would happen on the Judgment Day. He told them that He will come back to earth in all His glory at that time, and all the holy angels will be with Him. Then He will sit on His throne, and the dead of all nations will rise from their graves and stand before Him to be judged. And He will separate the righteous from the wicked, as a shepherd separates his sheep from the goats; He will place those who are good at His right hand, but those who are bad at His left.

Then He will say to those on His right hand, "Come, children of My Father, into the kingdom which has been waiting for you from the beginning of the world. For when I was hungry you gave me food; when I was thirsty you gave Me a drink; when I was poor and naked you clothed Me; when I was sick you visited Me; when I was in prison you came to Me and comforted Me."

Then those who are good will say to Him, "Lord, when did we ever see You hungry and feed you, or thirsty and give You a drink? When did we ever see You poor and naked, and clothe You? Or sick, or in prison, and comfort You?"

And Jesus will reply, "Whenever you did these things to any poor and suffering person who loved Me, it was the same as if you did it to Me."

Then He will turn to the wicked and say, "Go away; you are cursed, for I was hungry but you didn't feed me; I was thirsty but you gave Me nothing to drink; I was naked but you didn't give Me any clothes; I was sick and in prison, but you didn't visit Me."

They then will answer, "Lord, when did we ever see You hungry, or thirsty, or naked, or sick, or in prison, and not help You?"

And He will answer them, "When you didn't do it to the poor and suffering people who love Me, it was the same as if you didn't do it to Me." They will be sent away into everlasting punishment, but the righteous to eternal life.

Then Jesus told His disciples that in two days, at the celebration, He would be betrayed and killed. For the chief priests were anxious to arrest Him and kill Him. "But we can't do it during the holiday when all the people are around," they said, "or there will be a riot."

Jesus ate supper that night at Bethany with Mary, Martha, and Lazarus.

While He was there, Mary took a bottle of very rare, expensive perfume and poured it over Jesus' feet and wiped them with her hair; and the house was filled with the fragrance.

But Judas Iscariot, the disciple who later betrayed Him, complained about this. "Why wasn't this perfume sold, and the money given to the poor?" he growled. Judas didn't really care what happened to the poor, but he said this because he was the disciples' treasurer and carried their money, and often stole some of it.

But Jesus told him, "Let her alone. Why find fault with her? She has done a good thing. You will always have the poor with you, and whenever you want to you can do them good, but you will not always have Me."

Jesus then told His disciples that wherever the Good News about Him was preached throughout the whole world, this thing that Mary had done to Him would be talked about.

Then Judas Iscariot went to the chief priests and asked them, "How much will you give me if I take you to Jesus when He is alone, so that you can arrest Him quietly?"

They gladly promised him thirty pieces of silver. From that time on Judas was on the lookout for a time when Jesus would be away from the crowds, so that the chief priests could come and arrest Him without starting a riot.

QUESTIONS

What is the Judgment Day Jesus talked about?

Why is it like helping Jesus when we help other people?

What did Mary do with her expensive perfume? Why did Judas complain?

Why did Judas Iscariot go to the chief priests?

175

The First Communion Service

The Passover day finally came. This was a national Jewish holiday to celebrate the night so long before when the Israelis had escaped from Egypt. The angel of death had killed all the oldest boys in each Egyptian family that night, but he had passed over the houses where there was lamb's blood on the door. It was because the angel passed over them that the celebration was called the Passover.

Each year during the Passover celebration, every Israeli family took a lamb to the Temple and killed it as a sacrifice before the altar. Then the priests burned its fat on the altar, but the rest of the lamb was taken home, where it was roasted, and the family ate it that night, just as the Israelites had done so many hundreds of years before when they left Egypt.

The disciples asked Jesus where they should go to roast and eat the lamb, since Jesus had no home in Jerusalem—or anywhere else.

"Go into Jerusalem," He told them, "and as you enter the city you will see a man carrying a pitcher of water. Follow him into the house where he is going, and say to the man who lives there, 'The Master wants you to show us the room you have prepared for us.' He will take you upstairs to a large room all set up for you. Prepare the lamb there, for that is where we will eat it."

The disciples did as Jesus said, and sure enough, they met a man with a pitcher, and he took them to the room Jesus had told them about. There they prepared the lamb.

In the evening Jesus arrived with His other apostles and they all sat down for the supper. "I have wanted very much to eat this Passover supper with you before I die," He told them, "for I will not again eat a lamb that has been sacrificed until I Myself am sacrificed for the sins of the people."

But the apostles didn't understand Him. They didn't know what He was talking about. They still thought He

Only slaves washed people's feet in Bible times. Yet Jesus gladly washed His disciples' feet. He was showing them that they (and we) should lovingly help each other because everyone is important to God.

was going to become king of the Jews, and that the time for this was very near.

They began arguing among themselves, as they had before, as to which of them would be greatest in the kingdom. Then Jesus told them, "Here in this world the rulers and the wealthy are the greatest, but with you it is different. For whichever of you is the humblest will be the greatest. The one who wants to be the leader must be the servant of all!"

Then Jesus asked them which was greater, the master who ate at the table, or the servant who waited on him as he ate? They said it was the master. Then Jesus pointed out to them that He was their servant, even though he was their master; and they should serve each other as He served them. Then he demonstrated what He meant:

He got up from the table, wrapped a towel around his waist, poured water into a basin, and began to wash their feet and to wipe them with the towel. When He came to Peter, Peter didn't want Him to do it, for he didn't want Jesus to act like his servant. Jesus told him, "You don't understand now why I am doing it, but you will later."

"No," Peter told Him, "You shall never wash my feet."

Jesus replied, "If I don't, you can't be My disciple!"

"Then, Lord, don't wash just my feet, but my hands and my head too!" Peter exclaimed.

But Jesus told him, "When you have had a bath, it is only necessary to rewash the feet!"

After He had washed their feet and returned to the table again, He said to them, "Do you know what I have done to you? You call Me Master and Lord, and that is correct, for I am. If I, then, your Lord and Master, have washed your feet, you ought to wash each other's feet, for you should follow My example; you should do as I have done to you." He meant that we should help each other at all times.

As they ate the Passover supper Jesus said to them, "One of you sitting here eating with Me will betray Me." He meant that one of his disciples would tell the Jewish leaders where he was, so that they could come and arrest him when the people weren't around to protect Him from them.

The disciples were very much surprised and sad when they heard this. They looked at each other, wondering which one He was talking about. Peter motioned to the disciple sitting next to Jesus to find out who it was that Jesus meant. So he asked Jesus, "Lord, who is it who will do such a terrible thing?"

"It is the one I give this piece of bread to when I have dipped it in the dish," Jesus replied. Then He gave it to Judas Iscariot. After that Satan entered into Judas, and Jesus said to him, "What you are going to do, do quickly."

No one at the table knew what Jesus meant by these words. Some of them thought He was telling Judas to go

In this picture Jesus is eating with His disciples for the last time. He knows that tomorrow He will die on the cross. He is breaking the bread for them to eat with Him.

R. Hook

176
Jesus Is Arrested

Jesus and His apostles now sang a hymn together and went out to the Mount of Olives, a short distance from Jerusalem. There they went into a garden called the Garden of Gethsemane.

"Sit here while I go and pray," Jesus told them. Then He went a little distance away and kneeled down and prayed. And now He began to be in terrible anguish as He thought about being punished for our sins and separated from God, for He knew that in a few hours He would be crucified. Great drops of blood fell like sweat from His forehead to the ground. Then an angel came to help Him.

When He got up from prayer and went back to His disciples, He found them sleeping. "Asleep?" He asked. "Get up and pray so that you will not be tempted to do wrong." Then He went away and prayed again. When He came back He found them sleeping again. He went away a third time, and when He returned and they were asleep again, He told them, "Get up now, for My betrayer is near."

Judas had been watching when Jesus went to the garden. Because it was night, and because only a few of His followers were with Him, Judas decided that this was the best time to betray his Master. So he went to the Jewish government officials and told them that Jesus was alone with His disciples in the Garden of Gethsemane. They sent a gang of men with Judas to capture Jesus.

Judas was bringing the men to the garden now, and Jesus knew it, but He didn't run. He waited for them to come because it was the time for Him to die. While He was still talking with His disciples, Judas and the others arrived, carrying swords and clubs and lanterns.

"The one I kiss on the cheek is the

It is nighttime, and Jesus is in the Garden of Gethsemane. His disciples will soon run away for fear of their lives. Now Judas gives Him a "friendly kiss" to show the soldiers who He is, so that they can take Him away and kill Him. Judas was a traitor.

man you want," Judas told them. "Grab Him and don't let Him get away."

So Judas came up to Jesus, pretending to be His friend, and greeted Him with a kiss on the cheek, as is still the custom in eastern lands when men meet. Then the men grabbed Jesus and held Him.

"Lord, shall we use the sword?" the disciples cried out. And Peter drew his sword, and struck a servant of the High Priest, cutting off his ear.

"Put your sword away," Jesus told him. "Don't you realize that I could pray to My Father to send thousands of angels to fight for Me, and save Me from death? But then how could the words of the prophets come true, which say that I am to die for the people?" Then Jesus touched the man's ear and healed it.

Turning to the men holding Him, he asked, "Why the swords and clubs? If I am a thief why didn't you arrest Me in the Temple? I was there every day."

Then all the disciples left Him and ran away into the night.

Jesus was first taken to Caiaphas, who was the High Priest that year. All the Jewish government officials soon gathered at the High Priest's palace and Jesus was brought before them.

Peter had followed Jesus a long way off, hoping no one would recognize him; so now he too came along to the palace, and sat down among the palace servants beside a fire they had built in the courtyard because it was cold.

A servant girl came over to him and said, "You were with Jesus of Galilee!" Peter strongly denied it, and said it wasn't so. Then he went out onto the porch. Just then he heard a rooster crow.

Another servant girl saw him there and said to the others who were standing around, "This fellow was with Jesus of Nazareth!"

Again Peter denied it. "I don't even know the man!" he said.

After a while one of the servants of the High Priest, who was a relative of the man whose ear Peter had cut off, said, "Didn't I see you with Him in the Garden of Gethsemane?"

Peter denied it again. And just then he heard the rooster crow the second time, and Jesus turned around and looked at Peter.

Suddenly Peter remembered Jesus' words, "Before the cock crows twice, you will say three times that you don't even know Me." And he went out and cried bitterly.

The High Priest asked Jesus about His disciples, and about what He was teaching the people.

"Why do you ask?" Jesus replied. "You already know what I teach, for you have listened to Me in the Temple. Nothing I teach is a secret."

One of the police officers hit Him in the face for saying this. "Is that the way to talk to the High Priest?" he shouted.

"Should you strike a man for telling the truth?" Jesus asked him.

QUESTIONS

What were the disciples doing while Jesus prayed in the Garden of Gethsemane?
Why did Judas kiss Jesus on the cheek?
What did Peter and the other disciples do when the men grabbed Jesus?
Did Peter gladly tell people that he was one of Jesus' disciples?

177
Insults to the Son of God!

Early the next morning the men who had arrested Jesus brought Him before the Jewish Supreme Court. There the Jewish officials tried to get people to tell lies about Jesus, but no two of them could keep their stories straight. At last two false witnesses came who declared, "This fellow said, 'I am able to destroy the Temple and build it again in three days.' "

Then the High Priest said, "I demand that You tell us whether You are the Christ, the Son of God."

Jesus answered, "I am. And I tell you this, that you will see Me sitting at the right hand of God, and coming back to earth again in the clouds of heaven."

Then the High Priest tore his clothes and said, "We don't need any more witnesses. You yourselves have heard the wicked thing He said—that he is the Son of God. What should His punishment be?" And everyone shouted, "Kill him."

Then they spat in His face and mocked Him, and when they had blindfolded Him, they struck Him. "Tell us, You Christ, who hit You?" they laughed.

Now they tied Him up, and the entire Supreme Court led Him to Pontius Pilate, the Roman governor. "This man tells the Jews to rebel against the Romans," they lied. "He tells them not to pay taxes to the emperor, and says He is the king of the Jews."

"Are you a king?" Pilate asked Him.

"Yes," Jesus replied, "but My kingdom is not of this world, for if it were, My servants would fight to save Me."

Then Pilate went out and told the Court, "I find nothing wrong with this man."

But they were even more fierce, and yelled out, "Everywhere He goes He starts riots against the government, all the way from Galilee to Jerusalem."

When Pilate heard them speak of Galilee, he decided that since Jesus came from there, he would send Him to Herod, the governor of Galilee, for Herod was in Jerusalem at the time.

Herod was glad for the opportunity of seeing Jesus. He had long wanted to, having heard so much about Him, and he hoped to see Jesus do a miracle for him. Herod asked Jesus many questions, but Jesus remained silent as the High Priests and other Jewish leaders bitterly accused Him of many sins. Herod and his soldiers now made fun of Jesus and mocked Him, putting a royal purple robe on Him, because He had said he was a king.

Afterwards Herod sent Him back to Pilate again.

Then Pilate called together the Jewish leaders and said to them, "You have accused this man of starting riots, but I find him not guilty. Herod has also found him innocent. There is no reason at all to talk about giving him the death penalty."

Now every year, during the Passover, if any of the Jews were in prison for disobeying the Romans, the Roman governor used to set one of them free, and he let the Jews say which prisoner it should be. He did this to please them, and to make them more willing to let him rule over them.

At this time a Jew named Barabbas was in prison for murder. The people now began shouting to the governor to do as he had always done before and set one of the prisoners free.

"Which one?" Pilate asked, "Barabbas or Jesus?"

While Pilate was speaking with them, his wife sent this message to him: "Don't harm that innocent man. I had a terrible nightmare about Him last night."

The High Priests now persuaded the mob to demand the release of Barabbas.

"Then what shall I do with Jesus?" Pilate asked.

And everyone shouted, "Crucify him."

"But why, what has he done wrong?" Pilate asked.

"Crucify him! Crucify him!" they yelled.

When Pilate saw that he couldn't persuade them to ask him to free Jesus, he took some water and washed his hands while all the people watched, and said, "Don't ever blame me for this innocent man's death."

Then all the Jews answered, "Let the blame be on us and on our children."

But Pilate, by washing his hands, didn't rid himself of the blame. For he knew Jesus was innocent, but wouldn't let Him go free. He was afraid that if he offended the Jews they might want someone else than him to be their governor, and he would lose his job. That is why he gave Jesus to them, to crucify Him.

Before the Romans would crucify anyone they would whip him. He was stripped to the waist, His hands were bound to a low post or pillar in front of Him so as to make Him stoop forward, and while He stood in this way, He was cruelly beaten with rods or whips until His back was red with blood and open wounds. So now Pilate told his soldiers to whip Jesus in this way.

Afterwards, Pilate's soldiers made fun of Him just as Herod's soldiers had. They put a purple robe on Him and placed a crown of thorns upon His head. Then they bowed before Him, pretending He was their king, and shouted, "Hail, King of the Jews!" And they spat on Him, and struck Him on the head with a stick.

QUESTIONS

When the High Priest asked Jesus whether He was the Son of God, what did Jesus say?

Did Pilate think Jesus deserved to die? Then why did he let Him?

Why did Herod and his soldiers put a purple robe on Jesus?

Why was Barabbas, the murderer, let out of prison?

178

Jesus Is Killed

Pilate still hoped the Jewish Supreme Court would finally let Jesus go, so he spoke to them again. "Once more, I tell you that I find no fault in Him," he said.

Then he brought Jesus out to them, wearing the crown of thorns and the purple robe. But when the Jewish leaders saw Him, they shouted again, "Crucify him! Crucify him!"

"Take him yourselves, then, and crucify him, for I find no fault in him," Pilate told them.

The Jewish leaders answered, "By our law he ought to die because he says he is the Son of God."

Now Pilate was even more afraid to put Jesus to death.

"Where were you born?" he asked Jesus. But Jesus gave him no reply.

"Do you refuse to speak to me?" Pilate demanded. "Don't you know that I have power to crucify you, and power to let you go?"

"You can only do what God will let you do," Jesus answered.

From that time Pilate tried to set Him free. But Caesar, the emperor of Rome, was a jealous and cruel man and Pilate feared him. When the Jews saw that Pilate wanted to set Jesus free, they screamed out, "You are no friend of Caesar's if you free a man who claims he is a king. How will Caesar like that? What do you think he'll do to you?"

Then Pilate was afraid to let Jesus go, for fear the Jewish leaders would tell Caesar. So he gave Jesus to them to be crucified.

Then Judas Iscariot, the disciple who had betrayed Jesus, was afraid because of what he had done, and brought back to the Jewish leaders the thirty pieces of silver they had paid to him for telling them where Jesus was. "I have sinned," he said, "for I have betrayed an innocent man."

"So what?" they said. "That's your worry."

Then Judas threw down the thirty pieces of silver on the Temple floor, and went away and hanged himself and died.

The chief priests picked up the money. "It's against the law to put it into the treasury at the Temple," they said, "for it was paid for betraying a man to his death." So they used the money to buy a field where foreigners could be buried, who died while visiting in Jerusalem.

Then the soldiers took the purple robe from Jesus and gave Him His own clothes again, and led Him away to die. Jesus had to carry the heavy wooden cross up a hill outside the city, and when He stumbled, they made a man carry it whose name was Simon, who was coming in from the country. A crowd followed Him out to Skull Hill or Mount Calvary, just outside the city gates, where He was to die.

There they nailed His hands and feet to the cross and crucified Him. Yet in His agony He prayed for them. "Father, forgive them, for they don't know what they are doing," He pleaded. He meant that they didn't know how great their sin was in killing the Son of God, or how fearful their punishment would be. Then they gave Him a mixture of gall and vinegar to drink. This was given to people who were crucified so that they wouldn't feel their awful pain quite so much. But when Jesus had tasted it, He wouldn't drink it, for He was deliberately suffering those pains for all of us. They crucified two thieves with Him, one on His right side and the other on His left.

People who were crucified did not die suddenly; they lived in terrible pain for many hours, sometimes hanging on the cross for days before they died. Jesus was crucified in the morning, but hung in agony until the afternoon, while the soldiers who had crucified Him sat down and watched Him there. They took His clothes and divided them up among themselves, and threw dice for His coat.

Pilate told the soldiers to place this sign on the cross above Jesus' head: JESUS OF NAZARETH, THE KING OF THE JEWS. These words were read by many, for the place where He was crucified was near the city.

The people passing by felt no pity for Him, but mocked Him, saying, "If You are the Son of God, come down from the cross."

And one of the thieves who was crucified with Him said, "If you are the Christ, save yourself and us."

But the other thief said, "Lord, remember me when You come into Your kingdom."

Jesus told him, "Today you will be with Me in Paradise." Jesus meant that the sins of the thief were forgiven, and as soon as he died, even that very day, his real self would go to the hap-

Jesus is dying for our sins. He was crowned with thorns and then nailed to the cross. It is noontime, but everything is growing dark because the Son of God is dying.

py place where Jesus was going.

Jesus' mother and His disciple John were standing near the cross while Jesus died. Jesus saw them standing there and asked John to take care of His mother, since He was going to die and leave her. From that hour, John took her to his own home and cared for her just as though she was his own mother.

From twelve o'clock noon until three in the afternoon there was darkness over all the land. God sent the darkness because His son was being killed by wicked men.

About three o'clock, Jesus called out with a loud voice, "My God, why have You forsaken Me?" He said this because God seemed to have turned away from Him, and it was true. For God had turned away from our sins for which Jesus was dying.

When one of the men standing there heard His cry, he ran and got a sponge and filled it with sour wine and held it up on a stick to Jesus' mouth so that He could drink it. Jesus tasted it and then cried out, "It is finished," and bowed His head and died.

At that moment the curtain which hung in the Temple in front of the Holy of Holies was torn in two from top to bottom, and the earth shook, breaking great rocks. (And many people who loved the Lord came back to life, and when Jesus rose from the dead three days later, they came out of the tombs and walked into Jerusalem and were seen by many of their friends!)

When the Roman soldiers who were watching Jesus saw how He died, they were terrified, and one of them said, "Surely this man was the Son of God."

QUESTIONS

Who wanted Jesus to be crucified?
What did Simon do for Jesus?
Who else was crucified with Jesus?
What happened to the earth and sky when Jesus died?

179
Jesus Comes Alive Again

The Jewish leaders didn't want Jesus and the two robbers to be hanging on the cross the next day, for it was the Sabbath. So they asked Pilate to tell the soldiers to kill them there on their crosses, so that their bodies could be taken down and buried that day.

Pilate agreed, and told the soldiers to break their legs because this would make them die more quickly. So the soldiers broke the legs of the two thieves, but when they saw that Jesus was already dead, they didn't break his legs but instead they pierced His side with a spear, making blood and water flow out.

There was a garden near the place where Jesus was crucified, and in the garden there was a new burial place —a cave carved out of the rock. It belonged to a rich man named Joseph. Joseph was a disciple of Jesus, though he had never told anyone for fear of what people would say. But now after Jesus was dead he went boldly to Pilate and begged for Jesus' body, and Pilate said he could take it down and bury it. So Joseph took Jesus' body down from the cross and wrapped it in a new cloth he had bought, and laid it in the cave and rolled a huge stone across the door.

Meanwhile the Jewish leaders went to Pilate and said, "Sir, while that liar was still alive, He said, 'After three days I will rise again.' Please place a guard for the next three days at the cave where he is buried, so that His disciples can't come in the night and steal His body, and then tell everyone He has come back to life." So Pilate agreed, and soldiers were sent over to guard the cave so no one could get in and steal Jesus' body.

But during the night the angel of the Lord came down from heaven and rolled back the stone from the cave and sat upon it. His face was as bright as lightning, and his clothes were white as snow. The soldiers trembled for fear and became as weak and helpless as dead men. Then they ran into the city, terrified.

Early the next morning, as it was getting light, Mary Magdalene and the other Mary, and Salome, came to the tomb bringing spices to embalm Him, that is, to help keep His body from changing to dust. "But how can we ever roll away the stone from the door of the cave?" they were wondering; for it was *very* heavy. But when they got there, the stone was pushed aside! They went into the cave and there was an angel in a long white robe!

They were badly frightened, but the angel said to them, "Don't be afraid. Are you looking for Jesus? He isn't here; He has come back to life again! See, that is where His body lay. Now go and tell His disciples that He is alive again and that He will meet them in Galilee."

The women ran from the cave in great fear, and yet with great gladness, and went to tell His disciples what had happened. But as they were running, Jesus met them. "Hello there!" He greeted them. They came and held Him by the feet and worshipped Him. "Don't be afraid," He said, "but tell My brothers—My disciples, including Peter—to go to Galilee, for I will meet them there."

When the women told the disciples what the angel had said, Peter and John ran to the cave to see for themselves. John got there first and stooped down and looked in and saw the linen sheet lying there—the one Joseph had wrapped around Jesus' body—but he didn't go inside. Then Peter arrived and went right in. So then John went in too, and they finally realized that Jesus had come back to life again. Before that they hadn't understood what He meant when He had told them that He would be alive again three days after He died.

Meanwhile some of the guards reported to the Jewish leaders what had happened during the night. The Jewish leaders gave them money to get them to lie about what happened, and to say that His disciples had come during the night while they were asleep and had stolen Jesus' body! (How would the guards know what happened when they were asleep?)

"If the governor hears about it and wants to kill you for sleeping," (for soldiers were killed if they slept on duty), "we will persuade him to pardon you," they promised.

So the soldiers took the money and said what the Jewish leaders told them to. But of course, it was a lie, for they hadn't been asleep at all.

QUESTIONS

Where was Jesus buried?
Why were guards stationed at Jesus' grave?
What did the women see when they came to Jesus' grave?
What happened to Jesus?

Jesus was buried here in this cave. These women came to embalm His body—but it was gone! He had come back to life again and the angels had rolled away the stone in front so that His disciples could go in and see that He wasn't there. Afterward He came and talked to them and told them about the wonderful home in heaven He was going away to prepare for them.

FRANCES HOOK

180
Jesus Returns to Heaven

Late that afternoon as two of Jesus' friends were walking along to the village of Emmaus, which was about seven miles from Jerusalem, they were talking to each other about all the strange things that had happened that day. Then Jesus came and walked along with them.

But He looked different, so they didn't recognize Him.

"What are you talking about that makes you so sad?" He asked them.

One of them, whose name was Cleopas, answered, "Are you a stranger here, that you haven't heard all the things that have been happening the last few days?"

"What things?" Jesus asked.

"About Jesus of Nazareth," they replied, "He was a prophet and did great miracles. We thought He was the one who would free Israel from the Romans. But the chief priests and other Jewish leaders crucified Him. And now, early this morning, three days after He was killed, some women who are friends of ours went to the cave where He was buried and came back reporting that His body wasn't there, and that some angels told them He is alive! Some of our men went to the tomb afterwards and found it was as the women had said: Jesus' body wasn't there!"

Then Jesus reminded them about what the prophets had written concerning Christ–that He would be killed, and afterwards come back to life again. Then Jesus began at the beginning of the Bible and explained all that had been written about Him. But still his two friends didn't recognize Him.

As they neared the village where

Two of Jesus' friends were going home, talking about the terrible thing that had happened in Jerusalem that week—Jesus had been killed. Yet here He is, walking along, talking with them! He is alive again! (But they didn't recognize Him at first.)

they lived, He prepared to leave them and go on further. Thinking He was a traveller, they invited Him to spend the night with them, as it was getting late in the day. So He went home with them. As they were eating supper together, Jesus took a small loaf of bread, and after He had thanked God for it, He broke it and gave it to them. But as He did this, suddenly they recognized Him, and just then He disappeared!

Then they said to each other, "Didn't you feel warm inside while He was talking with us out there on the road, explaining what the prophets had said?"

They started back to Jerusalem and right away found Jesus' disciples and others with them, and told them how they had seen Jesus and talked with Him, and how they had recognized Him as He was breaking the bread at the supper table. And just then, while they were telling about it, Jesus Himself suddenly appeared among them and spoke to them! They were badly frightened, for they thought He was a ghost.

Then He said to them, "Look at the nail marks in My hands and My feet. Touch Me and see that it is I, Myself, for a ghost doesn't have flesh and bones as you see that I have!" They could hardly believe it for joy! Then He asked them for food and they watched Him as He ate it. Then He explained to them the Scriptures that told of His dying for the people, and coming back to life again. And now at last, although they had read those parts of the Bible before, they finally understood them.

One of the disciples, whose name was Thomas, wasn't there that evening, so he didn't get to see Jesus. The others told him about it afterwards.

But Thomas replied, "Unless I see the spear wound in His side, I won't believe it was He."

Eight days later as the disciples were meeting together behind locked doors, and Thomas was with them too, suddenly Jesus was standing there among them, and greeted them! Then He said to Thomas, "Poke your finger into the wounds in My hands and thrust your hand into My side, and believe!"

When Thomas heard His voice and realized it was Jesus, he exclaimed, "My Lord and my God!"

"Thomas," Jesus said to him, "you wouldn't believe until you saw Me; but blessed are those who believe even though they haven't seen Me."

A few days later Jesus appeared to His disciples on the shore of the Sea of Galilee. This is the way it happened: Peter, Thomas, Nathaniel, James, John, and two other disciples were there, and when Peter said he was going out to fish, they said they would go along. They did, but caught nothing all night. In the early morning, Jesus was standing on the shore, but the disciples didn't recognize Him.

"Did you catch any fish?" He asked them.

"No," they replied.

"Throw your net out on the right-

This is Jesus, the Good Shepherd. How He loves His little lambs! You and I can be His lambs, too, if we trust Him to be our Saviour. Then He will be our friend and guide forever.

R. Hook

hand side of the boat and you'll catch plenty of them!" Jesus told them.

They did, and now they couldn't drag the net into the boat, it was so full of fish!

John said to Peter, "It must be the Lord standing there on the shore!" When Peter heard that, he fastened his fisherman's coat around him and jumped into the water to get to shore faster. The other disciples came in the boat, dragging the net. As soon as they came to land, they saw a fire burning, and fish laid on it, and bread.

Jesus said to them, "Bring some of the fish you have caught." Then Peter pulled the net ashore and it was full of huge fish, more than one hundred and fifty of them, but though there were so many, the net wasn't broken.

"Come and have some breakfast," Jesus called. They were almost sure it was the Lord, but didn't want to ask Him! (By this time He had shown Himself to them on several occasions since He came back to life again.)

Another time He met them on a mountain in Galilee where He had told them to go, and when they saw Him they worshipped Him. He said to them, "God has given Me all power in heaven and on earth. Go and preach the Good News to the people of every nation, baptizing them in the name of the Father, the Son, and the Holy Spirit, and teaching them to do everything I have commanded you."

Jesus showed Himself not only to His disciples, but to more than five hundred others at one time.

Forty days after He came back to life, Jesus appeared to the disciples at Jerusalem again.

Then He walked with them to a place near the village of Bethany (where Mary, Martha and Lazarus lived) and blessed them. And while He was blessing them, He began to rise into the air until He disappeared into a cloud!

While the disciples stood there straining their eyes for another glimpse, two angels appeared, dressed in brilliant white, and said to them, "Why stand here looking at the sky? Jesus will return again someday, just as you have seen Him go!"

QUESTIONS

Why didn't Jesus' friends recognize Him right away?

What Good News were the disciples to tell all the world?

What made Thomas believe that Jesus was alive?

Who were some of the people who saw Jesus after He came back to life?

What happened forty days after Jesus came back to life? Where did He go?

Surprise! Jesus is on the way back to heaven to see His Father! He has been away for thirty-three years, but now His work down here on earth is finished and He will live forever with God. See how surprised His disciples are!

R.Hook

181

Arrested for Preaching!

After Jesus had gone back to heaven, the disciples returned to Jerusalem to wait until the Holy Spirit came upon them, for Jesus had told them to do this. They met in an upstairs room to pray and to give thanks to God. Other disciples were with them too, so that altogether there were about one hundred twenty people present.

Then Peter stood up and said to them, "Brothers, the prophets said that someone else should be chosen to replace Judas. Let's choose someone who, like us, has been with Him since He was baptized by John until He was taken up into heaven."

The other disciples agreed and selected two men named Joseph and Matthias, and asked God to guide them in their final choice. Then they drew straws and Matthias drew the long one, so he was the one who became the twelfth apostle instead of Judas.

When the annual Jewish holiday called Pentecost arrived, and the disciples were meeting together, suddenly they heard what sounded like the roar of a great wind storm. The noise came closer and closer until it was in every room of the house where they were meeting. Then what seemed to be flames of fire in the shape of tongues rested on the head of each of them and the Holy Spirit came into them as Jesus had promised, and they all began to speak in other languages that they had never known before!

At that time there were many Jews in Jerusalem who had come from other countries to attend the Passover celebration. These men and women were amazed to hear the disciples talking in their own languages. But others, who didn't understand what the disciples were saying, mocked them and said, "They're drunk."

Peter replied, "No, they aren't drunk, but God has sent His Holy Spirit into them. You killed Jesus of Nazareth who did such great miracles, but now God has brought Him back to life just as the Bible promised. And we, His apostles, have seen Him alive again. His coming back to life proves that He is the Saviour of the world whom the prophets told about."

Then everyone was sorry because they had helped kill Jesus. "What can we do now?" they asked Peter and the others.

Peter replied, "Be sorry for your sins and be baptized, and the Holy Spirit will be given to you just as He was to us, for God promised to send Him to you and to your children, and to all who will obey Him."

Great crowds believed on the Lord Jesus that day, and about three thousand were baptized. They began meeting regularly with the apostles to study the Bible and to pray and to learn more about Jesus. They all shared their money with each other—those who had a lot gave to those who didn't. They prayed together, ate together in each other's homes, and were very happy. God made everyone kind to them, and every day others turned to God and believed that Jesus was their Saviour, and came to the apostles to be baptized.

One afternoon Peter and John went together to the Temple at the hour of prayer. A man who was lame from birth was being carried along the street by his friends, and placed at the gate called the Beautiful Gate of the Temple. There he begged from all who came to worship. When he saw Peter and John about to go into the Temple, he asked them for some money.

Peter looked down at him and said, "Look here!" The man looked up expectantly, for he thought Peter was going to give him some money. But Peter said, "I have no money! But I'll give you what I have: in the name of Jesus Christ of Nazareth, stand up and walk!"

Then Peter took him by the right hand and helped him up, and immediately the lame man's feet and ankle bones were strengthened, and he leaped up, stood for a moment, and then started walking, leaping, and praising God as he went into the Temple with them! He didn't even have to learn to walk.

When all the people saw him, and realized he was the man who had sat begging at the Beautiful Gate of the Temple, they were filled with wonder at what had happened, and crowded around to see him. Then Peter preached them this sermon:

"You men of Israel, why be surprised by this? And why look at us as though we had made this man walk? It is Jesus who has given us the power to make him well. Brothers, turn to God and believe Jesus so that your sins will be forgiven."

There was one group of Jews who didn't believe there would ever be a Judgment Day, or that the dead would ever come back to life again. Some of these men belonged to the Jewish Supreme Court, and were part of the government. They rushed over to stop the disciples from preaching about Jesus. They arrested Peter and John and put them in jail. But it was too late, for about five thousand people who heard Peter's sermon that day believed in Jesus!

The Supreme Court met the next day, and Peter and John were brought in. "By what power did you heal that lame man?" the Court demanded of them.

Peter answered, "He was made well by the power of Jesus of Nazareth, the man you crucified. You counted Jesus as worthless, but God has made Him the ruler over all of us. No one else in all the world except Jesus can save us from being punished for our sins."

When the members of the Court realized that Peter and John were uneducated fishermen, and yet were so bold, they were amazed. And of course they couldn't deny that the man had been healed. Finally they told Peter and John to go out for a little while, so they could discuss the case among themselves and decide what to do.

They finally decided to tell them that if they ever again preached about Jesus, they would be punished severely. So they called them in and told them.

But Peter and John replied, "Should we obey you instead of God? We can't stop telling people about Jesus and what we have heard Him say, and have seen Him do."

Then the rulers threatened them again and finally let them go because they were afraid of riots among the people if they kept them in jail.

QUESTIONS

How was someone else chosen to take the place of Judas? What was his name?

What happened when the Holy Spirit came on the disciples?

What miracle did Peter do at the gate of the Temple?

What did the Supreme Court at Jerusalem tell Peter and John?

182

Lies!

Peter and John now went to the other friends of Jesus and told them what the rulers had said. "Lord," they all prayed, "help us not to be afraid to preach the Good News; and give us power to do more miracles in Jesus' name."

At the end of the prayer, the house where they were gathered began to shake, for God was telling them He had heard their prayers and would give them what they asked for. Then they went out and preached again, unafraid of what the rulers might do to them. Many who heard them believed, and all of these new believers joined the others in their Bible study and prayer meetings, and in helping each other. Those who owned houses or lands sold them and brought the money to the twelve disciples to give to those who were poor. (The twelve disciples were now called "apostles," meaning missionaries).

But when a man named Ananias with his wife Sapphira sold some land, they decided to bring only part of the money they received in payment, but to say it was all of it. They thought the apostles would like them better if they said they were giving so much, but they forgot that God wants us honest more than He wants our money.

They thought the apostles wouldn't know they were lying, but God told Peter about it. So when Ananias came with the money and told Peter the lie, Peter said to him, "Ananias, the land was yours. You didn't have to sell it. And the money you received was yours. You could have kept it all if you wanted it. Why have you let Satan tempt you to lie to the Holy Spirit?"

Instantly Ananias fell down dead! So the Lord punished him for his sin. Then the young men who were there carried him out and buried him.

About three hours later his wife, Sapphira, arrived, looking for her husband and not knowing what had happened. Peter asked her, "Was the money your husband brought to us the entire amount you received for the land?"

"Yes," she answered.

Then Peter said to her, "Why have you and your husband agreed together to try to fool the Spirit of the Lord? Look, the men who have just buried your husband are at the door, and they will carry you out."

Instantly she fell down dead at Peter's feet, and the young men came in and carried her out and buried her beside her husband.

After this the apostles continued to preach and do miracles, and many men and women believed as a result. And sick people were brought out onto the walks and laid on blankets and mats, for if even Peter's shadow fell upon them, they got well! Crowds came too from the villages around Jerusalem, bringing their sick folk, and those with evil spirits; and all were healed.

But soon the apostles were in jail again! The Jewish leaders were deeply concerned about the wild enthusiasm of the crowds, so they arrested them. However, that night the angel of the Lord came down and opened the prison doors, and brought them out!

"Go back to the Temple," the angel told them, "and preach the Good News to the people." So, early the next morning, they went up to the Temple again and began to preach.

Meanwhile, the Jewish leaders called together another session of the Supreme Court and sent for the apostles to be brought from the prison for trial. But of course they weren't there! The soldiers came back to say that the prison was shut and the guards were standing before the doors, but the prisoners were gone!

Instantly the Court was in great confusion, but while everyone was guessing how they had escaped, a messenger arrived to say, "They are preaching at the Temple!" Guards were sent at once to the Temple, with instructions to get the apostles, but to bring them quietly so as not to excite the people and start a riot. So the apostles were soon standing again before the Court.

"Didn't we tell you never again to speak about Jesus?" the High Priest yelled at them.

Then Peter and the other apostles replied, "We must obey God rather than men. You persecuted Jesus and cruelly killed Him on the cross, but God has brought Him back to life again, to be the Saviour and to give the Jews new hearts, and to forgive them their sins. And we, His apostles, are His messengers of this Good News.

This made the High Priest and the others raging mad, and there was talk of killing them. But Gamaliel, one of the rulers and a man deeply respected, stood up to ask that the apostles be sent out of the council room for a little while, so that he could speak freely.

Then he addressed the Court as follows:

"Rulers of Israel, be careful what you do to these men. Sometime ago there was a man named Theudas who created a great stir by pretending that he was someone great, and about four hundred men followed him and became his disciples. But before long he was killed and all of his followers were scattered. Afterwards another man named Judas, from Galilee, persuaded many to follow him, but he also died, and his disciples were scattered. I say, let these men alone and don't harm them. For if what they teach isn't true, it will soon come to nothing; but if God has indeed sent them, you can't stop them. If you try, you will be fighting against God."

The entire Court agreed to what Gamaliel said, but they whipped the apostles anyway, and again told them that they must stop preaching. Then they finally let them go, and the apostles went out rejoicing that they were allowed to suffer pain for Jesus' sake. By this time they had learned that Jesus had not come to be an earthly king, and that they would not be made rich and great by telling people about Him; they would still be poor and humble men. They knew now that they must expect to be hurt as Jesus was. Their reward would come later, in heaven.

QUESTIONS

What lie did Ananias and Sapphira tell? How were they punished?

What happened when the disciples were put in jail again?

What good advice did Gamaliel give?

183

Stephen Is Stoned to Death

Do you remember about the Christians selling their land and bringing the money to the apostles to give to the poor? Some of this money was given to widows, that is, to women whose husbands were dead. But there was a complaint that some needy widows weren't getting as much help as others.

So the apostles called together all of Jesus' friends and said to them, "It isn't right that we apostles should stop preaching the Good News in order to distribute this money; so you choose seven men who are honest and wise and full of the Holy Spirit, and let them take care of this business. Then we can spend all our time preaching and praying."

Everyone thought this was a good idea, and they chose seven men to decide who should get how much. Then the apostles prayed for them, asking God to help them and to give them wisdom in doing their work.

Stephen, who was one of these seven men, not only gave money to the poor, but also preached and did great miracles. But some Jews were angry with him for doing these good things, so they took him to court. They brought in witnesses to lie about him and to say, "This man is constantly saying things he shouldn't about the Temple and against God's law."

The High Priest asked Stephen if it was true that he was saying these bad things.

Stephen talked to them a long time about how wicked the Jews had been for hundreds of years. They had killed God's prophets and had worshipped idols.

Then Stephen told the men of the council, "You are wicked men just like your fathers were. Which prophet didn't they kill, and now you have killed the Saviour."

At this, the judges were furious, and gnashed their teeth at Stephen like wild animals. But he looked up into heaven and saw a glorious light, and then He saw Jesus standing there beside God. "I see the heavens opened, and Jesus standing at God's right hand!" he exclaimed.

Then the judges yelled and shouted and put their hands over their ears so that they couldn't hear his words. And they dragged him out of the city and killed him by throwing rocks at him.

But as they were stoning him, he knelt down and prayed, "Lord Jesus, forgive them for this sin."

The men who had lied about Stephen threw the first stones at him. They took off their outer robes so they could throw harder, and laid them at the feet of a young man named Saul, to keep for them until they had finished killing Stephen.

After Stephen's death everyone turned against Jesus' friends and tried to hurt them. But some good men dared to come and get Stephen's body, and to mourn over it, and bury it. As for Saul, the young man who had watched over the clothes of the witnesses, he began a great campaign against the Christians, for he went into every home to find those who believed that Jesus was their Saviour, and when he found them, he arrested them—men and women alike—and put them in jail. Many of Jesus' friends fled from Jerusalem to different parts of the country, and to other countries too; but wherever they went, they told everyone the Good News.

Philip, who was another of the seven men who gave the money to the widows, went at this time to the city of Samaria and preached to the people there; and they listened to him carefully when they saw the miracles he did. For evil spirits came screaming out of people when he told them to leave, and people who were sick or lame got well. So there was great joy in Samaria, and many people believed and were baptized.

When the apostles in Jerusalem heard how interested the people of Samaria were, they sent Peter and John to join Philip there, and to pray for the new Christians to receive the Holy Spirit. And when Peter and John laid their hands on the heads of these new believers, God sent His Holy Spirit into them.

QUESTIONS

What happened to Stephen because he preached about Jesus?

Why did the disciples choose the seven men to take care of business matters?

Stephen preached about Jesus. This made the Temple leaders angry. They killed Stephen by throwing rocks at him, but Stephen forgave them and asked God to forgive them too.

R. Hook

184
Saul Finds Life

In the city of Samaria there was a man named Simon who did wonderful things by magic. Everyone had always listened to whatever he said, for they thought God had given him special powers. But when Philip preached the Good News in that city, and many believed and were baptized, Simon did too! So Philip baptized him, and after that he stayed with Philip, marvelling at the miracles he did.

When Simon saw that people received the Holy Spirit when Peter and John placed their hands on them and prayed for them, he offered money if they would give him the power to do this too. But Peter told him it was wrong to think that God's powers could be bought. "Repent of your sin and ask to be forgiven," he told Simon, "for I can see that you are not right with God at all."

Then Simon answered, "Pray that God won't punish me."

The angel of the Lord now told Philip to leave Samaria and to go to the city of Gaza. He of course obeyed, but didn't know what he was supposed to do when he got there. But as he was walking along the dusty road toward the city, a black government official from the land of Ethiopia rode by in his chariot. He was a very important man in his country, for he took care of all the treasures of the queen of Ethiopia. He had been in Jerusalem to worship at the Temple, and now as he sat there in his chariot returning to his own land, he was reading from the Bible at the part where the prophet Isaiah told the people of Israel that a Saviour was going to come into the world to die for their sins.

The Holy Spirit told Philip to go over to the chariot and talk with the man. So Philip ran to the chariot, and heard him reading aloud.

"Do you understand what you are reading?" Philip called out to him.

"How can I unless someone comes and explains it to me?" the man ex-

The Holy Spirit told Philip to go to a distant road where he would see an important government official—a black from Ethiopia—reading about Jesus in the book of Isaiah.

F+R. Hook

claimed. Then he invited Philip to come and sit with him in the chariot and to talk to him about it.

As they were riding along, the treasurer asked him, "What did the prophet mean when he wrote these words? Was he speaking about himself or someone else?"

Then Philip explained what it all meant, and told him that Isaiah was talking about Jesus.

Further down the road they came to a pool of water beside the road, and the officer said, "Look! Water! What is there to keep me from being baptized?"

Philip replied, "If you believe with all your heart, you may."

"I believe that Jesus Christ is the Son of God," was the Ethiopian's answer. Then he told his driver to stop, and he stepped into the water with Philip, and Philip baptized him. When they came out again, the Holy Spirit took Philip away! He just suddenly disappeared! But the Ethiopian went home happy because now he had heard about Jesus and he was one of Jesus' disciples.

Philip now found himself in the city of Azotus. And he preached in all the cities from there to Caesarea.

Meanwhile, how Saul hated Jesus' disciples! He finally went to the High Priest at Jerusalem and asked him to write letters to the Jewish leaders in the city of Damascus, demanding that they help him arrest any disciples of Jesus he found there so that he could bring them in chains to Jerusalem to be punished for believing that Jesus was the Saviour.

The High Priest gave Saul the letters he asked for, and he started out to go to Damascus.

But as he neared the city, suddenly a brilliant light from heaven shone around him, and Jesus appeared to him. Saul was terribly frightened and fell flat on the ground. Then he heard a voice saying, "Saul, Saul, why are you trying to hurt me?"

"Who are you, sir?" Saul asked.

The voice answered, "I am Jesus, the One you are persecuting."

Then Saul, trembling and astonished, said, "Lord, what do You want me to do?"

The Lord replied, "Get up and go on into Damascus. You will be told there what to do next." (The men who were with Saul heard the voice but couldn't understand the words.)

Then Saul got up, and found himself blind. He couldn't see a thing. Those who were with him had to lead him by the hand and bring him to Damascus. He was there for three days without sight, and did not eat or drink anything.

QUESTIONS

What was the Ethiopian reading when Philip came to him?

Tell about what happened to Simon, and why?

What did Saul get permission to do to all of Jesus' disciples?

What happened to Saul on his way to Damascus to persecute the Christians?

Saul was walking along the road from Jerusalem to the city of Damascus when suddenly, around noontime, a great beam of light flashed down upon him from heaven, blinding him. Then Jesus talked to him from heaven. After that, Saul loved Jesus instead of hating Him as he had before.

185
Saul Preaches about Jesus

There was a disciple in Damascus named Ananias, and the Lord said to him, "Ananias, go down to Straight Street, and ask at the house of Judas for a man named Saul. He is praying to Me right now, and he has seen a vision of your coming to him and putting your hands on him, and giving him his sight!"

Ananias answered, "Lord, I have heard about this man and of all the harm he has done to Your people in Jerusalem. And now he has come here to Damascus with letters from the chief priests, giving him power to arrest everyone who believes in You."

But the Lord said, "Go and visit him, for I have chosen him to preach my Good News to the Gentiles, and to kings, and to the people of Israel. And I will show him how much he must suffer."

So Ananias went to the house of Judas, found Saul, and laid his hands on him, saying, "Brother Saul, the Lord Jesus who appeared to you as you were coming to Damascus has sent me to put my hands on you so that you can see again, and so that you will be filled with the Holy Spirit."

Immediately Saul's sight returned, and he was baptized, and after he had eaten some food he was strong again. Then he stayed with the disciples in Damascus, and went into the Jewish churches and preached to the Jews about Jesus, telling them that He is the Son of God.

The people in the city could hardly believe what they heard!

"Isn't this the man who persecuted the Christians in Jerusalem," they asked, "and came here to arrest all those who believe in Jesus, to take them back in chains to the chief priests for punishment?"

But Saul just preached all the more and proved from the Scriptures that Jesus is the Saviour.

After several days the angry Jews began to talk about killing Saul. They watched day and night at the city gates to capture him if he went out. But the Christians heard about it, and let him down at night in a basket from a window in the wall, so that he escaped and went into the desert for awhile to talk to God. Three years later he went to Jerusalem.

When he arrived at Jerusalem he went to find the disciples of Jesus, for now instead of hating them, he loved them and wanted to be with them. But they were all afraid of him and wouldn't believe he was really one of them. Then Barnabas, one of the men who had sold his land and given the money to the poor, brought Saul to them and told them how Saul had met Jesus on the road to Damascus, and how he had boldly preached the Good News.

Then the apostles welcomed Saul, and he stayed with them and preached in Jerusalem.

But some of the Jews at Jerusalem, like those at Damascus, determined to kill him. When the apostles heard about it they sent him away to the far-off city of Tarsus, his birthplace. After this the Christians had no more trouble for awhile, but were left in peace.

As Peter went through different parts of the land visiting the new churches, he came to the city of Lydda. He found there a man named Aeneas who had the palsy, and had been in bed for eight years.

Peter said to him, "Aeneas, Jesus Christ makes you well! Get up!" And immediately he stood up and was healed! Then many of the people who lived at Lydda and throughout that entire area believed in Jesus as their Saviour.

At Joppa, a city not far from Lydda, there was a disciple named Dorcas. This woman was very kind and good, always helping the poor. But she became sick and then died. Her friends sadly gathered in an upstairs room to prepare her for burial.

When the disciples in Joppa heard that Peter was not far away, over in Lydda, they sent two men to ask him to hurry and come to them, and he did.

They brought him to the house where the body of Dorcas lay. All the poor widows she had helped were there, crying and showing the coats and other clothes she had made for them.

But Peter asked them all to leave. After they had left the room he kneeled down and prayed, and then, turning to the dead body, he said, "Dorcas, get up!"

And she woke up as though she had been asleep, and sat up, and he gave her back to her friends!

QUESTIONS

How did Saul get his sight back?

Why was everyone so surprised to hear Saul preach about Jesus?

Who wanted to kill Saul?

What happened to Dorcas after she was already dead?

186
Peter Baptizes a Gentile

Over in the city of Caesarea was a man named Cornelius, an officer in the Roman army. He was a good man who feared God, and even though he wasn't a Jew, he taught his family about God. He gave many gifts to the poor, and spent much time in prayer. One day Cornelius saw an angel coming to him and calling him. He was terribly frightened. "What do you want, sir?" he asked.

The angel replied, "God has heard your prayers and seen the gifts you have given to the poor. Now send men to Joppa to find a man named Peter who is staying in the house of Simon, a tanner, by the seaside. Bring him here and he will tell you what to do."

So Cornelius called two of his servants and a godly soldier and told them what had happened and what the angel had said, and sent them to Joppa to find Peter.

The next day as they were arriving at Joppa, Peter went up to the housetop to pray, for the house had a flat roof and the people in that country used these roofs for porches. As he was praying, he grew very hungry, and while lunch was being prepared, God gave him a vision. He seemed to see the sky above him open, and something like a great sheet of canvas came down to the ground in front of him. On this sheet were all kinds of wild animals and snakes and birds. Then a voice said, "Kill them and eat them for dinner, Peter."

Do you remember that Moses told the people of Israel not to eat certain kinds of animals? Well, some of these animals were there on that canvas sheet, and in the vision, God told Peter to eat them! So Peter answered, "No, Lord, for I have never eaten anything You have told me not to."

But the voice came again, and said, "When God says it is all right, don't say it isn't!"

This happened three times, and then the sheet was pulled back to heaven again. It was God who sent the vision to Peter, and the reason He sent it was this: The Jews thought they were better than other nations because God had given them many special promises. So the Christians—all of them were Jewish—thought Jesus came to save only the Jews. They hadn't preached the Good News to others, but now God was using this vision to tell Peter that He wanted him to tell everyone, not just the Jews, about Jesus. The animals he saw in the vision meant the other nations, and God was showing Peter that he should not despise them and refuse to teach them about Jesus, for God had made all nations, and had sent Jesus to save everyone.

While Peter was trying to understand what the vision meant, the servants of Cornelius arrived at the house where Peter was staying. They were outside at the gate, asking if someone named Peter lived there. Then the Holy Spirit said to Peter, "Three men are looking for you. Go with them without fear, for I have sent them."

So Peter went downstairs to the men and said, "I'm the man you are looking for. What can I do for you?"

They answered, "Captain Cornelius, a good man who fears God and is well thought of by all the Jews, was told by a holy angel to send for you to come to his home, so that you could tell him what to do."

Then Peter asked the men to come in and stay there that night, and the next day he went with them, and some of the Christians who lived at Joppa went along with them.

They arrived at Caesarea the following day. Cornelius was expecting them and had invited his relatives and friends to be with him when Peter came. As Peter walked into his house, Cornelius fell down and worshipped him. But Peter said, "Stand up! I am only a man like yourself!"

Then after talking together awhile, Peter went inside and met many Gentiles—people who, like Cornelius, weren't Jews.

Peter told them, "You know that the Jews say it is wrong for us to associate with men of other nations, because we Jews think we are better, and we call everyone else heathen. But God has taught me in a vision that God loves all mankind, and not just the Jews. So I came as soon as I was sent for. And now, what is it you want? Why did you ask me to come?"

"Four days ago," Cornelius answered, "I was fasting and praying here in my house when suddenly an angel stood before me in bright clothing and said, 'Cornelius, God has heard your prayers and has seen your kind acts to the poor. Send messengers to Joppa to find a man named Peter. He is staying in the house of Simon, a tanner, living by the sea. When he comes he will tell you how you and all your family can be saved.'

"Immediately I sent for you and I appreciate your coming. We want to hear what God has told you to tell us."

Then Peter said, "I realize now that God doesn't choose one nation more than another, but in every nation there are those who worship Him, and do what is right, and are those He receives as His children.

"God sent Jesus into the world, and He went about doing good. Yet the Jewish leaders put Him to death. But God brought Him back to life again on the third day and allowed us to see Him. We even ate and drank with Him after He returned to life. He commanded us to go and preach to people everywhere and to tell them that God has appointed Jesus to be the ruler of all nations; for all who believe in Him have their sins forgiven."

While Peter was still speaking, the Holy Spirit came upon Cornelius and the other Gentiles who were with him. The Jews who had come with Peter from Joppa were greatly surprised, for the Gentiles began speaking in languages they hadn't learned, just as the apostles and other Jewish Christians did when the Holy Spirit came upon them.

Then Peter asked, "Shouldn't these men be baptized, since the Holy Spirit has come upon them just as He did upon us?" So he baptized them in the name of Jesus. Then they begged him to stay with them for several days.

But when the Christians at Jerusalem heard that Peter had gone to visit Cornelius and his friends at Caesarea, they scolded him. "You shouldn't preach to Gentiles or even eat with them," they said.

But Peter explained what had happened—how God had taught him by the vision that he should preach the Good News to the Gentiles too; and how God had told him to go with the messengers sent by Cornelius to find him; and that the Holy Spirit came upon them just as He had on the Jews who believed. "Since God sent His Spirit upon them, who was I to oppose Him?" Peter asked.

When the other Christians heard Peter's explanation, they stopped arguing and thanked God. "To think that God has given new hearts to the Gentiles too! And that they too can be saved as well as we!" they exclaimed.

QUESTIONS

Was Cornelius a Jew? Did he believe in God?

What was Peter's vision about? What did it mean?

Why was Peter surprised when the Holy Spirit came upon Cornelius?

Was it right for Peter to preach to the Gentiles?

187

Peter and the Angel

Some of the disciples who fled from Jerusalem at the time Stephen was put to death now went to the city of Antioch in the land of Syria, and preached there to men who weren't Jews, and God helped many of them to believe.

When news of this reached Jerusalem, the apostles sent Barnabas to Antioch to investigate the matter. He was glad when he saw how many of the people there believed, and he encouraged them to continue to earnestly worship and obey the Lord. For Barnabas was a good man whose heart was full of faith and of the Holy Spirit, and through his preaching many more believed in Jesus.

Then Barnabas went to the city of Tarsus to look for Saul, and when he found him he brought him back to Antioch. They stayed there a whole year, preaching the Good News. (It was in Antioch that the disciples were first called "Christians.")

While Saul and Barnabas were in Antioch, some believers who were prophets came from Jerusalem to visit them. One of these prophets, a man named Agabus, prophesied that a great famine was coming over all Judea. So the disciples at Antioch decided to send help to the Christians at Jerusalem. Each gave as much as he could, and Barnabas and Saul took their gifts to Jerusalem.

About that time King Herod began to persecute the Christians. He killed James, the apostle who was the brother of John, and because he saw how much this pleased the Jews, he arrested Peter too, and put him in jail, intending to execute him. Herod placed soldiers and guards all around the jail, night and day, so that Peter couldn't escape. But the church in Jerusalem kept praying for him.

The night before he was to be killed, Peter was sleeping between two soldiers, bound with two chains fastened to the soldiers' wrists, so that if he even moved they would know it.

Suddenly the prison was full of light and an angel was standing there! He touched Peter's side and wakened him. "Quick, get up!" he whispered. But the soldiers slept on as the chains fell off of Peter's hands! "Dress yourself and put on your shoes and follow me," the angel said to him. Peter followed along behind him, but thought it was only a dream! When they had passed the guards, they came to the iron gate that led out of the jail into the city, and it opened for them by itself! They walked on together down the street, and suddenly the angel was gone!

When Peter collected his thoughts, he said to himself, "Think of it! The Lord has sent His angel to save me!" He went over to the home of Mary, the mother of the disciple Mark, where many Christians were praying for him. Peter knocked at the gate, and a girl named Rhoda came to see who was there. But when she heard Peter's voice she was so excited and glad that she forgot to let him in, and ran back and told everyone that Peter was out there!

"Don't be foolish!" they said, "Peter is in prison!" But she insisted he was at the gate.

"Then it must be his spirit," they said. They thought he had already been killed, and his spirit was out there in the street trying to get in! Meanwhile, Peter kept on knocking! They finally opened the door and there he was. Then what excitement there was! But Peter quieted them and told them what had happened and asked them to tell the other apostles. Then he left and went to find a place to hide.

In the morning when the soldiers woke up at the jail, Peter was gone. King Herod questioned them closely, but they couldn't tell him what had happened, so he commanded them all to be killed for letting Peter escape.

One day not long afterwards, King Herod put on his royal robes and sat on his throne and made a speech to some of his people. "It is the voice of a god and not of a man!" they shouted. Herod was very proud and pleased when he heard them say this, and was glad that the people called him a god.

But the Lord was angry and sent His angel to punish Him. There came a dreadful disease upon him, and he was eaten with worms and died.

Barnabas and Saul had delivered the gifts from the Christians in Antioch to those in Jerusalem, then returned to Antioch. They brought along with them a young disciple named Mark.

One day while the Christians at Antioch were worshipping the Lord, the Holy Spirit spoke to them and told them to send Barnabas and Saul to other countries to preach the Good News to people everywhere. They all fasted and prayed together, and then put their hands on the heads of Barnabas and Saul to bless them, and sent them away as missionaries.

So Barnabas and Saul left Antioch and sailed away to the island of Cyprus.

There they met a Jew named Elymas, who was a false prophet and was the advisor to the governor of the country. The governor was a wise man and he sent for Barnabas and Saul to come and explain the Good News to him. But Elymas spoke against them, and tried to keep the governor from believing what they taught.

Then Saul, who was now called Paul, looked at Elymas, and said, "You child of the devil, full of all wickedness, will you never stop speaking against those things the Lord has commanded us to teach? And now the Lord has sent a punishment upon you, and you will be blind for a time, not able to see even the sun."

Immediately his sight was taken from him. He groped around like a person in the dark, and had to be led by the hand. Then the governor, when he saw the miracle that Paul had done, believed on Jesus.

QUESTIONS

In what city were the disciples first called Christians?

What happened to Peter the night before he was supposed to be killed?

How did God punish King Herod for pretending he was a god?

Whom did the Holy Spirit tell the church at Antioch to send out as missionaries?

What was Saul's new name?

Peter was put in jail for telling people that Jesus is alive again. But God sent an angel to get Peter out. You can see the angel telling Peter to get up and come! Peter is surprised. He didn't know God was going to help him like this.

188
Travelling Missionaries

Paul and Barnabas and Mark now sailed away from Cyprus and came to the city of Perga in Turkey. There Mark quit and went back to Jerusalem, for he decided the trip would be too hard. So Barnabas and Paul went on by themselves. They arrived at the city of Antioch and went into the Jewish church to teach. After the Scriptures had been read the pastor asked them to speak to the people.

So Paul stood up and said, "Men of Israel and all of you who fear God, listen to me. The God of the people of Israel chose our fathers to be His people, and by His mighty power He set them free when they were living as slaves in the land of Egypt. Afterwards He took care of them for forty years as they wandered around in the wilderness. Then He destroyed the wicked nations of Canaan, and divided the land among His people. He gave His people judges to rule over them for about 450 years, until the time of Samuel the prophet. But the people asked for a king, and God gave them King Saul; and afterwards He gave them King David.

"And now, just as God promised, He sent Jesus. But the people of Jerusalem and their rulers didn't realize who He really was, and they killed Him. But God brought Him back to life, and we talked to Him several times afterwards. And now we have come to tell you the Good News that this Jesus is the Saviour who was promised, and that all of your sins are forgiven if you believe in Him."

The Jews weren't too interested, and began to go away, but the Gentiles who were there begged Paul and Barnabas to preach to them again. And so on the next Sabbath almost the entire city came to hear them. But when the Jews saw the crowds they were jealous and displeased, and spoke against the things Paul said.

Then Paul and Barnabas spoke boldly to the Jews and said, "It was right for us to preach the Good News to you first, but since you won't hear it and don't care to be saved, we will preach it to the Gentiles instead. For that is what God has told us to do." They said that Jesus is the Saviour of all the nations, not just the Jews. When the Gentiles heard this they were glad, but the Jews started rioting until Paul and Barnabas had to flee for their lives to the city of Iconium.

At Iconium they went as usual to the Jewish church to teach the people about Jesus, and God gave them power to do miracles so that great numbers of both Jews and Gentiles believed. But in this city, too, the Jews who wouldn't believe stirred up the people until they were about to stone Paul and Barnabas to death.

Then Paul and Barnabas fled to another city, called Lystra, and preached there. A man was there who had been lame ever since he was born, and had never walked. Paul saw that the man had faith to believe, so he shouted, "Stand up!" And the man leaped up and walked!

When the people of Lystra saw this miracle, they cried out, "These are gods who have come down to us from heaven!" And they called Barnabas "Jupiter," and Paul "Mercury"—the names of their idols.

Then the priests from the idols' temple brought oxen covered with wreaths of flowers, intending to sacrifice them to the apostles in the same way that they sacrificed them to their idols.

But when Barnabas and Paul saw what was happening they tore their clothes to show their dismay, and ran among the people shouting, "Sirs, why do you do such things? For we are men like yourselves, and have come to preach to you and persuade you to turn from worshipping idols. We want you to worship only the true God who made heaven and earth and the sea, and everything in them. He is the God who sends us rain and sunshine, and makes the earth fertile, so that all may have food to eat and be glad." Yet even saying this could hardly keep the people from offering sacrifices to them.

But just then some Jews from Antioch and Iconium arrived at Lystra and shouted out that Barnabas and Paul were wicked men who were trying to fool everyone. Almost at once the same people who had just been wanting to worship them, tried to kill them. They stoned Paul and dragged him out of the city and left him for dead. But while the Christians were standing around him he got up and went back into the city again!

The next day he went with Barnabas to Derbe. After preaching there they went back to all the cities where the people had persecuted them, and preached to the Christians who lived there. Paul encouraged them to keep on believing in the Lord Jesus, and reminded them that they must expect trouble and sorrow when serving God.

Then they appointed elders to rule over the churches in each city, and finally they went back to Antioch to report to the church that had sent them on this journey. They called together the entire church and told everyone how they had told the Good News wherever they went, preaching it to the Gentiles as well as to the Jews. They stayed in Antioch with the disciples for a long while.

QUESTIONS

When Paul preached at Antioch, were the Jews or Gentiles more interested?

Why did the people of Lystra call Paul and Barnabas "Mercury" and "Jupiter"?

Who was stoned and left outside the city, supposedly dead? Then what happened?

189

Paul Meets Young Timothy

But now some believers from Jerusalem arrived at Antioch to preach, and they claimed that a person couldn't be saved without offering up animals as sacrifices.

For hundreds of years before Jesus came to earth, the Jews offered such sacrifices to show that their great Messiah was coming to save them. But when He came, there was no more need for these sacrifices; for we don't need anything to remind us that a person is coming when he is already here and we have seen him! Jesus is the Messiah, and He is the Lamb of God that takes away the sins of the world.

Paul and Barnabas talked with these men and tried to make them understand that sacrifices were no longer needed, but they wouldn't believe. So it was agreed that these men and Paul and Barnabas should go to Jerusalem to ask the elders of the church there to settle the question.

The apostles and elders met together in Jerusalem to discuss this problem, and the Holy Spirit told them that it is no longer necessary to offer up animal sacrifices.

Then the apostles and elders sent Judas and Silas to Antioch to tell the Christians there what had been decided. They also wrote a letter to be read to the Christians not only at Antioch, but in other cities too, telling them that they need no longer sacrifice lambs, oxen, or goats to the Lord. The time was past when the Lord wanted the people to worship Him in this way. What He wanted them to do now was to turn from their sins and to believe in His Son Jesus—loving Him in their hearts, and obeying His commandments.

So Paul, Barnabas, Judas, and Silas came to Antioch and called together all the believers, and gave them the letter from the apostles and elders, and explained it to them. Everyone was glad when they read it, for now they could worship God anywhere and not just in Jerusalem where the Temple was.

After this, Paul said to Barnabas, "Let's go out again and visit our brothers in all the cities where we preached before, and see how they are getting along."

Barnabas was willing, and he

wanted to take Mark with them; but Paul thought they shouldn't take Mark because he had deserted them and gone home when they took him with them before.

Paul and Barnabas disagreed so much about this that they decided not to stay together. Barnabas took Mark and sailed to the island of Cyprus, while Paul chose Silas and went to Syria to visit the churches there.

Arriving at Lystra, the city where he had healed the lame man, Paul met a young man named Timothy, whose mother was a Jewess, and a disciple of Jesus, but whose father was a Greek. Timothy was well thought of by the Christians there at Lystra, for he had lived a fine Christian life from the time he was a small child. When Paul saw how wise and good this young man was, he invited him to go along with him and Silas, and learn to be a minister and preach the Good News.

One night at Troas, a coastal city, Paul had a vision. In the vision he saw a man standing before him, pleading, "Come over to Macedonia and help us." Macedonia was over in Greece, across the Adriatic Sea. So Paul and those who were with him sailed from Troas and soon arrived in Philippi, a city of Macedonia.

On the Sabbath day they went out of the city a little way to a riverbank where people met to pray. They sat and talked with some women there, telling them about Jesus. A woman named Lydia, a saleswoman, was very interested and listened carefully to what Paul said, and believed in Jesus. When she and her family had been baptized, she begged Paul and his friends to come and stay at her home.

QUESTIONS

After Jesus died on the cross, was it still necessary for the Jews to offer up animals as sacrifices? Why not?

Why did Paul and Barnabas decide to go on separate trips?

Who went with Paul on his travels?

What made Paul decide to go to Macedonia?

190

Back to Jail!

At Philippi they met a young woman who had an evil spirit in her. She earned a lot of money for the men who owned her by telling fortunes. She would tell people what would happen to them in the future.

She followed along behind Paul and his companions and shouted, "These men are the servants of God; they will tell you how to be saved." This went on for several days.

But Paul didn't like it and finally turned around and said to the evil spirit inside her, "In the name of Jesus Christ, come out of her." And immediately the spirit came out and left her.

When her owners realized that she was healed and the evil spirit was gone, and that she could no longer earn money for them by telling people's fortunes, they were angry and grabbed Paul and Silas and brought them before the city judge. "These Jews are disturbing the peace of our city," they shouted. "They are teaching the people to do wicked things."

This was enough to start a riot and the judges commanded that Paul and Silas and Timothy be whipped. After they had been beaten until they had many painful wounds, they were put in prison. Their jailor was told to keep them safe; if they escaped, he would be killed. So he took them into the inner prison and fastened their feet in the stocks so they couldn't escape.

In the middle of the night as Paul and Silas were praying and singing praises to God, with the other prisoners listening, suddenly there was a great earthquake which shook the whole prison, and immediately all the doors opened of their own accord, and the chains that held the prisoners fell off! The jailor woke up, saw the prison doors open, and fearing he would be tortured and killed for letting the prisoners escape, he drew his sword to kill himself; for he supposed all the prisoners had run away. But Paul, down in the dark dungeon, knew what he was about to do, and

Wouldn't it be hard to sing and praise God in jail? Paul and Silas did this, and in the night God sent an earthquake to open the jail. Instead of running away, the men stayed and told their jailer how to be saved.

shouted up to him, "Do yourself no harm, for we are all here."

Then the jailor called for a light and came trembling into the dungeon where Paul and Silas were, and kneeled down before them, crying out, "Sirs, what must I do to be saved?"

They answered him, "Believe on the Lord Jesus Christ, and you will be saved, and your family." Then they told him and all his family about the Saviour, preaching the Good News to them. And they all believed and were baptized.

The jailor now washed the blood from their backs where they had been whipped, and brought them food. How happy he was because he and his family were Christians now, and all their sins forgiven.

In the morning the judges sent some officers to the prison to tell the jailor, "Let those men go."

When the jailor told Paul he could leave, Paul replied, "They had no right to beat us, for we are Roman citizens and had no trial. If they want us to go, let the judges themselves come and bring us out, so that the people will know we were unjustly whipped and thrown into prison."

When the judges heard that Paul was a Roman citizen, they were afraid they would be punished for what they had done to him; and they came and begged him to please leave their city. Then he and Silas left the prison and went to Lydia's house. After meeting with the disciples there and encouraging them, they left Philippi.

From there they went to Thessalonica, where Paul preached in the local Jewish church, called the synagogue, for three Sabbaths in a row. He explained the Scriptures and showed from them that Jesus was the Saviour. Some of the Jews believed, and many of the Gentiles too.

But the Jews who wouldn't believe were angry at those who did, for they were deserting the Jewish religion. So they started a riot, and a mob raided the house where Paul and Silas stayed, to bring them out to the people. When they couldn't find them, they caught the man who owned the house, a man named Jason, and brought him before the judges.

"These Christians," they shouted, "have caused trouble and confusion in every city of the empire, and now they have come here too. They won't obey the laws of Caesar, and say there is another king named Jesus. Yet Jason has let them come into his house."

The judges then made Jason promise that Paul and Silas wouldn't cause any more trouble, and let him go. Meanwhile, the Christians sent Paul and Silas away by night to the city of Beroea.

There, too, they went into the synagogue to preach to the Jews. The Jews in Beroea were more willing to learn than those in Thessalonica. They listened to the Good News and then searched the Scriptures to sec whether the things Paul and Silas told them were true. As a result, many believed, both men and women, Jews and Gentiles.

QUESTIONS

Who was angry when the evil spirit left the woman?

Did all the prisoners escape when their chains fell off?

How did Paul and Barnabas see the jailor when he was upstairs in another room?

How did the jailor and his family become Christians?

Why were the Jews so angry whenever people believed in Jesus?

191
Paul's Sermon

When the Jews of Thessalonica learned that Paul was preaching in Beroea, they went there to stir up the people against him. As a result, the Christians decided it would be best if he left the city, though Silas and Timothy stayed.

Paul and those with him went on to the capital of Greece. The people of Athens were considered the best thinkers of that time, and were known all over the world for their learning; yet they worshipped false gods. They made beautiful idols and built splendid temples and altars in different parts of their city. Among the altars was one with these words on it: "TO THE UNKNOWN GOD." For though they had many gods they thought there might be a God they had never heard of. That is why they built this altar to Him.

As Paul passed through the streets of Athens he noticed how full of idols the city was. He preached to the Jews in their synagogue, and went every day to the marketplace where the people of the city met to talk, and explained the Good News to them.

When the men of Athens heard him, some of them asked, "What is this fellow talking about?"

Others answered, "He seems to be telling about some new and strange god." They said this because he preached about Jesus and the resurrection.

So they invited him to Mars Hill, in the center of the city, to lecture to them about his religion.

"You are saying some strange things," they remarked, "and we would like to know what you mean." For the people of Athens liked nothing better than to tell or hear something new.

So Paul stood up and addressed them as follows:

"Men of Athens, I see that you think a great deal about the gods you worship, for as I walked through your city looking at your temples, altars, and images, I saw an altar with these words written on it: "TO THE UNKNOWN GOD." So now I want to tell you about this God you worship without knowing Him."

Then Paul told them about God—that He had made the world and everything else, but He doesn't live in temples built by men. He is not like the idols of gold, silver, and stone made by men. "People don't know any better than to worship such idols," Paul said, "so God hasn't destroyed them for doing it, but gives them food and clothing and everything they need. But now," Paul declared, "God tells everyone to quit worshipping idols and to repent of their sins and to believe on Jesus, for God has set the time when He will send Jesus to judge everyone, and the proof that He will do this is that He raised Jesus from the dead."

When the men of Athens heard Paul speak of the resurrection—the rising from the dead—some of them thought this was silly and they wouldn't listen to him anymore. But others told him, "We want to hear more."

Several of those who were there that morning believed, among them Dionysius, a member of the Supreme Court of Athens, and a woman named Damaris, and some others.

Paul now left Athens and came to the city of Corinth. There he found a Jew named Aquila, with his wife Priscilla, who were in the business of making tents. Paul was also a tent-maker, and whenever he needed money he made tents and sold them. So since he and Aquila were in the same kind of work, Paul went to stay and work with him.

But every Sabbath day he went into the Jewish church and taught the people, persuading both Jews and Gentiles to believe in the Saviour. When the Jews contradicted him and spoke against Jesus, he told them, "I have done my duty in telling you about Him. If you won't be saved, the fault is your own; from now on I am going to preach to the Gentiles."

Corinth, like Athens, was a great city, but the people who lived there were very wicked. One night the Lord spoke to Paul in a vision and told him that many Corinthians would become Christians. He told Paul to preach boldly, without fear, for the Lord would be with him and would take care of him and no one would hurt him.

Paul stayed in Corinth a year and six months preaching to the people. But the Jews who wouldn't believe finally got together and brought him before the governor. "This fellow," they told him, "teaches people to worship God in a way that is very wrong."

Paul started to defend himself, but the governor turned to those who had arrested him and said, "If this man had done something wrong, I would need to listen to you, but since it is only a question about your worship, handle it yourselves, for I refuse to judge such matters." And he drove them out of the courtroom.

QUESTIONS

Why did the people of Athens have an altar to the unknown God?

What were the people of Athens always doing?

What work did Paul do in Corinth?

What did Paul do every Sabbath?

192
Riot!

Paul stayed in Corinth a long time. Then, after saying good-bye to the Christian brothers there, he sailed to Ephesus in the land of Syria. He was in Ephesus for three years, preaching the Good News until all the people in that part of the world had heard it, both Jews and Gentiles. God gave him power to do wonderful miracles so that handkerchiefs or aprons he touched could be taken to sick people, and they got well!

Then some Jewish bums—seven brothers who spent their time loafing—when they saw Paul casting out demons, decided to try it themselves. Going over to a man possessed with an evil spirit, they said to the spirit, "In the name of Jesus we command you to come out!"

But the evil spirit answered them, "I know Jesus, and I know Paul, but who are you?" And he jumped on them and beat them up so that they fled out of the house wounded and with their clothes badly torn.

Of course, everyone soon heard about what happened, and as a result they believed and came to Paul confessing the evil they had done. Others, who were magicians, brought their magic books and publicly burned them.

The people of Ephesus worshipped the image of a Greek goddess named Diana—they thought this idol had fallen down from heaven. It was enshrined in a beautiful temple built of cedar, cypress wood, marble, and gold. It had taken 220 years to build this famous temple, known all over the world as a tourist attraction. People came from every land to visit it, for it was thought to be one of the most beautiful and wonderful buildings ever made.

Little models of this temple, called shrines, with an image of Diana inside, were manufactured at Ephesus. In fact, this was one of the main businesses of the city. The men who made the shrines sold them to the tourists, and in this way earned a lot of money. One day, Demetrius, one of these tradesmen, heard Paul telling some people that they shouldn't worship idols. Demetrius suddenly realized why his business was becoming so poor. The people weren't buying his idols anymore because of what

Paul was telling them about its being wrong! So Demetrius called together all the workmen who made silver shrines for Diana, and addressed them as follows:

"Gentlemen, you know that our living depends on selling these shrines. But this Paul has persuaded many people here, and in almost every other city in this country, that the idols we make are false gods. So there is danger that we cannot sell enough shrines to stay in business. But there is also danger that the great goddess Diana will no longer be worshipped, and that the people will not come to her beautiful temple anymore."

When the workmen heard what Demetrius said, they were very angry and shouted, "Great is Diana of the Ephesians!" The whole city was soon in confusion. Then the workmen caught Gaius and Aristarchus, two men who had come with Paul to Ephesus, and rushed them into the theatre where a great mob had gathered. Paul wanted to go in and try to reason with the mob, but the Christians wouldn't let him, fearing what might happen to him. And also some of the city's leaders who were his friends sent word to him not to do it.

Inside there was a great uproar, some people shouting one thing and some another, and many didn't even know why they were there!

A man named Alexander stood up and kept trying to get the people's attention so he could accuse Paul, but the crowd just kept on shouting for about two hours, "Great is Diana of the Ephesians; great is Diana of the Ephesians!"

Then the mayor of the city came in to address the crowd and the people finally quieted down. "Men of Ephesus," he said, "everyone knows that the people of our city are worshippers of the great goddess Diana, and of her image that fell down from heaven. And since no one denies this, you ought to be careful and do nothing in anger. For you have brought these men here called Christians, who have not robbed your temple nor spoken evil of your goddess. If Demetrius and the workmen who are with him have any complaint to make against them, let them go before the court and prove what evil they have done. We are in danger that the Roman government will send soldiers to harm us because of today's riot, for we can give no reason why we are here." Then he sent the people away and they left the building.

Paul then called together the disciples and told them good-bye, and went back to Macedonia, then on to Troas.

QUESTIONS

What did the people of Ephesus worship?

What did Demetrius and others do for a living?

Why did Demetrius start a riot against Paul?

193
Paul Says Good-bye

One Sunday evening as he was preaching a farewell sermon at Troas (for he was planning to leave the next day), Paul kept talking until midnight. There were many lanterns in the upstairs room where the meeting was held, and a young man named Eutychus, who was sitting on a window sill listening to Paul, fell asleep and fell to the ground three stories below. Everyone thought he was dead, but Paul went down and put his arms around him and said, "It's all right; he is alive." And he was!

Then they all went back upstairs to eat together, and Paul preached another long sermon, until finally it was morning. Then he left to sail with the others to the city of Miletus, not far from Ephesus. He didn't want to go to Ephesus at that time, so he sent for the leaders of the Ephesian church to meet with him at Miletus.

When they arrived he addressed them as follows:

"You know me well, for I stayed with you three years. All that time I served the Lord humbly while facing many sorrows and trials because of the Jews, who were always seeking to do me harm. And you know that when I preached to you I didn't keep back anything you needed to hear, even though it might offend you. I taught in the synagogue and in your own homes, telling both Jews and Gentiles that they must repent of their sins and believe in the Lord Jesus Christ.

"And now I am going to Jerusalem, not knowing what will happen to me there, except that wherever I go, the Holy Spirit keeps telling me that jail and persecution await me. But I am not afraid. I don't care if they kill me. I will die with joy, except for the fact that I will never see you again."

Then Paul kneeled down and prayed with them, and they all wept together, and as was the custom in those days, they embraced him and kissed his cheeks, sorrowing most of all because he said that they would never see him again. Then they went with him to the ship and watched him sail away.

Paul next came to the city of Tyre, where the ship was to unload. Finding some disciples there, he stayed with them seven days. When he left, they came with their wives and children and all kneeled together on the beach and prayed; then Paul and those travelling with him went aboard the ship and sailed on to the city of Caesarea. There they went to the home of Philip, one of the seven men appointed by the apostles to care for the widows in the church. This was the same Philip who preached the Good News to the Ethiopian as he rode in his chariot.

While Paul was in Philip's home, a prophet named Agabus came and took Paul's belt and bound his own hands and feet with it. Then he said, "The Holy Spirit has told me that the Jews at Jerusalem will bind the man who owns this belt, and give him to the Gentiles to torture him.

The Christians cried when they heard this, and begged Paul not to go to Jerusalem. But he said to them, "Why do you weep and break my heart? For I am not only ready to go to jail, but also to die at Jerusalem."

When they saw that they couldn't keep him from going, they stopped pleading and said, "May God's will be done."

Then Paul and his friends left Caesarea and went to Jerusalem, where they received a warm welcome from the church. The next day he went to the home of James, one of the apostles, and met there with the elders of the Jerusalem church. He reported to them about his trip, and how God had helped him so that many Gentiles believed as a result of his preaching. They were very happy about this and thanked God for what he had been able to do.

Then Paul went to the Temple. While he was there, some Jews from Turkey recognized him and grabbed him, crying out to all the people, "Men of Israel, help us! This man teaches the people to disobey the laws of Moses. He has brought Gentiles into the Temple!"

Soon the entire city was in an uproar. A mob formed and pulled Paul out of the Temple to kill him. But as they were doing it, someone told the captain of the Roman guard at the nearby barracks.

The captain took some of his soldiers with him and ran down among the people. When the men who were beating Paul saw the soldiers, they stopped, and the captain took him away from them and commanded him to be bound with chains, and asked who he was and what he had done. Some of the crowd yelled one thing and some another, so that no one could tell what the trouble was.

Then the captain ordered Paul taken into the barracks. As he was being carried up the stairs (for the soldiers were carrying Paul to protect him from the people), the crowd surged after him shouting, "Away with him! Kill him!"

QUESTIONS

Why did Eutychus fall from a third-story window? What happened afterward?

Why were the people of Ephesus so sad when Paul went to Jerusalem?

What did Agabus do with Paul's belt? What did this mean?

Was Paul safe when he got to Jerusalem?

194
Paul Talks to the People

Paul now spoke to the captain. "May I have a word with you?" he asked. "I would like to speak to the people."

The captain said he could, so Paul stood on the stairs where the people could see him, and motioned for silence. Then he spoke to them in Hebrew (which made the people even quieter). This is what he said:

"I am a Jew born in Tarsus, and brought up here in Jerusalem. I was taught all the wisdom of Moses by the great Gamaliel, and I used to be as anxious for everyone to obey Moses' laws as you are now. In fact, I persecuted and tried to kill every Christian I could lay my hands on, binding them and sending them away to prison and death, both men and women. The High Priest and all the Council will tell you that what I say is true, for they gave me letters to the Jews at Damascus permitting me to arrest all the Christians I found there, and to bring them in chains to Jerusalem to be punished.

"But as I was on the way to Damascus, one day about noon, suddenly a great light from heaven shone around me. I fell to the ground, and heard a voice saying, 'Saul, Saul, why are you hurting me?'

" 'Who are you?' I asked.

"He said, 'I am Jesus of Nazareth, the One you are hurting.' The men who were with me saw the light and were afraid, but couldn't understand the words that were spoken.

" 'What shall I do now, Lord?' I asked.

And He replied, 'Get up, and go to Damascus, and there you will be told what you must do.'

"I couldn't see, being blinded by the terrible light, so I was led by the hand into Damascus. After three days a disciple there named Ananias, who feared God and was well thought of by all the Jews, came and stood by me, and said, 'Brother Saul, receive your sight.'

"Immediately I could see him. And he said to me, 'God has allowed you to see Jesus and to hear Him speak so that you can go and tell all the nations about Him.'

"Later when I was in Jerusalem and was praying in the Temple, I saw Jesus again in a vision, and heard Him say, 'Hurry and get out of Jerusalem, for the Jews will not believe what you tell them about Me, and I will send you far away to preach among the Gentiles.' "

The crowd listened quietly until he said these words about preaching to the Gentiles. Instantly they began shouting, "Kill him! Kill him! Such a fellow isn't fit to live."

The captain then commanded that Paul be brought into the barracks and whipped, to make him confess what evil he had done.

But as they bound him and got ready to whip him, Paul said to the soldier in charge, "Is it legal for you to whip a Roman citizen before he has been tried and proved guilty?"

One of the soldiers ran over to the captain and warned him, "Be careful what you are doing, for this man is a Roman."

Then the captain came over and asked Paul, "Tell me, are you a Roman citizen?"

"Yes, I am," he replied.

"I am too," the captain said, "and I paid plenty for the privilege."

"But I was born free," Paul replied. Then the men who were about to whip him slipped away and disappeared, as did the captain, too! For he was afraid he might be punished for having even tied a Roman citizen.

The next day when the captain wanted to know for sure what the Jews were accusing Paul of, he commanded all the local Jewish religious leaders to appear, and brought Paul down and set him before them.

Paul looked at them very earnestly and said, "Men and brothers, my conscience is clear. I have done no wrong." Then Ananias, the High Priest, ordered those who stood near Paul to slap him on the mouth.

"You hypocrite!" Paul exclaimed. "God will punish you for pretending to give me a fair trial and yet commanding me to be hit before I am proved guilty!"

"Is that the way to talk to the High Priest?" they asked him.

"I didn't know he was the High Priest," Paul said, "for it is written in the Scriptures that we mustn't speak evil of those in authority over us."

Then Paul tried again to speak, but there was such an uproar that the captain, fearing Paul would be torn to pieces, told the soldiers to get him out of there and take him back to the barracks.

QUESTIONS

What did Paul tell the captain about how he came to believe in Jesus?

Why was the captain afraid to whip Paul?

Paul's enemies planned to ambush and kill him. His nephew found out about the plot in time to warn him and save his life.

R. Hook

195
Paul's Nephew and a Plot

The next night the Lord Jesus came and stood beside Paul and said, "Don't be afraid, Paul, for as you have spoken about Me to the people here in Jerusalem, so also you must speak about Me in the city of Rome."

In the morning, forty of the Jews promised one another that they wouldn't eat or drink until they had killed Paul. Then they went to the Chief Priest and elders and said to them, "We have agreed with one another that we will not eat or drink until we have killed Paul. So tell the captain to bring Paul down before the council tomorrow as though you wanted to ask him some more questions, and on the way we will ambush him and kill him."

But Paul's nephew heard about their plot and went into the barracks and told Paul. Paul called one of the soldiers and said, "Take this young man to the captain, for he has something to tell him."

So the soldier took him to the captain. "Paul, the prisoner, asked me to bring this young man to you," he said.

Then the captain led him to a place where they could be alone and asked him what he wanted to tell him. The young man answered, "The Jews have agreed to ask you to bring Paul before the council tomorrow, pretending they want to ask him some questions. But don't do it, for more than forty of them will be hiding along the road. They have promised each other that they won't eat or drink until they have killed him."

"Don't tell anyone you told me this," the captain warned.

The Roman governor of Judea was named Felix. He didn't live at Jerusalem, but in the city of Caesarea on the seacoast, about sixty miles from Jerusalem. When the captain heard that the Jews wanted to kill Paul, he decided to send him to the governor. So he called two of his officers and said, "Get ready 200 soldiers, and 70 horsemen and 200 spearmen, to go to Caesarea tonight. Have horses ready for Paul and the men who are with him to ride, and get him safely to the governor."

Then the captain wrote this letter to the governor: "The man I am sending to you was grabbed by the Jews and they were about to kill him. Then I went with soldiers and rescued him, for I heard he was a Roman. I wanted to know what they accused him of, so I brought him before their council, and found that he had done nothing worthy of death. When I learned they were still determined to kill him, I decided to send him to you, and have told the Jews who accused him to appear before you and tell you what they have against him. Farewell."

Then the soldiers brought Paul by night to the town of Antipatris, which was on the way to Caesarea. There the infantrymen left him, and returned to the barracks at Jerusalem, but the horsemen brought him to the governor the next day, and gave him the letter. After reading it, the governor told Paul he would hear his side of the story when the Jews came from Jerusalem to accuse him. Then he commanded that Paul be kept in prison until they arrived.

Five days later, Ananias the High Priest and some of the council came down from Jerusalem to Caesarea, bringing with them a lawyer named Tertullus to accuse Paul before the governor.

"We have found this fellow to be a wicked man," Tertullus said, "stirring up trouble and disorder among the Jews all over the world. He is a leader among those who believe in Jesus of Nazareth, and he took Gentiles into the Temple! We would have handled his case under our Jewish law, but the captain came with soldiers and took him from us by force, telling us to come to you to accuse him. Now we are here, ready to prove everything we charge him with."

Then Paul answered, "It was only twelve days ago that I went up to Jerusalem to worship, and they attacked me in the Temple; but I wasn't arguing with anyone, or trying to stir up the people; neither can they prove the things they have accused me of. But I confess this: that I worship God in a way different from theirs, although I believe everything that is written in their Scriptures. And I expect the dead, both the bad and the good, to rise up at the last day, just as the Jews believe. Believing this, I am trying constantly to do nothing that my conscience tells me is wrong.

"I have been away from Jerusalem for many years, and have come back at this time to bring gifts to the poor and an offering to God. But some Jews from Turkey attacked me there in the Temple, and they should be here now if they have anything against me. Or let these Jews who are present tell you whether they found any evil in me when I was taken before the council in Jerusalem, unless it was that I said I was on trial for preaching that the dead rise from their graves at the Judgment Day."

Then Governor Felix sent for the captain to explain what he knew about the affair. Felix told the soldiers to keep Paul in prison but to let him see any of his friends who might come to visit him.

QUESTIONS
How did Paul's nephew help Paul?
Who was Felix?
What did the Jews accuse Paul of doing?
What did Paul say he shouldn't have done?

196
Paul Preaches to a King

Several days later Felix sent for Paul to come and talk to him and his wife Drusilla, who was a Jewess, and to explain the Good News to them. As Paul spoke to them, persuading them to obey God and not to listen to temptation, and told them that they would be judged at the last day, Felix thought of his sins and was so afraid that he trembled. Yet he didn't repent of his sins, but sent Paul back to prison.

"Some other time when it is more convenient," he said, "I will send for you again to tell me more about these things."

Felix hoped too that Paul would offer him money to let him go free, and so he sent for him frequently to talk with him. But after two years, when another governor named Festus came to take Felix's place, instead of letting Paul go free, Felix left him in prison.

When Festus, the new governor, arrived at Caesarea, the Jews asked him to send Paul to Jerusalem to be tried, for they intended to have men hidden along the road to kill him.

But Festus said, "Paul shall stay here in Caesarea, and those who wish to accuse him may come here and say what they have against him."

So when they arrived, the governor commanded Paul to be brought before them, and the Jews stood and accused him of many things, but Paul denied everything.

Festus wanted to please the Jews so he asked Paul, "Are you willing to go to Jerusalem to be tried there for the things you are accused of?"

Now it was a law that any Roman who was sentenced to death might ask to be taken before Caesar, the emperor, for a final decision as to whether he should live or die. When Festus asked Paul if he was willing to go to Jerusalem to be tried, Paul knew what would happen, so he replied, "Jerusalem is not the place where I ought to be tried, for I have done no wrong to the Jews, as you know very well. I ask to be taken before Caesar."

Then Festus said, "You want to be tried by Caesar, do you? All right, to Caesar you shall go." He meant that Paul would be taken to the city of Rome, where the emperor lived.

Several days later, Agrippa, who

was the king of another part of the land of Israel, came with his sister Bernice to visit Festus at Caesarea. Festus told him about Paul. "There is a man here in prison," he said, "whom the High Priests and other leaders of the Jews have asked me to condemn to death."

Agrippa was a Jew and when the governor told him the Jews wanted to put Paul to death, he was interested. "I would like to hear what the man has to say," Agrippa said.

"Tomorrow you shall," the governor replied.

The next day Agrippa and Bernice came, dressed in their royal robes, with army officers and the principal men of the city around them. Then Festus sent for Paul to be brought from prison, and told him, "You have permission to speak for yourself, and to answer the things the Jews are saying against you."

Paul told King Agrippa that he was very glad to plead his case before him because the king knew all about the laws of the Jews, and would understand what he was talking about.

Then Paul told him, "The Jews themselves know very well what I have been like since childhood. For I am a Jew, and if they would tell the truth, they would say that I used to be one of the strictest among them. I, too, once thought that I ought to do many things against Jesus of Nazareth. I threw many of His disciples into prison, and when they were sentenced to death, I was one of those who spoke against them. I punished them in every church, and did all I could to make them speak against their Saviour. And being full of rage against them, I even went to other cities to search for them. But one day at noon, as I was nearing Damascus, I saw a bright light from heaven, brighter than the sun, that shone around me and the men who were with me. And we were all afraid and fell to the ground."

Then Paul told Agrippa and Festus and all who were listening to him how Jesus had spoken to him from heaven, and had said He would make Paul a missionary and send him to preach the Good News to the Gentiles, so that they too might repent and have their sins forgiven.

"And when I heard His voice," Paul said, "I did what He commanded—I went and preached to the Jews at Damascus and Jerusalem, and also to the Gentiles, telling them to repent and to obey God. And because I did this, the Jews caught me in the Temple and were about to kill me. But God saved me from them. I have kept preaching until this day to everyone, both poor and rich. Yet I have told them only those things the prophets said would happen: that Jesus would be put to death and afterwards rise from the dead, to be a Saviour of both the Jews and Gentiles."

While Paul was speaking, Governor Festus said with a loud voice, "Paul, you are crazy; you have studied so much that you have lost your mind."

But Paul answered, "I am not crazy, most noble Festus. I am only speaking the truth, and King Agrippa understands what I say, for I am sure he has heard all of these things."

Then Agrippa said to Paul, "With so little evidence do you expect me to become a Christian?"

Paul replied, "I wish that not only you but all these who are listening to me were Christians such as I am, except that they wouldn't have to wear these chains."

When Paul had said this, Agrippa stood up, and so everyone else did too, and Agrippa and Festus went off to talk with each other. "This man has done nothing worthy of prison or death," they agreed.

And King Agrippa added, "He could be set at liberty if he hadn't demanded to be taken to Rome, to appear before Caesar."

QUESTIONS
How long did Paul remain in jail while Felix was governor?
Where did Paul ask to be sent for a trial instead of to Jerusalem? Why?
Why did Governor Festus tell Paul he was crazy?
Did Agrippa and Festus think Paul deserved to die?

197
Shipwrecked, But Safe

When the time came for Paul to be sent to Rome, Festus turned him over to one of the captains of his guard, along with several other prisoners who were being sent to Rome at the same time. They went by ship from Caesarea and came the next day to the city of Sidon. Here they stopped for a while and the captain, whose name was Julius, treated Paul kindly, letting him go ashore to visit some of his friends.

Leaving Sidon they came to the city of Myra. There the captain placed his prisoners aboard another ship headed for Rome. After sailing slowly for several days they reached a place called Fair Havens, in the island of Crete. It was winter and the time for storms, and Paul said to the sailors, "Gentlemen, I prophesy that if we go on, there will be great danger not only to the ship but also to our lives." But the captain of the ship didn't believe Paul, and since Fair Havens wasn't a good harbor to stay in for the winter, he decided to leave it and to try to reach a place called Phoenix. The wind blew softly from the south that day, so everyone except Paul felt good about it. So, leaving Fair Havens, they sailed out to sea again.

But soon there was a storm, and the wind beat against the ship until the sailors could no longer steer, and they had to let the ship run before the wind. As they neared an island called Clauda, they wound cables around the ship to keep it from breaking to pieces. The storm grew worse, and the next day they threw out some of the cargo to make the ship lighter, to try to save it from sinking. On the following day they threw overboard all the ropes and sails that could be spared.

But the storm kept on day after day. No one could see the sun, moon, or stars at any time, because of the dark clouds that covered the sky. Finally everyone gave up all hope, thinking they would surely be drowned.

But after they had eaten nothing for a long, long time, Paul stood up among them and said, "Sirs, you should have listened to me and stayed at the island of Crete; then you wouldn't have come into this great danger. Nevertheless, don't be afraid, for there shall be no loss of any man's life among you, though the ship will go down. Last night the Lord sent His angel to tell me, 'Don't be afraid, Paul, for you will come safely to Rome and be brought before Caesar; and for your sake God will save the lives of all the men who are with you in the ship.' So, gentlemen, cheer up, for I believe what the angel told me. But we will be wrecked on an island."

On the fourteenth night of the storm, as the ship was driven along by the wind, the sailors thought they were near some land; they measured the depth of the water and found that they were right, for the water was getting more shallow. They were afraid of rocks near the beach, so they dropped four anchors out of the ship to keep it from being driven any further, and then waited for morning.

But some of the sailors thought the ship wouldn't last that long and would sink before morning, so they let down the lifeboat, intending to escape and leave the others to be drowned. But Paul said to the captain, "Unless these sailors stay on the ship, the rest of you cannot be saved." Then the soldiers cut the ropes that held the boat, and let it float away.

When it was morning Paul begged them all to eat something. "This is the fourteenth day since the storm began," he said, "and in all that time you have hardly eaten anything. Please take some food, for not one of you will be hurt." Then he took some bread and thanked God for it before them all, and began to eat. Suddenly everyone was more cheerful, and ate some too. Altogether there were 276 persons aboard. After they had eaten, they threw some of the cargo of wheat into the sea to lighten the ship even more.

When it was day, they saw the shore, but of course they didn't know what country they had come to. There was an inlet in front of them, and they decided to try to head the ship into it so as to avoid the rocks along the coast. After they had pulled up the anchors and hoisted the sail they steered toward the land, but before they reached it the ship ran aground, and the front part was held fast on the bottom of the sea and couldn't be moved, while the back part was broken by the great waves that dashed against it.

The soldiers shouted to the captain to have the prisoners killed for fear some of them might escape. But the captain wanted to save Paul and told them not to do it. He said for those who could swim to jump in and get to shore. The others followed clinging to boards and broken pieces of the ship. So everyone reached land safely.

QUESTIONS

Where was Paul going on the ship?

What warning did Paul give the sailors about their trip?

How long did the terrible storm last?

Did the ship's captain allow the prisoners to be killed so they couldn't escape?

How many were drowned while trying to get to shore?

God promised Paul that all the people on this sinking ship would reach land safely. He kept His promise, and not one person drowned!

198
Paul Arrives in Rome

They found they were on an island called Malta. The people of the island were very kind to them and helped them light a fire on the beach, because of the rain that was falling and because of the cold. Paul gathered a bundle of sticks and laid them on the fire, but suddenly a poisonous snake slithered out from the sticks and bit him, coiling onto his hand.

When the people of the island saw it hanging there they said, "No doubt this man is a murderer, and though he has escaped drowning in the sea he is being punished by the bite of the snake for the evil he has done."

But Paul shook off the snake into the fire and felt no harm. They watched him a long time, expecting his arm would swell or that he would fall down dead, but when no harm came to him, they changed their minds and said he was a god.

The governor of the island, Publius, invited Paul and those who were with him to his house, and they stayed there three days. Publius' father was sick with a fever, so Paul laid his hands on him and made him well. Then others who were sick came and were healed. They showed their gratitude by giving Paul and his friends many presents.

After three months the captain took Paul and the other prisoners aboard a ship that had been waiting at the island until the winter was over, and they sailed away to the city of Puteoli, where Paul was the guest of the local church for seven days. Then the prisoners were marched by land toward Rome. When the Christians at Rome heard that Paul was coming, they went out to welcome him at a place called the Three Taverns.

Upon arrival at Rome, the captain gave the prisoners into the care of the Roman guard. Paul was allowed to live in a house by himself, with the soldier who guarded him. Three days after his arrival in Rome he sent for the Jewish leaders who lived there and said to them, "Men and brothers, though I have done no wrong to the Jews, nor disobeyed the laws which Moses gave to our fathers, yet the Jews at Jerusalem gave me to the Romans as their prisoner. When the Romans tried me, they wanted to let me go because I had done nothing for which I deserved to die. But when the Jews still wanted to kill me, I asked to be taken before Caesar. Now I have sent for you so that I can tell you what I believe, for it is because I believe in the Saviour whom the prophets wrote about that I am bound with this chain."

The Jews replied, "We have had no letters about you, and the Jews who came from Jerusalem have not spoken against you. But we would like to hear what it is you preach—for we know these Christians are spoken against everywhere."

So they set a date and on that day many of the Jews came to Paul's house and he explained to them in an all-day Bible class what the prophets had written about Jesus. Some believed, but some didn't. As they argued, Paul told them that the prophet Isaiah had spoken the truth when he said that although a message from God would be brought to the people of Israel, many of them wouldn't listen to it because their hearts were wicked, and they didn't want to be God's children. Then he said that the Good News refused by the Jews would be preached to the Gentiles, and the Gentiles would accept it.

Paul stayed two years in Rome, living in a house he rented for himself. There he welcomed all who came to hear him, and he taught them fearlessly about Jesus, and no one tried to stop him.

The Bible does not tell us where Paul went after this, or how he died at last. But from accounts given in other books it is thought that he was set free at Rome and went back to Jerusalem, then travelled through other countries preaching the Good News and finally returned to Rome again.

Not many years after that, there was a great fire in Rome which continued burning for six or seven days. The people believed that their wicked emperor, Nero, had ordered the city to be set on fire. To save himself from the blame, Nero accused the Christians of doing it. Then the people rose up in a great fury against the Christians, and killed many of them. Among those who were killed, we are told, were the apostles Peter and Paul. Paul, it is said, was beheaded, and Peter crucified.

It made little difference to them how they died; they knew that afterwards they would be taken to heaven. And we will meet them there if we too are the disciples of Jesus. But if we are not His disciples, then He says to us as He said to the Jews who would not believe Him, "You cannot come where I am."

Will you let Him be your Saviour? Then you can be His disciple now and can live with Him forever in His home in heaven.

QUESTIONS

How long did Paul live after the poisonous snake bit him?

Did Paul ever get to Rome?

Does the Bible tell us what happened to Paul in Rome?

Are you a disciple of Jesus? Do you know how to be one?

SCRIPTURE REFERENCE INDEX

SCRIPTURE REFERENCE INDEX

Chap.	*Reference*
98	3–7
99	8–11
100	12
101	13
102	14, 15, 16
103	16, 17
104	18
105	18, 19
106	20, 21
107	22; 2 Kings 1
108	2 Kings 2
109	3, 4
110	4
111	5, 6
112	6, 7
113	8
114	9–13
115	14–15; also Book of Amos and Book of Hosea
116	1 Kings 14, 15
117	22; 2 Chronicles 18, 19, 20
118	2 Chronicles 21, 22
119	23, 24
120	24, 25
121	26; also Book of Isaiah
122	28, 29
123	30, 31
124	32
125	2 Kings 20; 2 Chronicles 32
126	2 Kings 22, 23; 2 Chronicles 34, 35
127	2 Kings 24; 2 Chronicles 36
128	2 Kings 25; 2 Chronicles 36; The Book of Jeremiah
129	2 Kings 25; also Book of Jeremiah
130, 131, 132	The Book of Ezekiel
133–137	The Book of Daniel
138–141	The Book of Ezra
142, 143, 144	The Book of Esther
145, 146, 147	The Book of Nehemiah
148, 149	Secular History
150	Luke 1
151	Matthew 2; Luke 2
152	Matthew 3, 4; Mark 1; Luke 2, 3, 4; John 1
153	Mark 6; John 2, 3
154	Luke 4; John 4
155	Matthew 8; Mark 1; Luke 4, 5
156	Matthew 9, 12; Mark 2, 3; Luke 5, 6; John 5
157	Matthew 5, 6, 7; Luke 6
158	Matthew 8; Luke 7
159	Matthew 13; Mark 4; Luke 8, 12
160	Matthew 8; Mark 4, 5; Luke 8
161	Matthew 9, 13; Mark 5, 6; Luke 8
162	Matthew 9–11, 14; Mark 6; Luke 9; John 6
163	Matthew 15, 16; Mark 7, 8
164	Matthew 16, 17; Mark 8, 9; Luke 9
165	Matthew 18; Mark 9; Luke 9, 17
166	Luke 10, 11
167	John 9
168	John 10, 11
169	Luke 14, 15
170	Matthew 19; Mark 10; Luke 16, 18
171	Matthew 20, 21; Mark 10, 11; Luke 18, 19
172	Matthew 21, 22; Mark 11, 12; Luke 20, 21
173	Matthew 25
174	Matthew 25, 26; Mark 14; Luke 22; John 12
175	Matthew 26; Mark 14; Luke 22; John 13, 14
176	Matthew 26; Mark 14; Luke 22; John 18
177	Matthew 26; Mark 14; Luke 22; John 18
178	Matthew 27; Mark 15; Luke 23; John 18, 19
179	Matthew 27, 28; Mark 15, 16; Luke 23, 24; John 19, 20
180	Mark 16; Luke 24; Acts 1
181	Acts 1–4
182	4, 5
183	6, 7, 8
184	8, 9
185	9
186	10, 11
187	11, 12, 13
188	13, 14
189	15, 16
190	16, 17
191	17, 18
192	19
193	20, 21
194	21, 22
195	23, 24
196	26
197	27
198	28